LINUX

NETWORK ADMINISTRATOR'S GUIDE

LINUX

NETWORK
ADMINISTRATOR'S
GUIDE

Second Edition

OLAF KIRCH & TERRY DAWSON

O'REILLY®

Beijing • Cambridge • Farnham • Köln • Paris • Sebastopol • Taipei • Tokyo

Linux Network Administrator's Guide, Second Edition

by Olaf Kirch and Terry Dawson

Printed in the United States of America.

Published by O'Reilly & Associates, Inc., 101 Morris Street, Sebastopol, CA 95472.

Editor: Andy Oram

Production Editor: Sarah Jane Shangraw

Cover Designer: Hanna Dyer

Printing History:

January 1995:	First Edition.
June 2000:	Second Edition.

Library of Congress Cataloging-in-Publication Data

Kirch, Olaf.
  Linux network administrator's guide / Olaf Kirch & Terry Dawson.—2nd ed.
     p. cm.
  Rev. ed. of: Linux system administration, 1999.
  ISBN: 1-56592-400-2
     1. Linux. 2. Operating systems (Computers) I. Dawson, Terry. II. Kirch, Olaf. Linux system administration. III. Title.

QA76.76.O63 K566 2000
005.4'469—dc21

                                                              00-041663

[DS]

TABLE OF CONTENTS

PREFACE

The Internet is now a household term in many countries. With otherwise serious people beginning to joyride along the Information Superhighway, computer networking seems to be moving toward the status of TV sets and microwave ovens. The Internet has unusually high media coverage, and social science majors are descending on Usenet newsgroups, online virtual reality environments, and the Web to conduct research on the new "Internet Culture."

Of course, networking has been around for a long time. Connecting computers to form local area networks has been common practice, even at small installations, and so have long-haul links using transmission lines provided by telecommunications companies. A rapidly growing conglomerate of world-wide networks has, however, made joining the global village a perfectly reasonable option for even small non-profit organizations of private computer users. Setting up an Internet host with mail and news capabilities offering dialup and ISDN access has become affordable, and the advent of DSL (Digital Subscriber Line) and Cable Modem technologies will doubtlessly continue this trend.

Talking about computer networks often means talking about Unix. Of course, Unix is not the only operating system with network capabilities, nor will it remain a frontrunner forever, but it has been in the networking business for a long time, and will surely continue to be for some time to come.

What makes Unix particularly interesting to private users is that there has been much activity to bring free Unix-like operating systems to the PC, such as 386BSD, FreeBSD, and Linux.

Linux is a freely distributable Unix clone for personal computers. It currently runs on a variety of machines that includes the Intel family of processors, but also Motorola 680x0 machines, such as the Commodore Amiga and Apple Macintosh;

Sun SPARC and Ultra-SPARC machines; Compaq Alphas; MIPS; PowerPCs, such as the new generation of Apple Macintosh; and StrongARM, like the rebel.com Netwinder and 3Com Palm machines. Linux has been ported to some relatively obscure platforms, like the Fujitsu AP-1000 and the IBM System 3/90. Ports to other interesting architectures are currently in progress in developers' labs, and the quest to move Linux into the embedded controller space promises success.

Linux was developed by a large team of volunteers across the Internet. The project was started in 1990 by Linus Torvalds, a Finnish college student, as an operating systems course project. Since that time, Linux has snowballed into a full-featured Unix clone capable of running applications as diverse as simulation and modeling programs, word processors, speech recognition systems, World Wide Web browsers, and a horde of other software, including a variety of excellent games. A great deal of hardware is supported, and Linux contains a complete implementation of TCP/IP networking, including SLIP, PPP, firewalls, a full IPX implementation, and many features and some protocols not found in any other operating system. Linux is powerful, fast, and free, and its popularity in the world beyond the Internet is growing rapidly.

The Linux operating system itself is covered by the GNU General Public License, the same copyright license used by software developed by the Free Software Foundation. This license allows anyone to redistribute or modify the software (free of charge or for a profit) as long as all modifications and distributions are freely distributable as well. The term "free software" refers to freedom of application, not freedom of cost.

Purpose and Audience for This Book

This book was written to provide a single reference for network administration in a Linux environment. Beginners and experienced users alike should find the information they need to cover nearly all important administration activities required to manage a Linux network configuration. The possible range of topics to cover is nearly limitless, so of course it has been impossible to include everything there is to say on all subjects. We've tried to cover the most important and common ones. We've found that beginners to Linux networking, even those with no prior exposure to Unix-like operating systems, have found this book good enough to help them successfully get their Linux network configurations up and running and get them ready to learn more.

There are many books and other sources of information from which you can learn any of the topics covered in this book (with the possible exception of some of the truly Linux-specific features, such as the new Linux firewall interface, which is not well documented elsewhere) in greater depth. We've provided a bibliography for you to use when you are ready to explore more.

Sources of Information

If you are new to the world of Linux, there are a number of resources to explore and become familiar with. Having access to the Internet is helpful, but not essential.

Linux Documentation Project guides

> The Linux Documentation Project is a group of volunteers who have worked to produce books (guides), HOWTO documents, and manual pages on topics ranging from installation to kernel programming. The LDP works include:

> *Linux Installation and Getting Started*

>> By Matt Welsh, et al. This book describes how to obtain, install, and use Linux. It includes an introductory Unix tutorial and information on systems administration, the X Window System, and networking.

> *Linux System Administrators Guide*

>> By Lars Wirzenius and Joanna Oja. This book is a guide to general Linux system administration and covers topics such as creating and configuring users, performing system backups, configuration of major software packages, and installing and upgrading software.

> *Linux System Adminstration Made Easy*

>> By Steve Frampton. This book describes day-to-day administration and maintenance issues of relevance to Linux users.

> *Linux Programmers Guide*

>> By B. Scott Burkett, Sven Goldt, John D. Harper, Sven van der Meer, and Matt Welsh. This book covers topics of interest to people who wish to develop application software for Linux.

> *The Linux Kernel*

>> By David A. Rusling. This book provides an introduction to the Linux Kernel, how it is constructed, and how it works. Take a tour of your kernel.

> *The Linux Kernel Module Programming Guide*

>> By Ori Pomerantz. This guide explains how to write Linux kernel modules.

> More manuals are in development. For more information about the LDP you should consult their World Wide Web server at *http://www.linuxdoc.org/* or one of its many mirrors.

HOWTO documents

> The Linux HOWTOs are a comprehensive series of papers detailing various aspects of the system—such as installation and configuration of the X Window System software, or how to write in assembly language programming under

Linux. These are generally located in the *HOWTO* subdirectory of the FTP sites listed later, or they are available on the World Wide Web at one of the many Linux Documentation Project mirror sites. See the Bibliography at the end of this book, or the file *HOWTO-INDEX* for a list of what's available.

You might want to obtain the *Installation HOWTO*, which describes how to install Linux on your system; the *Hardware Compatibility HOWTO*, which contains a list of hardware known to work with Linux; and the *Distribution HOWTO*, which lists software vendors selling Linux on diskette and CD-ROM.

The bibliography of this book includes references to the HOWTO documents that are related to Linux networking.

Linux Frequently Asked Questions
> The *Linux Frequently Asked Questions with Answers* (FAQ) contains a wide assortment of questions and answers about the system. It is a must-read for all newcomers.

Documentation Available via FTP

If you have access to anonymous FTP, you can obtain all Linux documentation listed above from various sites, including *metalab.unc.edu:/pub/Linux/docs* and *tsx-11.mit.edu:/pub/linux/docs*.

These sites are mirrored by a number of sites around the world.

Documentation Available via WWW

There are many Linux-based WWW sites available. The home site for the Linux Documentation Project can be accessed at *http://www.linuxdoc.org/*.

The Open Source Writers Guild (OSWG) is a project that has a scope that extends beyond Linux. The OSWG, like this book, is committed to advocating and facilitating the production of OpenSource documentation. The OSWG home site is at *http://www.oswg.org:8080/oswg*.

Both of these sites contain hypertext (and other) versions of many Linux related documents.

Documentation Available Commercially

A number of publishing companies and software vendors publish the works of the Linux Documentation Project. Two such vendors are:

Specialized Systems Consultants, Inc. (SSC)
http://www.ssc.com/
P.O. Box 55549 Seattle, WA 98155-0549
1-206-782-7733
1-206-782-7191 (FAX)
sales@ssc.com

and:

Linux Systems Labs
http://www.lsl.com/
18300 Tara Drive
Clinton Township, MI 48036
1-810-987-8807
1-810-987-3562 (FAX)
sales@lsl.com

Both companies sell compendiums of Linux HOWTO documents and other Linux documentation in printed and bound form.

O'Reilly & Associates publishes a series of Linux books. This one is a work of the Linux Documentation Project, but most have been independently authored. Their range includes:

Running Linux
　An installation and user guide to the system describing how to get the most out of personal computing with Linux.

Learning Debian GNU/Linux
Learning Red Hat Linux
　More basic than *Running Linux*, these books contain popular distributions on CD-ROM and offer robust directions for setting them up and using them.

Linux in a Nutshell
　Another in the successful "in a Nutshell" series, this book focuses on providing a broad reference text for Linux.

Linux Journal and Linux Magazine

Linux Journal and *Linux Magazine* are monthly magazines for the Linux community, written and published by a number of Linux activists. They contain articles ranging from novice questions and answers to kernel programming internals. Even if you have Usenet access, these magazines are a good way to stay in touch with the Linux community.

Linux Journal is the oldest magazine and is published by S.S.C. Incorporated, for which details were listed previously. You can also find the magazine on the World Wide Web at *http://www.linuxjournal.com/*.

Linux Magazine is a newer, independent publication. The home web site for the magazine is *http://www.linuxmagazine.com/*.

Linux Usenet Newsgroups

If you have access to Usenet news, the following Linux-related newsgroups are available:

comp.os.linux.announce
>   A moderated newsgroup containing announcements of new software, distributions, bug reports, and goings-on in the Linux community. All Linux users should read this group. Submissions may be mailed to *linux-announce@news.ornl.gov.*

comp.os.linux.help
>   General questions and answers about installing or using Linux.

comp.os.linux.admin
>   Discussions relating to systems administration under Linux.

comp.os.linux.networking
>   Discussions relating to networking with Linux.

comp.os.linux.development
>   Discussions about developing the Linux kernel and system itself.

comp.os.linux.misc
>   A catch-all newsgroup for miscellaneous discussions that don't fall under the previous categories.

There are also several newsgroups devoted to Linux in languages other than English, such as *fr.comp.os.linux* in French and *de.comp.os.linux* in German.

Linux Mailing Lists

There is a large number of specialist Linux mailing lists on which you will find many people willing to help with questions you might have.

The best-known of these are the lists hosted by Rutgers University. You may subscribe to these lists by sending an email message formatted as follows:

```
To: majordomo@vger.rutgers.edu
Subject: anything at all
Body:

subscribe listname
```

Some of the available lists related to Linux networking are:

linux-net
> Discussion relating to Linux networking

linux-ppp
> Discussion relating to the Linux PPP implementation

linux-kernel
> Discussion relating to Linux kernel development

Online Linux Support

There are many ways of obtaining help online, where volunteers from around the world offer expertise and services to assist users with questions and problems.

The OpenProjects IRC Network is an IRC network devoted entirely to Open Projects—Open Source and Open Hardware alike. Some of its channels are designed to provide online Linux support services. IRC stands for Internet Relay Chat, and is a network service that allows you to talk interactively on the Internet to other users. IRC networks support multiple channels on which groups of people talk. Whatever you type in a channel is seen by all other users of that channel.

There are a number of active channels on the OpenProjects IRC network where you will find users 24 hours a day, 7 days a week who are willing and able to help you solve any Linux problems you may have, or just chat. You can use this service by installing an IRC client like *irc-II*, connecting to servername **irc.openprojects.org:6667**, and joining the #linpeople channel.

Linux User Groups

Many Linux User Groups around the world offer direct support to users. Many Linux User Groups engage in activities such as installation days, talks and seminars, demonstration nights, and other completely social events. Linux User Groups are a great way of meeting other Linux users in your area. There are a number of published lists of Linux User Groups. Some of the better-known ones are:

Groups of Linux Users Everywhere
> *http://www.ssc.com/glue/groups/*

LUG list project
> *http://www.nllgg.nl/lugww/*

LUG registry
> *http://www.linux.org/users/*

Obtaining Linux

There is no single distribution of the Linux software; instead, there are many distributions, such as Debian, RedHat, Caldera, Corel, SuSE, and Slackware. Each distribution contains everything you need to run a complete Linux system: the kernel, basic utilities, libraries, support files, and applications software.

Linux distributions may be obtained via a number of online sources, such as the Internet. Each of the major distributions has its own FTP and web site. Some of these sites are:

Caldera

> *http://www.caldera.com/ftp://ftp.caldera.com/*

Corel

> *http://www.corel.com/ftp://ftp.corel.com/*

Debian

> *http://www.debian.org/ftp://ftp.debian.org/*

RedHat

> *http://www.redhat.com/ftp://ftp.redhat.com/*

Slackware

> *http://www.slackware.com/ftp://ftp.slackware.com/*

SuSE

> *http://www.suse.com/ftp://ftp.suse.com/*

Many of the popular general FTP archive sites also mirror various Linux distributions. The best-known of these sites are:

> *metalab.unc.edu:/pub/Linux/distributions/*
> *ftp.funet.fi:/pub/Linux/mirrors/*
> *tsx-11.mit.edu:/pub/linux/distributions/*
> *mirror.aarnet.edu.au:/pub/linux/distributions/*

Many of the modern distributions can be installed directly from the Internet. There is a lot of software to download for a typical installation, though, so you'd probably want to do this only if you have a high-speed, permanent network connection, or if you just need to update an existing installation.*

---

* ... or you are extremely impatient and know that the 24 hours it might take to download the software from the Internet is faster than the 72 hours it might take to wait for a CD-ROM to be delivered!

Linux may be purchased on CD-ROM from an increasing number of software vendors. If your local computer store doesn't have it, perhaps you should ask them to stock it! Most of the popular distributions can be obtained on CD-ROM. Some vendors produce products containing multiple CD-ROMs, each of which provides a different Linux distribution. This is an ideal way to try a number of different distributions before you settle on your favorite one.

File System Standards

In the past, one of the problems that afflicted Linux distributions, as well as the packages of software running on Linux, was the lack of a single accepted filesystem layout. This resulted in incompatibilities between different packages, and confronted users and administrators with the task of locating various files and programs.

To improve this situation, in August 1993, several people formed the Linux File System Standard Group (FSSTND). After six months of discussion, the group created a draft that presents a coherent file sytem structure and defines the location of the most essential programs and configuration files.

This standard was supposed to have been implemented by most major Linux distributions and packages. It is a little unfortunate that, while most distributions have made some attempt to work toward the FSSTND, there is a very small number of distributions that has actually adopted it fully. Throughout this book, we will assume that any files discussed reside in the location specified by the standard; alternative locations will be mentioned only when there is a long tradition that conflicts with this specification.

The Linux FSSTND continued to develop, but was replaced by the Linux File Hierarchy Standard (FHS) in 1997. The FHS addresses the multi-architecture issues that the FSSTND did not. The FHS can be obtained from the Linux documentation directory of all major Linux FTP sites and their mirrors, or at its home site at *http://www.pathname.com/fhs/*. Daniel Quinlan, the coordinator of the FHS group, can be reached at *quinlan@transmeta.com*.

Standard Linux Base

The vast number of different Linux distributions, while providing lots of healthy choice for Linux users, has created a problem for software developers—particularly developers of non-free software.

Each distribution packages and supplies certain base libraries, configuration tools, system applications, and configuration files. Unfortunately, differences in their versions, names, and locations make it very difficult to know what will exist on any distribution. This makes it hard to develop binary applications that will work reliably on all Linux distribution bases.

To help overcome this problem, a new project sprang up called the "Linux Standard Base." It aims to describe a standard base distribution that complying distributions will use. If a developer designs an application to work against the standard base platform, the application will work, and be portable to, any complying Linux distribution.

You can find information on the status of the Linux Standard Base project at its home web site at *http://www.linuxbase.org/*.

If you're concerned about interoperability, particularly of software from commercial vendors, you should ensure that your Linux distribution is making an effort to participate in the standardization project.

About This Book

When Olaf joined the Linux Documentation Project in 1992, he wrote two small chapters on UUCP and *smail*, which he meant to contribute to the System Administrator's Guide. Development of TCP/IP networking was just beginning, and when those "small chapters" started to grow, he wondered aloud whether it would be nice to have a Networking Guide. "Great!" everyone said. "Go for it!" So he went for it and wrote the first version of the Networking Guide, which was released in September 1993.

Olaf continued work on the Networking Guide and eventually produced a much enhanced version of the guide. Vince Skahan contributed the original *sendmail* mail chapter, which was completely replaced in this edition because of a new interface to the *sendmail* configuration.

The version of the guide that you are reading now is a revision and update prompted by O'Reilly & Associates and undertaken by Terry Dawson.* Terry has been an amateur radio operator for over 20 years and has worked in the telecommunications industry for over 15 of those. He was co-author of the original NET-FAQ, and has since authored and maintained various networking-related HOWTO documents. Terry has always been an enthusiastic supporter of the Network Administrators Guide project, and added a few new chapters to this version describing features of Linux networking that have been developed since the first edition, plus a bunch of changes to bring the rest of the book up to date.

The *exim* chapter was contributed by Philip Hazel,† who is a lead developer and maintainer of the package.

The book is organized roughly along the sequence of steps you have to take to configure your system for networking. It starts by discussing basic concepts of networks, and TCP/IP-based networks in particular. It then slowly works its way up

---

* Terry Dawson can be reached at *terry@linux.org.au*.

† Philip Hazel can be reached at *ph10@cus.cam.ac.uk*.

from configuring TCP/IP at the device level to firewall, accounting, and masquerade configuration, to the setup of common applications such as *rlogin* and friends, the Network File System, and the Network Information System. This is followed by a chapter on how to set up your machine as a UUCP node. Most of the remaining sections is dedicated to two major applications that run on top of TCP/IP and UUCP: electronic mail and news. A special chapter has been devoted to the IPX protocol and the NCP filesystem, because these are used in many corporate environments where Linux is finding a home.

The email part features an introduction to the more intimate parts of mail transport and routing, and the myriad of addressing schemes you may be confronted with. It describes the configuration and management of *exim*, a mail transport agent ideal for use in most situations not requiring UUCP, and *sendmail*, which is for people who have to do more complicated routing involving UUCP.

The news part gives you an overview of how Usenet news works. It covers INN and C News, the two most widely used news transport software packages at the moment, and the use of NNTP to provide newsreading access to a local network. The book closes with a chapter on the care and feeding of the most popular newsreaders on Linux.

Of course, a book can never exhaustively answer all questions you might have. So if you follow the instructions in this book and something still does not work, please be patient. Some of your problems may be due to mistakes on our part (see the section "Submitting Changes", later in this Preface), but they also may be caused by changes in the networking software. Therefore, you should check the listed information resources first. There's a good chance that you are not alone with your problems, so a fix or at least a proposed workaround is likely to be known. If you have the opportunity, you should also try to get the latest kernel and network release from one of the Linux FTP sites or a BBS near you. Many problems are caused by software from different stages of development, which fail to work together properly. After all, Linux is a "work in progress."

The Official Printed Version

In Autumn 1993, Andy Oram, who had been around the LDP mailing list from almost the very beginning, asked Olaf about publishing this book at O'Reilly & Associates. He was excited about this book, never having imagined that it would become this successful. He and Andy finally agreed that O'Reilly would produce an enhanced Official Printed Version of the Networking Guide, while Olaf retained the original copyright so that the source of the book could be freely distributed. This means that you can choose freely: you can get the various free forms of the document from your nearest Linux Documentation Project mirror site and print it out, or you can purchase the official printed version from O'Reilly.

Why, then, would you want to pay money for something you can get for free? Is Tim O'Reilly out of his mind for publishing something everyone can print and even sell themselves?* Is there any difference between these versions?

The answers are "it depends," "no, definitely not," and "yes and no." O'Reilly & Associates does take a risk in publishing the Networking Guide, and it seems to have paid off for them (they've asked us to do it again). We believe this project serves as a fine example of how the free software world and companies can cooperate to produce something both can benefit from. In our view, the great service O'Reilly is providing to the Linux community (apart from the book becoming readily available in your local bookstore) is that it has helped Linux become recognized as something to be taken seriously: a viable and useful alternative to other commercial operating systems. It's a sad technical bookstore that doesn't have at least one shelf stacked with O'Reilly Linux books.

Why are they publishing it? They see it as their kind of book. It's what they'd hope to produce if they contracted with an author to write about Linux. The pace, level of detail, and style fit in well with their other offerings.

The point of the LDP license is to make sure no one gets shut out. Other people can print out copies of this book, and no one will blame you if you get one of these copies. But if you haven't gotten a chance to see the O'Reilly version, try to get to a bookstore or look at a friend's copy. We think you'll like what you see, and will want to buy it for yourself.

So what about the differences between the printed and online versions? Andy Oram has made great efforts at transforming our ramblings into something actually worth printing. (He has also reviewed a few other books produced by the Linux Documentation Project, contributing whatever professional skills he can to the Linux community.)

Since Andy started reviewing the Networking Guide and editing the copies sent to him, the book has improved vastly from its original form, and with every round of submission and feedback it improves again. The opportunity to take advantage of a professional editor's skill is one not to be wasted. In many ways, Andy's contribution has been as important as that of the authors. The same is also true of the copyeditors, who got the book into the shape you see now. All these edits have been fed back into the online version, so there is no difference in content.

Still, the O'Reilly version *will* be different. It will be professionally bound, and while you may go to the trouble to print the free version, it is unlikely that you will get the same quality result, and even then it is more unlikely that you'll do it

---

* Note that while you are allowed to print out the online version, you may *not* run the O'Reilly book through a photocopier, much less sell any of its (hypothetical) copies.

for the price. Secondly, our amateurish attempts at illustration will have been replaced with nicely redone figures by O'Reilly's professional artists. Indexers have generated an improved index, which makes locating information in the book a much simpler process. If this book is something you intend to read from start to finish, you should consider reading the official printed version.

Overview

Chapter 1, *Introduction to Networking*, discusses the history of Linux and covers basic networking information on UUCP, TCP/IP, various protocols, hardware, and security. The next few chapters deal with configuring Linux for TCP/IP networking and running some major applications. We examine IP a little more closely in Chapter 2, *Issues of TCP/IP Networking*, before getting our hands dirty with file editing and the like. If you already know how IP routing works and how address resolution is performed, you can skip this chapter.

Chapter 3, *Configuring the Networking Hardware*, deals with very basic configuration issues, such as building a kernel and setting up your Ethernet card. The configuration of your serial ports is covered separately in Chapter 4, *Configuring the Serial Hardware*, because the discussion does not apply to TCP/IP networking only, but is also relevant for UUCP.

Chapter 5, *Configuring TCP/IP Networking*, helps you set up your machine for TCP/IP networking. It contains installation hints for standalone hosts with loopback enabled only, and hosts connected to an Ethernet. It also introduces you to a few useful tools you can use to test and debug your setup. Chapter 6, *Name Service and Resolver Configuration*, discusses how to configure hostname resolution and explains how to set up a name server.

Chapter 7, *Serial Line IP*, explains how to establish SLIP connections and gives a detailed reference for *dip*, a tool that allows you to automate most of the necessary steps. Chapter 8, *The Point-to-Point Protocol*, covers PPP and *pppd*, the PPP daemon.

Chapter 9, *TCP/IP Firewall*, extends our discussion on network security and describes the Linux TCP/IP firewall and its configuration tools: *ipfwadm*, *ipchains*, and *iptables*. IP firewalling provides a means of controlling who can access your network and hosts very precisely.

Chapter 10, *IP Accounting*, explains how to configure IP Accounting in Linux so you can keep track of how much traffic is going where and who is generating it.

Chapter 11, *IP Masquerade and Network Address Translation*, covers a feature of the Linux networking software called IP masquerade, which allows whole IP networks to connect to and use the Internet through a single IP address, hiding internal systems from outsiders in the process.

Chapter 12, *Important Network Features*, gives a short introduction to setting up some of the most important network applications, such as *rlogin, ssh*, etc. This chapter also covers how services are managed by the *inetd* superuser, and how you may restrict certain security-relevant services to a set of trusted hosts.

Chapter 13, *The Network Information System*, and Chapter 14, *The Network File System*, discuss NIS and NFS. NIS is a tool used to distribute administative information, such as user passwords in a local area network. NFS allows you to share filesystems between several hosts in your network.

In Chapter 15, *IPX and the NCP Filesystem*, we discuss the IPX protocol and the NCP filesystem. These allow Linux to be integrated into a Novell NetWare environment, sharing files and printers with non-Linux machines.

Chapter 16, *Managing Taylor UUCP*, gives you an extensive introduction to the administration of Taylor UUCP, a free implementation of the UUCP suite.

The remainder of the book is taken up by a detailed tour of electronic mail and Usenet news. Chapter 17, *Electronic Mail*, introduces you to the central concepts of electronic mail, like what a mail address looks like, and how the mail handling system manages to get your message to the recipient.

Chapter 18, *Sendmail*, and Chapter 19, *Getting Exim Up and Running*, cover the configuration of *sendmail* and *exim*, two mail transport agents you can use for Linux. This book explains both of them, because *exim* is easier to install for the beginner, while *sendmail* provides support for UUCP.

Chapter 20, *Netnews*, through Chapter 23, *Internet News*, explain the way news is managed in Usenet and how you install and use C News, *nntpd*, and INN: three popular software packages for managing Usenet news. After the brief introduction in Chapter 20, you can read Chapter 21, *C News*, if you want to transfer news using C News, a traditional service generally used with UUCP. The following chapters discuss more modern alternatives to C News that use the Internet-based protocol NNTP (Network News Transfer Protocol). Chapter 22, *NNTP and the nntpd Daemon* covers how to set up a simple NNTP daemon, *nntpd*, to provide news reading access for a local network, while Chapter 23 describes a more robust server for more extensive NetNews transfers, the InterNet News daemon (INN). And finally, Chapter 24, *Newsreader Configuration*, shows you how to configure and maintain various newsreaders.

Conventions Used in This Book

All examples presented in this book assume you are using a *sh* compatible shell. The *bash* shell is *sh* compatible and is the standard shell of all Linux distributions. If you happen to be a *csh* user, you will have to make appropriate adjustments.

The following is a list of the typographical conventions used in this book:

Italic

Used for file and directory names, program and command names, command-line options, email addresses and pathnames, URLs, and for emphasizing new terms.

Boldface

Used for machine names, hostnames, site names, usernames and IDs, and for occasional emphasis.

`Constant Width`

Used in examples to show the contents of code files or the output from commands and to indicate environment variables and keywords that appear in code.

`Constant Width Italic`

Used to indicate variable options, keywords, or text that the user is to replace with an actual value.

`Constant Width Bold`

Used in examples to show commands or other text that should be typed literally by the user.

Text appearing in this manner offers a warning. You can make a mistake here that hurts your system or is hard to recover from.

Submitting Changes

We have tested and verified the information in this book to the best of our ability, but you may find that features have changed (or even that we have made mistakes!). Please let us know about any errors you find, as well as your suggestions for future editions, by writing to:

O'Reilly & Associates, Inc.
101 Morris Street
Sebastopol, CA 95472
1-800-998-9938 (in the U.S. or Canada)
1-707-829-0515 (international or local)
1-707-829-0104 (FAX)

You can send us messages electronically. To be put on the mailing list or request a catalog, send email to:

info@oreilly.com

To ask technical questions or comment on the book, send email to:

bookquestions@oreilly.com

We have a web site for the book, where we'll list examples, errata, and any plans for future editions. You can access this page at:

http://www.oreilly.com/catalog/linag2

For more information about this book and others, see the O'Reilly web site:

http://www.oreilly.com

Acknowledgments

This edition of the Networking Guide owes almost everything to the outstanding work of Olaf and Vince. It is difficult to appreciate the effort that goes into researching and writing a book of this nature until you've had a chance to work on one yourself. Updating the book was a challenging task, but with an excellent base to work from, it was an enjoyable one.

This book owes very much to the numerous people who took the time to proofread it and help iron out many mistakes, both technical and grammatical (never knew that there was such a thing as a dangling participle). Phil Hughes, John Macdonald, and Erik Ratcliffe all provided very helpful (and on the whole, quite consistent) feedback on the content of the book.

We also owe many thanks to the people at O'Reilly we've had the pleasure to work with: Sarah Jane Shangraw, who got the book into the shape you can see now; Maureen Dempsey, who copyedited the text; Rob Romano, Rhon Porter, and Chris Reilley, who created all the figures; Hanna Dyer, who designed the cover; Alicia Cech, David Futato, and Jennifer Niedherst for the internal layout; Lars Kaufman for suggesting old woodcuts as a visual theme; Judy Hoer for the index; and finally, Tim O'Reilly for the courage to take up such a project.

We are greatly indebted to Andres Sepúlveda, Wolfgang Michaelis, Michael K. Johnson, and all developers who spared the time to check the information provided in the Networking Guide. Phil Hughes, John MacDonald, and Eric Ratcliffe contributed invaluable comments on the second edition. We also wish to thank all those who read the first version of the Networking Guide and sent corrections and suggestions. You can find a hopefully complete list of contributors in the file *Thanks* in the online distribution. Finally, this book would not have been possible without the support of Holger Grothe, who provided Olaf with the Internet connectivity he needed to make the original version happen.

Olaf would also like to thank the following groups and companies that printed the first edition of the Networking Guide and have donated money either to him or to the Linux Documentation Project as a whole: Linux Support Team, Erlangen, Germany; S.u.S.E. GmbH, Fuerth, Germany; and Linux System Labs, Inc., Clinton Twp., United States, RedHat Software, North Carolina, United States.

Terry thanks his wife, Maggie, who patiently supported him throughout his participation in the project despite the challenges presented by the birth of their first child, Jack. Additionally, he thanks the *many* people of the Linux community who either nurtured or suffered him to the point at which he could actually take part and actively contribute. "I'll help you if you promise to help someone else in return."

The Hall of Fame

Besides those we have already mentioned, a large number of people have contributed to the Networking Guide, by reviewing it and sending us corrections and suggestions. We are very grateful.

Here is a list of those whose contributions left a trace in our mail folders.

Al Longyear, Alan Cox, Andres Sepúlveda, Ben Cooper, Cameron Spitzer, Colin McCormack, D.J. Roberts, Emilio Lopes, Fred N. van Kempen, Gert Doering, Greg Hankins, Heiko Eissfeldt, J.P. Szikora, Johannes Stille, Karl Eichwalder, Les Johnson, Ludger Kunz, Marc van Diest, Michael K. Johnson, Michael Nebel, Michael Wing, Mitch D'Souza, Paul Gortmaker, Peter Brouwer, Peter Eriksson, Phil Hughes, Raul Deluth Miller, Rich Braun, Rick Sladkey, Ronald Aarts, Swen Thüemmler, Terry Dawson, Thomas Quinot, and Yury Shevchuk.

CHAPTER ONE

INTRODUCTION TO NETWORKING

History

The idea of networking is probably as old as telecommunications itself. Consider people living in the Stone Age, when drums may have been used to transmit messages between individuals. Suppose caveman A wants to invite caveman B over for a game of hurling rocks at each other, but they live too far apart for B to hear A banging his drum. What are A's options? He could 1) walk over to B's place, 2) get a bigger drum, or 3) ask C, who lives halfway between them, to forward the message. The last option is called *networking*.

Of course, we have come a long way from the primitive pursuits and devices of our forebears. Nowadays, we have computers talk to each other over vast assemblages of wires, fiber optics, microwaves, and the like, to make an appointment for Saturday's soccer match.* In the following description, we will deal with the means and ways by which this is accomplished, but leave out the wires, as well as the soccer part.

We will describe three types of networks in this guide. We will focus on TCP/IP most heavily because it is the most popular protocol suite in use on both Local Area Networks (LANs) and Wide Area Networks (WANs), such as the Internet. We will also take a look at UUCP and IPX. UUCP was once commonly used to transport news and mail messages over dialup telephone connections. It is less common today, but is still useful in a variety of situations. The IPX protocol is used most commonly in the Novell NetWare environment and we'll describe how to use

---

* The original spirit of which (see above) still shows on some occasions in Europe.

1

it to connect your Linux machine into a Novell network. Each of these protocols are networking protocols and are used to carry data between host computers. We'll discuss how they are used and introduce you to their underlying principles.

We define a network as a collection of *hosts* that are able to communicate with each other, often by relying on the services of a number of dedicated hosts that relay data between the participants. Hosts are often computers, but need not be; one can also think of X terminals or intelligent printers as hosts. Small agglomerations of hosts are also called *sites*.

Communication is impossible without some sort of language or code. In computer networks, these languages are collectively referred to as *protocols*. However, you shouldn't think of written protocols here, but rather of the highly formalized code of behavior observed when heads of state meet, for instance. In a very similar fashion, the protocols used in computer networks are nothing but very strict rules for the exchange of messages between two or more hosts.

TCP/IP Networks

Modern networking applications require a sophisticated approach to carrying data from one machine to another. If you are managing a Linux machine that has many users, each of whom may wish to simultaneously connect to remote hosts on a network, you need a way of allowing them to share your network connection without interfering with each other. The approach that a large number of modern networking protocols uses is called *packet-switching*. A *packet* is a small chunk of data that is transferred from one machine to another across the network. The switching occurs as the datagram is carried across each link in the network. A packet-switched network shares a single network link among many users by alternately sending packets from one user to another across that link.

The solution that Unix systems, and subsequently many non-Unix systems, have adopted is known as TCP/IP. When talking about TCP/IP networks you will hear the term *datagram*, which technically has a special meaning but is often used interchangeably with *packet*. In this section, we will have a look at underlying concepts of the TCP/IP protocols.

Introduction to TCP/IP Networks

TCP/IP traces its origins to a research project funded by the United States Defense Advanced Research Projects Agency (DARPA) in 1969. The ARPANET was an experimental network that was converted into an operational one in 1975 after it had proven to be a success.

In 1983, the new protocol suite TCP/IP was adopted as a standard, and all hosts on the network were required to use it. When ARPANET finally grew into the Internet (with ARPANET itself passing out of existence in 1990), the use of TCP/IP had spread to networks beyond the Internet itself. Many companies have now built corporate TCP/IP networks, and the Internet has grown to a point at which it could almost be considered a mainstream consumer technology. It is difficult to read a newspaper or magazine now without seeing reference to the Internet; almost everyone can now use it.

For something concrete to look at as we discuss TCP/IP throughout the following sections, we will consider Groucho Marx University (GMU), situated somewhere in Fredland, as an example. Most departments run their own Local Area Networks, while some share one and others run several of them. They are all interconnected and hooked to the Internet through a single high-speed link.

Suppose your Linux box is connected to a LAN of Unix hosts at the Mathematics department, and its name is **erdos**. To access a host at the Physics department, say **quark**, you enter the following command:

```
$ rlogin quark.physics
Welcome to the Physics Department at GMU
(ttyq2) login:
```

At the prompt, you enter your login name, say **andres**, and your password. You are then given a shell* on **quark**, to which you can type as if you were sitting at the system's console. After you exit the shell, you are returned to your own machine's prompt. You have just used one of the instantaneous, interactive applications that TCP/IP provides: remote login.

While being logged into **quark**, you might also want to run a graphical user interface application, like a word processing program, a graphics drawing program, or even a World Wide Web browser. The X windows system is a fully network-aware graphical user environment, and it is available for many different computing systems. To tell this application that you want to have its windows displayed on your host's screen, you have to set the DISPLAY environment variable:

```
$ DISPLAY=erdos.maths:0.0
$ export DISPLAY
```

If you now start your application, it will contact your X server instead of **quark**'s, and display all its windows on your screen. Of course, this requires that you have X11 runnning on **erdos**. The point here is that TCP/IP allows **quark** and **erdos** to send X11 packets back and forth to give you the illusion that you're on a single system. The network is almost transparent here.

---

* The shell is a command-line interface to the Unix operating system. It's similar to the DOS prompt in a Microsoft Windows environment, albeit much more powerful.

Another very important application in TCP/IP networks is NFS, which stands for *Network File System*. It is another form of making the network transparent, because it basically allows you to treat directory hierarchies from other hosts as if they were local file systems and look like any other directories on your host. For example, all users' home directories can be kept on a central server machine from which all other hosts on the LAN mount them. The effect is that users can log in to any machine and find themselves in the same home directory. Similarly, it is possible to share large amounts of data (such as a database, documentation or application programs) among many hosts by maintaining one copy of the data on a server and allowing other hosts to access it. We will come back to NFS in Chapter 14, *The Network File System*.

Of course, these are only examples of what you can do with TCP/IP networks. The possibilities are almost limitless, and we'll introduce you to more as you read on through the book.

We will now have a closer look at the way TCP/IP works. This information will help you understand how and why you have to configure your machine. We will start by examining the hardware, and slowly work our way up.

Ethernets

The most common type of LAN hardware is known as *Ethernet*. In its simplest form, it consists of a single cable with hosts attached to it through connectors, taps, or transceivers. Simple Ethernets are relatively inexpensive to install, which together with a net transfer rate of 10, 100, or even 1,000 Megabits per second, accounts for much of its popularity.

Ethernets come in three flavors: *thick, thin,* and *twisted pair.* Thin and thick Ethernet each use a coaxial cable, differing in diameter and the way you may attach a host to this cable. Thin Ethernet uses a T-shaped "BNC" connector, which you insert into the cable and twist onto a plug on the back of your computer. Thick Ethernet requires that you drill a small hole into the cable, and attach a transceiver using a "vampire tap." One or more hosts can then be connected to the transceiver. Thin and thick Ethernet cable can run for a maximum of 200 and 500 meters respectively, and are also called 10base-2 and 10base-5. The "base" refers to "baseband modulation" and simply means that the data is directly fed onto the cable without any modem. The number at the start refers to the speed in Megabits per second, and the number at the end is the maximum length of the cable in hundreds of metres. Twisted pair uses a cable made of two pairs of copper wires and usually requires additional hardware known as *active hubs.* Twisted pair is also known as 10base-T, the "T" meaning twisted pair. The 100 Megabits per second version is known as 100base-T.

To add a host to a thin Ethernet installation, you have to disrupt network service for at least a few minutes because you have to cut the cable to insert the connector. Although adding a host to a thick Ethernet system is a little complicated, it does not typically bring down the network. Twisted pair Ethernet is even simpler. It uses a device called a "hub," which serves as an interconnection point. You can insert and remove hosts from a hub without interrupting any other users at all.

Many people prefer thin Ethernet for small networks because it is very inexpensive; PC cards come for as little as US $30 (many companies are literally throwing them out now), and cable is in the range of a few cents per meter. However, for large-scale installations, either thick Ethernet or twisted pair is more appropriate. For example, the Ethernet at GMU's Mathematics Department originally chose thick Ethernet because it is a long route that the cable must take so traffic will not be disrupted each time a host is added to the network. Twisted pair installations are now very common in a variety of installations. The Hub hardware is dropping in price and small units are now available at a price that is attractive to even small domestic networks. Twisted pair cabling can be significantly cheaper for large installations, and the cable itself is much more flexible than the coaxial cables used for the other Ethernet systems. The network administrators in GMU's mathematics department are planning to replace the existing network with a twisted pair network in the coming finanical year because it will bring them up to date with current technology and will save them significant time when installing new host computers and moving existing computers around.

One of the drawbacks of Ethernet technology is its limited cable length, which precludes any use of it other than for LANs. However, several Ethernet segments can be linked to one another using repeaters, bridges, or routers. Repeaters simply copy the signals between two or more segments so that all segments together will act as if they are one Ethernet. Due to timing requirements, there may not be more than four repeaters between any two hosts on the network. Bridges and routers are more sophisticated. They analyze incoming data and forward it only when the recipient host is not on the local Ethernet.

Ethernet works like a bus system, where a host may send packets (or *frames*) of up to 1,500 bytes to another host on the same Ethernet. A host is addressed by a six-byte address hardcoded into the firmware of its Ethernet network interface card (NIC). These addresses are usually written as a sequence of two-digit hex numbers separated by colons, as in **aa:bb:cc:dd:ee:ff**.

A frame sent by one station is seen by all attached stations, but only the destination host actually picks it up and processes it. If two stations try to send at the same time, a *collision* occurs. Collisions on an Ethernet are detected very quickly by the electronics of the interface cards and are resolved by the two stations aborting the send, each waiting a random interval and re-attempting the transmission. You'll hear lots of stories about collisions on Ethernet being a problem and that utilization of Ethernets is only about 30 percent of the available bandwidth because of them. Collisions on Ethernet are a *normal* phenomenon, and on a very busy Ethernet network you shouldn't be surprised to see collision rates of up to about 30 percent. Utilization of Ethernet networks is more realistically limited to about 60 percent before you need to start worrying about it.*

Other Types of Hardware

In larger installations, such as Groucho Marx University, Ethernet is usually not the only type of equipment used. There are many other data communications protocols available and in use. All of the protocols listed are supported by Linux, but due to space constraints we'll describe them briefly. Many of the protocols have HOWTO documents that describe them in detail, so you should refer to those if you're interested in exploring those that we don't describe in this book.

At Groucho Marx University, each department's LAN is linked to the campus high-speed "backbone" network, which is a fiber optic cable running a network technology called *Fiber Distributed Data Interface* (FDDI). FDDI uses an entirely different approach to transmitting data, which basically involves sending around a number of *tokens*, with a station being allowed to send a frame only if it captures a token. The main advantage of a token-passing protocol is a reduction in collisions. Therefore, the protocol can more easily attain the full speed of the transmission medium, up to 100 Mbps in the case of FDDI. FDDI, being based on optical fiber, offers a significant advantage because its maximum cable length is much greater than wire-based technologies. It has limits of up to around 200 km, which makes it ideal for linking many buildings in a city, or as in GMU's case, many buildings on a campus.

Similarly, if there is any IBM computing equipment around, an IBM Token Ring network is quite likely to be installed. Token Ring is used as an alternative to Ethernet in some LAN environments, and offers the same sorts of advantages as FDDI in terms of achieving full wire speed, but at lower speeds (4 Mbps or 16 Mbps), and lower cost because it is based on wire rather than fiber. In Linux, Token Ring networking is configured in almost precisely the same way as Ethernet, so we don't cover it specifically.

Although it is much less likely today than in the past, other LAN technologies, such as ArcNet and DECNet, might be installed. Linux supports these too, but we don't cover them here.

Many national networks operated by Telecommunications companies support packet switching protocols. Probably the most popular of these is a standard named X.25. Many Public Data Networks, like Tymnet in the U.S., Austpac in

---

* The Ethernet FAQ at *http://www.faqs.org/faqs/LANs/ethernet-faq/* talks about this issue, and a wealth of detailed historical and technical information is available at Charles Spurgeon's Ethernet web site at *http://wwwhost.ots.utexas.edu/ethernet/*.

Australia, and Datex-P in Germany offer this service. X.25 defines a set of networking protocols that describes how data terminal equipment, such as a host, communicates with data communications equipment (an X.25 switch). X.25 requires a synchronous data link, and therefore special synchronous serial port hardware. It is possible to use X.25 with normal serial ports if you use a special device called a PAD (Packet Assembler Disassembler). The PAD is a standalone device that provides asynchronous serial ports and a synchronous serial port. It manages the X.25 protocol so that simple terminal devices can make and accept X.25 connections. X.25 is often used to carry other network protocols, such as TCP/IP. Since IP datagrams cannot simply be mapped onto X.25 (or vice versa), they are encapsulated in X.25 packets and sent over the network. There is an experimental implementation of the X.25 protocol available for Linux.

A more recent protocol commonly offered by telecommunications companies is called *Frame Relay.* The Frame Relay protocol shares a number of technical features with the X.25 protocol, but is much more like the IP protocol in behavior. Like X.25, Frame Relay requires special synchronous serial hardware. Because of their similarities, many cards support both of these protocols. An alternative is available that requires no special internal hardware, again relying on an external device called a Frame Relay Access Device (FRAD) to manage the encapsulation of Ethernet packets into Frame Relay packets for transmission across a network. Frame Relay is ideal for carrying TCP/IP between sites. Linux provides drivers that support some types of internal Frame Relay devices.

If you need higher speed networking that can carry many different types of data, such as digitized voice and video, alongside your usual data, ATM (Asynchronous Transfer Mode) is probably what you'll be interested in. ATM is a new network technology that has been specifically designed to provide a manageable, high-speed, low-latency means of carrying data, and provide control over the Quality of Service (Q.S.). Many telecommunications companies are deploying ATM network infrastructure because it allows the convergence of a number of different network services into one platform, in the hope of achieving savings in management and support costs. ATM is often used to carry TCP/IP. The Networking-HOWTO offers information on the Linux support available for ATM.

Frequently, radio amateurs use their radio equipment to network their computers; this is commonly called *packet radio.* One of the protocols used by amateur radio operators is called AX.25 and is loosely derived from X.25. Amateur radio operators use the AX.25 protocol to carry TCP/IP and other protocols, too. AX.25, like X.25, requires serial hardware capable of synchronous operation, or an external device called a "Terminal Node Controller" to convert packets transmitted via an asynchronous serial link into packets transmitted synchronously. There are a variety of different sorts of interface cards available to support packet radio operation; these cards are generally referred to as being "Z8530 SCC based," and are named after the most popular type of communications controller used in the designs. Two of the other protocols that are commonly carried by AX.25 are the NetRom and Rose protocols, which are network layer protocols. Since these protocols run over AX.25, they have the same hardware requirements. Linux supports a fully featured implementation of the AX.25, NetRom, and Rose protocols. The AX25-HOWTO is a good source of information on the Linux implementation of these protocols.

Other types of Internet access involve dialing up a central system over slow but cheap serial lines (telephone, ISDN, and so on). These require yet another protocol for transmission of packets, such as SLIP or PPP, which will be described later.

The Internet Protocol

Of course, you wouldn't want your networking to be limited to one Ethernet or one point-to-point data link. Ideally, you would want to be able to communicate with a host computer regardless of what type of physical network it is connected to. For example, in larger installations such as Groucho Marx University, you usually have a number of separate networks that have to be connected in some way. At GMU, the Math department runs two Ethernets: one with fast machines for professors and graduates, and another with slow machines for students. Both are linked to the FDDI campus backbone network.

This connection is handled by a dedicated host called a *gateway* that handles incoming and outgoing packets by copying them between the two Ethernets and the FDDI fiber optic cable. For example, if you are at the Math department and want to access **quark** on the Physics department's LAN from your Linux box, the networking software will not send packets to **quark** directly because it is not on the same Ethernet. Therefore, it has to rely on the gateway to act as a forwarder. The gateway (named **sophus**) then forwards these packets to its peer gateway **niels** at the Physics department, using the backbone network, with **niels** delivering it to the destination machine. Data flow between **erdos** and **quark** is shown in Figure 1-1.

This scheme of directing data to a remote host is called *routing*, and packets are often referred to as *datagrams* in this context. To facilitate things, datagram exchange is governed by a single protocol that is independent of the hardware used: IP, or *Internet Protocol*. In Chapter 2, *Issues of TCP/IP Networking*, we will cover IP and the issues of routing in greater detail.

The main benefit of IP is that it turns physically dissimilar networks into one apparently homogeneous network. This is called internetworking, and the resulting "meta-network" is called an *internet*. Note the subtle difference here between *an* internet and *the* Internet. The latter is the official name of one particular global internet.

Of course, IP also requires a hardware-independent addressing scheme. This is achieved by assigning each host a unique 32-bit number called the *IP address*. An IP address is usually written as four decimal numbers, one for each 8-bit portion, separated by dots. For example, **quark** might have an IP address of **0x954C0C04**,

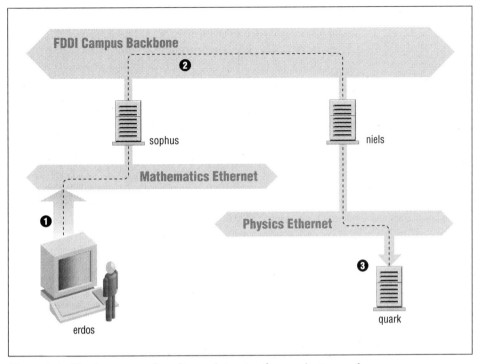

Figure 1-1. The three steps of sending a datagram from erdos to quark

which would be written as **149.76.12.4**. This format is also called *dotted decimal notation* and sometimes *dotted quad notation*. It is increasingly going under the name IPv4 (for Internet Protocol, Version 4) because a new standard called IPv6 offers much more flexible addressing, as well as other modern features. It will be at least a year after the release of this edition before IPv6 is in use.

You will notice that we now have three different types of addresses: first there is the host's name, like **quark**, then there are IP addresses, and finally, there are hardware addresses, like the 6-byte Ethernet address. All these addresses somehow have to match so that when you type *rlogin quark*, the networking software can be given **quark**'s IP address; and when IP delivers any data to the Physics department's Ethernet, it somehow has to find out what Ethernet address corresponds to the IP address.

We will deal with these situations in Chapter 2. For now, it's enough to remember that these steps of finding addresses are called *hostname resolution*, for mapping hostnames onto IP addresses, and *address resolution*, for mapping the latter to hardware addresses.

IP Over Serial Lines

On serial lines, a "de facto" standard exists known as SLIP, or *Serial Line IP*. A modification of SLIP known as CSLIP, or *Compressed SLIP*, performs compression of IP headers to make better use of the relatively low bandwidth provided by most serial links. Another serial protocol is PPP, or the *Point-to-Point Protocol*. PPP is more modern than SLIP and includes a number of features that make it more attractive. Its main advantage over SLIP is that it isn't limited to transporting IP datagrams, but is designed to allow just about any protocol to be carried across it.

The Transmission Control Protocol

Sending datagrams from one host to another is not the whole story. If you log in to **quark**, you want to have a reliable connection between your *rlogin* process on **erdos** and the shell process on **quark**. Thus, the information sent to and fro must be split up into packets by the sender and reassembled into a character stream by the receiver. Trivial as it seems, this involves a number of complicated tasks.

A very important thing to know about IP is that, by intent, it is not reliable. Assume that ten people on your Ethernet started downloading the latest release of Netscape's web browser source code from GMU's FTP server. The amount of traffic generated might be too much for the gateway to handle, because it's too slow and it's tight on memory. Now if you happen to send a packet to **quark**, **sophus** might be out of buffer space for a moment and therefore unable to forward it. IP solves this problem by simply discarding it. The packet is irrevocably lost. It is therefore the responsibility of the communicating hosts to check the integrity and completeness of the data and retransmit it in case of error.

This process is performed by yet another protocol, *Transmission Control Protocol* (TCP), which builds a reliable service on top of IP. The essential property of TCP is that it uses IP to give you the illusion of a simple connection between the two processes on your host and the remote machine, so you don't have to care about how and along which route your data actually travels. A TCP connection works essentially like a two-way pipe that both processes may write to and read from. Think of it as a telephone conversation.

TCP identifies the end points of such a connection by the IP addresses of the two hosts involved and the number of a *port* on each host. Ports may be viewed as attachment points for network connections. If we are to strain the telephone example a little more, and you imagine that cities are like hosts, one might compare IP addresses to area codes (where numbers map to cities), and port numbers to local codes (where numbers map to individual people's telephones). An individual host may support many different services, each distinguished by its own port number.

In the *rlogin* example, the client application (*rlogin*) opens a port on **erdos** and connects to port 513 on **quark**, to which the *rlogind* server is known to listen. This action establishes a TCP connection. Using this connection, *rlogind* performs the authorization procedure and then spawns the shell. The shell's standard input and output are redirected to the TCP connection, so that anything you type to *rlogin* on your machine will be passed through the TCP stream and be given to the shell as standard input.

The User Datagram Protocol

Of course, TCP isn't the only user protocol in TCP/IP networking. Although suitable for applications like *rlogin*, the overhead involved is prohibitive for applications like NFS, which instead uses a sibling protocol of TCP called UDP, or *User Datagram Protocol*. Just like TCP, UDP allows an application to contact a service on a certain port of the remote machine, but it doesn't establish a connection for this. Instead, you use it to send single packets to the destination service—hence its name.

Assume you want to request a small amount of data from a database server. It takes at least three datagrams to establish a TCP connection, another three to send and confirm a small amount of data each way, and another three to close the connection. UDP provides us with a means of using only two datagrams to achieve almost the same result. UDP is said to be connectionless, and it doesn't require us to establish and close a session. We simply put our data into a datagram and send it to the server; the server formulates its reply, puts the data into a datagram addressed back to us, and transmits it back. While this is both faster and more efficient than TCP for simple transactions, UDP was not designed to deal with datagram loss. It is up to the application, a name server for example, to take care of this.

More on Ports

Ports may be viewed as attachment points for network connections. If an application wants to offer a certain service, it attaches itself to a port and waits for clients (this is also called *listening* on the port). A client who wants to use this service allocates a port on its local host and connects to the server's port on the remote host. The same port may be open on many different machines, but on each machine only one process can open a port at any one time.

An important property of ports is that once a connection has been established between the client and the server, another copy of the server may attach to the server port and listen for more clients. This property permits, for instance, several concurrent remote logins to the same host, all using the same port 513. TCP is able to tell these connections from one another because they all come from different ports or hosts. For example, if you log in twice to **quark** from **erdos**, the first *rlogin* client will use the local port 1023, and the second one will use port 1022. Both, however, will connect to the same port 513 on **quark**. The two connections will be distinguished by use of the port numbers used at **erdos**.

This example shows the use of ports as rendezvous points, where a client contacts a specific port to obtain a specific service. In order for a client to know the proper port number, an agreement has to be reached between the administrators of both systems on the assignment of these numbers. For services that are widely used, such as *rlogin*, these numbers have to be administered centrally. This is done by the IETF (Internet Engineering Task Force), which regularly releases an RFC titled *Assigned Numbers* (RFC-1700). It describes, among other things, the port numbers assigned to well-known services. Linux uses a file called */etc/services* that maps service names to numbers.

It is worth noting that although both TCP and UDP connections rely on ports, these numbers do not conflict. This means that TCP port 513, for example, is different from UDP port 513. In fact, these ports serve as access points for two different services, namely *rlogin* (TCP) and *rwho* (UDP).

The Socket Library

In Unix operating systems, the software performing all the tasks and protocols described above is usually part of the kernel, and so it is in Linux. The programming interface most common in the Unix world is the *Berkeley Socket Library*. Its name derives from a popular analogy that views ports as sockets and connecting to a port as plugging in. It provides the *bind* call to specify a remote host, a transport protocol, and a service that a program can connect or listen to (using *connect, listen*, and *accept*). The socket library is somewhat more general in that it provides not only a class of TCP/IP-based sockets (the *AF_INET* sockets), but also a class that handles connections local to the machine (the *AF_UNIX* class). Some implementations can also handle other classes, like the XNS (*Xerox Networking System*) protocol or X.25.

In Linux, the socket library is part of the standard *libc* C library. It supports the *AF_INET* and *AF_INET6* sockets for TCP/IP and *AF_UNIX* for Unix domain sockets. It also supports *AF_IPX* for Novell's network protocols, *AF_X25* for the X.25 network protocol, *AF_ATMPVC* and *AF_ATMSVC* for the ATM network protocol and *AF_AX25*, *AF_NETROM*, and *AF_ROSE* sockets for Amateur Radio protocol support. Other protocol families are being developed and will be added in time.

UUCP Networks

Unix-to-Unix Copy (UUCP) started out as a package of programs that transferred files over serial lines, scheduled those transfers, and initiated execution of programs on remote sites. It has undergone major changes since its first implementation in the late seventies, but it is still rather spartan in the services it offers. Its main application is still in Wide Area Networks, based on periodic dialup telephone links.

UUCP was first developed by Bell Laboratories in 1977 for communication between their Unix development sites. In mid-1978, this network already connected over 80 sites. It was running email as an application, as well as remote printing. However, the system's central use was in distributing new software and bug fixes. Today, UUCP is not confined solely to the Unix environment. There are free and commercial ports available for a variety of platforms, including AmigaOS, DOS, and Atari's TOS.

One of the main disadvantages of UUCP networks is that they operate in batches. Rather than having a permanent connection established between hosts, it uses temporary connections. A UUCP host machine might dial in to another UUCP host only once a day, and then only for a short period of time. While it is connected, it will transfer all of the news, email, and files that have been queued, and then disconnect. It is this queuing that limits the sorts of applications that UUCP can be applied to. In the case of email, a user may prepare an email message and post it. The message will stay queued on the UUCP host machine until it dials in to another UUCP host to transfer the message. This is fine for network services such as email, but is no use at all for services such as *rlogin*.

Despite these limitations, there are still many UUCP networks operating all over the world, run mainly by hobbyists, which offer private users network access at reasonable prices. The main reason for the longtime popularity of UUCP was that it was very cheap compared to having your computer directly connected to the Internet. To make your computer a UUCP node, all you needed was a modem, a working UUCP implementation, and another UUCP node that was willing to feed you mail and news. Many people were prepared to provide UUCP feeds to individuals because such connections didn't place much demand on their existing network.

We cover the configuration of UUCP in a chapter of its own later in the book, but we won't focus on it too heavily, as it's being replaced rapidly with TCP/IP, now that cheap Internet access has become commonly available in most parts of the world.

Linux Networking

As it is the result of a concerted effort of programmers around the world, Linux wouldn't have been possible without the global network. So it's not surprising that in the early stages of development, several people started to work on providing it with network capabilities. A UUCP implementation was running on Linux almost from the very beginning, and work on TCP/IP-based networking started around autumn 1992, when Ross Biro and others created what has now become known as Net-1.

After Ross quit active development in May 1993, Fred van Kempen began to work on a new implementation, rewriting major parts of the code. This project was known as Net-2. The first public release, Net-2d, was made in the summer of 1993 (as part of the 0.99.10 kernel), and has since been maintained and expanded by several people, most notably Alan Cox.* Alan's original work was known as Net-2Debugged. After heavy debugging and numerous improvements to the code, he changed its name to Net-3 after Linux 1.0 was released. The Net-3 code was further developed for Linux 1.2 and Linux 2.0. The 2.2 and later kernels use the Net-4 version network support, which remains the standard official offering today.

The Net-4 Linux Network code offers a wide variety of device drivers and advanced features. Standard Net-4 protocols include SLIP and PPP (for sending network traffic over serial lines), PLIP (for parallel lines), IPX (for Novell compatible networks, which we'll discuss in Chapter 15, *IPX and the NCP Filesystem*), Appletalk (for Apple networks) and AX.25, NetRom, and Rose (for amateur radio networks). Other standard Net-4 features include IP firewalling, IP accounting (discussed later in Chapter 9, *TCP/IP Firewall* and Chapter 10, *IP Accounting*), and IP Masquerade (discussed later in Chapter 11, *IP Masquerade and Network Address Translation*. IP tunnelling in a couple of different flavors and advanced policy routing are supported. A very large variety of Ethernet devices is supported, in addition to support for some FDDI, Token Ring, Frame Relay, and ISDN, and ATM cards.

Additionally, there are a number of other features that greatly enhance the flexibility of Linux. These features include an implementation of the SMB filesystem, which interoperates with applications like *lanmanager* and Microsoft Windows, called Samba, written by Andrew Tridgell, and an implementation of the Novell NCP (NetWare Core Protocol).†

---

* Alan can be reached at *alan@lxorguk.ukuu.org.uk*

† NCP is the protocol on which Novell file and print services are based.

Different Streaks of Development

There have been, at various times, varying network development efforts active for Linux.

Fred continued development after Net-2Debugged was made the official network implementation. This development led to the Net-2e, which featured a much revised design of the networking layer. Fred was working toward a standardized Device Driver Interface (DDI), but the Net-2e work has ended now.

Yet another implementation of TCP/IP networking came from Matthias Urlichs, who wrote an ISDN driver for Linux and FreeBSD. For this driver, he integrated some of the BSD networking code in the Linux kernel. That project, too is no longer being worked on.

There has been a lot of rapid change in the Linux kernel networking implementation, and change is still the watchword as development continues. Sometimes this means that changes also have to occur in other software, such as the network configuration tools. While this is no longer as large a problem as it once was, you may still find that upgrading your kernel to a later version means that you must upgrade your network configuration tools, too. Fortunately, with the large number of Linux distributions available today, this is a quite simple task.

The Net-4 network implementation is now quite mature and is in use at a very large number of sites around the world. Much work has been done on improving the performance of the Net-4 implementation, and it now competes with the best implementations available for the same hardware platforms. Linux is proliferating in the Internet Service Provider environment, and is often used to build cheap and reliable World Wide Web servers, mail servers, and news servers for these sorts of organizations. There is now sufficient development interest in Linux that it is managing to keep abreast of networking technology as it changes, and current releases of the Linux kernel offer the next generation of the IP protocol, IPv6, as a standard offering.

Where to Get the Code

It seems odd now to remember that in the early days of the Linux network code development, the standard kernel required a huge patch kit to add the networking support to it. Today, network development occurs as part of the mainstream Linux kernel development process. The latest stable Linux kernels can be found on **ftp.kernel.org** in */pub/linux/kernel/v2.x/*, where *x* is an even number. The latest experimental Linux kernels can be found on **ftp.kernel.org** in */pub/linux/kernel/v2.y/*, where *y* is an odd number. There are Linux kernel source mirrors all over the world. It is now hard to imagine Linux without standard network support.

Maintaining Your System

Throughout this book, we will mainly deal with installation and configuration issues. Administration is, however, much more than that—after setting up a service, you have to keep it running, too. For most services, only a little attendance will be necessary, while some, like mail and news, require that you perform routine tasks to keep your system up to date. We will discuss these tasks in later chapters.

The absolute minimum in maintenance is to check system and per-application log files regularly for error conditions and unusual events. Often, you will want to do this by writing a couple of administrative shell scripts and periodically running them from *cron*. The source distributions of some major applications, like *inn* or C News, contain such scripts. You only have to tailor them to suit your needs and preferences.

The output from any of your *cron* jobs should be mailed to an administrative account. By default, many applications will send error reports, usage statistics, or log file summaries to the **root** account. This makes sense only if you log in as **root** frequently; a much better idea is to forward **root**'s mail to your personal account by setting up a mail alias as described in Chapter 19, *Getting Exim Up and Running* or Chapter 18, *Sendmail*.

However carefully you have configured your site, Murphy's law guarantees that some problem *will* surface eventually. Therefore, maintaining a system also means being available for complaints. Usually, people expect that the system administrator can at least be reached via email as *root*, but there are also other addresses that are commonly used to reach the person responsible for a specific aspect of maintenence. For instance, complaints about a malfunctioning mail configuration will usually be addressed to *postmaster*, and problems with the news system may be reported to *newsmaster* or *usenet*. Mail to *hostmaster* should be redirected to the person in charge of the host's basic network services, and the DNS name service if you run a name server.

System Security

Another very important aspect of system administration in a network environment is protecting your system and users from intruders. Carelessly managed systems offer malicious people many targets. Attacks range from password guessing to Ethernet snooping, and the damage caused may range from faked mail messages to data loss or violation of your users' privacy. We will mention some particular problems when discussing the context in which they may occur and some common defenses against them.

This section will discuss a few examples and basic techniques for dealing with system security. Of course, the topics covered cannot treat all security issues you may be faced with in detail; they merely serve to illustrate the problems that may arise. Therefore, reading a good book on security is an absolute must, especially in a networked system.

System security starts with good system administration. This includes checking the ownership and permissions of all vital files and directories and monitoring use of privileged accounts. The COPS program, for instance, will check your file system and common configuration files for unusual permissions or other anomalies. It is also wise to use a password suite that enforces certain rules on the users' passwords that make them hard to guess. The shadow password suite, for instance, requires a password to have at least five letters and to contain both upper- and lowercase numbers, as well as non-alphabetic characters.

When making a service accessible to the network, make sure to give it "least privilege"; don't permit it to do things that aren't required for it to work as designed. For example, you should make programs setuid to **root** or some other privileged account only when necessary. Also, if you want to use a service for only a very limited application, don't hesitate to configure it as restrictively as your special application allows. For instance, if you want to allow diskless hosts to boot from your machine, you must provide *Trivial File Transfer Protocol* (TFTP) so that they can download basic configuration files from the */boot* directory. However, when used unrestrictively, TFTP allows users anywhere in the world to download any world-readable file from your system. If this is not what you want, restrict TFTP service to the */boot* directory.*

You might also want to restrict certain services to users from certain hosts, say from your local network. In Chapter 12, we introduce *tcpd*, which does this for a variety of network applications. More sophisticated methods of restricting access to particular hosts or services will be explored later in Chapter 9.

Another important point is to avoid "dangerous" software. Of course, any software you use can be dangerous because software may have bugs that clever people might exploit to gain access to your system. Things like this happen, and there's no complete protection against it. This problem affects free software and commercial products alike.† However, programs that require special privilege are inherently more dangerous than others, because any loophole can have drastic consequences.‡ If you install a setuid program for network purposes, be doubly

---

* We will come back to this topic in Chapter 12, *Important Network Features.*

† There have been commercial Unix systems (that you have to pay lots of money for) that came with a setuid-**root** shell script, which allowed users to gain **root** privilege using a simple standard trick.

‡ In 1988, the RTM worm brought much of the Internet to a grinding halt, partly by exploiting a gaping hole in some programs including the *sendmail* program. This hole has long since been fixed.

careful to check the documentation so that you don't create a security breach by accident.

Another source of concern should be programs that enable login or command execution with limited authentication. The *rlogin, rsh,* and *rexec* commands are all very useful, but offer very limited authentication of the calling party. Authentication is based on trust of the calling host name obtained from a name server (we'll talk about these later), which can be faked. Today it should be standard practice to disable the *r* commands completely and replace them with the *ssh* suite of tools. The *ssh* tools use a much more reliable authentication method and provide other services, such as encryption and compression, as well.

You can never rule out the possibility that your precautions might fail, regardless of how careful you have been. You should therefore make sure you detect intruders early. Checking the system log files is a good starting point, but the intruder is probably clever enough to anticipate this action and will delete any obvious traces he or she left. However, there are tools like *tripwire*, written by Gene Kim and Gene Spafford, that allow you to check vital system files to see if their contents or permissions have been changed. *tripwire* computes various strong checksums over these files and stores them in a database. During subsequent runs, the checksums are recomputed and compared to the stored ones to detect any modifications.

## CHAPTER TWO

ISSUES OF TCP/IP NETWORKING

In this chapter we turn to the configuration decisions you'll need to make when connecting your Linux machine to a TCP/IP network, including dealing with IP addresses, hostnames, and routing issues. This chapter gives you the background you need in order to understand what your setup requires, while the next chapters cover the tools you will use.

To learn more about TCP/IP and the reasons behind it, refer to the three-volume set *Internetworking with TCP/IP*, by Douglas R. Comer (Prentice Hall). For a more detailed guide to managing a TCP/IP network, see *TCP/IP Network Administration* by Craig Hunt (O'Reilly).

Networking Interfaces

To hide the diversity of equipment that may be used in a networking environment, TCP/IP defines an abstract *interface* through which the hardware is accessed. This interface offers a set of operations that is the same for all types of hardware and basically deals with sending and receiving packets.

For each peripheral networking device, a corresponding interface has to be present in the kernel. For example, Ethernet interfaces in Linux are called by such names as *eth0* and *eth1*; PPP (discussed in Chapter 8, *The Point-to-Point Protocol*) interfaces are named *ppp0* and *ppp1*; and FDDI interfaces are given names like *fddi0* and *fddi1*. These interface names are used for configuration purposes when you want to specify a particular physical device in a configuration command, and they have no meaning beyond this use.

Before being used by TCP/IP networking, an interface must be assigned an IP address that serves as its identification when communicating with the rest of the world. This address is different from the interface name mentioned previously; if you compare an interface to a door, the address is like the nameplate pinned on it.

Other device parameters may be set, like the maximum size of datagrams that can be processed by a particular piece of hardware, which is referred to as *Maximum Transfer Unit* (MTU). Other attributes will be introduced later. Fortunately, most attributes have sensible defaults.

IP Addresses

As mentioned in Chapter 1, *Introduction to Networking*, the IP networking protocol understands addresses as 32-bit numbers. Each machine must be assigned a number unique to the networking environment.* If you are running a local network that does not have TCP/IP traffic with other networks, you may assign these numbers according to your personal preferences. There are some IP address ranges that have been reserved for such private networks. These ranges are listed in Table 2-1. However, for sites on the Internet, numbers are assigned by a central authority, the *Network Information Center* (NIC).†

IP addresses are split up into four eight-bit numbers called *octets* for readability. For example, **quark.physics.groucho.edu** has an IP address of **0x954C0C04**, which is written as **149.76.12.4**. This format is often referred to as *dotted quad notation*.

Another reason for this notation is that IP addresses are split into a *network* number, which is contained in the leading octets, and a *host* number, which is the remainder. When applying to the NIC for IP addresses, you are not assigned an address for each single host you plan to use. Instead, you are given a network number and allowed to assign all valid IP addresses within this range to hosts on your network according to your preferences.

The size of the host part depends on the size of the network. To accommodate different needs, several classes of networks, defining different places to split IP addresses, have been defined. The class networks are described here:

---

* The version of the Internet Protocol most frequently used on the Internet is Version 4. A lot of effort has been expended in designing a replacement called IP Version 6. IPv6 uses a different addressing scheme and larger addresses. Linux has an implementation of IPv6, but it isn't ready to document it in this book yet. The Linux kernel support for IPv6 is good, but a large number of network applications need to be modified to support it as well. Stay tuned.

† Frequently, IP addresses will be assigned to you by the provider from whom you buy your IP connectivity. However, you may also apply to the NIC directly for an IP address for your network by sending email to *hostmaster@internic.net*, or by using the form at *http://www.internic.net/*.

Class A

Class A comprises networks 1.0.0.0 through 127.0.0.0. The network number is contained in the first octet. This class provides for a 24-bit host part, allowing roughly 1.6 million hosts per network.

Class B

Class B contains networks 128.0.0.0 through 191.255.0.0; the network number is in the first two octets. This class allows for 16,320 nets with 65,024 hosts each.

Class C

Class C networks range from 192.0.0.0 through 223.255.255.0, with the network number contained in the first three octets. This class allows for nearly 2 million networks with up to 254 hosts.

Classes D, E, and F

Addresses falling into the range of 224.0.0.0 through 254.0.0.0 are either experimental or are reserved for special purpose use and don't specify any network. IP Multicast, which is a service that allows material to be transmitted to many points on an internet at one time, has been assigned addresses from within this range.

If we go back to the example in Chapter 1, we find that 149.76.12.4, the address of **quark**, refers to host 12.4 on the class B network 149.76.0.0.

You may have noticed that not all possible values in the previous list were allowed for each octet in the host part. This is because octets 0 and 255 are reserved for special purposes. An address where all host part bits are 0 refers to the network, and an address where all bits of the host part are 1 is called a *broadcast address*. This refers to all hosts on the specified network simultaneously. Thus, 149.76.255.255 is not a valid host address, but refers to all hosts on network 149.76.0.0.

A number of network addresses are reserved for special purposes. 0.0.0.0 and 127.0.0.0 are two such addresses. The first is called the *default route*, and the latter is the *loopback address*. The default route has to do with the way the IP routes datagrams.

Network 127.0.0.0 is reserved for IP traffic local to your host. Usually, address 127.0.0.1 will be assigned to a special interface on your host, the *loopback interface*, which acts like a closed circuit. Any IP packet handed to this interface from TCP or UDP will be returned to them as if it had just arrived from some network. This allows you to develop and test networking software without ever using a "real" network. The loopback network also allows you to use networking software on a standalone host. This may not be as uncommon as it sounds; for instance, many UUCP sites don't have IP connectivity at all, but still want to run the INN news system. For proper operation on Linux, INN requires the loopback interface.

Some address ranges from each of the network classes have been set aside and designated "reserved" or "private" address ranges. These addresses are reserved for use by private networks and are not routed on the Internet. They are commonly used by organizations building their own intranet, but even small networks often find them useful. The reserved network addresses appear in Table 2-1.

Table 2-1. IP Address Ranges Reserved for Private Use

Class	Networks
A	10.0.0.0 through 10.255.255.255
B	172.16.0.0 through 172.31.0.0
C	192.168.0.0 through 192.168.255.0

Address Resolution

Now that you've seen how IP addresses are composed, you may be wondering how they are used on an Ethernet or Token Ring network to address different hosts. After all, these protocols have their own addresses to identify hosts that have absolutely nothing in common with an IP address, don't they? Right.

A mechanism is needed to map IP addresses onto the addresses of the underlying network. The mechanism used is the *Address Resolution Protocol* (ARP). In fact, ARP is not confined to Ethernet or Token Ring, but is used on other types of networks, such as the amateur radio AX.25 protocol. The idea underlying ARP is exactly what most people do when they have to find Mr. X in a throng of 150 people: the person who wants him calls out loudly enough that everyone in the room can hear them, expecting him to respond if he is there. When he responds, we know which person he is.

When ARP wants to find the Ethernet address corresponding to a given IP address, it uses an Ethernet feature called *broadcasting*, in which a datagram is addressed to all stations on the network simultaneously. The broadcast datagram sent by ARP contains a query for the IP address. Each receiving host compares this query to its own IP address and if it matches, returns an ARP reply to the inquiring host. The inquiring host can now extract the sender's Ethernet address from the reply.

You may wonder how a host can reach an Internet address that may be on a different network halfway around the world. The answer to this question involves *routing*, namely finding the physical location of a host in a network. We will discuss this issue further in the next section.

Let's talk a little more about ARP. Once a host has discovered an Ethernet address, it stores it in its ARP cache so that it doesn't have to query for it again the next time it wants to send a datagram to the host in question. However, it is unwise to keep this information forever; the remote host's Ethernet card may be replaced because of technical problems, so the ARP entry becomes invalid. Therefore, entries in the ARP cache are discarded after some time to force another query for the IP address.

Sometimes it is also necessary to find the IP address associated with a given Ethernet address. This happens when a diskless machine wants to boot from a server on the network, which is a common situation on Local Area Networks. A diskless client, however, has virtually no information about itself—except for its Ethernet address! So it broadcasts a message containing a request asking a boot server to provide it with an IP address. There's another protocol for this situation named *Reverse Address Resolution Protocol* (RARP). Along with the BOOTP protocol, it serves to define a procedure for bootstrapping diskless clients over the network.

IP Routing

We now take up the question of finding the host that datagrams go to based on the IP address. Different parts of the address are handled in different ways; it is your job to set up the files that indicate how to treat each part.

IP Networks

When you write a letter to someone, you usually put a complete address on the envelope specifying the country, state, and Zip Code. After you put it in the mailbox, the post office will deliver it to its destination: it will be sent to the country indicated, where the national service will dispatch it to the proper state and region. The advantage of this hierarchical scheme is obvious: wherever you post the letter, the local postmaster knows roughly which direction to forward the letter, but the postmaster doesn't care which way the letter will travel once it reaches its country of destination.

IP networks are structured similarly. The whole Internet consists of a number of proper networks, called *autonomous systems.* Each system performs routing between its member hosts internally so that the task of delivering a datagram is reduced to finding a path to the destination host's network. As soon as the datagram is handed to *any* host on that particular network, further processing is done exclusively by the network itself.

Subnetworks

This structure is reflected by splitting IP addresses into a host and network part, as explained previously. By default, the destination network is derived from the network part of the IP address. Thus, hosts with identical IP *network* numbers should be found within the same network.*

It makes sense to offer a similar scheme *inside* the network, too, since it may consist of a collection of hundreds of smaller networks, with the smallest units being physical networks like Ethernets. Therefore, IP allows you to subdivide an IP network into several *subnets*.

A subnet takes responsibility for delivering datagrams to a certain range of IP addresses. It is an extension of the concept of splitting bit fields, as in the A, B, and C classes. However, the network part is now extended to include some bits from the host part. The number of bits that are interpreted as the subnet number is given by the so-called *subnet mask*, or *netmask*. This is a 32-bit number too, which specifies the bit mask for the network part of the IP address.

The campus network of Groucho Marx University is an example of such a network. It has a class B network number of **149.76.0.0**, and its netmask is therefore **255.255.0.0**.

Internally, GMU's campus network consists of several smaller networks, such various ous departments' LANs. So the range of IP addresses is broken up into 254 subnets, **149.76.1.0** through **149.76.254.0**. For example, the department of Theoretical Physics has been assigned **149.76.12.0**. The campus backbone is a network in its own right, and is given **149.76.1.0**. These subnets share the same IP network number, while the third octet is used to distinguish between them. They will thus use a subnet mask of **255.255.255.0**.

Figure 2-1 shows how **149.76.12.4**, the address of **quark**, is interpreted differently when the address is taken as an ordinary class B network and when used with subnetting.

It is worth noting that *subnetting* (the technique of generating subnets) is only an *internal division* of the network. Subnets are generated by the network owner (or the administrators). Frequently, subnets are created to reflect existing boundaries, be they physical (between two Ethernets), administrative (between two departments), or geographical (between two locations), and authority over each subnet is delegated to some contact person. However, this structure affects only the network's internal behavior, and is completely invisible to the outside world.

---

* Autonomous systems are slightly more general. They may comprise more than one IP network.

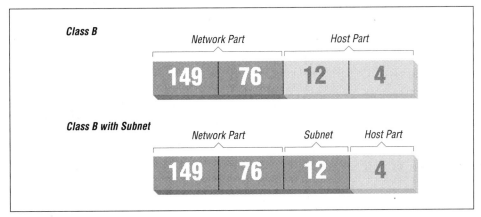

Figure 2-1. Subnetting a class B network

Gateways

Subnetting is not only a benefit to the organization; it is frequently a natural consequence of hardware boundaries. The viewpoint of a host on a given physical network, such as an Ethernet, is a very limited one: it can only talk to the host of the network it is on. All other hosts can be accessed only through special-purpose machines called *gateways*. A gateway is a host that is connected to two or more physical networks simultaneously and is configured to switch packets between them.

Figure 2-2 shows part of the network topology at Groucho Marx University (GMU). Hosts that are on two subnets at the same time are shown with both addresses.

Different physical networks have to belong to different IP networks for IP to be able to recognize if a host is on a local network. For example, the network number 149.76.4.0 is reserved for hosts on the mathematics LAN. When sending a datagram to **quark**, the network software on **erdos** immediately sees from the IP address 149.76.12.4 that the destination host is on a different physical network, and therefore can be reached only through a gateway (**sophus** by default).

sophus itself is connected to two distinct subnets: the Mathematics department and the campus backbone. It accesses each through a different interface, *eth0* and *fddi0*, respectively. Now, what IP address do we assign it? Should we give it one on subnet 149.76.1.0, or on 149.76.4.0?

The answer is: "both." **sophus** has been assigned the address 149.76.1.1 for use on the 149.76.1.0 network and address 149.76.4.1 for use on the 149.76.4.0 network. A gateway must be assigned one IP address for each network it belongs to. These

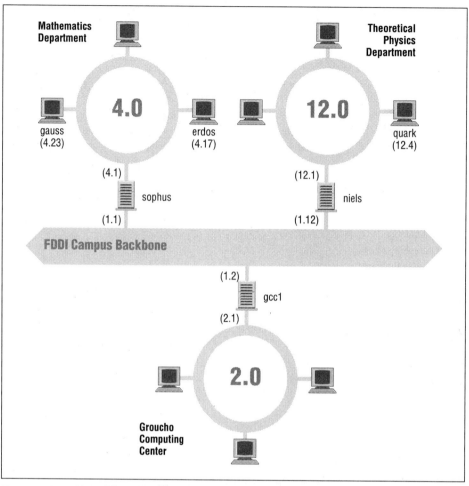

Figure 2-2. A part of the net topology at Groucho Marx University

addresses—along with the corresponding netmask—are tied to the interface through which the subnet is accessed. Thus, the interface and address mapping for **sophus** would look like this:

Interface	Address	Netmask
eth0	149.76.4.1	255.255.255.0
fddi0	149.76.1.1	255.255.255.0
lo	127.0.0.1	255.0.0.0

The last entry describes the loopback interface *lo*, which we talked about earlier.

Generally, you can ignore the subtle difference between attaching an address to a host or its interface. For hosts that are on one network only, like **erdos**, you would generally refer to the host as having this-and-that IP address, although strictly speaking, it's the Ethernet interface that has this IP address. The distinction is really important only when you refer to a gateway.

The Routing Table

We now focus our attention on how IP chooses a gateway to use to deliver a datagram to a remote network.

We have seen that **erdos**, when given a datagram for **quark**, checks the destination address and finds that it is not on the local network. **erdos** therefore sends the datagram to the default gateway **sophus**, which is now faced with the same task. **sophus** recognizes that **quark** is not on any of the networks it is connected to directly, so it has to find yet another gateway to forward it through. The correct choice would be **niels**, the gateway to the Physics department. **sophus** thus needs information to associate a destination network with a suitable gateway.

IP uses a table for this task that associates networks with the gateways by which they may be reached. A catch-all entry (the *default route*) must generally be supplied too; this is the gateway associated with network 0.0.0.0. All destination addresses match this route, since none of the 32 bits are required to match, and therefore packets to an unknown network are sent through the default route. On **sophus**, the table might look like this:

Network	Netmask	Gateway	Interface
149.76.1.0	255.255.255.0	-	*fddi0*
149.76.2.0	255.255.255.0	149.76.1.2	*fddi0*
149.76.3.0	255.255.255.0	149.76.1.3	*fddi0*
149.76.4.0	255.255.255.0	-	*eth0*
149.76.5.0	255.255.255.0	149.76.1.5	*fddi0*
...	...	...	...
0.0.0.0	0.0.0.0	149.76.1.2	*fddi0*

If you need to use a route to a network that **sophus** is directly connected to, you don't need a gateway; the gateway column here contains a hyphen.

The process for identifying whether a particular destination address matches a route is a mathematical operation. The process is quite simple, but it requires an understanding of binary arithmetic and logic: A route matches a destination if the network address logically ANDed with the netmask precisely equals the destination address logically ANDed with the netmask.

Translation: a route matches if the number of bits of the network address specified by the netmask (starting from the left-most bit, the high order bit of byte one of the address) match that same number of bits in the destination address.

When the IP implementation is searching for the best route to a destination, it may find a number of routing entries that match the target address. For example, we know that the default route matches every destination, but datagrams destined for locally attached networks will match their local route, too. How does IP know which route to use? It is here that the netmask plays an important role. While both routes match the destination, one of the routes has a larger netmask than the other. We previously mentioned that the netmask was used to break up our address space into smaller networks. The larger a netmask is, the more specifically a target address is matched; when routing datagrams, we should always choose the route that has the largest netmask. The default route has a netmask of zero bits, and in the configuration presented above, the locally attached networks have a 24-bit netmask. If a datagram matches a locally attached network, it will be routed to the appropriate device in preference to following the default route because the local network route matches with a greater number of bits. The only datagrams that will be routed via the default route are those that don't match any other route.

You can build routing tables by a variety of means. For small LANs, it is usually most efficient to construct them by hand and feed them to IP using the *route* command at boot time (see Chapter 5, *Configuring TCP/IP Networking*). For larger networks, they are built and adjusted at runtime by *routing daemons*; these daemons run on central hosts of the network and exchange routing information to compute "optimal" routes between the member networks.

Depending on the size of the network, you'll need to use different routing protocols. For routing inside autonomous systems (such as the Groucho Marx campus), the *internal routing protocols* are used. The most prominent one of these is the *Routing Information Protocol* (RIP), which is implemented by the BSD *routed* daemon. For routing between autonomous systems, *external routing protocols* like *External Gateway Protocol* (EGP) or *Border Gateway Protocol* (BGP) have to be used; these protocols, including RIP, have been implemented in the University of Cornell's *gated* daemon.

Metric Values

We depend on dynamic routing to choose the best route to a destination host or network based on the number of *hops*. Hops are the gateways a datagram has to pass before reaching a host or network. The shorter a route is, the better RIP rates it. Very long routes with 16 or more hops are regarded as unusable and are discarded.

RIP manages routing information internal to your local network, but you have to run *gated* on all hosts. At boot time, *gated* checks for all active network interfaces. If there is more than one active interface (not counting the loopback interface), it assumes the host is switching packets between several networks and will actively exchange and broadcast routing information. Otherwise, it will only passively receive RIP updates and update the local routing table.

When broadcasting information from the local routing table, *gated* computes the length of the route from the so-called *metric value* associated with the routing table entry. This metric value is set by the system administrator when configuring the route, and should reflect the actual route cost.* Therefore, the metric of a route to a subnet that the host is directly connected to should always be zero, while a route going through two gateways should have a metric of two. You don't have to bother with metrics if you don't use *RIP* or *gated*.

The Internet Control Message Protocol

IP has a companion protocol that we haven't talked about yet. This is the *Internet Control Message Protocol* (ICMP), used by the kernel networking code to communicate error messages to other hosts. For instance, assume that you are on **erdos** again and want to *telnet* to port 12345 on **quark**, but there's no process listening on that port. When the first TCP packet for this port arrives on **quark**, the networking layer will recognize this arrival and immediately return an ICMP message to **erdos** stating "Port Unreachable."

The ICMP protocol provides several different messages, many of which deal with error conditions. However, there is one very interesting message called the Redirect message. It is generated by the routing module when it detects that another host is using it as a gateway, even though a much shorter route exists. For example, after booting, the routing table of **sophus** may be incomplete. It might contain the routes to the Mathematics network, to the FDDI backbone, and the default route pointing at the Groucho Computing Center's gateway (gcc1). Thus, packets for **quark** would be sent to **gcc1** rather than to **niels**, the gateway to the Physics department. When receiving such a datagram, **gcc1** will notice that this is a poor choice of route and will forward the packet to **niels**, meanwhile returning an ICMP Redirect message to **sophus** telling it of the superior route.

This seems to be a very clever way to avoid manually setting up any but the most basic routes. However, be warned that relying on dynamic routing schemes, be it RIP or ICMP Redirect messages, is not always a good idea. ICMP Redirect and RIP

---

* The cost of a route can be thought of, in a simple case, as the number of hops required to reach the destination. Proper calculation of route costs can be a fine art in complex network designs.

offer you little or no choice in verifying that some routing information is indeed authentic. This situation allows malicious good-for-nothings to disrupt your entire network traffic, or even worse. Consequently, the Linux networking code treats Network Redirect messages as if they were Host Redirects. This minimizes the damage of an attack by restricting it to just one host, rather than the whole network. On the flip side, it means that a little more traffic is generated in the event of a legitimate condition, as each host causes the generation of an ICMP Redirect message. It is generally considered bad practice to rely on ICMP redirects for anything these days.

Resolving Host Names

As described previously, addressing in TCP/IP networking, at least for IP Version 4, revolves around 32-bit numbers. However, you will have a hard time remembering more than a few of these numbers. Therefore, hosts are generally known by "ordinary" names such as **gauss** or **strange**. It becomes the application's duty to find the IP address corresponding to this name. This process is called *hostname resolution.*

When an application needs to find the IP address of a given host, it relies on the library functions *gethostbyname(3)* and *gethostbyaddr(3)*. Traditionally, these and a number of related procedures were grouped in a separate library called the *resolverlibrary*; on Linux, these functions are part of the standard *libc*. Colloquially, this collection of functions is therefore referred to as "the resolver." Resolver name configuration is detailed in Chapter 6, *Name Service and Resolver Configuration.*

On a small network like an Ethernet or even a cluster of Ethernets, it is not very difficult to maintain tables mapping hostnames to addresses. This information is usually kept in a file named */etc/hosts*. When adding or removing hosts, or reassigning addresses, all you have to do is update the *hosts* file on all hosts. Obviously, this will become burdensome with networks that comprise more than a handful of machines.

One solution to this problem is the *Network Information System* (NIS), developed by Sun Microsystems, colloquially called YP or Yellow Pages. NIS stores the *hosts* file (and other information) in a database on a master host from which clients may retrieve it as needed. Still, this approach is suitable only for medium-sized networks such as LANs, because it involves maintaining the entire *hosts* database centrally and distributing it to all servers. NIS installation and configuration is discussed in detail in Chapter 13, *The Network Information System.*

On the Internet, address information was initially stored in a single *HOSTS.TXT* database, too. This file was maintained at the *Network Information Center* (NIC), and had to be downloaded and installed by all participating sites. When the network grew, several problems with this scheme arose. Besides the administrative overhead involved in installing *HOSTS.TXT* regularly, the load on the servers that distributed it became too high. Even more severe, all names had to be registered with the NIC, which made sure that no name was issued twice.

This is why a new name resolution scheme was adopted in 1994: the *Domain Name System*. DNS was designed by Paul Mockapetris and addresses both problems simultaneously. We discuss the Domain Name System in detail in Chapter 6.

CHAPTER THREE

CONFIGURING THE NETWORKING HARDWARE

We've been talking quite a bit about network interfaces and general TCP/IP issues, but we haven't really covered what happens when the "networking code" in the kernel accesses a piece of hardware. In order to describe this accurately, we have to talk a little about the concept of interfaces and drivers.

First, of course, there's the hardware itself, for example an Ethernet, FDDI or Token Ring card: this is a slice of Epoxy cluttered with lots of tiny chips with strange numbers on them, sitting in a slot of your PC. This is what we generally call a physical device.

For you to use a network card, special functions have to be present in your Linux kernel that understand the particular way this device is accessed. The software that implements these functions is called a *device driver*. Linux has device drivers for many different types of network interface cards: ISA, PCI, MCA, EISA, Parallel port, PCMCIA, and more recently, USB.

But what do we mean when we say a driver "handles" a device? Let's consider an Ethernet card. The driver has to be able to communicate with the peripheral's on-card logic somehow: it has to send commands and data to the card, while the card should deliver any data received to the driver.

In IBM-style personal computers, this communication takes place through a cluster of I/O addresses that are mapped to registers on the card and/or through shared or direct memory transfers. All commands and data the kernel sends to the card have to go to these addresses. I/O and memory addresses are generally described by providing the starting or *base address*. Typical base addresses for ISA bus Ethernet cards are 0x280 or 0x300. PCI bus network cards generally have their I/O address automatically assigned.

Usually you don't have to worry about any hardware issues such as the base address because the kernel makes an attempt at boot time to detect a card's location. This is called *auto probing*, which means that the kernel reads several memory or I/O locations and compares the data it reads there with what it would expect to see if a certain network card were installed at that location. However, there may be network cards it cannot detect automatically; this is sometimes the case with cheap network cards that are not-quite clones of standard cards from other manufacturers. Also, the kernel will normally attempt to detect only one network device when booting. If you're using more than one card, you have to tell the kernel about the other cards explicitly.

Another parameter that you might have to tell the kernel about is the interrupt request line. Hardware components usually interrupt the kernel when they need to be taken care of—for example, when data has arrived or a special condition occurs. In an ISA bus PC, interrupts may occur on one of 15 interrupt channels numbered 0, 1, and 3 through 15. The interrupt number assigned to a hardware component is called its *interrupt request number* (IRQ).*

As described in Chapter 2, *Issues of TCP/IP Networking*, the kernel accesses a piece of network hardware through a software construct called an *interface*. Interfaces offer an abstract set of functions that are the same across all types of hardware, such as sending or receiving a datagram.

Interfaces are identified by means of names. In many other Unix-like operating systems, the network interface is implemented as a special device file in the */dev/* directory. If you type the `ls -las /dev/` command, you will see what these device files look like. In the file permissions (second) column you will see that device files begin with a letter rather than the hyphen seen for normal files. This character indicates the device type. The most common device types are `b`, which indicates the device is a *block* device and handles whole blocks of data with each read and write, and `c`, which indicates the device is a *character* device and handles data one character at a time. Where you would normally see the file length in the *ls* output, you instead see two numbers, called the major and minor device numbers. These numbers indicate the actual device with which the device file is associated.

Each device driver registers a unique major number with the kernel. Each *instance* of that device registers a unique minor number for that major device. The `tty` interfaces, */dev/tty**, are a character mode device indicated by the "`c`", and each have a major number of `4`, but */dev/tty1* has a minor number of 1, and */dev/tty2* has a minor number of 2. Device files are very useful for many types of devices, but can be clumsy to use when trying to find an unused device to open.

---

* IRQs 2 and 9 are the same because the IBM PC design has two cascaded interrupt processors with eight IRQs each; the secondary processor is connected to IRQ 2 of the primary one.

Linux interface names are defined internally in the kernel and are not device files in the */dev* directory. Some typical device names are listed later in "A Tour of Linux Network Devices." The assignment of interfaces to devices usually depends on the order in which devices are configured. For instance, the first Ethernet card installed will become *eth0*, and the next will be *eth1*. SLIP interfaces are handled differently from others because they are assigned dynamically. Whenever a SLIP connection is established, an interface is assigned to the serial port.

Figure 3-1 illustrates the relationship between the hardware, device drivers, and interfaces.

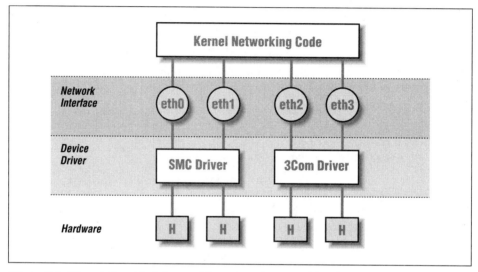

Figure 3-1. The relationship between drivers, interfaces, and hardware

When booting, the kernel displays the devices it detects and the interfaces it installs. The following is an excerpt from typical boot messages:

```
   .
   . This processor honors the WP bit even when in supervisor mode./
     Good.
Swansea University Computer Society NET3.035 for Linux 2.0
NET3: Unix domain sockets 0.13 for Linux NET3.035.
Swansea University Computer Society TCP/IP for NET3.034
IP Protocols: IGMP,ICMP, UDP, TCP
Swansea University Computer Society IPX 0.34 for NET3.035
IPX Portions Copyright (c) 1995 Caldera, Inc.
Serial driver version 4.13 with no serial options enabled
tty00 at 0x03f8 (irq = 4) is a 16550A
tty01 at 0x02f8 (irq = 3) is a 16550A
CSLIP: code copyright 1989 Regents of the University of California
PPP: Version 2.2.0 (dynamic channel allocation)
```

```
PPP Dynamic channel allocation code copyright 1995 Caldera, Inc.
PPP line discipline registered.
eth0: 3c509 at 0x300 tag 1, 10baseT port, address 00 a0 24 0e e4 e0,/
    IRQ 10.
3c509.c:1.12 6/4/97 becker@cesdis.gsfc.nasa.gov
Linux Version 2.0.32 (root@perf) (gcc Version 2.7.2.1)
#1 Tue Oct 21 15:30:44 EST 1997
```
.
.

This example shows that the kernel has been compiled with TCP/IP enabled, and it includes drivers for SLIP, CSLIP, and PPP. The third line from the bottom says that a 3C509 Ethernet card was detected and installed as interface *eth0*. If you have some other type of network card—perhaps a D-Link pocket adaptor, for example—the kernel will usually print a line starting with its device name—*dl0* in the D-Link example—followed by the type of card detected. If you have a network card installed but don't see any similar message, the kernel is unable to detect your card properly. This situation will be discussed later in the section "Ethernet Autoprobing."

Kernel Configuration

Most Linux distributions are supplied with boot disks that work for all common types of PC hardware. Generally, the supplied kernel is highly modularized and includes nearly every possible driver. This is a great idea for boot disks, but is probably not what you'd want for long-term use. There isn't much point in having drivers cluttering up your disk that you will never use. Therefore, you will generally roll your own kernel and include only those drivers you actually need or want; that way you save a little disk space and reduce the time it takes to compile a new kernel.

In any case, when running a Linux system, you should be familiar with building a kernel. Think of it as a right of passage, an affirmation of the one thing that makes free software as powerful as it is—you have the source. It isn't a case of, "I have to compile a kernel," rather it's a case of, "I *can* compile a kernel." The basics of compiling a Linux kernel are explained in Matt Welsh's book, *Running Linux* (O'Reilly). Therefore, we will discuss only configuration options that affect networking in this section.

One important point that does bear repeating here is the way the kernel version numbering scheme works. Linux kernels are numbered in the following format: 2.2.14. The first digit indicates the *major* version number. This digit changes when there are large and significant changes to the kernel design. For example, the kernel changed from major 1 to 2 when the kernel obtained support for machines other than Intel machines. The second number is the *minor* version number. In many respects, this number is the most important number to look at.

The Linux development community has adopted a standard at which *even* minor version numbers indicate *production,* or *stable,* kernels and *odd* minor version numbers indicate *development,* or *unstable,* kernels. The stable kernels are what you should use on a machine that is important to you, as they have been more thoroughly tested. The development kernels are what you should use if you are interested in experimenting with the newest features of Linux, but they may have problems that haven't yet been found and fixed. The third number is simply incremented for each release of a minor version.*

When running *make menuconfig,* you are presented with a text-based menu that offers lists of configuration questions, such as whether you want kernel math emulation. One of these queries asks you whether you want TCP/IP networking support. You must answer this with y to get a kernel capable of networking.

Kernel Options in Linux 2.0 and Higher

After the general option section is complete, the configuration will go on to ask whether you want to include support for various features, such as SCSI drivers or sound cards. The prompt will indicate what options are available. You can press ? to obtain a description of what the option is actually offering. You'll always have the option of yes (y) to statically include the component in the kernel, or no (n) to exclude the component completely. You'll also see the module (m) option for those components that may be compiled as a run-time loadable module. Modules need to be loaded before they can be used, and are useful for drivers of components that you use infrequently.

The subsequent list of questions deal with networking support. The exact set of configuration options is in constant flux due to ongoing development. A typical list of options offered by most kernel versions around 2.0 and 2.1 looks like this:

```
*
* Network device support
*
Network device support (CONFIG_NETDEVICES) [Y/n/?]
```

You must answer this question with y if you want to use *any* type of networking devices, whether they are Ethernet, SLIP, PPP, or whatever. When you answer the question with y, support for Ethernet-type devices is enabled automatically. You must answer additional questions if you want to enable support for other types of network drivers:

---

* People should use development kernels and report bugs if they are found; this is a very useful thing to do if you have a machine you can use as a test machine. Instructions on how to report bugs are detailed in */usr/src/linux/REPORTING-BUGS* in the Linux kernel source.

```
PLIP (parallel port) support (CONFIG_PLIP) [N/y/m/?] y
PPP (point-to-point) support (CONFIG_PPP) [N/y/m/?] y
*
* CCP compressors for PPP are only built as modules.
*
SLIP (serial line) support (CONFIG_SLIP) [N/y/m/?] m
 CSLIP compressed headers (CONFIG_SLIP_COMPRESSED) [N/y/?] (NEW) y
 Keepalive and linefill (CONFIG_SLIP_SMART) [N/y/?] (NEW) y
 Six bit SLIP encapsulation (CONFIG_SLIP_MODE_SLIP6) [N/y/?] (NEW) y
```

These questions concern the various link layer protocols that Linux supports. Both PPP and SLIP allow you to transport IP datagrams across serial lines. PPP is actually a suite of protocols used to send network traffic across serial lines. Some of the protocols that form PPP manage the way that you authenticate yourself to the dial-in server, while others manage the way certain protocols are carried across the link—PPP is not limited to carrying TCP/IP datagrams; it may also carry other protocol such as IPX.

If you answer y or m to SLIP support, you will be prompted to answer the three questions that appear below it. The compressed header option provides support for CSLIP, a technique that compresses TCP/IP headers to as little as three bytes. Note that this kernel option does not turn on CSLIP automatically; it merely provides the necessary kernel functions for it. The `Keepalive and linefill` option causes the SLIP support to periodically generate activity on the SLIP line to avoid it being dropped by an inactivity timer. The `Six bit SLIP encapsulation` option allows you to run SLIP over lines and circuits that are not capable of transmitting the whole 8-bit data set cleanly. This is similar to the uuencoding or binhex technique used to send binary files by electronic mail.

PLIP provides a way to send IP datagrams across a parallel port connection. It is mostly used to communicate with PCs running DOS. On typical PC hardware, PLIP can be faster than PPP or SLIP, but it requires much more CPU overhead to perform, so while the transfer rate might be good, other tasks on the machine may be slow.

The following questions address network cards from various vendors. As more drivers are being developed, you are likely to see questions added to this section. If you want to build a kernel you can use on a number of different machines, or if your machine has more than one type of network card installed, you can enable more than one driver:

```
    .
    .
Ethernet (10 or 100Mbit) (CONFIG_NET_ETHERNET) [Y/n/?]
3COM cards (CONFIG_NET_VENDOR_3COM) [Y/n/?]
3c501 support (CONFIG_EL1) [N/y/m/?]
3c503 support (CONFIG_EL2) [N/y/m/?]
3c509/3c579 support (CONFIG_EL3) [Y/m/n/?]
3c590/3c900 series (592/595/597/900/905) "Vortex/Boomerang" support/
    (CONFIG_VORTEX) [N/y/m/?]
```

```
AMD LANCE and PCnet (AT1500 and NE2100) support (CONFIG_LANCE) [N/y/?]
AMD PCInet32 (VLB and PCI) support (CONFIG_LANCE32) [N/y/?] (NEW)
Western Digital/SMC cards (CONFIG_NET_VENDOR_SMC) [N/y/?]
WD80*3 support (CONFIG_WD80x3) [N/y/m/?] (NEW)
SMC Ultra support (CONFIG_ULTRA) [N/y/m/?] (NEW)
SMC Ultra32 support (CONFIG_ULTRA32) [N/y/m/?] (NEW)
SMC 9194 support (CONFIG_SMC9194) [N/y/m/?] (NEW)
Other ISA cards (CONFIG_NET_ISA) [N/y/?]
Cabletron E21xx support (CONFIG_E2100) [N/y/m/?] (NEW)
DEPCA, DE10x, DE200, DE201, DE202, DE422 support (CONFIG_DEPCA) [N/y/m/?]/
    (NEW)
EtherWORKS 3 (DE203, DE204, DE205) support (CONFIG_EWRK3) [N/y/m/?] (NEW)
EtherExpress 16 support (CONFIG_EEXPRESS) [N/y/m/?] (NEW)
HP PCLAN+ (27247B and 27252A) support (CONFIG_HPLAN_PLUS) [N/y/m/?] (NEW)
HP PCLAN (27245 and other 27xxx series) support (CONFIG_HPLAN) [N/y/m/?]/
    (NEW)
HP 10/100VG PCLAN (ISA, EISA, PCI) support (CONFIG_HP100) [N/y/m/?] (NEW)
NE2000/NE1000 support (CONFIG_NE2000) [N/y/m/?] (NEW)
SK_G16 support (CONFIG_SK_G16) [N/y/?] (NEW)
EISA, VLB, PCI and on card controllers (CONFIG_NET_EISA) [N/y/?]
Apricot Xen-II on card ethernet (CONFIG_APRICOT) [N/y/m/?] (NEW)
Intel EtherExpress/Pro 100B support (CONFIG_EEXPRESS_PRO100B) [N/y/m/?]/
    (NEW)
DE425, DE434, DE435, DE450, DE500 support (CONFIG_DE4X5) [N/y/m/?] (NEW)
DECchip Tulip (dc21x4x) PCI support (CONFIG_DEC_ELCP) [N/y/m/?] (NEW)
Digi Intl. RightSwitch SE-X support (CONFIG_DGRS) [N/y/m/?] (NEW)
Pocket and portable adaptors (CONFIG_NET_POCKET) [N/y/?]
AT-LAN-TEC/RealTek pocket adaptor support (CONFIG_ATP) [N/y/?] (NEW)
D-Link DE600 pocket adaptor support (CONFIG_DE600) [N/y/m/?] (NEW)
D-Link DE620 pocket adaptor support (CONFIG_DE620) [N/y/m/?] (NEW)
Token Ring driver support (CONFIG_TR) [N/y/?]
IBM Tropic chipset based adaptor support (CONFIG_IBMTR) [N/y/m/?] (NEW)
FDDI driver support (CONFIG_FDDI) [N/y/?]
Digital DEFEA and DEFPA adapter support (CONFIG_DEFXX) [N/y/?] (NEW)
ARCnet support (CONFIG_ARCNET) [N/y/m/?]
  Enable arc0e (ARCnet "Ether-Encap" packet format) (CONFIG_ARCNET_ETH)/
      [N/y/?] (NEW)
  Enable arc0s (ARCnet RFC1051 packet format) (CONFIG_ARCNET_1051)/
      [N/y/?] (NEW)
   .
   .
```

Finally, in the file system section, the configuration script will ask you whether you want support for NFS, the networking file system. NFS lets you export file systems to several hosts, which makes the files appear as if they were on an ordinary hard disk attached to the host:

```
NFS file system support (CONFIG_NFS_FS) [y]
```

We describe NFS in detail in Chapter 14, *The Network File System.*

Kernel Networking Options in Linux 2.0.0 and Higher

Linux 2.0.0 marked a significant change in Linux Networking. Many features were made a standard part of the Kernel, such as support for IPX. A number of options were also added and made configurable. Many of these options are used only in very special circumstances and we won't cover them in detail. The Networking HOWTO probably addresses what is not covered here. We'll list a number of useful options in this section, and explain when you'd want to use each one:

Basics

To use TCP/IP networking, you must answer this question with y. If you answer with n, however, you will still be able to compile the kernel with IPX support:

```
Networking options  --->
    [*] TCP/IP networking
```

Gateways

You have to enable this option if your system acts as a gateway between two networks or between a LAN and a SLIP link, etc. It doesn't hurt to enable this by default, but you may want to disable it to configure a host as a so-called *firewall*. Firewalls are hosts that are connected to two or more networks, but don't route traffic between them. They're commonly used to provide users with Internet access at minimal risk to the internal network. Users are allowed to log in to the firewall and use Internet services, but the company's machines are protected from outside attacks because incoming connections can't cross the firewall (firewalls are covered in detail in Chapter 9, *TCP/IP Firewall*):

```
    [*] IP: forwarding/gatewaying
```

Virtual hosting

These options together allow to you configure more than one IP address onto an interface. This is sometimes useful if you want to do "virtual hosting," through which a single machine can be configured to look and act as though it were actually many separate machines, each with its own network personality. We'll talk more about IP aliasing in a moment:

```
    [*] Network aliasing
        <*> IP: aliasing support
```

Accounting

This option enables you to collect data on the volume of IP traffic leaving and arriving at your machine (we cover this is detail in Chapter 10, *IP Accounting*):

```
[*] IP: accounting
```

PC bug

This option works around an incompatibility with some versions of PC/TCP, a commercial TCP/IP implementation for DOS-based PCs. If you enable this option, you will still be able to communicate with normal Unix machines, but performance may be hurt over slow links:

```
--- (it is safe to leave these untouched)
[*] IP: PC/TCP compatibility mode
```

Diskless booting

This function enables *Reverse Address Resolution Protocol* (RARP). RARP is used by diskless clients and X terminals to request their IP address when booting. You should enable RARP if you plan to serve this sort of client. A small program called *rarp*, included with the standard networking utilities, is used to add entries to the kernel RARP table:

```
<*> IP: Reverse ARP
```

MTU

When sending data over TCP, the kernel has to break up the stream into blocks of data to pass to IP. The size of the block is called the *Maximum Transmission Unit*, or MTU. For hosts that can be reached over a local network such as an Ethernet, it is typical to use an MTU as large as the maximum length of an Ethernet packet—1,500 bytes. When routing IP over a Wide Area Network like the Internet, it is preferable to use smaller-sized datagrams to ensure that they don't need to be further broken down along the route through a process called *IP fragmentation*.* The kernel is able to automatically determine the smallest MTU of an IP route and to automatically configure a TCP connection to use it. This behavior is on by default. If you answer y to this option this feature will be disabled.

If you do want to use smaller packet sizes for data sent to specific hosts (because, for example, the data goes through a SLIP link), you can do so using the *mss* option of the *route* command, which is briefly discussed at the end of this chapter:

```
[ ] IP: Disable Path MTU Discovery (normally enabled)
```

Security feature

The IP protocol supports a feature called *Source Routing*. Source routing allows you to specify the route a datagram should follow by coding the route into the datagram itself. This was once probably useful before routing protocols such as RIP and OSPF became commonplace. But today it's considered a security threat because it can provide clever attackers with a way of

---

* Remember, the IP protocol can be carried over many different types of network, and not all network types will support packet sizes as large as Ethernet.

circumventing certain types of firewall protection by bypassing the routing table of a router. You would normally want to filter out source routed datagrams, so this option is normally enabled:

```
[*] IP: Drop source routed frames
```

Novell support

This option enables support for IPX, the transport protocol Novell Networking uses. Linux will function quite happily as an IPX router and this support is useful in environments where you have Novell fileservers. The NCP filesystem also requires IPX support enabled in your kernel; if you wish to attach to and mount your Novell filesystems you must have this option enabled (we'll dicuss IPX and the NCP filesystem in Chapter 15, *IPX and the NCP Filesystem*):

```
<*> The IPX protocol
```

Amateur radio

These three options select support for the three Amateur Radio protocols supported by Linux: AX.25, NetRom and Rose (we don't describe them in this book, but they are covered in detail in the AX25 HOWTO):

```
<*> Amateur Radio AX.25 Level 2
<*> Amateur Radio NET/ROM
<*> Amateur Radio X.25 PLP (Rose)
```

Linux supports another driver type: the dummy driver. The following question appears toward the start of the device-driver section:

```
<*> Dummy net driver support
```

The dummy driver doesn't really do much, but it is quite useful on standalone or PPP/SLIP hosts. It is basically a masqueraded loopback interface. On hosts that offer PPP/SLIP but have no other network interface, you want to have an interface that bears your IP address all the time. This is discussed in a little more detail in "The Dummy Interface" in Chapter 5, *Configuring TCP/IP Networking*. Note that today you can achieve the same result by using the IP alias feature and configuring your IP address as an alias on the loopback interface.

A Tour of Linux Network Devices

The Linux kernel supports a number of hardware drivers for various types of equipment. This section gives a short overview of the driver families available and the interface names they use.

There is a number of standard names for interfaces in Linux, which are listed here. Most drivers support more than one interface, in which case the interfaces are numbered, as in *eth0* and *eth1*:

lo   This is the local loopback interface. It is used for testing purposes, as well as a couple of network applications. It works like a closed circuit in that any datagram written to it will immediately be returned to the host's networking layer. There's always one loopback device present in the kernel, and there's little sense in having more.

eth0, eth1, ...
These are the Ethernet card interfaces. They are used for most Ethernet cards, including many of the parallel port Ethernet cards.

tr0, tr1, ...
These are the Token Ring card interfaces. They are used for most Token Ring cards, including non-IBM manufactured cards.

sl0, sl1, ...
These are the SLIP interfaces. SLIP interfaces are associated with serial lines in the order in which they are allocated for SLIP.

ppp0, ppp1, ...
These are the PPP interfaces. Just like SLIP interfaces, a PPP interface is associated with a serial line once it is converted to PPP mode.

plip0, plip1, ...
These are the PLIP interfaces. PLIP transports IP datagrams over parallel lines. The interfaces are allocated by the PLIP driver at system boot time and are mapped onto parallel ports. In the *2.0.x* kernels there is a direct relationship between the device name and the I/O port of the parallel port, but in later kernels the device names are allocated sequentially, just as for SLIP and PPP devices.

ax0, ax1, ...
These are the AX.25 interfaces. AX.25 is the primary protocol used by amateur radio operators. AX.25 interfaces are allocated and mapped in a similar fashion to SLIP devices.

There are many other types of interfaces available for other network drivers. We've listed only the most common ones.

During the next few sections, we will discuss the details of using the drivers described previously. The Networking HOWTO provides details on how to configure most of the others, and the AX25 HOWTO explains how to configure the Amateur Radio network devices.

Ethernet Installation

The current Linux network code supports a large variety of Ethernet cards. Most drivers were written by Donald Becker, who authored a family of drivers for cards based on the National Semiconductor 8390 chip; these have become known as the Becker Series Drivers. Many other developers have contributed drivers, and today there are few common Ethernet cards that aren't supported by Linux. The list of supported Ethernet cards is growing all the time, so if your card isn't supported yet, chances are it will be soon.

Sometime earlier in Linux's history we would have attempted to list all supported Ethernet cards, but that would now take too much time and space. Fortunately, Paul Gortmaker maintains the Ethernet HOWTO, which lists each of the supported cards and provides useful information about getting each of them running under Linux.* It is posted monthly to the *comp.os.linux.answers* newsgroup, and is also available on any of the Linux Documentation Project mirror sites.

Even if you are confident you know how to install a particular type of Ethernet card in your machine, it is often worthwhile taking a look at what the Ethernet HOWTO has to say about it. You will find information that extends beyond simple configuration issues. For example, it could save you a lot of headaches to know the behavior of some DMA-based Ethernet cards that use the same DMA channel as the Adaptec 1542 SCSI controller by default. Unless you move one of them to a different DMA channel, you will wind up with the Ethernet card writing packet data to arbitrary locations on your hard disk.

To use any of the supported Ethernet cards with Linux, you may use a precompiled kernel from one of the major Linux distributions. These generally have modules available for all of the supported drivers, and the installation process usually allows you to select which drivers you want loaded. In the long term, however, it's better to build your own kernel and compile only those drivers you actually need; this saves disk space and memory.

Ethernet Autoprobing

Many of the Linux Ethernet drivers are smart enough to know how to search for the location of your Ethernet card. This saves you having to tell the kernel where it is manually. The Ethernet HOWTO lists whether a particular driver uses autoprobing and in which order it searches the I/O address for the card.

There are three limitations to the autoprobing code. First, it may not recognize all cards properly. This is especially true for some of the cheaper clones of common cards. Second, the kernel won't autoprobe for more than one card unless specifically instructed. This was a conscious design decision, as it is assumed you will want to have control over which card is assigned to which interface. The best way to do this reliably is to manually configure the Ethernet cards in your machine. Third, the driver may not probe at the address that your card is configured for. Generally speaking, the drivers will autoprobe at the addresses that the particular device is capable of being configured for, but sometimes certain addresses are

---

* Paul can be reached at *gpg109@rsphy1.anu.edu.au.*

ignored to avoid hardware conflicts with other types of cards that commonly use that same address.

PCI network cards should be reliably detected. But if you are using more than one card, or if the autoprobe should fail to detect your card, you have a way to explicitly tell the kernel about the card's base address and name.

At boot time you can supply arguments and information to the kernel that any of the kernel components may read. This mechanism allows you to pass information to the kernel that Ethernet drivers can use to locate your Ethernet hardware without making the driver probe.

If you use lilo to boot your system, you can pass parameters to the kernel by specifying them through the `append` option in the *lilo.conf* file. To inform the kernel about an Ethernet device, you can pass the following parameters:

```
ether=irq,base_addr,[param1,][param2,]name
```

The first four parameters are numeric, while the last is the device name. The *irq*, *base_addr*, and *name* parameters are required, but the two *param* parameters are optional. Any of the numeric values may be set to zero, which causes the kernel to determine the value by probing.

The first parameter sets the IRQ assigned to the device. By default, the kernel will try to autodetect the device's IRQ channel. The 3c503 driver, for example, has a special feature that selects a free IRQ from the list 5, 9, 3, 4 and configures the card to use this line. The *base_addr* parameter gives the I/O base address of the card; a value of zero tells the kernel to probe the addresses listed above.

Different drivers use the next two parameters differently. For shared-memory cards, such as the WD80x3, they specify starting and ending addresses of the shared memory area. Other cards commonly use *param1* to set the level at which debugging information is displayed. Values of 1 through 7 denote increasing levels of verbosity, while 8 turns them off altogether; 0 denotes the default. The 3c503 driver uses *param2* to choose between the internal transceiver (default) or an external transceiver (a value of 1). The former uses the card's BNC connector; the latter uses its AUI port. The *param* arguments need not be included at all if you don't have anything special to configure.

The first non-numeric argument is interpreted by the kernel as the device name. You must specify a device name for each Ethernet card you describe.

If you have two Ethernet cards, you can have Linux autodetect one card and pass the second card's parameters with *lilo*, but you'll probably want to manually configure both cards. If you decide to have the kernel probe for one and manually configure the second, you must make sure the kernel doesn't accidentally find the second card first, or else the other one won't be registered at all. You do this by passing *lilo* a `reserve` option, which explicitly tells the kernel to avoid probing the I/O space taken up by the second card. For instance, to make Linux install a second Ethernet card at `0x300` as *eth1*, you would pass the following parameters to the kernel:

```
reserve=0x300,32 ether=0,0x300,eth1
```

The *reserve* option makes sure no driver accesses the second card's I/O space when probing for some device. You may also use the kernel parameters to override autoprobing for *eth0*:

```
reserve=0x340,32 ether=0,0x340,eth0
```

You can turn off autoprobing altogether. You might do this, for example, to stop a kernel probing for an Ethernet card you might have temporarily removed. Disabling autoprobing is as simple as specifying a *base_addr* argument of –1:

```
ether=0,-1,eth0
```

To supply these parameters to the kernel at boot time, you enter the parameters at the lilo "boot:" prompt. To have *lilo* give you the "`boot:`" at the prompt, you must press any one of the Control, Alt or Shift keys while *lilo* is booting. If you press the Tab key at the prompt, you will be presented with a list of kernels that you may boot. To boot a kernel with parameters supplied, enter the name of the kernel you wish to boot, followed by a space, then followed by the parameters you wish to supply. When you press the Enter key, *lilo* will load that kernel and boot it with the parameters you've supplied.

To make this change occur automatically on each reboot, enter the parameters into the */etc/lilo.conf* using the `append=` keyword. An example might look like this:

```
boot=/dev/hda
root=/dev/hda2
install=/boot/boot.b
map=/boot/map
vga=normal
delay=20
append="ether=10,300,eth0"

image=/boot/vmlinuz-2.2.14
label=2.2.14
read-only
```

After you've edited *lilo.conf*, you must rerun the *lilo* command to activate the change.

The PLIP Driver

Parallel Line IP (PLIP) is a cheap way to network when you want to connect only two machines. It uses a parallel port and a special cable, achieving speeds of 10 kilobytes per second to 20 kilobytes per second.

PLIP was originally developed by Crynwr, Inc. Its design at the time was rather ingenious (or, if you prefer, a hack), because the original parallel ports on IBM PCs were designed to spend their time being unidirectional printer ports; the eight data lines could be used only to send data from the PC to the peripheral device, but not the other way around.* The Cyrnwr PLIP design worked around this limitation by using the port's five status lines for input, which limited it to transferring all data as nibbles (half bytes) only, but allowed for bidirectional transfer. This mode of operation was called PLIP "mode 0." Today, the parallel ports supplied on PC hardware cater to full bidirectional 8-bit data transfer, and PLIP has been extended to accomodate this with the addition of PLIP "mode 1."

Linux kernels up to and including Version 2.0 support PLIP mode 0 only, and an enhanced parallel port driver exists as a patch against the 2.0 kernel and as a standard part of the 2.2 kernel code to provide PLIP mode 1 operation, too. ‡ Unlike earlier versions of the PLIP code, the driver now attempts to be compatible with the PLIP implementations from Crynwr, as well as the PLIP driver in NCSA *telnet*.§ To connect two machines using PLIP, you need a special cable sold at some shops as a Null Printer or Turbo Laplink cable. You can, however, make one yourself fairly easily; Appendix B, *Useful Cable Configurations* shows you how.

The PLIP driver for Linux is the work of almost countless persons. It is currently maintained by Niibe Yutaka. If compiled into the kernel, it sets up a network interface for each of the possible printer ports, with *plip0* corresponding to parallel port *lp0*, *plip1* corresponding to *lp1*, etc. The mapping of interfaces to ports differs in the 2.0 kernels and the 2.2 kernels. In the 2.0 kernels, the mapping was

---

* Fight to clear the hacking name! Always use "cracker" when you are referring to people who are consciously trying to defeat the security of a system, and "hacker" when you are referring to people who have found a clever way of solving a problem. Hackers can be crackers, but the two should never be confused. Consult the New Hackers Dictionary (popularly found as the Jargon file) for a more complete understanding of the terms.

‡ The enhanced parallel port adaptor patch for 2.0 kernel is available from *http://www.cyberelk.demon.co.uk/parport.html*.

§ NCSA *telnet* is a popular program for DOS that runs TCP/IP over Ethernet or PLIP, and supports *telnet* and FTP.

Niibe can be reached at *gniibe@mri.co.jp*.

hardwired in the *drivers/net/Spacd.c* file in the kernel source. The default mappings in this file are:

Interface	I/O Port	IRQ
plip0	0x3BC	7
plip1	0x378	7
plip2	0x278	5

If you configured your printer port in a different way, you must change these values in *drivers/net/Space.c* in the Linux kernel source and build a new kernel.

In the 2.2 kernels, the PLIP driver uses the "parport" parallel port sharing driver developed by Philip Blundell.* The new driver allocates the PLIP network device names serially, just as for the Ethernet or PPP drivers, so the first PLIP device created is *plip0*, the second is *plip1*, and so on. The physical parallel port hardware is also allocated serially. By default, the parallel port driver will attempt to detect your parallel port hardware with an autoprobe routine, recording the physical device information in the order found. It is better practice to explicitly tell the kernel the physical I/O parameters. You can do this by supplying arguments to the *parport_pc.o* module as you load it, or if you have compiled the driver into your kernel, using lilo to supply arguments to the kernel at boot time. The IRQ setting of any device may be changed later by writing the new IRQ value to the related */proc/parport/*/irq* file.

Configuring the physical I/O parameters in a 2.2 kernel when loading the module is straightforward. For instance, to tell the driver that you have two PC-style parallel ports at I/O addresses 0x278 and 0c378 and IRQs 5 and 7, respectively, you would load the module with the following arguments:

```
modprobe parport_pc io=0x278,0x378 irq=5,7
```

The corresponding arguments to pass to the kernel for a compiled-in driver are:

```
parport=0x278,5 parport=0x378,7
```

You would use the lilo **append** keyword to have these arguments passed to the kernel automatically at boot time.

When the PLIP driver is initialized, either at boot time if it is built-in, or when the *plip.o* module is loaded, each of the parallel ports will have a *plip* network device associated with it. *plip0* will be assigned to the first parallel port device, *plip1* the second, and so on. You can manually override this automatic assignment using another set of kernel arguments. For instance, to assign **parport0** to network

---

* You can reach Philip at *Philip.Blundell@pobox.com*.

device `plip0`, and `parport1` to network device `plip1`, you would use kernel arguments of:

```
plip=parport1 plip=parport0
```

This mapping does not mean, however, that you cannot use these parallel ports for printing or other purposes. The physical parallel port devices are used by the PLIP driver only when the corresponding interface is configured up.

The PPP and SLIP Drivers

Point-to-Point Protocol (PPP) and Serial Line IP (SLIP) are widely used protocols for carrying IP packets over a serial link. A number of institutions offer dialup PPP and SLIP access to machines that are on the Internet, thus providing IP connectivity to private persons (something that's otherwise hardly affordable).

No hardware modifications are necessary to run PPP or SLIP; you can use any serial port. Since serial port configuration is not specific to TCP/IP networking, we have devoted a separate chapter to this. Please refer to Chapter 4, *Configuring the Serial Hardware*, for more information. We cover PPP in detail in Chapter 8, *The Point-to-Point Protocol*, and SLIP in Chapter 7, *Serial Line IP*.

Other Network Types

Most other network types are configured similarly to Ethernet. The arguments passed to the loadable modules will be different and some drivers may not support more than one card, but just about everything else is the same. Documentation for these cards is generally available in the */usr/src/linux/Documentation/ networking/* directory of the Linux kernel source.

CHAPTER FOUR

CONFIGURING THE SERIAL HARDWARE

The Internet is growing at an incredible rate. Much of this growth is attributed to Internet users who can't afford high-speed permanent network connections and who use protocols such as SLIP, PPP, or UUCP to dial in to a network provider to retrieve their daily dose of email and news.

This chapter is intended to help all people who rely on modems to maintain their link to the outside world. We won't cover the mechanics of how to configure your modem (the manual that came with it will tell you more about it than we can), but we will cover most of the Linux-specific aspects of managing devices that use serial ports. Topics include serial communications software, creating the serial device files, serial hardware, and configuring serial devices using the *setserial* and *stty* commands. Many other related topics are covered in the Serial HOWTO by David Lawyer.*

Communications Software for Modem Links

There are a number of communications packages available for Linux. Many of these packages are *terminal programs*, which allow a user to dial in to another computer as if she were sitting in front of a simple terminal. The traditional terminal program for Unix-like environments is *kermit*. It is, however, fairly ancient now, and would probably be considered difficult to use. There are more comfortable programs available that support features, like telephone-dialing dictionaries, script languages to automate dialing and logging in to remote computer systems,

---

* David can be reached at *bf347@lafn.org.*

and a variety of file exchange protocols. One of these programs is *minicom*, which was modeled after some of the most popular DOS terminal programs. X11 users are accommodated, too. *seyon* is a fully featured X11-based communications program.

Terminal programs aren't the only type of serial communication programs available. Other programs let you connect to a host and download news and email in a single bundle, to read and reply later at your leisure. This can save a lot of time, and is especially useful if you are unfortunate enough to live in an area where your local calls are time-charged. All of the reading and replying time can be spent offline, and when you are ready, you can redial and upload your responses in a single bundle. This all consumes a bit more hard disk because all of the messages have to be stored to your disk before you can read them, but this could be a reasonable trade-off at today's hard drive prices.

UUCP epitomizes this communication software style. It is a program suite that copies files from one host to another and executes programs on a remote host. It is frequently used to transport mail or news in private networks. Ian Taylor's UUCP package, which also runs under Linux, is described in detail in Chapter 16, *Managing Taylor UUCP*. Other noninteractive communications software is used throughout networks such as Fidonet. Fidonet application ports like *ifmail* are also available, although we expect that not many people still use them.

PPP and SLIP are in between, allowing both interactive and noninteractive use. Many people use PPP or SLIP to dial in to their campus network or other Internet Service Provider to run FTP and read web pages. PPP and SLIP are also, however, commonly used over permanent or semipermanent connections for LAN-to-LAN coupling, although this is really only interesting with ISDN or other high-speed network connections.

Introduction to Serial Devices

The Unix kernel provides devices for accessing serial hardware, typically called *tty* devices (pronounced as it is spelled: T-T-Y). This is an abbreviation for *Teletype device*, which used to be one of the major manufacturers of terminal devices in the early days of Unix. The term is used now for any character-based data terminal. Throughout this chapter, we use the term to refer exclusively to the Linux device files rather than the physical terminal.

Linux provides three classes of tty devices: serial devices, virtual terminals (all of which you can access in turn by pressing Alt-F1 through Alt-F*nn* on the local console), and pseudo-terminals (similar to a two-way pipe, used by applications such as X11). The former were called tty devices because the original character-based terminals were connected to the Unix machine by a serial cable or telephone line and modem. The latter two were named after the tty device because they were created to behave in a similar fashion from the programmer's perspective.

SLIP and PPP are most commonly implemented in the kernel. The kernel doesn't really treat the *tty* device as a network device that you can manipulate like an Ethernet device, using commands such as *ifconfig*. However, it does treat tty devices as places where network devices can be bound. To do this, the kernel changes what is called the "line discipline" of the tty device. Both SLIP and PPP are line disciplines that may be enabled on tty devices. The general idea is that the serial driver handles data given to it differently, depending on the line discipline it is configured for. In its default line discipline, the driver simply transmits each character it is given in turn. When the SLIP or PPP line discipline is selected, the driver instead reads a block of data, wraps a special header around it that allows the remote end to identify that block of data in a stream, and transmits the new data block. It isn't too important to understand this yet; we'll cover both SLIP and PPP in later chapters, and it all happens automatically for you anyway.

Accessing Serial Devices

Like all devices in a Unix system, serial ports are accessed through device special files, located in the */dev* directory. There are two varieties of device files related to serial drivers, and there is one device file of each type for each port. The device will behave slightly differently, depending on which of its device files we open. We'll cover the differences because it will help you understand some of the configurations and advice that you might see relating to serial devices, but in practice you need to use only one of these. At some point in the future, one of them may even disappear completely.

The most important of the two classes of serial device has a major number of 4, and its device special files are named *ttyS0*, *ttyS1*, etc. The second variety has a major number of 5, and was designed for use when dialing out (calling out) through a port; its device special files are called *cua0*, *cua1*, etc. In the Unix world, counting generally starts at zero, while laypeople tend to start at one. This creates a small amount of confusion for people because COM1: is represented by */dev/ttyS0*, COM2: by */dev/ttyS1*, etc. Anyone familiar with IBM PC-style hardware knows that COM3: and greater were never really standardized anyway.

The *cua*, or "callout," devices were created to solve the problem of avoiding conflicts on serial devices for modems that have to support both incoming and outgoing connections. Unfortunately, they've created their own problems and are now likely to be discontinued. Let's briefly look at the problem.

Linux, like Unix, allows a device, or any other file, to be opened by more than one process simultaneously. Unfortunately, this is rarely useful with tty devices, as the two processes will almost certainly interfere with each other. Luckily, a mechanism was devised to allow a process to check if a tty device had already been opened by another device before opening it. The mechanism uses what are called *lock files.* The idea was that when a process wanted to open a tty device, it would check for the existence of a file in a special location, named similarly to the device it intends to open. If the file does not exist, the process creates it and opens the tty device. If the file does exist, the process assumes another process already has the tty device open and takes appropriate action. One last clever trick to make the lock file management system work was writing the process ID (pid) of the process that had created the lock file into the lock file itself; we'll talk more about that in a moment.

The lock file mechanism works perfectly well in circumstances in which you have a defined location for the lock files and all programs know where to find them. Alas, this wasn't always the case for Linux. It wasn't until the Linux Filesystem Standard defined a standard location for lock files when *tty* lock files began to work correctly. At one time there were at least four, and possibly more locations chosen by software developers to store lock files: */usr/spool/locks/*, */var/spool/locks/*, */var/lock/*, and */usr/lock/*. Confusion caused chaos. Programs were opening lock files in different locations that were meant to control a single tty device; it was as if lock files weren't being used at all.

The *cua* devices were created to provide a solution to this problem. Rather than relying on the use of lock files to prevent clashes between programs wanting to use the serial devices, it was decided that the kernel could provide a simple means of arbitrating who should be given access. If the *ttyS* device were already opened, an attempt to open the *cua* would result in an error that a program could interpret to mean the device was already being used. If the *cua* device were already open and an attempt was made to open the *ttyS*, the request would block; that is, it would be put on hold and wait until the *cua* device was closed by the other process. This worked quite well if you had a single modem that you had configured for dial-in access and you occasionally wanted to dial out on the same device. But it did not work very well in environments where you had multiple programs wanting to call out on the same device. The only way to solve the contention problem was to use lock files! Back to square one.

Suffice it to say that the Linux Filesystem Standard came to the rescue and now mandates that lock files be stored in the */var/lock* directory, and that by convention, the lock file name for the *ttyS1* device, for instance, is *LCK..ttyS1*. The *cua* lock files should also go in this directory, but use of *cua* devices is now discouraged.

The *cua* devices will probably still be around for some time to provide a period of backward compatibility, but in time they will be retired. If you are wondering what to use, stick to the *ttyS* device and make sure that your system is Linux FSSTND compliant, or at the very least that all programs using the serial devices agree on where the lock files are located. Most software dealing with serial tty devices provides a compile-time option to specify the location of the lock files. More often than not, this will appear as a variable called something like LOCKDIR in the *Makefile* or in a configuration header file. If you're compiling the software yourself, it is best to change this to agree with the FSSTND-specified location. If you're using a precompiled binary and you're not sure where the program will write its lock files, you can use the following command to gain a hint:

strings binaryfile | *grep* lock

If the location found does not agree with the rest of your system, you can try creating a symbolic link from the lock directory that the foreign executable wants to use back to */var/lock/*. This is ugly, but it will work.

The Serial Device Special Files

Minor numbers are identical for both types of serial devices. If you have your modem on one of the ports COM1: through COM4:, its minor number will be the COM port number plus 63. If you are using special serial hardware, such as a high-performance multiple port serial controller, you will probably need to create special device files for it; it probably won't use the standard device driver. The Serial-HOWTO should be able to assist you in finding the appropriate details.

Assume your modem is on COM2:. Its minor number will be 65, and its major number will be 4 for normal use. There should be a device called *ttyS1* that has these numbers. List the serial ttys in the */dev/* directory. The fifth and sixth columns show the major and minor numbers, respectively:

```
$ ls -l /dev/ttyS*
0 crw-rw----   1 uucp     dialout    4,  64 Oct 13  1997 /dev/ttyS0
0 crw-rw----   1 uucp     dialout    4,  65 Jan 26 21:55 /dev/ttyS1
0 crw-rw----   1 uucp     dialout    4,  66 Oct 13  1997 /dev/ttyS2
0 crw-rw----   1 uucp     dialout    4,  67 Oct 13  1997 /dev/ttyS3
```

If there is no device with major number 4 and minor number 65, you will have to create one. Become the superuser and type:

```
# mknod -m 666 /dev/ttyS1 c 4 65
# chown uucp.dialout /dev/ttyS1
```

The various Linux distributions use slightly differing strategies for who should own the serial devices. Sometimes they will be owned by *root*, and other times they will be owned by another user, such as **uucp** in our example. Modern distributions have a group specifically for dial-out devices, and any users who are allowed to use them are added to this group.

Some people suggest making */dev/modem* a symbolic link to your modem device so that casual users don't have to remember the somewhat unintuitive *ttyS1*. However, you cannot use *modem* in one program and the real device file name in another. Their lock files would have different names and the locking mechanism wouldn't work.

Serial Hardware

RS-232 is currently the most common standard for serial communications in the PC world. It uses a number of circuits for transmitting single bits, as well as for synchronization. Additional lines may be used for signaling the presence of a carrier (used by modems) and for handshaking. Linux supports a wide variety of serial cards that use the RS-232 standard.

Hardware handshake is optional, but very useful. It allows either of the two stations to signal whether it is ready to receive more data, or if the other station should pause until the receiver is done processing the incoming data. The lines used for this are called "Clear to Send" (CTS) and "Ready to Send" (RTS), respectively, which explains the colloquial name for hardware handshake: "RTS/CTS." The other type of handshake you might be familiar with is called "XON/XOFF" handshaking. XON/XOFF uses two nominated characters, conventionally Ctrl-S and Ctrl-Q, to signal to the remote end that it should stop and start transmitting data, respectively. While this method is simple to implement and okay for use by dumb terminals, it causes great confusion when you are dealing with binary data, as you may want to transmit those characters as part of your data stream, and not have them interpreted as flow control characters. It is also somewhat slower to take effect than hardware handshake. Hardware handshake is clean, fast, and recommended in preference to XON/XOFF when you have a choice.

In the original IBM PC, the RS-232 interface was driven by a UART chip called the 8250. PCs around the time of the 486 used a newer version of the UART called the 16450. It was slightly faster than the 8250. Nearly all Pentium-based machines have been supplied with an even newer version of the UART called the 16550. Some brands (most notably internal modems equipped with the Rockwell chip set) use completely different chips that emulate the behavior of the 16550 and can be treated similarly. Linux supports all of these in its standard serial port driver.*

The 16550 was a significant improvement over the 8250 and the 16450 because it offered a 16-byte FIFO buffer. The 16550 is actually a family of UART devices, comprising the 16550, the 16550A, and the 16550AFN (later renamed PC16550DN). The differences relate to whether the FIFO actually works; the 16550AFN is the one that is sure to work. There was also an NS16550, but its FIFO never really worked either.

The 8250 and 16450 UARTs had a simple 1-byte buffer. This means that a 16450 generates an interrupt for every character transmitted or received. Each interrupt

---

* Note that we are not talking about WinModem™ here! WinModems have very simple hardware and rely completely on the main CPU of your computer instead of dedicated hardware to do all of the hard work. If you're purchasing a modem, it is our strongest recommendation to *not* purchase such a modem; get a real modem. You may find Linux support for WinModems, but that makes them only a marginally more attractive solution.

takes a short period of time to service, and this small delay limits 16450s to a reliable maximum bit speed of about 9,600 bps in a typical ISA bus machine.

In the default configuration, the kernel checks the four standard serial ports, COM1: through COM4:. The kernel is also able to automatically detect what UART is used for each of the standard serial ports, and will make use of the enhanced FIFO buffer of the 16550, if it is available.

Using the Configuration Utilities

Now let's spend some time looking at the two most useful serial device configuration utilities: *setserial* and *stty*.

The setserial Command

The kernel will make its best effort to correctly determine how your serial hardware is configured, but the variations on serial device configuration makes this determination difficult to achieve 100 percent reliably in practice. A good example of where this is a problem is the internal modems we talked about earlier. The UART they use has a 16-byte FIFO buffer, but it looks like a 16450 UART to the kernel device driver: unless we specifically tell the driver that this port is a 16550 device, the kernel will not make use of the extended buffer. Yet another example is that of the dumb 4-port cards that allow sharing of a single IRQ among a number of serial devices. We may have to specifically tell the kernel which IRQ port it's supposed to use, and that IRQs may be shared.

setserial was created to configure the serial driver at runtime. The *setserial* command is most commonly executed at boot time from a script called *0setserial* on some distributions, and *rc.serial* on others. This script is charged with the responsibility of initializing the serial driver to accommodate any nonstandard or unusual serial hardware in the machine.

The general syntax for the *setserial* command is:

```
setserial device [parameters]
```

in which the device is one of the serial devices, such as *ttyS0.*

The *setserial* command has a large number of parameters. The most common of these are described in Table 4-1. For information on the remainder of the parameters, you should refer to the *setserial* manual page.

Table 4-1. setserial Command-Line Parameters

Parameter	Description
port *port_number*	Specify the I/O port address of the serial device. Port numbers should be specified in hexadecimal notation, e.g., 0x2f8.
irq *num*	Specify the interrupt request line the serial device is using.
uart *uart_type*	Specify the UART type of the serial device. Common values are 16450, 16550, etc. Setting this value to none will disable this serial device.
fourport	Specifying this parameter instructs the kernel serial driver that this port is one port of an AST Fourport card.
spd_hi	Program the UART to use a speed of 57.6 kbps when a process requests 38.4 kbps.
spd_vhi	Program the UART to use a speed of 115 kbps when a process requests 38.4 kbps.
spd_normal	Program the UART to use the default speed of 38.4 kbps when requested. This parameter is used to reverse the effect of a spd_hi or spd_vhi performed on the specified serial device.
auto_irq	This parameter will cause the kernel to attempt to automatically determine the IRQ of the specified device. This attempt may not be completely reliable, so it is probably better to think of this as a request for the kernel to guess the IRQ. If you know the IRQ of the device, you should specify that it use the irq parameter instead.
autoconfig	This parameter must be specified in conjunction with the port parameter. When this parameter is supplied, *setserial* instructs the kernel to attempt to automatically determine the UART type located at the supplied port address. If the auto_irq parameter is also supplied, the kernel attempts to automatically determine the IRQ, too.
skip_test	This parameter instructs the kernel not to bother performing the UART type test during auto-configuration. This is necessary when the UART is incorrectly detected by the kernel.

A typical and simple *rc* file to configure your serial ports at boot time might look something like that shown in Example 4-1. Most Linux distributions will include something slightly more sophisticated than this one.

Example 4-1: Example rc.serial setserial Commands

```
# /etc/rc.serial - serial line configuration script.
#
# Configure serial devices
/sbin/setserial /dev/ttyS0 auto_irq skip_test autoconfig
```

Example 4-1: Example rc.serial setserial Commands (continued)

```
/sbin/setserial /dev/ttyS1 auto_irq skip_test autoconfig
/sbin/setserial /dev/ttyS2 auto_irq skip_test autoconfig
/sbin/setserial /dev/ttyS3 auto_irq skip_test autoconfig
#
# Display serial device configuration
/sbin/setserial -bg /dev/ttyS*
```

The `-bg /dev/ttyS*` argument in the last command will print a neatly formatted summary of the hardware configuration of all active serial devices. The output will look like that shown in Example 4-2.

Example 4-2: Output of setserial -bg /dev/ttyS Command

```
/dev/ttyS0 at 0x03f8 (irq = 4) is a 16550A
/dev/ttyS1 at 0x02f8 (irq = 3) is a 16550A
```

The stty Command

The name *stty* probably means "set tty," but the *stty* command can also be used to display a terminal's configuration. Perhaps even more so than *setserial*, the *stty* command provides a bewildering number of characteristics you can configure. We'll cover the most important of these in a moment. You can find the rest described in the *stty* manual page.

The *stty* command is most commonly used to configure terminal parameters, such as whether characters will be echoed or what key should generate a break signal. We explained earlier that serial devices are tty devices and the *stty* command is therefore equally applicable to them.

One of the more important uses of the *stty* for serial devices is to enable hardware handshaking on the device. We talked briefly about hardware handshaking earlier. The default configuration for serial devices is for hardware handshaking to be disabled. This setting allows "three wire" serial cables to work; they don't support the necessary signals for hardware handshaking, and if it were enabled by default, they'd be unable to transmit any characters to change it.

Surprisingly, some serial communications programs don't enable hardware handshaking, so if your modem supports hardware handshaking, you should configure the modem to use it (check your modem manual for what command to use), and also configure your serial device to use it. The *stty* command has a `crtscts` flag that enables hardware handshaking on a device; you'll need to use this. The command is probably best issued from the *rc.serial* file (or equivalent) at boot time using commands like those shown in Example 4-3.

Example 4-3: Example rc.serial stty Commands

```
#
stty crtscts < /dev/ttyS0
stty crtscts < /dev/ttyS1
stty crtscts < /dev/ttyS2
stty crtscts < /dev/ttyS3
#
```

The *stty* command works on the current terminal by default, but by using the input redirection ("<") feature of the shell, we can have *stty* manipulate any tty device. It's a common mistake to forget whether you are supposed to use "<" or ">"; modern versions of the *stty* command have a much cleaner syntax for doing this. To use the new syntax, we'd rewrite our sample configuration to look like that shown in Example 4-4.

Example 4-4: Example rc.serial stty Commands Using Modern Syntax

```
#
stty crtscts -F /dev/ttyS0
stty crtscts -F /dev/ttyS1
stty crtscts -F /dev/ttyS2
stty crtscts -F /dev/ttyS3
#
```

We mentioned that the *stty* command can be used to display the terminal configuration parameters of a tty device. To display all of the active settings on a tty device, use:

$ **stty -a -F /dev/ttyS1**

The output of this command, shown in Example 4-5, gives you the status of all flags for that device; a flag shown with a preceding minus, as in *−crtscts*, means that the flag has been turned off.

Example 4-5: Output of stty -a Command

```
speed 19200 baud; rows 0; columns 0; line = 0;
intr = ^C; quit = ^\; erase = ^?; kill = ^U; eof = ^D; eol = <undef>;
        eol2 = <undef>; start = ^Q; stop = ^S; susp = ^Z; rprnt = ^R;
        werase = ^W; lnext = ^V; flush = ^O; min = 1; time = 0;
-parenb -parodd cs8 hupcl -cstopb cread clocal -crtscts
-ignbrk -brkint -ignpar -parmrk -inpck -istrip -inlcr -igncr -icrnl -ixon
        -ixoff -iuclc -ixany -imaxbel
-opost -olcuc -ocrnl onlcr -onocr -onlret -ofill -ofdel nl0 cr0 tab0
        bs0 vt0 ff0
-isig -icanon iexten echo echoe echok -echonl -noflsh -xcase -tostop
        -echoprt echoctl echoke
```

A description of the most important of these flags is given in Table 4-2. Each of these flags is enabled by supplying it to *stty* and disabled by supplying it to *stty* with the – character in front of it. Thus, to disable hardware handshaking on the ttyS0 device, you would use:

```
$ stty -crtscts -F /dev/ttyS0
```

Table 4-2. stty Flags Most Relevant to Configuring Serial Devices

Flags	Description
N	Set the line speed to N bits per second.
crtsdts	Enable/Disable hardware handshaking.
ixon	Enable/Disable XON/XOFF flow control.
clocal	Enable/Disable modem control signals such as DTR/DTS and DCD. This is necessary if you are using a "three wire" serial cable because it does not supply these signals.
cs5 cs6 cs7 cs8	Set number of data bits to 5, 6, 7, or 8, respectively.
parodd	Enable odd parity. Disabling this flag enables even parity.
parenb	Enable parity checking. When this flag is negated, no parity is used.
cstopb	Enable use of two stop bits per character. When this flag is negated, one stop bit per character is used.
echo	Enable/Disable echoing of received characters back to sender.

The next example combines some of these flags and sets the *ttyS0* device to 19,200 bps, 8 data bits, no parity, and hardware handshaking with echo disabled:

```
$ stty 19200 cs8 -parenb crtscts -echo -F /dev/ttyS0
```

Serial Devices and the login: Prompt

It was once very common that a Unix installation involved one server machine and many "dumb" character mode terminals or dial-up modems. Today that sort of installation is less common, which is good news for many people interested in operating this way, because the "dumb" terminals are now very cheap to acquire. Dial-up modem configurations are no less common, but these days they would probably be used to support a SLIP or PPP login (discussed in Chapter 7, *Serial Line IP* and Chapter 8, *The Point-to-Point Protocol*) than to be used for a simple login. Nevertheless, each of these configurations can make use of a simple program called a *getty* program.

The term *getty* is probably a contraction of "get tty." A *getty* program opens a serial device, configures it appropriately, optionally configures a modem, and waits for a connection to be made. An active connection on a serial device is usually indicated by the Data Carrier Detect (DCD) pin on the serial device being raised.

When a connection is detected, the *getty* program issues a `login:` prompt, and then invokes the *login* program to handle the actual system login. Each of the virtual terminals (e.g., */dev/tty1*) in Linux has a *getty* running against it.

There are a number of different *getty* implementations, each designed to suit some configurations better than others. The *getty* that we'll describe here is called *mgetty*. It is quite popular because it has all sorts of features that make it especially modem-friendly, including support for automatic fax programs and voice modems. We'll concentrate on configuring *mgetty* to answer conventional data calls and leave the rest for you to explore at your convenience.

Configuring the mgetty Daemon

The *mgetty* daemon is available in source form from *ftp://alpha.greenie.net/pub/ mgetty/source/*, and is available in just about all Linux distributions in prepackaged form. The *mgetty* daemon differs from most other *getty* implementations in that it has been designed specifically for Hayes-compatible modems. It still supports direct terminal connections, but is best suited for dialup applications. Rather than using the DCD line to detect an incoming call, it listens for the `RING` message generated by modern modems when they detect an incoming call and are not configured for auto-answer.

The main executable program is called */usr/sbin/mgetty*, and its main configuration file is called */etc/mgetty/mgetty.config*. There are a number of other binary programs and configuration files that cover other *mgetty* features.

For most installations, configuration is a matter of editing the */etc/mgetty/ mgetty.config* file and adding appropriate entries to the */etc/inittab* file to execute *mgetty* automatically.

Example 4-6 shows a very simple *mgetty* configuration file. This example configures two serial devices. The first, */dev/ttyS0*, supports a Hayes-compatible modem at 38,400 bps. The second, */dev/ttyS0*, supports a directly connected VT100 terminal at 19,200 bps.

Example 4-6: Sample /etc/mgetty/mgetty.config File

```
#
# mgetty configuration file
#
# this is a sample configuration file, see mgetty.info for details
#
# comment lines start with a "#", empty lines are ignored
#
# ----- global section -----
#
# In this section, you put the global defaults, per-port stuff is below
#
# access the modem(s) with 38400 bps
```

Example 4-6: Sample /etc/mgetty/mgetty.config File (continued)

```
speed 38400
#
# set the global debug level to "4" (default from policy.h)
debug 4
#

# ----- port specific section -----
#
# Here you can put things that are valid only for one line, not the others
#
#
# Hayes modem connected to ttyS0: don't do fax, less logging
#
port ttyS0
  debug 3
  data-only y
#
# direct connection of a VT100 terminal which doesn't like DTR drops
#
port ttyS1
  direct y
  speed 19200
  toggle-dtr n
#
```

The configuration file supports global and port-specific options. In our example we used a global option to set the speed to 38,400 bps. This value is inherited by the *ttyS0* port. Ports we apply *mgetty* to use this speed setting unless it is overwritten by a port-specific speed setting, as we have done in the *ttyS1* configuration.

The `debug` keyword controls the verbosity of *mgetty* logging. The `data-only` keyword in the *ttyS0* configuration causes *mgetty* to ignore any modem fax features, to operate just as a data modem. The `direct` keyword in the *ttyS1* configuration instructs *mgetty* not to attempt any modem initialization on the port. Finally, the `toggle-dtr` keyword instructs *mgetty* not to attempt to hang up the line by dropping the DTR (Data Terminal Ready) pin on the serial interface; some terminals don't like this to happen.

You can also choose to leave the *mgetty.config* file empty and use command-line arguments to specify most of the same parameters. The documentation accompanying the application includes a complete description of the *mgetty* configuration file parameters and command-line arguments. See the following example.

We need to add two entries to the */etc/inittab* file to activate this configuration. The *inittab* file is the configuration file of the Unix System V *init* command. The *init* command is responsible for system initialization; it provides a means of automatically executing programs at boot time and re-executing them when they terminate. This is ideal for the goals of running a *getty* program.

```
T0:23:respawn:/sbin/mgetty ttyS0
T1:23:respawn:/sbin/mgetty ttyS1
```

Each line of the */etc/inittab* file contains four fields, separated by colons. The first field is an identifier that uniquely labels an entry in the file; traditionally it is two characters, but modern versions allow four. The second field is the list of run levels at which this entry should be active. A run level is a means of providing alternate machine configurations and is implemented using trees of startup scripts stored in directories called */etc/rc1.d, /etc/rc2.d,* etc. This feature is typically implemented very simply, and you should model your entries on others in the file or refer to your system documentation for more information. The third field describes when to take action. For the purposes of running a *getty* program, this field should be set to `respawn`, meaning that the command should be re-executed automatically when it dies. There are several other options, as well, but they are not useful for our purposes here. The fourth field is the actual command to execute; this is where we specify the *mgetty* command and any arguments we wish to pass it. In our simple example we're starting and restarting *mgetty* whenever the system is operating at either of run levels two or three, and are supplying as an argument just the name of the device we wish it to use. The *mgetty* command assumes the */dev/*, so we don't need to supply it.

This chapter was a quick introduction to *mgetty* and how to offer login prompts to serial devices. You can find more extensive information in the Serial-HOWTO.

After you've edited the configuration files, you need to reload *init* to make the changes take effect. Simply send a hangup signal to the *init* process; it always has a process ID of one, so you can use the following command safely:

```
# kill -HUP 1
```

CHAPTER FIVE

CONFIGURING TCP/IP NETWORKING

In this chapter, we walk you through all the necessary steps to set up TCP/IP networking on your machine. Starting with the assignment of IP addresses, we slowly work our way through the configuration of TCP/IP network interfaces and introduce a few tools that come in handy when hunting down network installation problems.

Most of the tasks covered in this chapter will generally have to be done only once. Afterward, you have to touch most configuration files only when adding a new system to your network or when you reconfigure your system entirely. Some of the commands used to configure TCP/IP, however, have to be executed each time the system is booted. This is usually done by invoking them from the system */etc/ rc** scripts.

Commonly, the network-specific part of this procedure is contained in a script. The name of this script varies in different Linux distributions. In many older Linux distributions, it is known as *rc.net* or *rc.inet*. Sometimes you will also see two scripts named *rc.inet1* and *rc.inet2*; the former initializes the kernel part of networking and the latter starts basic networking services and applications. In modern distributions, the *rc* files are structured in a more sophisticated arrangement; here you may find scripts in the */etc/init.d/* (or */etc/rc.d/init.d/*) directory that create the network devices and other *rc* files that run the network application programs. This book's examples are based on the latter arrangement.

This chapter discusses parts of the script that configure your network interfaces, while applications will be covered in later chapters. After finishing this chapter, you should have established a sequence of commands that properly configure TCP/IP networking on your computer. You should then replace any sample commands in your configuration scripts with your commands, make sure the script is executed from the basic *rc* script at startup time, and reboot your machine. The networking *rc* scripts that come along with your favorite Linux distribution should provide a solid example from which to work.

Mounting the /proc Filesystem

Some of the configuration tools of the Linux NET-2 and NET-3 release rely on the */proc* filesystem for communicating with the kernel. This interface permits access to kernel runtime information through a filesystem-like mechanism. When mounted, you can list its files like any other filesystem, or display their contents. Typical items include the *loadavg* file, which contains the system load average, and *meminfo*, which shows current core memory and swap usage.

To this, the networking code adds the *net* directory. It contains a number of files that show things like the kernel ARP tables, the state of TCP connections, and the routing tables. Most network administration tools get their information from these files.

The *proc* filesystem (or *procfs*, as it is also known) is usually mounted on */proc* at system boot time. The best method is to add the following line to */etc/fstab*:

```
# procfs mount point:
none            /proc          proc    defaults
```

Then execute *mount /proc* from your */etc/rc* script.

The *procfs* is now configured into most kernels by default. If the *procfs* is not in your kernel, you will get a message such as: `mount: fs type procfs not supported by kernel`. You will then have to recompile the kernel and answer "yes" when asked for *procfs* support.

Installing the Binaries

If you are using one of the prepackaged Linux distributions, it will contain the major networking applications and utilities along with a coherent set of sample files. The only case in which you might have to obtain and install new utilities is when you install a new kernel release. As they occasionally involve changes in the kernel networking layer, you will need to update the basic configuration tools. This update at least involves recompiling, but sometimes you may also be required to obtain the latest set of binaries. These binaries are available at their official home site at *ftp.inka.de/pub/comp/Linux/networking/NetTools/*, packaged in an archive called *net-tools-XXX.tar.gz*, where *XXX* is the version number. The release matching Linux 2.0 is *net-tools-1.45*.

If you want to compile and install the standard TCP/IP network applications yourself, you can obtain the sources from most Linux FTP servers. All modern Linux distributions include a fairly comprehensive range of TCP/IP network applications, such as World Wide Web browsers, *telnet* and *ftp* programs, and other network applications, such as *talk*. If you do find something that you do need to compile yourself, the chances are good that it will compile under Linux from source quite simply if you follow the instructions included in the source package.

Setting the Hostname

Most, if not all, network applications rely on you to set the local host's name to some reasonable value. This setting is usually made during the boot procedure by executing the *hostname* command. To set the hostname to *name*, enter:

```
# hostname name
```

It is common practice to use the unqualified hostname without specifying the domain name. For instance, hosts at the Virtual Brewery (described in Appendix A, *Example Network: The Virtual Brewery*) might be called **vale.vbrew.com** or **vlager.vbrew.com**. These are their official *fully qualified domain names* (FQDNs). Their local hostnames would be the first component of the name, such as **vale**. However, as the local hostname is frequently used to look up the host's IP address, you have to make sure that the resolver library is able to look up the host's IP address. This usually means that you have to enter the name in */etc/hosts*.

Some people suggest using the *domainname* command to set the kernel's idea of a domain name to the remaining part of the FQDN. This way you could combine the output from *hostname* and *domainname* to get the FQDN again. However, this is at best only half correct. *domainname* is generally used to set the host's NIS domain, which may be entirely different from the DNS domain to which your host belongs. Instead, to ensure that the short form of your hostname is resolvable with all recent versions of the *hostname* command, either add it as an entry in your local Domain Name Server or place the fully qualified domain name in the */etc/hosts* file. You may then use the −*fqdn* argument to the *hostname* command, and it will print the fully qualifed domain name.

Assigning IP Addresses

If you configure the networking software on your host for standalone operation (for instance, to be able to run the INN Netnews software), you can safely skip this section, because the only IP address you will need is for the loopback interface, which is always **127.0.0.1**.

Things are a little more complicated with real networks like Ethernets. If you want to connect your host to an existing network, you have to ask its administrators to give you an IP address on this network. When setting up a network all by yourself, you have to assign IP addresses yourself.

Hosts within a local network should usually share addresses from the same logical IP network. Hence, you have to assign an IP network address. If you have several physical networks, you have to either assign them different network numbers, or use subnetting to split your IP address range into several subnetworks. Subnetting will be revisited in the next section, "Creating Subnets."

When picking an IP network number, much depends on whether you intend to get on the Internet in the near future. If so, you should obtain an official IP address *now*. Ask your network service provider to help you. If you want to obtain a network number, just in case you might get on the Internet someday, request a Network Address Application Form from *hostmaster@internic.net*, or your country's own Network Information Center, if there is one.

If your network is not connected to the Internet and won't be in the near future, you are free to choose any legal network address. Just make sure no packets from your internal network escape to the real Internet. To make sure no harm can be done even if packets *did* escape, you should use one of the network numbers reserved for private use. The Internet Assigned Numbers Authority (IANA) has set aside several network numbers from classes A, B, and C that you can use without registering. These addresses are valid only within your private network and are not routed between real Internet sites. The numbers are defined by RFC 1597 and are listed in Table 2-1 in Chapter 2, *Issues of TCP/IP Networking*. Note that the second and third blocks contain 16 and 256 networks, respectively.

Picking your addresses from one of these network numbers is not only useful for networks completely unconnected to the Internet; you can still implement a slightly more restricted access using a single host as a gateway. To your local network, the gateway is accessible by its internal IP address, while the outside world knows it by an officially registered address (assigned to you by your provider). We come back to this concept in connection with the IP masquerade facility in Chapter 11, *IP Masquerade and Network Address Translation*.

Throughout the remainder of the book, we will assume that the brewery's network manager uses a class B network number, say **172.16.0.0**. Of course, a class C network number would definitely suffice to accommodate both the Brewery's and the Winery's networks. We'll use a class B network here for the sake of simplicity; it will make the subnetting examples in the next section of this chapter a little more intuitive.

Creating Subnets

To operate several Ethernets (or other networks, once a driver is available), you have to split your network into subnets. Note that subnetting is required only if you have more than one *broadcast network*—point-to-point links don't count. For instance, if you have one Ethernet, and one or more SLIP links to the outside world, you don't need to subnet your network. This is explained in more detail in Chapter 7, *Serial Line IP*.

To accommodate the two Ethernets, the Brewery's network manager decides to use 8 bits of the host part as additional subnet bits. This leaves another 8 bits for the host part, allowing for 254 hosts on each of the subnets. She then assigns subnet number 1 to the brewery, and gives the winery number 2. Their respective network addresses are thus **172.16.1.0** and **172.16.2.0**. The subnet mask is **255.255.255.0**.

vlager, which is the gateway between the two networks, is assigned a host number of 1 on both of them, which gives it the IP addresses **172.16.1.1** and **172.16.2.1**, respectively.

Note that in this example we are using a class B network to keep things simple, but a class C network would be more realistic. With the new networking code, subnetting is not limited to byte boundaries, so even a class C network may be split into several subnets. For instance, you could use two bits of the host part for the netmask, giving you 4 possible subnets with 64 hosts on each.*

Writing hosts and networks Files

After you have subnetted your network, you should prepare for some simple sort of hostname resolution using the */etc/hosts* file. If you are not going to use DNS or NIS for address resolution, you have to put all hosts in the *hosts* file.

Even if you want to run DNS or NIS during normal operation, you should have some subset of all hostnames in */etc/hosts*. You should have some sort of name resolution, even when no network interfaces are running, for example, during boot time. This is not only a matter of convenience, but it allows you to use symbolic hostnames in your network *rc* scripts. Thus, when changing IP addresses, you only have to copy an updated *hosts* file to all machines and reboot, rather than edit a large number of *rc* files separately. Usually you put all local hostnames and addresses in *hosts*, adding those of any gateways and NIS servers used.†

---

* The first number on each subnet is the subnetwork address, and the last number on each subnet is reserved as the broadcast address, so it's actually 62 hosts per subnet.

† You need the address of an NIS server only if you use Peter Eriksson's NYS. Other NIS implementations locate their servers only at runtime by using *ypbind*.

You should make sure your resolver only uses information from the *hosts* file during initial testing. Sample files that come with your DNS or NIS software may produce strange results. To make all applications use */etc/hosts* exclusively when looking up the IP address of a host, you have to edit the */etc/host.conf* file. Comment out any lines that begin with the keyword `order` by preceding them with a hash sign, and insert the line:

```
order hosts
```

The configuration of the resolver library is covered in detail in Chapter 6, *Name Service and Resolver Configuration.*

The *hosts* file contains one entry per line, consisting of an IP address, a hostname, and an optional list of aliases for the hostname. The fields are separated by spaces or tabs, and the address field must begin in the first column. Anything following a hash sign (#) is regarded as a comment and is ignored.

Hostnames can be either fully qualified or relative to the local domain. For **vale**, you would usually enter the fully qualified name, **vale.vbrew.com**, and **vale** by itself in the *hosts* file, so that it is known by both its official name and the shorter local name.

This is an example how a *hosts* file at the Virtual Brewery might look. Two special names are included, **vlager-if1** and **vlager-if2**, which give the addresses for both interfaces used on **vlager**:

```
#
# Hosts file for Virtual Brewery/Virtual Winery
#
# IP           FQDN                  aliases
#
127.0.0.1      localhost
#
172.16.1.1     vlager.vbrew.com      vlager vlager-if1
172.16.1.2     vstout.vbrew.com      vstout
172.16.1.3     vale.vbrew.com        vale
#
172.16.2.1     vlager-if2
172.16.2.2     vbeaujolais.vbrew.com vbeaujolais
172.16.2.3     vbardolino.vbrew.com  vbardolino
172.16.2.4     vchianti.vbrew.com    vchianti
```

Just as with a host's IP address, you should sometimes use a symbolic name for network numbers, too. Therefore, the *hosts* file has a companion called */etc/networks* that maps network names to network numbers, and vice versa. At the Virtual Brewery, we might install a *networks* file like this:*

---

* Note that names in *networks* must not collide with hostnames from the *hosts* file, or else some programs may produce strange results.

```
# /etc/networks for the Virtual Brewery
brew-net       172.16.1.0
wine-net       172.16.2.0
```

Interface Configuration for IP

After setting up your hardware as explained in Chapter 4, *Configuring the Serial Hardware*, you have to make these devices known to the kernel networking software. A couple of commands are used to configure the network interfaces and initialize the routing table. These tasks are usually performed from the network initialization script each time you boot the system. The basic tools for this process are called *ifconfig* (where "if" stands for interface) and *route*.

ifconfig is used to make an interface accessible to the kernel networking layer. This involves the assignment of an IP address and other parameters, and activation of the interface, also known as "bringing up" the interface. Being active here means that the kernel will send and receive IP datagrams through the interface. The simplest way to invoke it is with:

```
ifconfig interface ip-address
```

This command assigns `ip-address` to `interface` and activates it. All other parameters are set to default values. For instance, the default network mask is derived from the network class of the IP address, such as **255.255.0.0** for a class B address. *ifconfig* is described in detail in the section "All About ifconfig."

route allows you to add or remove routes from the kernel routing table. It can be invoked as:

```
route [add|del] [-net|-host] target [if]
```

The *add* and *del* arguments determine whether to add or delete the route to `target`. The *-net* and *-host* arguments tell the route command whether the target is a network or a host (a host is assumed if you don't specify). The *if* argument is again optional, and allows you to specify to which network interface the route should be directed—the Linux kernel makes a sensible guess if you don't supply this information. This topic will be explained in more detail in succeeding sections.

The Loopback Interface

The very first interface to be activated is the loopback interface:

 # ifconfig lo 127.0.0.1

Occasionally, you will see the dummy hostname **localhost** being used instead of the IP address. *ifconfig* will look up the name in the *hosts* file, where an entry should declare it as the hostname for **127.0.0.1**:

```
# Sample /etc/hosts entry for localhost
localhost      127.0.0.1
```

To view the configuration of an interface, you invoke *ifconfig*, giving it only the interface name as argument:

```
$ ifconfig lo
lo          Link encap:Local Loopback
            inet addr:127.0.0.1  Mask:255.0.0.0
            UP LOOPBACK RUNNING  MTU:3924  Metric:1
            RX packets:0 errors:0 dropped:0 overruns:0 frame:0
            TX packets:0 errors:0 dropped:0 overruns:0 carrier:0
            Collisions:0
```

As you can see, the loopback interface has been assigned a netmask of **255.0.0.0**, since **127.0.0.1** is a class A address.

Now you can almost start playing with your mini-network. What is still missing is an entry in the routing table that tells IP that it may use this interface as a route to destination **127.0.0.1**. This is accomplished by using:

```
# route add 127.0.0.1
```

Again, you can use **localhost** instead of the IP address, provided you've entered it into your */etc/hosts.*

Next, you should check that everything works fine, for example by using *ping.* *ping* is the networking equivalent of a sonar device.* The command is used to verify that a given address is actually reachable, and to measure the delay that occurs when sending a datagram to it and back again. The time required for this process is often referred to as the "round-trip time":

```
# ping localhost
PING localhost (127.0.0.1): 56 data bytes
64 bytes from 127.0.0.1: icmp_seq=0 ttl=255 time=0.4 ms
64 bytes from 127.0.0.1: icmp_seq=1 ttl=255 time=0.4 ms
64 bytes from 127.0.0.1: icmp_seq=2 ttl=255 time=0.4 ms
^C
--- localhost ping statistics ---
3 packets transmitted, 3 packets received, 0% packet loss
round-trip min/avg/max = 0.4/0.4/0.4 ms
#
```

When you invoke *ping* as shown here, it will continue emitting packets forever, unless interrupted by the user. The ^C marks the place where we pressed Ctrl-C.

The previous example shows that packets for **127.0.0.1** are properly delivered and a reply is returned to *ping* almost instantaneously. This shows that you have successfully set up your first network interface.

---

* Anyone remember Pink Floyd's "Echoes"?

If the output you get from *ping* does not resemble that shown in the previous example, you are in trouble. Check any errors if they indicate that some file hasn't been installed properly. Check that the *ifconfig* and *route* binaries you use are compatible with the kernel release you run, and above all, that the kernel has been compiled with networking enabled (you see this from the presence of the */proc/net* directory). If you get an error message saying "Network unreachable," you probably got the *route* command wrong. Make sure you use the same address you gave to *ifconfig*.

The steps previously described are enough to use networking applications on a standalone host. After adding the lines mentioned earlier to your network initialization script and making sure it will be executed at boot time, you may reboot your machine and try out various applications. For instance, *telnet localhost* should establish a *telnet* connection to your host, giving you a `login:` prompt.

However, the loopback interface is useful not only as an example in networking books, or as a test bed during development, but is actually used by some applications during normal operation.* Therefore, you always have to configure it, regardless of whether your machine is attached to a network or not.

Ethernet Interfaces

Configuring an Ethernet interface is pretty much the same as the loopback interface; it just requires a few more parameters when you are using subnetting.

At the Virtual Brewery, we have subnetted the IP network, which was originally a class B network, into class C subnetworks. To make the interface recognize this, the *ifconfig* incantation would look like this:

```
# ifconfig eth0 vstout netmask 255.255.255.0
```

This command assigns the *eth0* interface the IP address of **vstout (172.16.1.2)**. If we omitted the netmask, *ifconfig* would deduce the netmask from the IP network class, which would result in an incorrect netmask of **255.255.0.0**. Now a quick check shows:

```
# ifconfig eth0
eth0      Link encap 10Mps Ethernet  HWaddr  00:00:C0:90:B3:42
          inet addr 172.16.1.2 Bcast 172.16.1.255 Mask 255.255.255.0
          UP BROADCAST RUNNING  MTU 1500  Metric 1
          RX packets 0 errors 0 dropped 0 overrun 0
          TX packets 0 errors 0 dropped 0 overrun 0
```

You can see that *ifconfig* automatically sets the broadcast address (the `Bcast` field) to the usual value, which is the host's network number with all the host bits set. Also, the maximum transmission unit (the maximum size of IP datagrams the

---

* For example, all applications based on RPC use the loopback interface to register themselves with the *portmapper* daemon at startup. These applications include NIS and NFS.

kernel will generate for this interface) has been set to the maximum size of Ethernet packets: 1,500 bytes. The defaults are usually what you will use, but all these values can be overidden if required, with special options that will be described under "All About ifconfig".

Just as for the loopback interface, you now have to install a routing entry that informs the kernel about the network that can be reached through *eth0*. For the Virtual Brewery, you might invoke *route* as:

```
# route add -net 172.16.1.0
```

At first this looks a little like magic, because it's not really clear how *route* detects which interface to route through. However, the trick is rather simple: the kernel checks all interfaces that have been configured so far and compares the destination address (**172.16.1.0** in this case) to the network part of the interface address (that is, the bitwise AND of the interface address and the netmask). The only interface that matches is *eth0*.

Now, what's that *−net* option for? This is used because *route* can handle both routes to networks and routes to single hosts (as you saw before with **localhost**). When given an address in dotted quad notation, *route* attempts to guess whether it is a network or a hostname by looking at the host part bits. If the address's host part is zero, *route* assumes it denotes a network; otherwise, *route* takes it as a host address. Therefore, *route* would think that **172.16.1.0** is a host address rather than a network number, because it cannot know that we use subnetting. We have to tell *route* explicitly that it denotes a network, so we give it the *−net* flag.

Of course, the *route* command is a little tedious to type, and it's prone to spelling mistakes. A more convenient approach is to use the network names we defined in */etc/networks*. This approach makes the command much more readable; even the *−net* flag can be omitted because *route* knows that **172.16.1.0** denotes a network:

```
# route add brew-net
```

Now that you've finished the basic configuration steps, we want to make sure that your Ethernet interface is indeed running happily. Choose a host from your Ethernet, for instance **vlager**, and type:

```
# ping vlager
PING vlager: 64 byte packets
64 bytes from 172.16.1.1: icmp_seq=0. time=11. ms
64 bytes from 172.16.1.1: icmp_seq=1. time=7. ms
64 bytes from 172.16.1.1: icmp_seq=2. time=12. ms
64 bytes from 172.16.1.1: icmp_seq=3. time=3. ms
^C
----vstout.vbrew.com PING Statistics----
4 packets transmitted, 4 packets received, 0
round-trip (ms)  min/avg/max = 3/8/12
```

If you don't see similar output, something is broken. If you encounter unusual packet loss rates, this hints at a hardware problem, like bad or missing terminators.

If you don't receive any replies at all, you should check the interface configuration with *netstat* described later in "The netstat Command". The packet statistics displayed by *ifconfig* should tell you whether any packets have been sent out on the interface at all. If you have access to the remote host too, you should go over to that machine and check the interface statistics. This way you can determine exactly where the packets got dropped. In addition, you should display the routing information with *route* to see if both hosts have the correct routing entry. *route* prints out the complete kernel routing table when invoked without any arguments (*–n* just makes it print addresses as dotted quad instead of using the hostname):

```
# route -n
Kernel routing table
Destination  Gateway   Genmask          Flags Metric Ref Use     Iface
127.0.0.1    *         255.255.255.255  UH    1      0      112  lo
172.16.1.0   *         255.255.255.0    U     1      0       10  eth0
```

The detailed meaning of these fields is explained later in "The netstat Command." The `Flags` column contains a list of flags set for each interface. `U` is always set for active interfaces, and `H` says the destination address denotes a host. If the `H` flag is set for a route that you meant to be a network route, you have to reissue the *route* command with the *–net* option. To check whether a route you have entered is used at all, check to see if the `Use` field in the second to last column increases between two invocations of *ping*.

Routing Through a Gateway

In the previous section, we covered only the case of setting up a host on a single Ethernet. Quite frequently, however, one encounters networks connected to one another by gateways. These gateways may simply link two or more Ethernets, but may also provide a link to the outside world, such as the Internet. In order to use a gateway, you have to provide additional routing information to the networking layer.

The Ethernets of the Virtual Brewery and the Virtual Winery are linked through such a gateway, namely the host **vlager**. Assuming that **vlager** has already been configured, we just have to add another entry to **vstout**'s routing table that tells the kernel it can reach all hosts on the Winery's network through **vlager**. The appropriate incantation of *route* is shown below; the `gw` keyword tells it that the next argument denotes a gateway:

```
# route add wine-net gw vlager
```

Of course, any host on the Winery network you wish to talk to must have a routing entry for the Brewery's network. Otherwise you would only be able to send data to the Winery network from the Brewery network, but the hosts on the Winery would be unable to reply.

This example describes only a gateway that switches packets between two isolated Ethernets. Now assume that **vlager** also has a connection to the Internet (say, through an additional SLIP link). Then we would want datagrams to *any* destination network other than the Brewery to be handed to **vlager**. This action can be accomplished by making it the default gateway for **vstout**:

```
# route add default gw vlager
```

The network name **default** is a shorthand for 0.0.0.0, which denotes the default route. The default route matches every destination and will be used if there is no more specific route that matches. You do not have to add this name to */etc/networks* because it is built into *route*.

If you see high packet loss rates when pinging a host behind one or more gateways, this may hint at a very congested network. Packet loss is not so much due to technical deficiencies as to temporary excess loads on forwarding hosts, which makes them delay or even drop incoming datagrams.

Configuring a Gateway

Configuring a machine to switch packets between two Ethernets is pretty straightforward. Assume we're back at **vlager**, which is equipped with two Ethernet cards, each connected to one of the two networks. All you have to do is configure both interfaces separately, giving them their respective IP addresses and matching routes, and that's it.

It is quite useful to add information on the two interfaces to the *hosts* file as shown in the following example, so we have handy names for them, too:

```
172.16.1.1      vlager.vbrew.com      vlager vlager-if1
172.16.2.1      vlager-if2
```

The sequence of commands to set up the two interfaces is then:

```
# ifconfig eth0 vlager-if1
# route add brew-net
# ifconfig eth1 vlager-if2
# route add wine-net
```

If this sequence doesn't work, make sure your kernel has been compiled with support for IP forwarding enabled. One good way to do this is to ensure that the first number on the second line of */proc/net/snmp* is set to 1.

The PLIP Interface

A PLIP link used to connect two machines is a little different from an Ethernet. PLIP links are an example of what are called *point-to-point* links, meaning that there is a single host at each end of the link. Networks like Ethernet are called *broadcast* networks. Configuration of point-to-point links is different because unlike broadcast networks, point-to-point links don't support a network of their own.

PLIP provides very cheap and portable links between computers. As an example, we'll consider the laptop computer of an employee at the Virtual Brewery that is connected to **vlager** via PLIP. The laptop itself is called **vlite** and has only one parallel port. At boot time, this port will be registered as *plip1*. To activate the link, you have to configure the *plip1* interface using the following commands:*

```
# ifconfig plip1 vlite pointopoint vlager
# route add default gw vlager
```

The first command configures the interface, telling the kernel that this is a point-to-point link, with the remote side having the address of **vlager**. The second installs the default route, using **vlager** as gateway. On **vlager**, a similar *ifconfig* command is necessary to activate the link (a *route* invocation is not needed):

```
# ifconfig plip1 vlager pointopoint vlite
```

Note that the *plip1* interface on **vlager** does not need a separate IP address, but may also be given the address **172.16.1.1**. Point-to-point networks don't support a network directly, so the interfaces don't require an address on any supported network. The kernel uses the interface information in the routing table to avoid any possible confusion.†

Now we have configured routing from the laptop to the Brewery's network; what's still missing is a way to route from any of the Brewery's hosts to **vlite**. One particularly cumbersome way is to add a specific route to every host's routing table that names **vlager** as a gateway to **vlite**:

```
# route add vlite gw vlager
```

Dynamic routing offers a much better option for temporary routes. You could use *gated*, a routing daemon, which you would have to install on each host in the network in order to distribute routing information dynamically. The easiest option, however, is to use *proxy ARP* (Address Resolution Protocol). With proxy ARP, **vlager** will respond to any ARP query for **vlite** by sending its own Ethernet address. All packets for **vlite** will wind up at **vlager**, which then forwards them to the laptop. We will come back to proxy ARP in the section "Checking the ARP Tables."

---

* Note that **pointopoint** is not a typo. It's really spelled like this.

† As a matter of caution, you should configure a PLIP or SLIP link only after you have completely set up the routing table entries for your Ethernets. With some older kernels, your network route might otherwise end up pointing at the point-to-point link.

Current *net-tools* releases contain a tool called *plipconfig*, which allows you to set certain PLIP timing parameters. The IRQ to be used for the printer port can be set using the *ifconfig* command.

The SLIP and PPP Interfaces

Although SLIP and PPP links are only simple point-to-point links like PLIP connections, there is much more to be said about them. Usually, establishing a SLIP connection involves dialing up a remote site through your modem and setting the serial line to SLIP mode. PPP is used in a similar fashion. We discuss SLIP and PPP in detail in Chapter 7 and Chapter 8, *The Point-to-Point Protocol.*

The Dummy Interface

The dummy interface is a little exotic, but rather useful nevertheless. Its main benefit is with standalone hosts and machines whose only IP network connection is a dialup link. In fact, the latter are standalone hosts most of the time, too.

The dilemma with standalone hosts is that they only have a single network device active, the loopback device, which is usually assigned the address 127.0.0.1. On some occasions, however, you must send data to the "official" IP address of the local host. For instance, consider the laptop **vlite**, which was disconnected from a network for the duration of this example. An application on **vlite** may now want to send data to another application on the same host. Looking up **vlite** in */etc/hosts* yields an IP address of 172.16.1.65, so the application tries to send to this address. As the loopback interface is currently the only active interface on the machine, the kernel has no idea that 172.16.1.65 actually refers to itself! Consequently, the kernel discards the datagram and returns an error to the application.

This is where the dummy device steps in. It solves the dilemma by simply serving as the alter ego of the loopback interface. In the case of **vlite**, you simply give it the address 172.16.1.65 and add a host route pointing to it. Every datagram for 172.16.1.65 is then delivered locally. The proper invocation is:*

```
# ifconfig dummy vlite
# route add vlite
```

IP Alias

New kernels support a feature that can completely replace the dummy interface and serve other useful functions. *IP Alias* allows you to configure multiple IP addresses onto a physical device. In the simplest case, you could replicate the

---

* The dummy device is called *dummy0* if you have loaded it as a module rather than choosing it as an inbuilt kernel option. This is because you are able to load multiple modules and have more than one dummy device.

function of the dummy interface by configuring the host address as an alias onto the loopback interface and completely avoid using the dummy interface. In more complex uses, you could configure your host to look like many different hosts, each with its own IP address. This configuration is sometimes called "Virtual Hosting," although technically it is also used for a variety of other techniques.[*]

To configure an alias for an interface, you must first ensure that your kernel has been compiled with support for IP Alias (check that you have a */proc/net/ip_alias* file; if not, you will have to recompile your kernel). Configuration of an IP alias is virtually identical to configuring a real network device; you use a special name to indicate it's an alias that you want. For example:

```
# ifconfig lo:0 172.16.1.1
```

This command would produce an alias for the loopback interface with the address 172.16.1.1. IP aliases are referred to by appending :*n* to the actual network device, in which "n" is an integer. In our example, the network device we are creating the alias on is lo, and we are creating an alias numbered zero for it. This way, a single physical device may support a number of aliases.

Each alias may be treated as though it is a separate device, and as far as the kernel IP software is concerned, it will be; however, it will be sharing its hardware with another interface.

All About ifconfig

There are many more parameters to *ifconfig* than we have described so far. Its normal invocation is this:

```
ifconfig interface [address [parameters]]
```

interface is the interface name, and *address* is the IP address to be assigned to the interface. This may be either an IP address in dotted quad notation or a name that *ifconfig* will look up in */etc/hosts*.

If *ifconfig* is invoked with only the interface name, it displays that interface's configuration. When invoked without any parameters, it displays all interfaces you have configured so far; a *–a* option forces it to show the inactive ones as well. A sample invocation for the Ethernet interface *eth0* may look like this:

---

[*] More correctly, using IP aliasing is known as network layer virtual hosting. It is more common in the WWW and STMP worlds to use application layer virtual hosting, in which the same IP address is used for each virtual host, but a different hostname is passed with each application layer request. Services like FTP are not capable of operating in this way, and they demand network layer virtual hosting.

```
# ifconfig eth0
eth0      Link encap 10Mbps Ethernet  HWaddr 00:00:C0:90:B3:42
          inet addr 172.16.1.2 Bcast 172.16.1.255 Mask 255.255.255.0
          UP BROADCAST RUNNING  MTU 1500  Metric 0
          RX packets 3136 errors 217 dropped 7 overrun 26
          TX packets 1752 errors 25 dropped 0 overrun 0
```

The `MTU` and `Metric` fields show the current MTU and metric value for that inter-face. The metric value is traditionally used by some operating systems to compute the cost of a route. Linux doesn't use this value yet, but defines it for compatibility, nevertheless.

The `RX` and `TX` lines show how many packets have been received or transmitted error free, how many errors occurred, how many packets were dropped (probably because of low memory), and how many were lost because of an overrun. Receiver overruns usually occur when packets come in faster than the kernel can service the last interrupt. The flag values printed by *ifconfig* roughly correspond to the names of its command-line options; they will be explained later.

The following is a list of parameters recognized by *ifconfig* with the corresponding flag names. Options that simply turn on a feature also allow it to be turned off again by preceding the option name by a dash (–).

up This option makes an interface accessible to the IP layer. This option is implied when an *address* is given on the command line. It may also be used to reenable an interface that has been taken down temporarily using the `down` option.

   This option corresponds to the flags *UP* and *RUNNING*.

down
   This option marks an interface inaccessible to the IP layer. This effectively dis-ables any IP traffic through the interface. Note that this option will also auto-matically delete all routing entries that use this interface.

netmask *mask*
   This option assigns a subnet mask to be used by the interface. It may be given as either a 32-bit hexadecimal number preceded by 0x, or as a dotted quad of decimal numbers. While the dotted quad format is more common, the hex-adecimal representation is often easier to work with. Netmasks are essentially binary, and it is easier to do binary-to-hexadecimal than binary-to-decimal conversion.

pointopoint *address*
   This option is used for point-to-point IP links that involve only two hosts. This option is needed to configure SLIP or PLIP interfaces, for example. If a point-to-point address has been set, *ifconfig* displays the *POINTOPOINT* flag.

broadcast *address*

> The broadcast address is usually made up from the network number by setting all bits of the host part. Some IP implementations (systems derived from BSD 4.2, for instance) use a different scheme in which all host part bits are cleared instead. The *broadcast* option adapts to these strange environments. If a broadcast address has been set, *ifconfig* displays the *BROADCAST* flag.

irq

> This option allows you to set the IRQ line used by certain devices. This is especially useful for PLIP, but may also be useful for certain Ethernet cards.

metric *number*

> This option may be used to assign a metric value to the routing table entry created for the interface. This metric is used by the Routing Information Protocol (RIP) to build routing tables for the network.* The default metric used by *ifconfig* is zero. If you don't run a RIP daemon, you don't need this option at all; if you do, you will rarely need to change the metric value.

mtu *bytes*

> This sets the Maximum Transmission Unit, which is the maximum number of octets the interface is able to handle in one transaction. For Ethernets, the MTU defaults to 1,500 (the largest allowable size of an Ethernet packet); for SLIP interfaces, it is 296. (There is no constraint on the MTU of SLIP links; this value is a good compromise.)

arp

> This is an option specific to broadcast networks such as Ethernets or packet radio. It enables the use of the Address Resolution Protocol (ARP) to detect the physical addresses of hosts attached to the network. For broadcast networks, it is on by default. If ARP is disabled, *ifconfig* displays the *NOARP* flag.

-arp

> This option disables the use of ARP on this interface.

promisc

> This option puts the interface in promiscuous mode. On a broadcast network, this makes the interface receive all packets, regardless of whether they were destined for this host or not. This allows network traffic analysis using packet filters and such, also called *Ethernet snooping*. Usually, this is a good technique for hunting down network problems that are otherwise hard to detect. Tools such as *tcpdump* rely on this.

---

* RIP chooses the optimal route to a given host based on the "length" of the path. It is computed by summing up the individual metric values of each host-to-host link. By default, a hop has length 1, but this may be any positive integer less than 16. (A route length of 16 is equal to infinity. Such routes are considered unusable.) The *metric* parameter sets this hop cost, which is then broadcast by the routing daemon.

On the other hand, this option allows attackers to do nasty things, such as skim the traffic of your network for passwords. You can protect against this type of attack by prohibiting just anyone from plugging their computers into your Ethernet. You could also use secure authentication protocols, such as Kerberos or the secure shell login suite.* This option corresponds to the *PROMISC* flag.

-promisc

This option turns promiscuous mode off.

allmulti

Multicast addresses are like Ethernet broadcast addresses, except that instead of automatically including everybody, the only people who receive packets sent to a multicast address are those programmed to listen to it. This is useful for applications like Ethernet-based videoconferencing or network audio, to which only those interested can listen. Multicast addressing is supported by most, but not all, Ethernet drivers. When this option is enabled, the interface receives and passes multicast packets for processing. This option corresponds to the *ALLMULTI* flag.

-allmulti

This option turns multicast addresses off.

The netstat Command

netstat is a useful tool for checking your network configuration and activity. It is in fact a collection of several tools lumped together. We discuss each of its functions in the following sections.

Displaying the Routing Table

When you invoke *netstat* with the *−r* flag, it displays the kernel routing table in the way we've been doing with *route*. On **vstout**, it produces:

```
# netstat -nr
Kernel IP routing table
Destination     Gateway         Genmask         Flags MSS Window  irtt Iface
127.0.0.1       *               255.255.255.255 UH      0 0          0 lo
172.16.1.0      *               255.255.255.0   U       0 0          0 eth0
172.16.2.0      172.16.1.1      255.255.255.0   UG      0 0          0 eth0
```

The *−n* option makes *netstat* print addresses as dotted quad IP numbers rather than the symbolic host and network names. This option is especially useful when you want to avoid address lookups over the network (e.g., to a DNS or NIS server).

---

* ssh can be obtained from **ftp.cs.hut.fi** in */pub/ssh*.

The second column of *netstat*'s output shows the gateway to which the routing entry points. If no gateway is used, an asterisk is printed instead. The third column shows the "generality" of the route, i.e., the network mask for this route. When given an IP address to find a suitable route for, the kernel steps through each of the routing table entries, taking the bitwise AND of the address and the genmask before comparing it to the target of the route.

The fourth column displays the following flags that describe the route:

G   The route uses a gateway.

U   The interface to be used is up.

H   Only a single host can be reached through the route. For example, this is the case for the loopback entry 127.0.0.1.

D   This route is dynamically created. It is set if the table entry has been generated by a routing daemon like *gated* or by an ICMP redirect message (see the section "The Internet Control Message Protocol" in Chapter 2).

M   This route is set if the table entry was modified by an ICMP redirect message.

!   The route is a reject route and datagrams will be dropped.

The next three columns show the MSS, Window and irtt that will be applied to TCP connections established via this route. The MSS is the Maximum Segment Size and is the size of the largest datagram the kernel will construct for transmission via this route. The Window is the maximum amount of data the system will accept in a single burst from a remote host. The acronym `irtt` stands for "initial round trip time." The TCP protocol ensures that data is reliably delivered between hosts by retransmitting a datagram if it has been lost. The TCP protocol keeps a running count of how long it takes for a datagram to be delivered to the remote end, and an acknowledgement to be received so that it knows how long to wait before assuming a datagram needs to retransmitted; this process is called the round-trip time. The initial round-trip time is the value that the TCP protocol will use when a connection is first established. For most network types, the default value is okay, but for some slow networks, notably certain types of amateur packet radio networks, the time is too short and causes unnecessary retransmission. The `irtt` value can be set using the *route* command. Values of zero in these fields mean that the default is being used.

Finally, the last field displays the network interface that this route will use.

Displaying Interface Statistics

When invoked with the *−i* flag, *netstat* displays statistics for the network interfaces currently configured. If the *−a* option is also given, it prints *all* interfaces present in the kernel, not only those that have been configured currently. On **vstout**, the output from *netstat* will look like this:

```
# netstat -i
Kernel Interface table
Iface MTU Met   RX-OK RX-ERR RX-DRP RX-OVR   TX-OK TX-ERR TX-DRP TX-OVR Flags
lo       0  0    3185      0      0      0    3185      0      0      0 BLRU
eth0 1500   0 972633     17     20    120  628711    217      0      0 BRU
```

The MTU and Met fields show the current MTU and metric values for that interface. The RX and TX columns show how many packets have been received or
transmitted error-free (RX-OK/TX-OK) or damaged (RX-ERR/TX-ERR); how many
were dropped (RX-DRP/TX-DRP); and how many were lost because of an overrun (RX-OVR/TX-OVR).

The last column shows the flags that have been set for this interface. These characters are one-character versions of the long flag names that are printed when you
display the interface configuration with *ifconfig*:

B   A broadcast address has been set.

L   This interface is a loopback device.

M   All packets are received (promiscuous mode).

O   ARP is turned off for this interface.

P   This is a point-to-point connection.

R   Interface is running.

U   Interface is up.

Displaying Connections

netstat supports a set of options to display active or passive sockets. The options
−*t*, −*u*, −*w*, and −*x* show active TCP, UDP, RAW, or Unix socket connections. If you
provide the −*a* flag in addition, sockets that are waiting for a connection (i.e., listening) are displayed as well. This display will give you a list of all servers that are
currently running on your system.

Invoking *netstat -ta* on **vlager** produces this output:

```
$ netstat -ta
Active Internet Connections
Proto Recv-Q Send-Q Local Address      Foreign Address      (State)
tcp        0      0 *:domain           *:*                  LISTEN
tcp        0      0 *:time             *:*                  LISTEN
tcp        0      0 *:smtp             *:*                  LISTEN
tcp        0      0 vlager:smtp        vstout:1040          ESTABLISHED
tcp        0      0 *:telnet           *:*                  LISTEN
tcp        0      0 localhost:1046     vbardolino:telnet    ESTABLISHED
tcp        0      0 *:chargen          *:*                  LISTEN
tcp        0      0 *:daytime          *:*                  LISTEN
tcp        0      0 *:discard          *:*                  LISTEN
```

```
tcp        0      0 *:echo          *:*                LISTEN
tcp        0      0 *:shell         *:*                LISTEN
tcp        0      0 *:login         *:*                LISTEN
```

This output shows most servers simply waiting for an incoming connection. However, the fourth line shows an incoming SMTP connection from **vstout**, and the sixth line tells you there is an outgoing *telnet* connection to **vbardolino**.*

Using the *–a* flag by itself will display all sockets from all families.

Checking the ARP Tables

On some occasions, it is useful to view or alter the contents of the kernel's ARP tables, for example when you suspect a duplicate Internet address is the cause for some intermittent network problem. The *arp* tool was made for situations like this. Its command-line options are:

```
arp [-v] [-t hwtype] -a [hostname]
arp [-v] [-t hwtype] -s hostname hwaddr
arp [-v] -d hostname [hostname...]
```

All `hostname` arguments may be either symbolic hostnames or IP addresses in dotted quad notation.

The first invocation displays the ARP entry for the IP address or host specified, or all hosts known if no `hostname` is given. For example, invoking *arp* on **vlager** may yield:

```
# arp -a
IP address        HW type            HW address
172.16.1.3        10Mbps Ethernet    00:00:C0:5A:42:C1
172.16.1.2        10Mbps Ethernet    00:00:C0:90:B3:42
172.16.2.4        10Mbps Ethernet    00:00:C0:04:69:AA
```

which shows the Ethernet addresses of **vlager**, **vstout** and **vale**.

You can limit the display to the hardware type specified using the *–t* option. This may be `ether`, `ax25`, or `pronet`, standing for 10 Mbps Ethernet; AMPR AX.25, and IEEE 802.5 token ring equipment, respectively.

The *–s* option is used to permanently add `hostname`'s Ethernet address to the ARP tables. The `hwaddr` argument specifies the hardware address, which is by default expected to be an Ethernet address specified as six hexadecimal bytes separated by colons. You may also set the hardware address for other types of hardware, using the *–t* option.

---

* You can tell whether a connection is outgoing from the port numbers. The port number shown for the *calling* host will always be a simple integer. On the host being called, a well-known service port will be in use for which *netstat* uses the symbolic name such as `smtp`, found in */etc/services*.

For some reason, ARP queries for the remote host sometimes fail, for instance when its ARP driver is buggy or there is another host in the network that erroneously identifies itself with that host's IP address; this problem requires you to manually add an IP address to the ARP table. Hard-wiring IP addresses in the ARP table is also a (very drastic) measure to protect yourself from hosts on your Ethernet that pose as someone else.

Invoking *arp* using the *−d* switch deletes all ARP entries relating to the given host. This switch may be used to force the interface to re-attempt obtaining the Ethernet address for the IP address in question. This is useful when a misconfigured system has broadcasted wrong ARP information (of course, you have to reconfigure the broken host first).

The *−s* option may also be used to implement *proxy* ARP. This is a special technique through which a host, say **gate**, acts as a gateway to another host named **fnord** by pretending that both addresses refer to the same host, namely **gate**. It does so by publishing an ARP entry for **fnord** that points to its own Ethernet interface. Now when a host sends out an ARP query for **fnord**, **gate** will return a reply containing its own Ethernet address. The querying host will then send all datagrams to **gate**, which dutifully forwards them to **fnord**.

These contortions may be necessary when you want to access **fnord** from a DOS machine with a broken TCP implementation that doesn't understand routing too well. When you use proxy ARP, it will appear to the DOS machine as if **fnord** was on the local subnet, so it doesn't have to know about how to route through a gateway.

Another useful application of proxy ARP is when one of your hosts acts as a gateway to some other host only temporarily, for instance, through a dial-up link. In a previous example, we encountered the laptop **vlite**, which was connected to **vlager** through a PLIP link from time to time. Of course, this application will work only if the address of the host you want to provide proxy ARP for is on the same IP subnet as your gateway. **vstout** could proxy ARP for any host on the Brewery subnet (**172.16.1.0**), but never for a host on the Winery subnet (**172.16.2.0**).

The proper invocation to provide proxy ARP for **fnord** is given below; of course, the given Ethernet address must be that of **gate**:

```
# arp -s fnord 00:00:c0:a1:42:e0 pub
```

The proxy ARP entry may be removed again by invoking:

```
# arp -d fnord
```

CHAPTER SIX
NAME SERVICE AND RESOLVER CONFIGURATION

As we discussed in Chapter 2, *Issues of TCP/IP Networking*, TCP/IP networking may rely on different schemes to convert names into addresses. The simplest way is a host table stored in */etc/hosts*. This is useful only for small LANs that are run by one single administrator and otherwise have no IP traffic with the outside world. The format of the *hosts* file has already been described in Chapter 5, *Configuring TCP/IP Networking*.

Alternatively, you can use the *Berkeley Internet Name Domain service* (BIND) for resolving hostnames to IP addresses. Configuring BIND can be a real chore, but once you've done it, you can easily make changes in the network topology. On Linux, as on many other Unixish systems, name service is provided through a program called *named*. At startup, it loads a set of master files into its internal cache and waits for queries from remote or local user processes. There are different ways to set up BIND, and not all require you to run a name server on every host.

This chapter can do little more than give a rough sketch of how DNS works and how to operate a name server. It should be sufficient if you have a small LAN and an Internet uplink. For the most current information, you may want to check the documentation contained in the BIND source package, which supplies manual pages, release notes, and the *BIND Operator's Guide* (BOG). Don't let this name scare you off; it's actually a very useful document. For a more comprehensive coverage of DNS and associated issues, you may find *DNS and BIND* by Paul Albitz and Cricket Liu (O'Reilly) a useful reference. DNS questions may be answered in a newsgroup called *comp.protocols.tcp-ip.domains*. For technical details, the Domain Name System is defined by RFC numbers 1033, 1034, and 1035.

The Resolver Library

The term *resolver* refers not to a special application, but to the resolver library. This is a collection of functions that can be found in the standard C library. The central routines are *gethostbyname(2)* and *gethostbyaddr(2)*, which look up all IP addresses associated with a host name, and vice versa. They may be configured to simply look up the information in *hosts*, to query a number of DNS name servers, or to use the *hosts* database of Network Information Service (NIS).

The resolver functions read configuration files when they are invoked. From these configuration files, they determine what databases to query, in which order, and other details relevant to how you've configured your environment. The older Linux standard library, libc, used */etc/host.conf* as its master configuration file, but Version 2 of the GNU standard library, glibc, uses */etc/nsswitch.conf*. We'll describe each in turn, since both are commonly used.

The host.conf File

The */etc/host.conf* tells the older Linux standard library resolver functions which services to use, and in what order.

Options in *host.conf* must appear on separate lines. Fields may be separated by white space (spaces or tabs). A hash sign (#) introduces a comment that extends to the next newline. The following options are available:

order
> This option determines the order in which the resolving services are tried. Valid options are bind for querying the name server, *hosts* for lookups in */etc/hosts*, and nis for NIS lookups. Any or all of them may be specified. The order in which they appear on the line determines the order in which the respective services are tried.

multi
> multi takes on or off as options. This determines if a host in */etc/hosts* is allowed to have several IP addresses, which is usually referred to as being "multi-homed." The default is off. This flag has no effect on DNS or NIS queries.

nospoof
> As we'll explain in the section "Reverse Lookups," DNS allows you to find the hostname belonging to an IP address by using the **in-addr.arpa** domain. Attempts by name servers to supply a false hostname are called *spoofing*. To guard against this, the resolver can be configured to check whether the original IP address is in fact associated with the obtained hostname. If not, the name is rejected and an error is returned. This behavior is turned on by setting nospoof on.

`alert`

> This option takes `on` or `off` as arguments. If it is turned on, any spoof attempts will cause the resolver to log a message to the *syslog* facility.

`trim`

> This option takes an argument specifying a domain name that will be removed from hostnames before lookup. This is useful for *hosts* entries, for which you might only want to specify hostnames without a local domain. If you specify your local domain name here, it will be removed from a lookup of a host with the local domain name appended, thus allowing the lookup in */etc/hosts* to succeed. The domain name you add must end with the (.) character (e.g., `:linux.org.au.`) if `trim` is to work correctly.
>
> `trim` options accumulate; you can consider your host as being local to several domains.

A sample file for **vlager** is shown in Example 6-1.

Example 6-1: Sample host.conf File

```
# /etc/host.conf
# We have named running, but no NIS (yet)
order   bind,hosts
# Allow multiple addrs
multi   on
# Guard against spoof attempts
nospoof on
# Trim local domain (not really necessary).
trim    vbrew.com.
```

Resolver environment variables

The settings from *host.conf* may be overridden using a number of environment variables:

`RESOLV_HOST_CONF`

> This variable specifies a file to be read instead of */etc/host.conf*.

`RESOLV_SERV_ORDER`

> This variable overrides the `order` option given in *host.conf*. Services are given as `hosts`, `bind`, and `nis`, separated by a space, comma, colon, or semicolon.

`RESOLV_SPOOF_CHECK`

> This variable determines the measures taken against spoofing. It is completely disabled by `off`. The values `warn` and `warn off` enable spoof checking by turning logging on and off, respectively. A value of `*` turns on spoof checks, but leaves the logging facility as defined in *host.conf*.

RESOLV_MULTI

This variable uses a value of on or off to override the multi options from *host.conf*.

RESOLV_OVERRIDE_TRIM_DOMAINS

This variable specifies a list of trim domains that override those given in *host.conf*. Trim domains were explained earlier when we discussed the trim keyword.

RESOLV_ADD_TRIM_DOMAINS

This variable specifies a list of trim domains that are added to those given in *host.conf*.

The nsswitch.conf File

Version 2 of the GNU standard library includes a more powerful and flexible replacement for the older *host.conf* mechanism. The concept of the name service has been extended to include a variety of different types of information. Configuration options for all of the different functions that query these databases have been brought back into a single configuration file; the *nsswitch.conf* file.

The *nsswitch.conf* file allows the system administrator to configure a wide variety of different databases. We'll limit our discussion to options that relate to host and network IP address resolution. You can easily find more information about the other features by reading the GNU standard library documentation.

Options in *nsswitch.conf* must appear on separate lines. Fields may be separated by whitespace (spaces or tabs). A hash sign (#) introduces a comment that extends to the next newline. Each line describes a particular service; hostname resolution is one of these. The first field in each line is the name of the database, ending with a colon. The database name associated with host address resolution is hosts. A related database is networks, which is used for resolution of network names into network addresses. The remainder of each line stores options that determine the way lookups for that database are performed.

The following options are available:

dns

Use the Domain Name System (DNS) service to resolve the address. This makes sense only for host address resolution, not network address resolution. This mechanism uses the */etc/resolv.conf* file that we'll describe later in the chapter.

files

Search a local file for the host or network name and its corresponding address. This option uses the traditional */etc/hosts* and */etc/network* files.

nis *or* nisplus
> Use the Network Information System (NIS) to resolve the host or network address. NIS and NIS+ are discussed in detail in Chapter 13, *The Network Information System.*

The order in which the services to be queried are listed determines the order in which they are queried when attempting to resolve a name. The query-order list is in the service description in the */etc/nsswitch.conf* file. The services are queried from left to right and by default searching stops when a resolution is successful.

A simple example of host and network database specification that would mimic our configuration using the older libc standard library is shown in Example 6-2.

Example 6-2: Sample nsswitch.conf File

```
# /etc/nsswitch.conf
#
# Example configuration of GNU Name Service Switch functionality.
# Information about this file is available in the 'libc6-doc' package.

hosts:          dns files
networks:       files
```

This example causes the system to look up hosts first in the Domain Name System, and the */etc/hosts* file, if that can't find them. Network name lookups would be attempted using only the */etc/networks* file.

You are able to control the lookup behavior more precisely using "action items" that describe what action to take given the result of the previous lookup attempt. Action items appear between service specifications, and are enclosed within square brackets, [ ]. The general syntax of the action statement is:

```
[ [!] status = action ... ]
```

There are two possible actions:

return
> Controls returns to the program that attempted the name resolution. If a lookup attempt was successful, the resolver will return with the details, otherwise it will return a zero result.

continue
> The resolver will move on to the next service in the list and attempt resolution using it.

The optional (!) character specifies that the status value should be inverted before testing; that is, it means "not."

The available status values on which we can act are:

`success`
> The requested entry was found without error. The default action for this status is `return`.

`notfound`
> There was no error in the lookup, but the target host or network could not be found. The default action for this status is `continue`.

`unavail`
> The service queried was unavailable. This could mean that the *hosts* or *networks* file was unreadable for the `files` service or that a name server or NIS server did not respond for the `dns` or `nis` services. The default action for this status is `continue`.

`tryagain`
> This status means the service is temporarily unavailable. For the `files` files service, this would usually indicate that the relevant file was locked by some process. For other services, it may mean the server was temporarily unable to accept connections. The default action for this status is `continue`.

A simple example of how you might use this mechanism is shown in Example 6-3.

Example 6-3: Sample nsswitch.conf File Using an Action Statement

```
# /etc/nsswitch.conf
#
# Example configuration of GNU Name Service Switch functionality.
# Information about this file is available in the 'libc6-doc' package.

hosts:          dns [!UNAVAIL=return] files
networks:       files
```

This example attempts host resolution using the Domain Name Service system. If the return status is anything other than unavailable, the resolver returns whatever it has found. If, and only if, the DNS lookup attempt returns an unavailable status, the resolver attempts to use the local */etc/hosts*. This means that we should use the *hosts* file only if our name server is unavailable for some reason.

Configuring Name Server Lookups Using resolv.conf

When configuring the resolver library to use the BIND name service for host lookups, you also have to tell it which name servers to use. There is a separate file for this called *resolv.conf*. If this file does not exist or is empty, the resolver assumes the name server is on your local host.

To run a name server on your local host, you have to set it up separately, as will be explained in the following section. If you are on a local network and have the opportunity to use an existing name server, this should always be preferred. If you use a dialup IP connection to the Internet, you would normally specify the name server of your service provider in the *resolv.conf* file.

The most important option in *resolv.conf* is `name server`, which gives the IP address of a name server to use. If you specify several name servers by giving the `name server` option several times, they are tried in the order given. You should therefore put the most reliable server first. The current implementation allows you to have up to three `name server` statements in *resolv.conf*. If no `name server` option is given, the resolver attempts to connect to the name server on the local host.

Two other options, `domain` and `search`, let you use shortcut names for hosts in your local domain. Usually, when just telnetting to another host in your local domain, you don't want to type in the fully qualified hostname, but use a name like **gauss** on the command line and have the resolver tack on the **mathematics.groucho.edu** part.

This is just the `domain` statement's purpose. It lets you specify a default domain name to be appended when DNS fails to look up a hostname. For instance, when given the name **gauss**, the resolver fails to find **gauss.** in DNS, because there is no such top-level domain. When given **mathematics.groucho.edu** as a default domain, the resolver repeats the query for **gauss** with the default domain appended, this time succeeding.

That's just fine, you may think, but as soon you get out of the Math department's domain, you're back to those fully qualified domain names. Of course, you would also want to have shorthands like **quark.physics** for hosts in the Physics department's domain.

This is when the *search list* comes in. A search list can be specified using the `search` option, which is a generalization of the `domain` statement. Where the latter gives a single default domain, the former specifies a whole list of them, each to be tried in turn until a lookup succeeds. This list must be separated by blanks or tabs.

The `search` and `domain` statements are mutually exclusive and may not appear more than once. If neither option is given, the resolver will try to guess the default domain from the local hostname using the *getdomainname(2)* system call. If the local hostname doesn't have a domain part, the default domain will be assumed to be the root domain.

If you decide to put a `search` statement into *resolv.conf,* you should be careful about what domains you add to this list. Resolver libraries prior to BIND 4.9 used to construct a default search list from the domain name when no search list was given. This default list was made up of the default domain itself, plus all of its parent domains up to the root. This caused some problems because DNS requests wound up at name servers that were never meant to see them.

Assume you're at the Virtual Brewery and want to log in to **foot.groucho.edu**. By a slip of your fingers, you mistype **foot** as **foo**, which doesn't exist. GMU's name server will therefore tell you that it knows no such host. With the old-style search list, the resolver would now go on trying the name with **vbrew.com** and **com** appended. The latter is problematic because **groucho.edu.com** might actually be a valid domain name. Their name server might then even find **foo** in their domain, pointing you to one of their hosts—which clearly was not intended.

For some applications, these bogus host lookups can be a security problem. Therefore, you should usually limit the domains on your search list to your local organization, or something comparable. At the Mathematics department of Groucho Marx University, the search list would commonly be set to **maths.groucho.edu** and **groucho.edu**.

If default domains sound confusing to you, consider this sample *resolv.conf* file for the Virtual Brewery:

```
# /etc/resolv.conf
# Our domain
domain          vbrew.com
#
# We use vlager as central name server:
name server     172.16.1.1
```

When resolving the name **vale**, the resolver looks up **vale** and, failing this, **vale.vbrew.com**.

Resolver Robustness

When running a LAN inside a larger network, you definitely should use central name servers if they are available. The name servers develop rich caches that speed up repeat queries, since all queries are forwarded to them. However, this scheme has a drawback: when a fire destroyed the backbone cable at Olaf's university, no more work was possible on his department's LAN because the resolver could no longer reach any of the name servers. This situation caused difficulties with most network services, such as X terminal logins and printing.

Although it is not very common for campus backbones to go down in flames, one might want to take precautions against cases like this.

One option is to set up a local name server that resolves hostnames from your local domain and forwards all queries for other hostnames to the main servers. Of course, this is applicable only if you are running your own domain.

Alternatively, you can maintain a backup host table for your domain or LAN in */etc/hosts*. This is very simple to do. You simply ensure that the resolver library queries DNS first, and the hosts file next. In an */etc/host.conf* file you'd use "order bind,hosts", and in an */etc/nsswitch.conf* file you'd use "hosts: dns files", to make the resolver fall back to the hosts file if the central name server is unreachable.

How DNS Works

DNS organizes hostnames in a domain hierarchy. A *domain* is a collection of sites that are related in some sense—because they form a proper network (e.g., all machines on a campus, or all hosts on BITNET), because they all belong to a certain organization (e.g., the U.S. government), or because they're simply geographically close. For instance, universities are commonly grouped in the **edu** domain, with each university or college using a separate *subdomain*, below which their hosts are subsumed. Groucho Marx University have the **groucho.edu** domain, while the LAN of the Mathematics department is assigned **maths.groucho.edu**. Hosts on the departmental network would have this domain name tacked onto their hostname, so **erdos** would be known as **erdos.maths.groucho.edu**. This is called the *fully qualified domain name* (FQDN), which uniquely identifies this host worldwide.

Figure 6-1 shows a section of the namespace. The entry at the root of this tree, which is denoted by a single dot, is quite appropriately called the *root domain* and encompasses all other domains. To indicate that a hostname is a fully qualified domain name, rather than a name relative to some (implicit) local domain, it is sometimes written with a trailing dot. This dot signifies that the name's last component is the root domain.

Depending on its location in the name hierarchy, a domain may be called top-level, second-level, or third-level. More levels of subdivision occur, but they are rare. This list details several top-level domains you may see frequently:

Domain	Description
edu	(Mostly U.S.) educational institutions like universities.
com	Commercial organizations and companies.
org	Non-commercial organizations. Private UUCP networks are often in this domain.
net	Gateways and other administrative hosts on a network.
mil	U.S. military institutions.
gov	U.S. government institutions.
uucp	Officially, all site names formerly used as UUCP names without domains have been moved to this domain.

Historically, the first four of these were assigned to the U.S., but recent changes in policy have meant that these domains, named global Top Level Domains (gTLD), are now considered global in nature. Negotiations are currently underway to broaden the range of gTLDs, which may result in increased choice in the future.

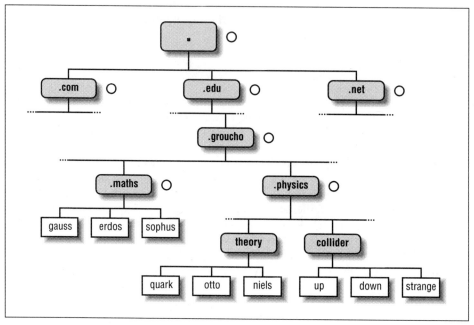

Figure 6-1. A part of the domain namespace

Outside the U.S., each country generally uses a top-level domain of its own named after the two-letter country code defined in ISO-3166. Finland, for instance, uses the **fi** domain; **fr** is used by France, **de** by Germany, and **au** by Australia. Below this top-level domain, each country's NIC is free to organize hostnames in whatever way they want. Australia has second-level domains similar to the international top-level domains, named **com.au** and **edu.au**. Other countries, like Germany, don't use this extra level, but have slightly long names that refer directly to the organizations running a particular domain. It's not uncommon to see hostnames like **ftp.informatik.uni-erlangen.de**. Chalk that up to German efficiency.

Of course, these national domains do not imply that a host below that domain is actually located in that country; it means only that the host has been registered with that country's NIC. A Swedish manufacturer might have a branch in Australia and still have all its hosts registered with the **se** top-level domain.

Organizing the namespace in a hierarchy of domain names nicely solves the problem of name uniqueness; with DNS, a hostname has to be unique only within its domain to give it a name different from all other hosts worldwide. Furthermore, fully qualified names are easy to remember. Taken by themselves, these are already very good reasons to split up a large domain into several subdomains.

DNS does even more for you than this. It also allows you to delegate authority over a subdomain to its administrators. For example, the maintainers at the Groucho Computing Center might create a subdomain for each department; we already encountered the **math** and **physics** subdomains above. When they find the network at the Physics department too large and chaotic to manage from outside (after all, physicists are known to be an unruly bunch of people), they may simply pass control of the **physics.groucho.edu** domain to the administrators of this network. These administrators are free to use whatever hostnames they like and assign them IP addresses from their network in whatever fashion they desire, without outside interference.

To this end, the namespace is split up into *zones*, each rooted at a domain. Note the subtle difference between a *zone* and a *domain*: the domain **groucho.edu** encompasses all hosts at Groucho Marx University, while the zone **groucho.edu** includes only the hosts that are managed by the Computing Center directly; those at the Mathematics department, for example. The hosts at the Physics department belong to a different zone, namely **physics.groucho.edu**. In Figure 6-1, the start of a zone is marked by a small circle to the right of the domain name.

Name Lookups with DNS

At first glance, all this domain and zone fuss seems to make name resolution an awfully complicated business. After all, if no central authority controls what names are assigned to which hosts, how is a humble application supposed to know?

Now comes the really ingenious part about DNS. If you want to find the IP address of **erdos**, DNS says, "Go ask the people who manage it, and they will tell you."

In fact, DNS is a giant distributed database. It is implemented by so-called name servers that supply information on a given domain or set of domains. For each zone there are at least two, or at most a few, name servers that hold all authoritative information on hosts in that zone. To obtain the IP address of **erdos**, all you have to do is contact the name server for the **groucho.edu** zone, which will then return the desired data.

Easier said than done, you might think. So how do I know how to reach the name server at Groucho Marx University? In case your computer isn't equipped with an address-resolving oracle, DNS provides for this, too. When your application wants to look up information on **erdos**, it contacts a local name server, which conducts a so-called iterative query for it. It starts off by sending a query to a name server for the root domain, asking for the address of **erdos.maths.groucho.edu**. The root name server recognizes that this name does not belong to its zone of authority, but rather to one below the **edu** domain. Thus, it tells you to contact an **edu** zone name server for more information and encloses a list of all **edu** name servers along with their addresses. Your local name server will then go on and query one of those, for instance, **a.isi.edu**. In a manner similar to the root name server, **a.isi.edu** knows that the **groucho.edu** people run a zone of their own, and points you to their servers. The local name server will then present its query for **erdos** to one of these, which will finally recognize the name as belonging to its zone, and return the corresponding IP address.

This looks like a lot of traffic being generated for looking up a measly IP address, but it's really only miniscule compared to the amount of data that would have to be transferred if we were still stuck with *HOSTS.TXT*. There's still room for improvement with this scheme, however.

To improve response time during future queries, the name server stores the information obtained in its local *cache*. So the next time anyone on your local network wants to look up the address of a host in the **groucho.edu** domain, your name server will go directly to the **groucho.edu** name server.*

Of course, the name server will not keep this information forever; it will discard it after some time. The expiration interval is called the *time to live*, or TTL. Each datum in the DNS database is assigned such a TTL by administrators of the responsible zone.

Types of Name Servers

Name servers that hold all information on hosts within a zone are called *authoritative* for this zone, and sometimes are referred to as *master name servers*. Any query for a host within this zone will end up at one of these master name servers.

Master servers must be fairly well synchronized. Thus, the zone's network administrator must make one the *primary* server, which loads its zone information from data files, and make the others *secondary* servers, which transfer the zone data from the primary server at regular intervals.

Having several name servers distributes workload; it also provides backup. When one name server machine fails in a benign way, like crashing or losing its network connection, all queries will fall back to the other servers. Of course, this scheme doesn't protect you from server malfunctions that produce wrong replies to all DNS requests, such as from software bugs in the server program itself.

You can also run a name server that is not authoritative for any domain.† This is useful, as the name server will still be able to conduct DNS queries for the applications running on the local network and cache the information. Hence it is called a *caching-only* server.

---

* If information weren't cached, then DNS would be as inefficient as any other method because each query would involve the root name servers.

† Well, almost. A name server has to provide at least name service for **localhost** and reverse lookups of **127.0.0.1**.

The DNS Database

We have seen that DNS not only deals with IP addresses of hosts, but also exchanges information on name servers. DNS databases may have, in fact, many different types of entries.

A single piece of information from the DNS database is called a *resource record* (RR). Each record has a type associated with it describing the sort of data it represents, and a class specifying the type of network it applies to. The latter accommodates the needs of different addressing schemes, like IP addresses (the IN class), Hesiod addresses (used by MIT's Kerberos system), and a few more. The prototypical resource record type is the A record, which associates a fully qualified domain name with an IP address.

A host may be known by more than one name. For example you might have a server that provides both FTP and World Wide Web servers, which you give two names: **ftp.machine.org** and **www.machine.org**. However, one of these names must be identified as the official or *canonical* hostname, while the others are simply aliases referring to the official hostname. The difference is that the canonical hostname is the one with an associated A record, while the others only have a record of type CNAME that points to the canonical hostname.

We will not go through all record types here, but we will give you a brief example. Example 6-4 shows a part of the domain database that is loaded into the name servers for the **physics.groucho.edu** zone.

Example 6-4: An Excerpt from the named.hosts File for the Physics Department

```
; Authoritative Information on physics.groucho.edu.
@   IN  SOA niels.physics.groucho.edu. janet.niels.physics.groucho.edu. {
                    1999090200          ; serial no
                    360000              ; refresh
                    3600                ; retry
                    3600000             ; expire
                    3600                ; default ttl
                }
;
; Name servers
                IN      NS          niels
                IN      NS          gauss.maths.groucho.edu.
gauss.maths.groucho.edu. IN A 149.76.4.23
;
; Theoretical Physics (subnet 12)
niels           IN      A           149.76.12.1
                IN      A           149.76.1.12
name server     IN      CNAME       niels
otto            IN      A           149.76.12.2
quark           IN      A           149.76.12.4
down            IN      A           149.76.12.5
strange         IN      A           149.76.12.6
```

Example 6-4: An Excerpt from the named.hosts File for the Physics Department (continued)

```
...
; Collider Lab. (subnet 14)
boson        IN    A      149.76.14.1
muon         IN    A      149.76.14.7
bogon        IN    A      149.76.14.12
...
```

Apart from the A and CNAME records, you can see a special record at the top of the file, stretching several lines. This is the SOA resource record signaling the *Start of Authority*, which holds general information on the zone the server is authoritative for. The SOA record comprises, for instance, the default time to live for all records.

Note that all names in the sample file that do not end with a dot should be interpreted relative to the **physics.groucho.edu** domain. The special name (@) used in the SOA record refers to the domain name by itself.

We have seen earlier that the name servers for the **groucho.edu** domain somehow have to know about the **physics** zone so that they can point queries to their name servers. This is usually achieved by a pair of records: the NS record that gives the server's FQDN, and an A record that associates an address with that name. Since these records are what holds the namespace together, they are frequently called *glue records*. They are the only instances of records in which a parent zone actually holds information on hosts in the subordinate zone. The glue records pointing to the name servers for **physics.groucho.edu** are shown in Example 6-5.

Example 6-5: An Excerpt from the named.hosts File for GMU

```
; Zone data for the groucho.edu zone.
@  IN  SOA vax12.gcc.groucho.edu. joe.vax12.gcc.groucho.edu. {
                    1999070100       ; serial no
                    360000           ; refresh
                    3600             ; retry
                    3600000          ; expire
                    3600             ; default ttl
            }
....
;
; Glue records for the physics.groucho.edu zone
physics         IN    NS      niels.physics.groucho.edu.
                IN    NS      gauss.maths.groucho.edu.
niels.physics   IN    A       149.76.12.1
gauss.maths     IN    A       149.76.4.23
...
```

Reverse Lookups

Finding the IP address belonging to a host is certainly the most common use for the Domain Name System, but sometimes you'll want to find the canonical host-name corresponding to an address. Finding this hostname is called *reverse mapping*, and is used by several network services to verify a client's identity. When using a single *hosts* file, reverse lookups simply involve searching the file for a host that owns the IP address in question. With DNS, an exhaustive search of the namespace is out of the question. Instead, a special domain, **in-addr.arpa**, has been created that contains the IP addresses of all hosts in a reversed dotted quad notation. For instance, an IP address of 149.76.12.4 corresponds to the name 4.12.76.149.in-addr.arpa. The resource-record type linking these names to their canonical hostnames is PTR.

Creating a zone of authority usually means that its administrators have full control over how they assign addresses to names. Since they usually have one or more IP networks or subnets at their hands, there's a one-to-many mapping between DNS zones and IP networks. The Physics department, for instance, comprises the subnets 149.76.8.0, 149.76.12.0, and 149.76.14.0.

Consequently, new zones in the **in-addr.arpa** domain have to be created along with the **physics** zone, and delegated to the network administrators at the department: **8.76.149.in-addr.arpa**, **12.76.149.in-addr.arpa**, and **14.76.149.in-addr.arpa**. Otherwise, installing a new host at the Collider Lab would require them to contact their parent domain to have the new address entered into their **in-addr.arpa** zone file.

The zone database for subnet 12 is shown in Example 6-6. The corresponding glue records in the database of their parent zone are shown in Example 6-7.

Example 6-6: An Excerpt from the named.rev File for Subnet 12

```
; the 12.76.149.in-addr.arpa domain.
@   IN  SOA  niels.physics.groucho.edu.  janet.niels.physics.groucho.edu. {
                    1999090200 360000 3600 3600000 3600
            }
2           IN      PTR         otto.physics.groucho.edu.
4           IN      PTR         quark.physics.groucho.edu.
5           IN      PTR         down.physics.groucho.edu.
6           IN      PTR         strange.physics.groucho.edu.
```

Example 6-7: An Excerpt from the named.rev File for Network 149.76

```
; the 76.149.in-addr.arpa domain.
@   IN  SOA  vax12.gcc.groucho.edu.  joe.vax12.gcc.groucho.edu. {
                    1999070100 360000 3600 3600000 3600
            }
...
; subnet 4: Mathematics Dept.
1.4         IN      PTR         sophus.maths.groucho.edu.
```

Example 6-7: An Excerpt from the named.rev File for Network 149.76 (continued)

```
17.4        IN    PTR        erdos.maths.groucho.edu.
23.4        IN    PTR        gauss.maths.groucho.edu.
...
; subnet 12: Physics Dept, separate zone
12          IN    NS         niels.physics.groucho.edu.
            IN    NS         gauss.maths.groucho.edu.
niels.physics.groucho.edu. IN  A 149.76.12.1
gauss.maths.groucho.edu. IN  A   149.76.4.23
...
```

in-addr.arpa system zones can only be created as supersets of IP networks. An even more severe restriction is that these networks' netmasks have to be on byte boundaries. All subnets at Groucho Marx University have a netmask of **255.255.255.0**, hence an **in-addr.arpa** zone could be created for each subnet. However, if the netmask were **255.255.255.128** instead, creating zones for the subnet **149.76.12.128** would be impossible, because there's no way to tell DNS that the **12.76.149.in-addr.arpa** domain has been split into two zones of authority, with hostnames ranging from **1** through **127**, and **128** through **255**, respectively.

Running named

named (pronounced *name-dee*) provides DNS on most Unix machines. It is a server program originally developed for BSD to provide name service to clients, and possibly to other name servers. BIND Version 4 was around for some time and appeared in most Linux distributions. The new release, Version 8, has been introduced in most Linux distributions, and is a big change from previous versions.* It has many new features, such as support for DNS dynamic updates, DNS change notifications, much improved performance, and a new configuration file syntax. Please check the documentation contained in the source distribution for details.

This section requires some understanding of the way DNS works. If the following discussion is all Greek to you, you may want to reread the section "How DNS Works."

named is usually started at system boot time and runs until the machine goes down again. Implementations of BIND prior to Version 8 take their information from a configuration file called */etc/named.boot* and various files that map domain names to addresses. The latter are called *zone files*. Versions of BIND from Version 8 onwards use */etc/named.conf* in place of */etc/named.boot*.

---

* BIND 4.9 was developed by Paul Vixie, *paul@vix.com*, but BIND is now maintained by the Internet Software Consortium, *bind-bugs@isc.org*.

To run *named* at the prompt, enter:

```
# /usr/sbin/named
```

named will come up and read the *named.boot* file and any zone files specified therein. It writes its process ID to */var/run/named.pid* in ASCII, downloads any zone files from primary servers, if necessary, and starts listening on port 53 for DNS queries.

The named.boot File

The BIND configuration file prior to Version 8 was very simple in structure. BIND Version 8 has a very different configuration file syntax to deal with many of the new features introduced. The name of the configuration file changed from */etc/named.boot*, in older versions of BIND, to */etc/named.conf* in BIND Version 8. We'll focus on configuring the older version because it is probably what most distributions are still using, but we'll present an equivalent *named.conf* to illustrate the differences, and we'll talk about how to convert the old format into the new one.

The *named.boot* file is generally small and contains little but pointers to master files containing zone information and pointers to other name servers. Comments in the boot file start with the (#) or (;) characters and extend to the next newline. Before we discuss the format of *named.boot* in more detail, we will take a look at the sample file for **vlager** given in Example 6-8.

Example 6-8: The named.boot File for vlager

```
;
; /etc/named.boot file for vlager.vbrew.com
;
directory       /var/named
;
;               domain                  file
;-----------------
cache           .                       named.ca
primary         vbrew.com               named.hosts
primary         0.0.127.in-addr.arpa    named.local
primary         16.172.in-addr.arpa     named.rev
```

Let's look at each statement individually. The `directory` keyword tells *named* that all filenames referred to later in this file, zone files for example, are located in the */var/named* directory. This saves a little typing.

The `primary` keyword shown in this example loads information into *named*. This information is taken from the master files specified as the last of the parameters. These files represent DNS resource records, which we will look at next.

In this example, we configured *named* as the primary name server for three domains, as indicated by the three `primary` statements. The first of these statements instructs *named* to act as a primary server for **vbrew.com**, taking the zone data from the file *named.hosts*.

The `cache` keyword is very special and should be present on virtually all machines running a name server. It instructs *named* to enable its cache and to load the *root name server hints* from the cache file specified (*named.ca* in our example). We will come back to the name server hints in the following list.

Here's a list of the most important options you can use in *named.boot*:

directory

> This option specifies a directory in which zone files reside. Names of files in other options may be given relative to this directory. Several directories may be specified by repeatedly using `directory`. The Linux file system standard suggests this should be */var/named*.

primary

> This option takes a domain name and filename as an argument, declaring the local server authoritative for the named domain. As a primary server, *named* loads the zone information from the given master file.

> There will always be at least one `primary` entry in every boot file used for reverse mapping of network **127.0.0.0**, which is the local loopback network.

secondary

> This statement takes a domain name, an address list, and a filename as an argument. It declares the local server a secondary master server for the specified domain.

> A secondary server holds authoritative data on the domain, too, but it doesn't gather it from files; instead, it tries to download it from the primary server. The IP address of at least one primary server thus must be given to *named* in the address list. The local server contacts each of them in turn until it successfully transfers the zone database, which is then stored in the backup file given as the third argument. If none of the primary servers responds, the zone data is retrieved from the backup file instead.

> *named* then attempts to refresh the zone data at regular intervals. This process is explained later in connection with the SOA resource record type.

cache

> This option takes a domain name and filename as arguments. This file contains the root server hints, which is a list of records pointing to the root name servers. Only NS and A records will be recognized. The `domain` should be the root domain name, a simple period (.).

This information is absolutely crucial to *named*; if the `cache` statement does not occur in the boot file, *named* will not develop a local cache at all. This situation/lack of development will severely degrade performance and increase network load if the next server queried is not on the local net. Moreover, *named* will not be able to reach any root name servers, and thus won't resolve any addresses except those it is authoritative for. An exception from this rule involves forwarding servers (see the `forwarders` option that follows).

`forwarders`
> This statement takes a whitespace-separated list of addresses as an argument. The IP addresses in this list specify a list of name servers that *named* may query if it fails to resolve a query from its local cache. They are tried in order until one of them responds to the query. Typically, you would use the name server of your network provider or another well-known server as a forwarder.

`slave`
> This statement makes the name server a *slave* server. It never performs recursive queries itself, but only forwards them to servers specified in the `forwarders` statement.

There are two options that we will not describe here: `sortlist` and `domain`. Two other directives may also be used inside these database files: `$INCLUDE` and `$ORIGIN`. Since they are rarely needed, we will not describe them here, either.

The BIND 8 host.conf File

BIND Version 8 introduced a range of new features, and with these came a new configuration file syntax. The *named.boot*, with its simple single line statements, was replaced by the *named.conf* file, with a syntax like that of *gated* and resembling C source syntax.

The new syntax is more complex, but fortunately a tool has been provided that automates conversion from the old syntax to the new syntax. In the BIND 8 source package, a *perl* program called *named-bootconf.pl* is provided that will read your existing *named.boot* file from `stdin` and convert it into the equivalent *named.conf* format on `stdout`. To use it, you must have the *perl* interpreter installed.

You should use the script somewhat like this:

```
# cd /etc
# named-bootconf.pl <named.boot >named.conf
```

The script then produces a *named.conf* that looks like that shown in Example 6-9. We've cleaned out a few of the helpful comments the script includes to help show the almost direct relationship between the old and the new syntax.

Example 6-9: The BIND 8 equivalent named.conf File for vlager

```
//
// /etc/named.boot file for vlager.vbrew.com
options {
        directory "/var/named";
};

zone "." {
        type hint;
        file "named.ca";
};

zone "vbrew.com" {
        type master;
        file "named.hosts";
};

zone "0.0.127.in-addr.arpa" {
        type master;
        file "named.local";
};

zone "16.172.in-addr.arpa" {
        type master;
        file "named.rev";
};
```

If you take a close look, you will see that each of the one-line statements in *named.boot* has been converted into a C-like statement enclosed within {} characters in the *named.conf* file.

The comments, which in the *named.boot* file were indicated by a semicolon (;), are now indicated by two forward slashes (//).

The `directory` statement has been translated into an `options` paragraph with a `directory` clause.

The `cache` and `primary` statements have been converted into `zone` paragraphs with `type` clauses of `hint` and `master`, respectively.

The zone files do not need to be modified in any way; their syntax remains unchanged.

The new configuration syntax allows for many new options that we haven't covered here. If you'd like information on the new options, the best source of information is the documentation supplied with the BIND Version 8 source package.

The DNS Database Files

Master files included with *named*, like *named.hosts*, always have a domain associated with them, which is called the *origin*. This is the domain name specified with the `cache` and `primary` options. Within a master file, you are allowed to specify domain and host names relative to this domain. A name given in a configuration file is considered *absolute* if it ends in a single dot, otherwise it is considered relative to the origin. The origin by itself may be referred to using (@).

The data contained in a master file is split up in *resource records*(RRs). RRs are the smallest units of information available through DNS. Each resource record has a type. A records, for instance, map a hostname to an IP address, and a CNAME record associates an alias for a host with its official hostname. To see an example, look at Example 6-11, which shows the *named.hosts* master file for the Virtual Brewery.

Resource record representations in master files share a common format:

```
[domain] [ttl] [class] type rdata
```

Fields are separated by spaces or tabs. An entry may be continued across several lines if an opening brace occurs before the first newline and the last field is followed by a closing brace. Anything between a semicolon and a newline is ignored. A description of the format terms follows:

domain

> This term is the domain name to which the entry applies. If no domain name is given, the RR is assumed to apply to the domain of the previous RR.

ttl

> In order to force resolvers to discard information after a certain time, each RR is associated a time to live (*ttl*). The ttl field specifies the time in seconds that the information is valid after it has been retrieved from the server. It is a decimal number with at most eight digits.

> If no ttl value is given, the field value defaults to that of the *minimum* field of the preceding SOA record.

class

> This is an address class, like IN for IP addresses or HS for objects in the Hesiod class. For TCP/IP networking, you have to specify IN.

> If no class field is given, the class of the preceding RR is assumed.

type

> This describes the type of the RR. The most common types are A, SOA, PTR, and NS. The following sections describe the various types of RRs.

rdata

This holds the data associated with the RR. The format of this field depends on the type of RR. In the following discussion, it will be described for each RR separately.

The following is partial list of RRs to be used in DNS master files. There are a couple more of them that we will not explain; they are experimental and of little use, generally.

SOA

This RR describes a zone of authority (SOA means "Start of Authority"). It signals that the records following the SOA RR contain authoritative information for the domain. Every master file included by a **primary** statement must contain an SOA record for this zone. The resource data contains the following fields:

origin

This field is the canonical hostname of the primary name server for this domain. It is usually given as an absolute name.

contact

This field is the email address of the person responsible for maintaining the domain, with the "@" sign replaced by a dot. For instance, if the responsible person at the Virtual Brewery were **janet**, this field would contain `janet.vbrew.com`.

serial

This field is the version number of the zone file, expressed as a single decimal number. Whenever data is changed in the zone file, this number should be incremented. A common convention is to use a number that reflects the date of the last update, with a version number appended to it to cover the case of multiple updates occurring on a single day, e.g., 2000012600 being update 00 that occurred on January 26, 2000.

The serial number is used by secondary name servers to recognize zone information changes. To stay up to date, secondary servers request the primary server's SOA record at certain intervals and compare the serial number to that of the cached SOA record. If the number has changed, the secondary servers transfer the whole zone database from the primary server.

refresh

This field specifies the interval in seconds that the secondary servers should wait between checking the SOA record of the primary server. Again, this is a decimal number with at most eight digits.

Generally, the network topology doesn't change too often, so this number should specify an interval of roughly a day for larger networks, and even more for smaller ones.

retry

> This number determines the intervals at which a secondary server should retry contacting the primary server if a request or a zone refresh fails. It must not be too low, or a temporary failure of the server or a network problem could cause the secondary server to waste network resources. One hour, or perhaps one-half hour, might be a good choice.

expire

> This field specifies the time in seconds after which a secondary server should finally discard all zone data if it hasn't been able to contact the primary server. You should normally set this field to at least a week (604,800 seconds), but increasing it to a month or more is also reasonable.

minimum

> This field is the default *ttl* value for resource records that do not explicitly contain one. The ttl value specifies the maximum amount of time other name servers may keep the RR in their cache. This time applies only to normal lookups, and has nothing to do with the time after which a secondary server should try to update the zone information.
>
> If the topology of your network does not change frequently, a week or even more is probably a good choice. If single RRs change more frequently, you could still assign them smaller ttls individually. If your network changes frequently, you may want to set *minimum* to one day (86,400 seconds).

A   This record associates an IP address with a hostname. The resource data field contains the address in dotted quad notation.

> For each hostname, there must be only one A record. The hostname used in this A record is considered the official or *canonical* hostname. All other hostnames are aliases and must be mapped onto the canonical hostname using a CNAME record. If the canonical name of our host were **vlager**, we'd have an A record that associated that hostname with its IP address. Since we may also want another name associated with that address, say **news**, we'd create a CNAME record that associates this alternate name with the canonical name. We'll talk more about CNAME records shortly.

NS   NS records are used to specify a zone's primary server and all its secondary servers. An NS record points to a master name server of the given zone, with the resource data field containing the hostname of the name server.

> You will meet NS records in two situations: The first situation is when you delegate authority to a subordinate zone; the second is within the master zone database of the subordinate zone itself. The sets of servers specified in both the parent and delegated zones should match.

The NS record specifies the name of the primary and secondary name servers for a zone. These names must be resolved to an address so they can be used. Sometimes the servers belong to the domain they are serving, which causes a "chicken and egg" problem; we can't resolve the address until the name server is reachable, but we can't reach the name server until we resolve its address. To solve this dilemma, we can configure special A records directly into the name server of the parent zone. The A records allow the name servers of the parent domain to resolve the IP address of the delegated zone name servers. These records are commonly called *glue records* because they provide the "glue" that binds a delegated zone to its parent.

CNAME

This record associates an alias with a host's *canonical hostname*. It provides an alternate name by which users can refer to the host whose canonical name is supplied as a parameter. The canonical hostname is the one the master file provides an A record for; aliases are simply linked to that name by a CNAME record, but don't have any other records of their own.

PTR

This type of record is used to associate names in the **in-addr.arpa** domain with hostnames. It is used for reverse mapping of IP addresses to hostnames. The hostname given must be the canonical hostname.

MX

This RR announces a *mail exchanger* for a domain. Mail exchangers are discussed in "Mail Routing on the Internet." The syntax of an MX record is:

```
[domain] [ttl] [class] MX preference host
```

host names the mail exchanger for *domain*. Every mail exchanger has an integer *preference* associated with it. A mail transport agent that wants to deliver mail to *domain* tries all hosts who have an MX record for this domain until it succeeds. The one with the lowest preference value is tried first, then the others, in order of increasing preference value.

HINFO

This record provides information on the system's hardware and software. Its syntax is:

```
[domain] [ttl] [class] HINFO hardware software
```

The *hardware* field identifies the hardware used by this host. Special conventions are used to specify this. A list of valid "machine names" is given in the Assigned Numbers RFC (RFC-1700). If the field contains any blanks, it must be enclosed in double quotes. The *software* field names the operating system software used by the system. Again, a valid name from the Assigned Numbers RFC should be chosen.

An `HINFO` record to describe an Intel-based Linux machine should look something like:

```
tao    36500  IN  HINFO  IBM-PC  LINUX2.2
```

and `HINFO` records for Linux running on Motorola 68000-based machines might look like:

```
cevad 36500 IN  HINFO  ATARI-104ST LINUX2.0
jedd 36500 IN  HINFO  AMIGA-3000  LINUX2.0
```

Caching-only named Configuration

There is a special type of *named* configuration that we'll talk about before we explain how to build a full name server configuration. It is called a *caching-only* configuration. It doesn't really serve a domain, but acts as a relay for all DNS queries produced on your host. The advantage of this scheme is that it builds up a cache so only the first query for a particular host is actually sent to the name servers on the Internet. Any repeated request will be answered directly from the cache in your local name server. This may not seem useful yet, but it will when you are dialing in to the Internet, as described in Chapter 7, *Serial Line IP* and Chapter 8, *The Point-to-Point Protocol*.

A *named.boot* file for a caching-only server looks like this:

```
; named.boot file for caching-only server
directory                       /var/named
primary       0.0.127.in-addr.arpa  named.local ; localhost network
cache         .                     named.ca    ; root servers
```

In addition to this *named.boot* file, you must set up the *named.ca* file with a valid list of root name servers. You could copy and use Example 6-10 for this purpose. No other files are needed for a caching-only server configuration.

Writing the Master Files

Example 6-10, Example 6-11, Example 6-12, and Example 6-13 give sample files for a name server at the brewery, located on **vlager**. Due to the nature of the network discussed (a single LAN), the example is pretty straightforward.

The *named.ca* cache file shown in Example 6-10 shows sample hint records for a root name server. A typical cache file usually describes about a dozen name servers. You can obtain the current list of name servers for the root domain using the *nslookup* tool described in the next section.*

---

* Note that you can't query your name server for the root servers if you don't have any root server hints installed. To escape this dilemma, you can either make *nslookup* use a different name server, or use the sample file in Example 6-10 as a starting point, and then obtain the full list of valid servers.

Example 6-10: The named.ca File

```
;
; /var/named/named.ca          Cache file for the brewery.
;               We're not on the Internet, so we don't need
;               any root servers. To activate these
;               records, remove the semicolons.
;
;.                     3600000  IN  NS   A.ROOT-SERVERS.NET.
;A.ROOT-SERVERS.NET.   3600000      A    198.41.0.4
;.                     3600000      NS   B.ROOT-SERVERS.NET.
;B.ROOT-SERVERS.NET.   3600000      A    128.9.0.107
;.                     3600000      NS   C.ROOT-SERVERS.NET.
;C.ROOT-SERVERS.NET.   3600000      A    192.33.4.12
;.                     3600000      NS   D.ROOT-SERVERS.NET.
;D.ROOT-SERVERS.NET.   3600000      A    128.8.10.90
;.                     3600000      NS   E.ROOT-SERVERS.NET.
;E.ROOT-SERVERS.NET.   3600000      A    192.203.230.10
;.                     3600000      NS   F.ROOT-SERVERS.NET.
;F.ROOT-SERVERS.NET.   3600000      A    192.5.5.241
;.                     3600000      NS   G.ROOT-SERVERS.NET.
;G.ROOT-SERVERS.NET.   3600000      A    192.112.36.4
;.                     3600000      NS   H.ROOT-SERVERS.NET.
;H.ROOT-SERVERS.NET.   3600000      A    128.63.2.53
;.                     3600000      NS   I.ROOT-SERVERS.NET.
;I.ROOT-SERVERS.NET.   3600000      A    192.36.148.17
;.                     3600000      NS   J.ROOT-SERVERS.NET.
;J.ROOT-SERVERS.NET.   3600000      A    198.41.0.10
;.                     3600000      NS   K.ROOT-SERVERS.NET.
;K.ROOT-SERVERS.NET.   3600000      A    193.0.14.129
;.                     3600000      NS   L.ROOT-SERVERS.NET.
;L.ROOT-SERVERS.NET.   3600000      A    198.32.64.12
;.                     3600000      NS   M.ROOT-SERVERS.NET.
;M.ROOT-SERVERS.NET.   3600000      A    202.12.27.33
;
```

Example 6-11: The named.hosts File

```
;
; /var/named/named.hosts       Local hosts at the brewery
;                              Origin is vbrew.com
;
@           IN  SOA   vlager.vbrew.com. janet.vbrew.com. (
                      2000012601 ; serial
                      86400      ; refresh: once per day
                      3600       ; retry:   one hour
                      3600000    ; expire:  42 days
                      604800     ; minimum: 1 week
                      )
            IN  NS    vlager.vbrew.com.
;
; local mail is distributed on vlager
```

Example 6-11: .The named.hosts File (continued)

```
                IN   MX    10 vlager
;
; loopback address
localhost.      IN   A     127.0.0.1
;
; Virtual Brewery Ethernet
vlager          IN   A     172.16.1.1
vlager-if1      IN   CNAME vlager
; vlager is also news server
news            IN   CNAME vlager
vstout          IN   A     172.16.1.2
vale            IN   A     172.16.1.3
;
; Virtual Winery Ethernet
vlager-if2      IN   A     172.16.2.1
vbardolino      IN   A     172.16.2.2
vchianti        IN   A     172.16.2.3
vbeaujolais     IN   A     172.16.2.4
;
; Virtual Spirits (subsidiary) Ethernet
vbourbon        IN   A     172.16.3.1
vbourbon-if1    IN   CNAME vbourbon
```

Example 6-12: The named.local File

```
;
; /var/named/named.local      Reverse mapping of 127.0.0
;                             Origin is 0.0.127.in-addr.arpa.
;
@            IN   SOA   vlager.vbrew.com. joe.vbrew.com. (
                       1          ; serial
                       360000     ; refresh: 100 hrs
                       3600       ; retry:   one hour
                       3600000    ; expire:  42 days
                       360000     ; minimum: 100 hrs
                       )
             IN   NS    vlager.vbrew.com.
1            IN   PTR   localhost.
```

Example 6-13: The named.rev File

```
;
; /var/named/named.rev        Reverse mapping of our IP addresses
;                             Origin is 16.172.in-addr.arpa.
;
@            IN   SOA   vlager.vbrew.com. joe.vbrew.com. (
                       16         ; serial
                       86400      ; refresh: once per day
                       3600       ; retry:   one hour
                       3600000    ; expire:  42 days
```

Example 6-13: The named.rev File (continued)

```
                              604800      ; minimum: 1 week
                              )
                 IN   NS     vlager.vbrew.com.
; brewery
1.1              IN   PTR    vlager.vbrew.com.
2.1              IN   PTR    vstout.vbrew.com.
3.1              IN   PTR    vale.vbrew.com.
; winery
1.2              IN   PTR    vlager-if2.vbrew.com.
2.2              IN   PTR    vbardolino.vbrew.com.
3.2              IN   PTR    vchianti.vbrew.com.
4.2              IN   PTR    vbeaujolais.vbrew.com.
```

Verifying the Name Server Setup

nslookup is a great tool for checking the operation of your name server setup. It can be used both interactively with prompts and as a single command with immediate output. In the latter case, you simply invoke it as:

```
$ nslookup
hostname
```

nslookup queries the name server specified in *resolv.conf* for `hostname`. (If this file names more than one server, *nslookup* chooses one at random.)

The interactive mode, however, is much more exciting. Besides looking up individual hosts, you may query for any type of DNS record and transfer the entire zone information for a domain.

When invoked without an argument, *nslookup* displays the name server it uses and enters interactive mode. At the > prompt, you may type any domain name you want to query. By default, it asks for class A records, those containing the IP address relating to the domain name.

You can look for record types by issuing:

```
> set type=type
```

in which `type` is one of the resource record names described earlier, or ANY.

You might have the following *nslookup* session:

```
$ nslookup
Default Server:  tao.linux.org.au
Address:  203.41.101.121

> metalab.unc.edu
Server:  tao.linux.org.au
Address:  203.41.101.121
```

```
Name:     metalab.unc.edu
Address:  152.2.254.81

>
```

The output first displays the DNS server being queried, and then the result of the query.

If you try to query for a name that has no IP address associated with it, but other records were found in the DNS database, *nslookup* returns with an error message saying "`No type A records found.`" However, you can make it query for records other than type A by issuing the *set type* command. To get the SOA record of **unc.edu**, you would issue:

```
> unc.edu
Server:  tao.linux.org.au
Address:  203.41.101.121

*** No address (A) records available for unc.edu
> set type=SOA
> unc.edu
Server:  tao.linux.org.au
Address:  203.41.101.121

unc.edu
        origin = ns.unc.edu
        mail addr = host-reg.ns.unc.edu
        serial = 1998111011
        refresh = 14400 (4H)
        retry   = 3600 (1H)
        expire  = 1209600 (2W)
        minimum ttl = 86400 (1D)
unc.edu name server = ns2.unc.edu
unc.edu name server = ncnoc.ncren.net
unc.edu name server = ns.unc.edu
ns2.unc.edu     internet address = 152.2.253.100
ncnoc.ncren.net internet address = 192.101.21.1
ncnoc.ncren.net internet address = 128.109.193.1
ns.unc.edu      internet address = 152.2.21.1
```

In a similar fashion, you can query for MX records:

```
> set type=MX
> unc.edu
Server:  tao.linux.org.au
Address:  203.41.101.121

unc.edu preference = 0, mail exchanger = conga.oit.unc.edu
unc.edu preference = 10, mail exchanger = imsety.oit.unc.edu
unc.edu name server = ns.unc.edu
unc.edu name server = ns2.unc.edu
unc.edu name server = ncnoc.ncren.net
```

```
conga.oit.unc.edu        internet address = 152.2.22.21
imsety.oit.unc.edu       internet address = 152.2.21.99
ns.unc.edu      internet address = 152.2.21.1
ns2.unc.edu     internet address = 152.2.253.100
ncnoc.ncren.net internet address = 192.101.21.1
ncnoc.ncren.net internet address = 128.109.193.1
```

Using a type of ANY returns all resource records associated with a given name.

A practical application of *nslookup*, besides debugging, is to obtain the current list of root name servers. You can obtain this list by querying for all NS records associated with the root domain:

```
> set type=NS
> .
Server:  tao.linux.org.au
Address:  203.41.101.121

Non-authoritative answer:
(root)   name server = A.ROOT-SERVERS.NET
(root)   name server = H.ROOT-SERVERS.NET
(root)   name server = B.ROOT-SERVERS.NET
(root)   name server = C.ROOT-SERVERS.NET
(root)   name server = D.ROOT-SERVERS.NET
(root)   name server = E.ROOT-SERVERS.NET
(root)   name server = I.ROOT-SERVERS.NET
(root)   name server = F.ROOT-SERVERS.NET
(root)   name server = G.ROOT-SERVERS.NET
(root)   name server = J.ROOT-SERVERS.NET
(root)   name server = K.ROOT-SERVERS.NET
(root)   name server = L.ROOT-SERVERS.NET
(root)   name server = M.ROOT-SERVERS.NET

Authoritative answers can be found from:
A.ROOT-SERVERS.NET      internet address = 198.41.0.4
H.ROOT-SERVERS.NET      internet address = 128.63.2.53
B.ROOT-SERVERS.NET      internet address = 128.9.0.107
C.ROOT-SERVERS.NET      internet address = 192.33.4.12
D.ROOT-SERVERS.NET      internet address = 128.8.10.90
E.ROOT-SERVERS.NET      internet address = 192.203.230.10
I.ROOT-SERVERS.NET      internet address = 192.36.148.17
F.ROOT-SERVERS.NET      internet address = 192.5.5.241
G.ROOT-SERVERS.NET      internet address = 192.112.36.4
J.ROOT-SERVERS.NET      internet address = 198.41.0.10
K.ROOT-SERVERS.NET      internet address = 193.0.14.129
L.ROOT-SERVERS.NET      internet address = 198.32.64.12
M.ROOT-SERVERS.NET      internet address = 202.12.27.33
```

To see the complete set of available commands, use the *help* command in *nslookup*.

Other Useful Tools

There are a few tools that can help you with your tasks as a BIND administrator. We will briefly describe two of them here. Please refer to the documentation that comes with these tools for more information on how to use them.

hostcvt helps you with your initial BIND configuration by converting your */etc/hosts* file into master files for *named*. It generates both the forward (A) and reverse mapping (PTR) entries, and takes care of aliases. Of course, it won't do the whole job for you, as you may still want to tune the timeout values in the SOA record, for example, or add MX records. Still, it may help you save a few aspirins. *hostcvt* is part of the BIND source, but can also be found as a standalone package on a few Linux FTP servers.

After setting up your name server, you may want to test your configuration. Some good tools that make this job much simpler: the first is called *dnswalk*, which is a Perl-based package. The second is called *nslint*. They both walk your DNS database looking for common mistakes and verify that the information they find is consistent. Two other useful tools are *host* and *dig*, which are general purpose DNS database query tools. You can use these tools to manually inspect and diagnose DNS database entries.

These tools are likely to be available in prepackaged form. *dnswalk* and *nslint* are available in source from *http://www.visi.com/~barr/dnswalk/* and *ftp://ftp.ee.lbl.gov/nslint.tar.Z*. The *host* and *dig* source codes can be found at *ftp://ftp.nikhef.nl/pub/network/* and *ftp://ftp.is.co.za/networking/ip/dns/dig/*.

## CHAPTER SEVEN

SERIAL LINE IP

Packet protocols like IP or IPX rely upon the receiver host knowing where the start and end of each packet are in the data stream. The mechanism used to mark and detect the start and end of packets is called *delimitation*. The Ethernet protocol manages this mechanism in a LAN environment, and the SLIP and PPP protocols manage it for serial communications lines.

The comparatively low cost of low-speed dialup modems and telephone circuits has made the serial line IP protocols immensely popular, especially for providing connectivity to end users of the Internet. The hardware required to run SLIP or PPP is simple and readily available. All that is required is a modem and a serial port equipped with a FIFO buffer.

The SLIP protocol is very simple to implement and at one time was the more common of the two. Today almost everyone uses the PPP protocol instead. The PPP protocol adds a host of sophisticated features that contribute to its popularity today, and we'll look at the most important of these later.

Linux supports kernel-based drivers for both SLIP and PPP. The drivers have both been around for some time and are stable and reliable. In this chapter and the next, we'll discuss both protocols and how to configure them.

General Requirements

To use SLIP or PPP, you have to configure some basic networking features as described in the previous chapters. You must set up the loopback interface and configure the name resolver. When connecting to the Internet, you will want to use DNS. Your options here are the same as for PPP: you can perform your DNS queries across your serial link by configuring your Internet Service Provider's IP address into your */etc/resolv.conf* file, or configure a caching-only name server as described under "Caching-only named Configuration," in Chapter 6, *Name Service and Resolver Configuration.*"

SLIP Operation

Dialup IP servers frequently offer SLIP service through special user accounts. After logging in to such an account, you are not dropped into the common shell; instead, a program or shell script is executed that enables the server's SLIP driver for the serial line and configures the appropriate network interface. Then you have to do the same at your end of the link.

On some operating systems, the SLIP driver is a user-space program; under Linux, it is part of the kernel, which makes it a lot faster. This speed requires, however, that the serial line be converted to the SLIP mode explicitly. This conversion is done by means of a special tty line discipline, SLIPDISC. While the tty is in normal line discipline (DISC0), it exchanges data only with user processes, using the normal *read(2)* and *write(2)* calls, and the SLIP driver is unable to write to or read from the tty. In SLIPDISC, the roles are reversed: now any user-space processes are blocked from writing to or reading from the tty, while all data coming in on the serial port is passed directly to the SLIP driver.

The SLIP driver itself understands a number of variations on the SLIP protocol. Apart from ordinary SLIP, it also understands CSLIP, which performs the so-called Van Jacobson header compression (described in RFC-1144) on outgoing IP packets. This compression improves throughput for interactive sessions noticeably. There are also six-bit versions for each of these protocols.

A simple way to convert a serial line to SLIP mode is by using the *slattach* tool. Assume you have your modem on */dev/ttyS3* and have logged in to the SLIP server successfully. You will then execute:

```
# slattach /dev/ttyS3 &
```

This tool switches the line discipline of *ttyS3* to SLIPDISC and attaches it to one of the SLIP network interfaces. If this is your first active SLIP link, the line will be attached to *sl0*; the second will be attached to *sl1*, and so on. The current kernels support a default maximum of 256 simultaneous SLIP links.

The default line discipline chosen by *slattach* is CSLIP. You may choose any other discipline using the *–p* switch. To use normal SLIP (no compression), you use:

```
# slattach -p slip /dev/ttyS3 &
```

The disciplines available are listed in Table 7-1. A special pseudo-discipline is available called adaptive, which causes the kernel to automatically detect which type of SLIP encapsulation is being used by the remote end.

Table 7-1. Linux Slip-Line Disciplines

Disciplipe	Description
slip	Traditional SLIP encapsulation.
cslip	SLIP encapsulation with Van Jacobsen header compression.
slip6	SLIP encapsulation with six-bit encoding. The encoding method is similar to that used by the *uuencode* command, and causes the SLIP datagram to be converted into printable ASCII characters. This conversion is useful when you do not have a serial link that is eight bit clean.
cslip6	SLIP encapsulation with Van Jacobsen header compression and six-bit encoding.
adaptive	This is not a real line discipline; instead, it causes the kernel to attempt to identify the line discipline being used by the remote machine and to match it.

Note that you must use the same encapsulation as your peer. For example, if **cowslip** uses CSLIP, you also have to do so. If your SLIP connection doesn't work, the first thing you should do is ensure that both ends of the link agree on whether to use header compression or not. If you are unsure what the remote end is using, try configuring your host for adaptive slip. The kernel might figure out the right type for you.

slattach lets you enable not only SLIP, but other protocols that use the serial line, like PPP or KISS (another protocol used by ham radio people). Doing this is not common, though, and there are better tools available to support these protocols. For details, please refer to the *slattach(8)* manual page.

After turning over the line to the SLIP driver, you must configure the network interface. Again, you do this using the standard *ifconfig* and *route* commands. Assume that we have dialed up a server named **cowslip** from **vlager**. On **vlager** you would execute:

```
# ifconfig sl0 vlager-slip pointopoint cowslip
# route add cowslip
# route add default gw cowslip
```

The first command configures the interface as a point-to-point link to **cowslip**, while the second and third add the route to **cowslip** and the default route, using **cowslip** as a gateway.

Two things are worth noting about the *ifconfig* invocation: The `pointopoint` option that specifies the address of the remote end of a point-to-point link and our use of **vlager-slip** as the address of the local SLIP interface.

We have mentioned that you can use the same address you assigned to **vlager**'s Ethernet interface for your SLIP link, as well. In this case, **vlager-slip** might just be another alias for address **172.16.1.1**. However, it is also possible that you have to use an entirely different address for your SLIP link. One such case is when your network uses an unregistered IP network address, as the Brewery does. We will return to this scenario in greater detail in the next section.

For the remainder of this chapter we will always use **vlager-slip** to refer to the address of the local SLIP interface.

When taking down the SLIP link, you should first remove all routes through **cowslip** using *route* with the *del* option, then take the interface down, and send *slattach* the hangup signal. The you must hang up the modem using your terminal program again:

```
# route del default
# route del cowslip
# ifconfig sl0 down
# kill -HUP 516
```

Note that the *516* should be replaced with the process id (as shown in the output of **ps ax**) of the *slattach* command controlling the slip device you wish to take down.

Dealing with Private IP Networks

You will remember from Chapter 5, *Configuring TCP/IP Networking*, that the Virtual Brewery has an Ethernet-based IP network using unregistered network numbers that are reserved for internal use only. Packets to or from one of these networks are not routed on the Internet; if we were to have **vlager** dial into **cowslip** and act as a router for the Virtual Brewery network, hosts within the Brewery's network could not talk to real Internet hosts directly because their packets would be dropped silently by the first major router.

To work around this dilemma, we will configure **vlager** to act as a kind of launch pad for accessing Internet services. To the outside world, it will present itself as a normal SLIP-connected Internet host with a registered IP address (probably assigned by the network provider running **cowslip**). Anyone logged in to **vlager** can use text-based programs like *ftp*, *telnet*, or even *lynx* to make use of the Internet. Anyone on the Virtual Brewery LAN can therefore telnet and log in to **vlager** and use the programs there. For some applications, there may be solutions that avoid logging in to **vlager**. For WWW users, for example, we could run a so-called *proxy server* on **vlager**, which would relay all requests from your users to their respective servers.

Having to log in to **vlager** to make use of the Internet is a little clumsy. But apart from eliminating the paperwork (and cost) of registering an IP network, it has the added benefit of going along well with a firewall setup. Firewalls are dedicated hosts used to provide limited Internet access to users on your local network without exposing the internal hosts to network attacks from the outside world. Simple firewall configuration is covered in more detail in Chapter 9, *TCP/IP Firewall*. In Chapter 11, *IP Masquerade and Network Address Translation*, we'll discuss a Linux feature called "IP masquerade" that provides a powerful alternative to proxy servers.

Assume that the Brewery has been assigned the IP address **192.168.5.74** for SLIP access. All you have to do to realize that the setup discussed above is to enter this address into your */etc/hosts* file, naming it **vlager-slip**. The procedure for bringing up the SLIP link itself remains unchanged.

Using dip

Now that was rather simple. Nevertheless, you might want to automate the steps previously described. It would be much better to have a simple command that performs all the steps necessary to open the serial device, cause the modem to dial the provider, log in, enable the SLIP line discipline, and configure the network interface. This is what the *dip* command is for.

dip means *Dialup IP*. It was written by Fred van Kempen and has been patched very heavily by a number of people. Today there is one strain that is used by almost everyone: Version `dip337p-uri`, which is included with most modern Linux distributions, or is available from the **metalab.unc.edu** FTP archive.

dip provides an interpreter for a simple scripting language that can handle the modem for you, convert the line to SLIP mode, and configure the interfaces. The script language is powerful enough to suit most configurations.

To be able to configure the SLIP interface, *dip* requires root privilege. It would now be tempting to make *dip* setuid to **root** so that all users can dial up some SLIP server without having to give them root access. This is very dangerous, though, because setting up bogus interfaces and default routes with *dip* may disrupt routing on your network. Even worse, this action would give your users power to connect to *any* SLIP server and launch dangerous attacks on your network. If you want to allow your users to fire up a SLIP connection, write small wrapper programs for each prospective SLIP server and have these wrappers invoke *dip* with the specific script that establishes the connection. Carefully written wrapper programs can then safely be made setuid to **root**.* An alternative, more flexible approach is to give trusted users root access to *dip* using a program like *sudo*.

---

* *diplogin* must be run as setuid to **root**, too. See the section at the end of this chapter.

A Sample Script

Assume that the host to which we make our SLIP connection is **cowslip**, and that we have written a script for *dip* to run called *cowslip.dip* that makes our connection. We invoke *dip* with the script name as argument:

```
# dip cowslip.dip
DIP: Dialup IP Protocol Driver version 3.3.7 (12/13/93)
Written by Fred N. van Kempen, MicroWalt Corporation.
connected to cowslip.moo.com with addr 192.168.5.74
#
```

The script itself is shown in Example 7-1.

Example 7-1: A Sample dip Script

```
# Sample dip script for dialing up cowslip
# Set local and remote name and address
        get $local vlager-slip
        get $remote cowslip
        port ttyS3                    # choose a serial port
        speed 38400                   # set speed to max
        modem HAYES                   # set modem type
        reset                         # reset modem and tty
        flush                         # flush out modem response
# Prepare for dialing.
        send ATQ0V1E1X1\r
        wait OK 2
        if $errlvl != 0 goto error
        dial 41988
        if $errlvl != 0 goto error
        wait CONNECT 60
        if $errlvl != 0 goto error
# Okay, we're connected now
        sleep 3
        send \r\n\r\n
        wait ogin: 10
        if $errlvl != 0 goto error
        send Svlager\n
        wait ssword: 5
        if $errlvl != 0 goto error
        send knockknock\n
        wait running 30
        if $errlvl != 0 goto error
# We have logged in, and the remote side is firing up SLIP.
        print Connected to $remote with address $rmtip
        default                       # Make this link our default route
        mode SLIP                     # We go to SLIP mode, too
# fall through in case of error
error:
        print SLIP to $remote failed.
```

After connecting to **cowslip** and enabling SLIP, *dip* will detach from the terminal and go to the background. You can then start using the normal networking services on the SLIP link. To terminate the connection, simply invoke *dip* with the *–k* option. This sends a hangup signal to *dip*, using the process ID *dip* records in */etc/ dip.pid*:

```
# dip -k
```

In *dip*'s scripting language, keywords prefixed with a dollar symbol denote variable names. *dip* has a predefined set of variables, which will be listed below. `$remote` and `$local`, for instance, contain the hostnames of the remote and local hosts involved in the SLIP link.

The first two statements in the sample script are *get* commands, which is *dip*'s way to set a variable. Here, the local and remote hostnames are set to **vlager** and **cowslip**, respectively.

The next five statements set up the terminal line and the modem. `reset` sends a reset string to the modem. The next statement flushes out the modem response so that the login chat in the next few lines works properly. This chat is pretty straightforward: it simply dials 41988, the phone number of **cowslip**, and logs in to the account `Svlager` using the password `knockknock`. The `wait` command makes *dip* wait for the string given as its first argument; the number given as its second argument makes the wait time out after that many seconds if no such string is received. The `if` commands interspersed in the login procedure check that no error occurred while executing the command.

The final commands executed after logging in are `default`, which makes the SLIP link the default route to all hosts, and `mode`, which enables SLIP mode on the line and configures the interface and routing table for you.

A dip Reference

In this section, we will give a reference for most of *dip*'s commands. You can get an overview of all the commands it provides by invoking *dip* in test mode and entering the `help` command. To learn about the syntax of a command, you may enter it without any arguments. Remember that this does not work with commands that take no arguments. The following example illustrates the `help` command:

```
# dip -t
DIP: Dialup IP Protocol Driver version 3.3.7p-uri (25 Dec 96)
Written by Fred N. van Kempen, MicroWalt Corporation.
Debian version 3.3.7p-2 (debian).

DIP> help
DIP knows about the following commands:

        beep        bootp       break       chatkey     config
        databits    dec         default     dial        echo
```

```
flush      get        goto       help       if
inc        init       mode       modem      netmask
onexit     parity     password   proxyarp   print
psend      port       quit       reset      securidfixed
securid    send       shell      skey       sleep
speed      stopbits   term       timeout    wait
```

```
DIP> echo
Usage: echo on|off
DIP>
```

Throughout the following section, examples that display the *DIP>* prompt show how to enter a command in test mode and what output it produces. Examples lacking this prompt should be taken as script excerpts.

The modem commands

dip provides a number of commands that configure your serial line and modem. Some of these are obvious, such as `port`, which selects a serial port, and `speed`, `databits`, `stopbits`, and `parity`, which set the common line parameters. The `modem` command selects a modem type. Currently, the only type supported is HAYES (capitalization required). You have to provide *dip* with a modem type, or else it will refuse to execute the `dial` and `reset` commands. The `reset` command sends a reset string to the modem; the string used depends on the modem type selected. For Hayes-compatible modems, this string is ATZ.

The `flush` code can be used to flush out all responses the modem has sent so far. Otherwise, a chat script following `reset` might be confused because it reads the OK responses from earlier commands.

The `init` command selects an initialization string to be passed to the modem before dialing. The default for Hayes modems is "ATE0 Q0 V1 X1", which turns on echoing of commands and long result codes, and selects blind dialing (no checking of dial tone). Modern modems have a good factory default configuration, so this is a little unnecessary, though it does no harm.

The `dial` command sends the initialization string to the modem and dials up the remote system. The default dial command for Hayes modems is ATD.

The echo command

The `echo` command serves as a debugging aid. Calling `echo on` makes *dip* echo to the console everything it sends to the serial device. This can be turned off again by calling `echo off`.

dip also allows you to leave script mode temporarily and enter terminal mode. In this mode, you can use *dip* just like any ordinary terminal program, writing the characters you type to the serial line, reading data from the serial line, and displaying the characters. To leave this mode, enter Ctrl-].

The get command

The `get` command is *dip's* way of setting a variable. The simplest form is to set a variable to a constant, as we did in *cowslip.dip*. You may, however, also prompt the user for input by specifying the keyword `ask` instead of a value:

```
DIP> get $local ask
Enter the value for $local: _
```

A third method is to obtain the value from the remote host. Bizarre as it seems at first, this is very useful in some cases. Some SLIP servers will not allow you to use your own IP address on the SLIP link, but will rather assign you one from a pool of addresses whenever you dial in, printing some message that informs you about the address you have been assigned. If the message looks something like "`Your address: 192.168.5.74`", the following piece of *dip* code would let you pick up the address:

```
# finish login
wait address: 10
get $locip remote
```

The print command

This is the command used to echo text to the console from which *dip* was started. Any of *dip's* variables may be used in print commands. Here's an example:

```
DIP> print Using port $port at speed $speed
Using port ttyS3 at speed 38400
```

Variable names

dip understands only a predefined set of variables. A variable name always begins with a dollar symbol and must be written in lowercase letters.

The `$local` and `$locip` variables contain the local host's name and IP address. When you store the canonical hostname in `$local`, *dip* will automatically attempt to resolve the hostname to an IP address and to store it in the `$locip` variable. A similar but backward process occurs when you assign an IP address to the `$locip` variable; *dip* will attempt to perform a reverse lookup to identify the name of the host and store it in the `$local` variable.

The `$remote` and `$rmtip` variables operate in the same way for the remote host's name and address. `$mtu` contains the MTU value for the connection.

These five variables are the only ones that may be assigned values directly using the `get` command. A number of other variables are set as a result of the configuration commands bearing the same name, but may be used in `print` statements; these variables are `$modem`, `$port`, and `$speed`.

`$errlvl` is the variable through which you can access the result of the last command executed. An error level of 0 indicates success, while a nonzero value denotes an error.

The if and goto commands

The `if` command is a conditional branch, rather than a full-featured programming *if* statement. Its syntax is:

```
if var op number goto label
```

The expression must be a simple comparison between one of the variables `$errlvl`, `$locip`, and `$rmtip`. *var* must be an integer number; the operator *op* may be one of ==, !=, <, >, <=, and >=.

The `goto` command makes the execution of the script continue at the line following that bearing the *label*. A label must be the first word on the line and must be followed immediately by a colon.

send, wait, and sleep

These commands help implement simple chat scripts in *dip*. The `send` command outputs its arguments to the serial line. It does not support variables, but understands all C-style backslash character sequences, such as \n for newline and \b for backspace. The tilde character (˜) can be used as an abbreviation for carriage return/newline.

The `wait` command takes a word as an argument and will read all input on the serial line until it detects a sequence of characters that match this word. The word itself may not contain any blanks. Optionally, you may give `wait` a timeout value as a second argument; if the expected word is not received within that many seconds, the command will return with an `$errlvl` value of 1. This command is used to detect login and other prompts.

The `sleep` command may be used to wait for a certain amount of time; for instance, to patiently wait for any login sequence to complete. Again, the interval is specified in seconds.

mode and default

These commands are used to flip the serial line to SLIP mode and configure the interface.

The `mode` command is the last command executed by *dip* before going into daemon mode. Unless an error occurs, the command does not return.

mode takes a protocol name as argument. *dip* currently recognizes SLIP, CSLIP, SLIP6, CSLIP6, PPP, and TERM as valid names. The current version of *dip* does not understand adaptive SLIP, however.

After enabling SLIP mode on the serial line, *dip* executes *ifconfig* to configure the interface as a point-to-point link, and invokes *route* to set the route to the remote host.

If, in addition, the script executes the default command before mode, *dip* creates a default route that points to the SLIP link.

Running in Server Mode

Setting up your SLIP client was the hard part. Configuring your host to act as a SLIP server is much easier.

There are two ways of configuring a SLIP server. Both ways require that you set up one login account per SLIP client. Assume you provide SLIP service to Arthur Dent at **dent.beta.com**. You might create an account named **dent** by adding the following line to your *passwd* file:

```
dent:*:501:60:Arthur Dent's SLIP account:/tmp:/usr/sbin/diplogin
```

Afterwards, you would set **dent**'s password using the *passwd* utility.

The *dip* command can be used in server mode by invoking it as *diplogin*. Usually *diplogin* is a link to *dip*. Its main configuration file is */etc/diphosts*, which is where you specify what IP address a SLIP user will be assigned when he or she dials in. Alternatively, you can also use the *sliplogin* command, a BSD-derived tool featuring a more flexible configuration scheme that lets you execute shell scripts whenever a host connects and disconnects.

When our SLIP user **dent** logs in, *dip* starts up as a server. To find out if he is indeed permitted to use SLIP, it looks up the username in */etc/diphosts*. This file details the access rights and connection parameter for each SLIP user. The general format for an */etc/diphosts* entry looks like:

```
# /etc/diphosts
user:password:rem-addr:loc-addr:netmask:comments:protocol,MTU
#
```

Each of the fields is described in Table 7-2.

Table 7-2. /etc/diphosts Field Description

Field	Description
user	The username of the user invoking *dip* that this entry will apply to.
password	Field 2 of the */etc/diphosts* file is used to add an extra layer of password-based security on the connection. You can place a password in encrypted form here (just as in */etc/passwd*) and *diplogin* will prompt for the user to enter the password before allowing SLIP access. Note that this password is used in addition to the normal *login*-based password the user will enter.
rem-addr	The address that will be assigned to the remote machine. This address may be specified either as a hostname that will be resolved or an IP address in dotted quad notation.
loc-addr	The IP address that will be used for this end of the SLIP link. This may also be specified as a resolvable hostname or in dotted quad format.
netmask	The netmask that will be used for routing purposes. Many people are confused by this entry. The netmask doesn't apply to the SLIP link itself, but is used in combination with the rem-addr field to produce a route to the remote site. The netmask should be that used by the network supported by that of the remote host.
comments	This field is free-form text that you may use to help document the */etc/diphosts* file. It serves no other purpose.
protocol	This field is where you specify what protocol or line discipline you want applied to this connection. Valid entries here are the same as those valid for the *−p* argument to the *slattach* command.
MTU	The maximum transmission unit that this link will carry. This field describes the largest datagram that will be transmitted across the link. Any datagram routed to the SLIP device that is larger than the MTU will be fragmented into datagrams no larger than this value. Usually, the MTU is configured identically at both ends of the link.

A sample entry for **dent** could look like this:

```
dent::dent.beta.com:vbrew.com:255.255.255.0:Arthur Dent:CSLIP,296
```

Our example gives our user **dent** access to SLIP with no additional password required. He will be assigned the IP address associated with **dent.beta.com** with a netmask of 255.255.255.0. His default route should be directed to the IP address of **vbrew.com**, and he will use the CSLIP protocol with an MTU of 296 bytes.

When **dent** logs in, *diplogin* extracts the information on him from the *diphosts* file. If the second field contains a value, *diplogin* will prompt for an "external security password." The string entered by the user is encrypted and compared to the password from *diphosts*. If they do not match, the login attempt is rejected. If the password field contains the string `s/key`, and *dip* was compiled with S/Key support, S/Key authentication will take place. S/Key authentication is described in the documentation that comes in the *dip* source package.

After a successful login, *diplogin* proceeds by flipping the serial line to CSLIP or SLIP mode, and sets up the interface and route. This connection remains established until the user disconnects and the modem drops the line. *diplogin* then returns the line to normal line discipline and exits.

diplogin requires superuser privilege. If you don't have *dip* running setuid **root**, you should make *diplogin* a separate copy of *dip* instead of a simple link. *diplogin* can then safely be made setuid without affecting the status of *dip* itself.

CHAPTER EIGHT
THE POINT-TO-POINT PROTOCOL

Like SLIP, PPP is a protocol used to send datagrams across a serial connection; however, it addresses a couple of the deficiencies of SLIP. First, it can carry a large number of protocols and is thus not limited to the IP protocol. It provides error detection on the link itself, while SLIP accepts and forwards corrupted datagrams as long as the corruption does not occur in the header. Equally important, it lets the communicating sides negotiate options, such as the IP address and the maximum datagram size at startup time, and provides client authorization. This built-in negotiation allows reliable automation of the connection establishment, while the authentication removes the need for the clumsy user login accounts that SLIP requires. For each of these capabilities, PPP has a separate protocol. In this chapter, we briefly cover these basic building blocks of PPP. This discussion of PPP is far from complete; if you want to know more about PPP, we urge you to read its RFC specification and the dozen or so companion RFCs.* There is also a comprehensive O'Reilly book on the topic of *Using & Managing PPP*, by Andrew Sun.

At the very bottom of PPP is the *High-Level Data Link Control* (HDLC) protocol, which defines the boundaries around the individual PPP frames and provides a 16-bit checksum.† As opposed to the more primitive SLIP encapsulation, a PPP frame is capable of holding packets from protocols other than IP, such as Novell's IPX or Appletalk. PPP achieves this by adding a protocol field to the basic HDLC frame that identifies the type of packet carried by the frame.

The *Link Control Protocol*, (LCP) is used on top of HDLC to negotiate options pertaining to the data link. For instance, the *Maximum Receive Unit* (MRU), states the maximum datagram size that one side of the link agrees to receive.

An important step at the configuration stage of a PPP link is client authorization. Although it is not mandatory, it is really a must for dialup lines in order to keep

---

* Relevant RFCs are listed in the Bibiliography at the end of this book.

† In fact, HDLC is a much more general protocol devised by the International Standards Organization (ISO) and is also an essential component of the X.25 specification.

out intruders. Usually the called host (the server) asks the client to authorize itself by proving it knows some secret key. If the caller fails to produce the correct secret, the connection is terminated. With PPP, authorization works both ways; the caller may also ask the server to authenticate itself. These authentication procedures are totally independent of each other. There are two protocols for different types of authorization, which we will discuss further in this chapter: *Password Authentication Protocol* (PAP) and *Challenge Handshake Authentication Protocol* (CHAP).

Each network protocol that is routed across the data link (like IP and AppleTalk) is configured dynamically using a corresponding *Network Control Protocol* (NCP). To send IP datagrams across the link, both sides running PPP must first negotiate which IP address each of them uses. The control protocol used for this negotiation is the *Internet Protocol Control Protocol* (IPCP).

Besides sending standard IP datagrams across the link, PPP also supports Van Jacobson header compression of IP datagrams. This technique shrinks the headers of TCP packets to as little as three bytes. It is also used in CSLIP, and is more colloquially referred to as VJ header compression. The use of compression may be negotiated at startup time through IPCP, as well.

PPP on Linux

On Linux, PPP functionality is split into two parts: a kernel component that handles the low-level protocols (HDLC, IPCP, IPXCP, etc.) and the user space *pppd* daemon that handles the various higher-level protocols, such as PAP and CHAP. The current release of the PPP software for Linux contains the PPP daemon *pppd* and a program named *chat* that automates the dialing of the remote system.

The PPP kernel driver was written by Michael Callahan and reworked by Paul Mackerras. *pppd* was derived from a free PPP implementation* for Sun and 386BSD machines that was written by Drew Perkins and others, and is maintained by Paul Mackerras. It was ported to Linux by Al Longyear. *chat* was written by Karl Fox.†

Like SLIP, PPP is implemented by a special line discipline. To use a serial line as a PPP link, you first establish the connection over your modem as usual, and subsequently convert the line to PPP mode. In this mode, all incoming data is passed to

---

* If you have any general questions about PPP, ask the people on the Linux-net mailing list at **vger.rutgers.edu**.

† Karl can be reached at *karl@morningstar.com*.

the PPP driver, which checks the incoming HDLC frames for validity (each HDLC frame carries a 16-bit checksum), and unwraps and dispatches them. Currently, PPP is able to transport both the IP protocol, optionally using Van Jacobson header compression, and the IPX protocol.

pppd aids the kernel driver, performing the initialization and authentication phase that is necessary before actual network traffic can be sent across the link. *pppd*'s behavior may be fine-tuned using a number of options. As PPP is rather complex, it is impossible to explain all of them in a single chapter. This book therefore cannot cover all aspects of *pppd*, but only gives you an introduction. For more information, consult *Using & Managing PPP* or the *pppd* manual pages, and *README*s in the *pppd* source distribution, which should help you sort out most questions this chapter fails to discuss. The PPP-HOWTO might also be of use.

Probably the greatest help you will find in configuring PPP will come from other users of the same Linux distribution. PPP configuration questions are very common, so try your local usergroup mailing list or the IRC Linux channel. If your problems persist even after reading the documentation, you could try the *comp.protocols.ppp* newsgroup. This is the place where you can find most of the people involved in *pppd* development.

Running pppd

When you want to connect to the Internet through a PPP link, you have to set up basic networking capabilities, such as the loopback device and the resolver. Both have been covered in Chapter 5, *Configuring TCP/IP Networking*, and Chapter 6, *Name Service and Resolver Configuration*. You can simply configure the name server of your Internet Service Provider in the */etc/resolv.conf* file, but this will mean that every DNS request is sent across your serial link. This situation is not optimal; the closer (network-wise) you are to your name server, the faster the name lookups will be. An alternative solution is to configure a caching-only name server at a host on your network. This means that the first time you make a DNS query for a particular host, your request will be sent across your serial link, but every subsequent request will be answered directly by your local name server, and will be much faster. This configuration is described in Chapter 6, in "Caching-only named Configuration."

As an introductory example of how to establish a PPP connection with *pppd*, assume you are at **vlager** again. First, dial in to the PPP server **c3po** and log in to the **ppp** account. **c3po** will execute its PPP driver. After exiting the communications program you used for dialing, execute the following command, substituting the name of the serial device you used for the `ttyS3` shown here:

```
# pppd /dev/ttyS3 38400 crtscts defaultroute
```

This command flips the serial line *ttyS3* to the PPP line discipline and negotiates an IP link with **c3po**. The transfer speed used on the serial port will be 38,400 bps.

The `crtscts` option turns on hardware handshake on the port, which is an absolute must at speeds above 9,600 bps.

The first thing *pppd* does after starting up is negotiate several link characteristics with the remote end using LCP. Usually, the default set of options *pppd* tries to negotiate will work, so we won't go into this here. Expect to say that part of this negotiation involves requesting or assigning the IP addresses at each end of the link.

For the time being, we also assume that **c3po** doesn't require any authentication from us, so the configuration phase is completed successfully.

pppd will then negotiate the IP parameters with its peer using IPCP, the IP control protocol. Since we didn't specify any particular IP address to *pppd* earlier, it will try to use the address obtained by having the resolver look up the local hostname. Both will then announce their addresses to each other.

Usually, there's nothing wrong with these defaults. Even if your machine is on an Ethernet, you can use the same IP address for both the Ethernet and the PPP interface. Nevertheless, *pppd* allows you to use a different address, or even to ask your peer to use some specific address. These options are discussed later in the "IP Configuration Options" section.

After going through the IPCP setup phase, *pppd* will prepare your host's networking layer to use the PPP link. It first configures the PPP network interface as a point-to-point link, using *ppp0* for the first PPP link that is active, *ppp1* for the second, and so on. Next, it sets up a routing table entry that points to the host at the other end of the link. In the previous example, *pppd* made the default network route point to **c3po**, because we gave it the `defaultroute` option.* The default route simplifies your routing by causing any IP datagram destined to a nonlocal host to be sent to **c3po**; this makes sense since it is the only way they can be reached. There are a number of different routing schemes *pppd* supports, which we will cover in detail later in this chapter.

Using Options Files

Before *pppd* parses its command-line arguments, it scans several files for default options. These files may contain any valid command-line arguments spread out across an arbitrary number of lines. Hash signs introduce comments.

The first options file is */etc/ppp/options*, which is always scanned when *pppd* starts up. Using it to set some global defaults is a good idea, because it allows you to keep your users from doing several things that may compromise security. For instance, to make *pppd* require some kind of authentication (either PAP or CHAP) from the peer, you add the *auth* option to this file. This option cannot be

---

* The default network route is installed only if none is already present.

overridden by the user, so it becomes impossible to establish a PPP connection with any system that is not in your authentication databases. Note, however, that some options can be overridden; the `connect` string is a good example.

The other options file, which is read after */etc/ppp/options*, is *.ppprc* in the user's home directory. It allows each user to specify her own set of default options.

A sample */etc/ppp/options* file might look like this:

```
# Global options for pppd running on vlager.vbrew.com
lock                    # use UUCP-style device locking
auth                    # require authentication
usehostname             # use local hostname for CHAP
domain vbrew.com        # our domain name
```

The `lock` keyword makes *pppd* comply to the standard UUCP method of device locking. With this convention, each process that accesses a serial device, say */dev/ttyS3*, creates a lock file with a name like *LCK..ttyS3* in a special lock-file directory to signal that the device is in use. This is necessary to prevent signal other programs, such as *minicom* or *uucico*, from opening the serial device while it is used by PPP.

The next three options relate to authentication and, therefore, to system security. The authentication options are best placed in the global configuration file because they are "privileged" and cannot be overridden by users' ˜*/.ppprc* options files.

Using chat to Automate Dialing

One of the things that may have struck you as inconvenient in the previous example is that you had to establish the connection manually before you could fire up *pppd*. Unlike *dip*, *pppd* does not have its own scripting language for dialing the remote system and logging in, but relies on an external program or shell script to do this. The command to be executed can be given to *pppd* with the `connect` command-line option. *pppd* will redirect the command's standard input and output to the serial line.

The *pppd* software package is supplied with a very simple program called *chat*, which is capable of being used in this way to automate simple login sequences. We'll talk about this command in some detail.

If your login sequence is complex, you will need something more powerful than *chat*. One useful alternative you might consider is *expect*, written by Don Libes. It has a very powerful language based on Tcl, and was designed exactly for this sort of application. Those of you whose login sequence requires, for example, challenge/response authentication involving calculator-like key generators will find *expect* powerful enough to handle the task. Since there are so many possible variations on this theme, we won't describe how to develop an appropriate expect script in this book. Suffice it to say, you'd call your expect script by specifying its name using the *pppd* `connect` option. It's also important to note that when the script is running, the standard input and output will be attached to the modem, not to the terminal that invoked *pppd*. If you require user interaction, you should manage it by opening a spare virtual terminal, or arrange some other means.

The *chat* command lets you specify a UUCP-style chat script. Basically, a chat script consists of an alternating sequence of strings that we expect to receive from the remote system, and the answers we are to send. We will call them *expect* and *send* strings, respectively. This is a typical excerpt from a chat script:

```
ogin: b1ff ssword: s3|<r1t
```

This script tells *chat* to wait for the remote system to send the login prompt and return the login name **b1ff**. We wait only for `ogin:` so that it doesn't matter if the login prompt starts with an uppercase or lowercase l, or if it arrives garbled. The following string is another expect string that makes *chat* wait for the password prompt and send our response password.

This is basically what chat scripts are all about. A complete script to dial up a PPP server would, of course, also have to include the appropriate modem commands. Assume that your modem understands the Hayes command set, and the server's telephone number is 318714. The complete *chat* invocation to establish a connection with **c3po** would then be:

```
$ chat -v '' ATZ OK ATDT318714 CONNECT '' ogin: ppp word: GaGariN
```

By definition, the first string must be an expect string, but as the modem won't say anything before we have kicked it, we make *chat* skip the first expect by specifying an empty string. We then send `ATZ`, the reset command for Hayes-compatible modems, and wait for its response (`OK`). The next string sends the *dial* command along with the phone number to *chat*, and expects the `CONNECT` message in response. This is followed by an empty string again because we don't want to send anything now, but rather wait for the login prompt. The remainder of the chat script works exactly as described previously. This description probably looks a bit confusing, but we'll see in a moment that there is a way to make chat scripts a lot easier to understand.

The *–v* option makes *chat* log all activities to the *syslog* daemon `local2` facility.*

Specifying the chat script on the command line bears a certain risk because users can view a process's command line with the *ps* command. You can avoid this risk by putting the chat script in a file like *dial-c3po*. You make *chat* read the script from the file instead of the command line by giving it the *–f* option, followed by

---

* If you edit *syslog.conf* to redirect these log messages to a file, make sure this file isn't world readable, as *chat* also logs the entire chat script by default—including passwords.

the filename. This action has the added benefit of making our chat expect
sequences easier to understand. To convert our example, our *dial-c3po* file would
look like:

```
' '     ATZ
OK      ATDT318714
CONNECT ' '
ogin:   ppp
word:   GaGariN
```

When we use a chat script file in this way, the string we expect to receive is on
the left and the response we will send is on the right. They are much easier to
read and understand when presented this way.

The complete *pppd* incantation would now look like this:

```
# pppd connect "chat -f dial-c3po" /dev/ttyS3 38400 -detach \
    crtscts modem defaultroute
```

Besides the `connect` option that specifies the dialup script, we have added two
more options to the command line: `-detach`, which tells *pppd* not to detach from
the console and become a background process, and the `modem` keyword, which
makes it perform modem-specific actions on the serial device, like disconnecting
the line before and after the call. If you don't use this keyword, *pppd* will not
monitor the port's DCD line and will therefore not detect whether the remote end
hangs up unexpectedly.

The examples we have shown are rather simple; *chat* allows for much more complex scripts. For instance, it can specify strings on which to abort the chat with an
error. Typical abort strings are messages like `BUSY` or `NO CARRIER` that your
modem usually generates when the called number is busy or doesn't answer. To
make *chat* recognize these messages immediately rather than timing out, you can
specify them at the beginning of the script using the `ABORT` keyword:

```
$ chat -v ABORT BUSY ABORT 'NO CARRIER' ' ' ATZ OK ...
```

Similarly, you can change the timeout value for parts of the chat scripts by insert-
ing `TIMEOUT` options.

Sometimes you also need to have conditional execution for parts of the chat script:
when you don't receive the remote end's login prompt, you might want to send a
BREAK or a carriage return. You can achieve this by appending a subscript to an
expect string. The subscript consists of a sequence of send and expect strings, just
like the overall script itself, which are separated by hyphens. The subscript is executed whenever the expected string it is appended to is not received in time. In
the example above, we would modify the chat script as follows:

```
ogin:-BREAK-ogin: ppp ssword: GaGariN
```

When *chat* doesn't see the remote system send the login prompt, the subscript is executed by first sending a BREAK, and then waiting for the login prompt again. If the prompt now appears, the script continues as usual; otherwise, it will terminate with an error.

IP Configuration Options

IPCP is used to negotiate a number of IP parameters at link configuration time. Usually, each peer sends an IPCP Configuration Request packet, indicating which values it wants to change from the defaults and the new value. Upon receipt, the remote end inspects each option in turn and either acknowledges or rejects it.

pppd gives you a lot of control over which IPCP options it will try to negotiate. You can tune it through various command-line options that we will discuss in this section.

Choosing IP Addresses

All IP interfaces require IP addresses assigned to them; a PPP device always has an IP address. The PPP suite of protocols provides a mechanism that allows the automatic assignment of IP addresses to PPP interfaces. It is possible for the PPP program at one end of a point-to-point link to assign an IP address for the remote end to use, or each may use its own.

Some PPP servers that handle a lot of client sites assign addresses dynamically; addresses are assigned to systems only when calling in and are reclaimed after they have logged off again. This allows the number of IP addresses required to be limited to the number of dialup lines. While limitation is convenient for managers of the PPP dialup server, it is often less convenient for users who are dialing in. We discussed the way that hostnames are mapped to IP addresses by use of a database in Chapter 6. In order for people to connect to your host, they must know your IP address or the hostname associated with it. If you are a user of a PPP service that assigns you an IP address dynamically, this knowledge is difficult without providing some means of allowing the DNS database to be updated after you are assigned an IP address. Such systems do exist, but we won't cover them in detail here; instead, we will look at the more preferable approach, which involves you being able to use the same IP address each time you establish your network connection.*

In the previous example, we had *pppd* dial up **c3po** and establish an IP link. No provisions were taken to choose a particular IP address on either end of the link. Instead, we let *pppd* take its default action. It attempts to resolve the local

---

* More information on two dynamic host assignment mechanisms can be found at *http://www.dynip.com/* and *http://www.justlinux.com/dynamic_dns.html*.

hostname, **vlager** in our example, to an IP address, which it uses for the local end, while letting the remote machine, **c3po**, provide its own. PPP supports several alternatives to this arrangement.

To ask for particular addresses, you generally provide *pppd* with the following option:

```
local_addr:remote_addr
```

`local_addr` and `remote_addr` may be specified either in dotted quad notation or as hostnames.* This option makes *pppd* attempt to use the first address supplied as its own IP address, and the second as the peer's. If the peer rejects either of the addresses during IPCP negotiation, no IP link will be established.†

If you are dialing in to a server and expect it to assign you an IP address, you should ensure that *pppd* does not attempt to negotiate one for itself. To do this, use the *noipdefault* option and leave the `local_addr` blank. The *noipdefault* option will stop *pppd* from trying to use the IP address associated with the hostname as the local address.

If you want to set only the local address but accept any address the peer uses, simply leave out the `remote_addr` part. To make **vlager** use the IP address **130.83.4.27** instead of its own, give it *130.83.4.27:* on the command line. Similarly, to set the remote address only, leave the `local_addr` field blank. By default, *pppd* will then use the address associated with your hostname.

Routing Through a PPP Link

After setting up the network interface, *pppd* will usually set up a host route to its peer only. If the remote host is on a LAN, you certainly want to be able to connect to hosts "behind" your peer as well; in that case, a network route must be set up.

We have already seen that *pppd* can be asked to set the default route using the *defaultroute* option. This option is very useful if the PPP server you dialed up acts as your Internet gateway.

The reverse case, in which your system acts as a gateway for a single host, is also relatively easy to accomplish. For example, take some employee at the Virtual Brewery whose home machine is called **oneshot**. Let's also assume that we've configured **vlager** as a dialin PPP server. If we've configured **vlager** to dynamically assign an IP address that belongs to the Brewery's subnet, then we can use the

---

* Using hostnames in this option has consequences for CHAP authentication. Please refer to the "Authentication with PPP" section later in this chapter.

† The *ipcp-accept-local* and *ipcp-accept-remote* options instruct your *pppd* to accept the local and remote IP addresses being offered by the remote PPP, even if you've supplied some in your configuration. If these options are not configured, your *pppd* will reject any attempt to negotiate the IP addresses used.

proxyarp option with *pppd*, which will install a proxy ARP entry for **oneshot**. This automatically makes **oneshot** accessible from all hosts at the Brewery and the Winery.

However, things aren't always that simple. Linking two local area networks usually requires adding a specific network route because these networks may have their own default routes. Besides, having both peers use the PPP link as the default route would generate a loop, through which packets to unknown destinations would ping-pong between the peers until their time to live expired.

Suppose the Virtual Brewery opens a branch in another city. The subsidiary runs an Ethernet of its own using the IP network number **172.16.3.0**, which is subnet 3 of the Brewery's class B network. The subsidiary wants to connect to the Brewery's network via PPP to update customer databases. Again, **vlager** acts as the gateway for the brewery network and will support the PPP link; its peer at the new branch is called **vbourbon** and has an IP address of **172.16.3.1**. This network is illustrated in Figure A-2 in Appendix A, *Example Network: The Virtual Brewery*.

When **vbourbon** connects to **vlager**, it makes the default route point to **vlager** as usual. On **vlager**, however, we will have only the point-to-point route to **vbourbon** and will have to specially configure a network route for subnet 3 that uses **vbourbon** as its gateway. We could do this manually using the *route* command by hand after the PPP link is established, but this is not a very practical solution. Fortunately, we can configure the route automatically by using a feature of *pppd* that we haven't discussed yet—the *ip-up* command. This command is a shell script or program located in */etc/ppp* that is executed by *pppd* after the PPP interface has been configured. When present, it is invoked with the following parameters:

```
ip-up iface device speed local_addr remote_addr
```

The following table summarizes the meaning of each of the arguments (in the first column, we show the number used by the shell script to refer to each argument):

Argument	Name	Purpose
$1	`iface`	The network interface used, e.g., `ppp0`
$2	`device`	The pathname of the serial device file used (*/dev/tty*, if stdin/stdout are used)
$3	`speed`	The speed of the serial device in bits per second
$4	`local_addr`	The IP address of the link's remote end in dotted quad notation
$5	`remote_addr`	The IP address of the remote end of the link in dotted quad notation

In our case, the *ip-up* script may contain the following code fragment:*

```
#!/bin/sh
case $5 in
172.16.3.1)                 # this is vbourbon
        route add -net 172.16.3.0 gw 172.16.3.1;;
...
esac
exit 0
```

Similarly, */etc/ppp/ip-down* can be used to undo any actions of *ip-up* after the PPP link has been taken down again. So in our */etc/ppp/ip-down* script we would have a *route* command that removed the route we created in the */etc/ppp/ip-up* script.

However, the routing scheme is not yet complete. We have set up routing table entries on both PPP hosts, but so far none of the hosts on either network knows anything about the PPP link. This is not a big problem if all hosts at the subsidiary have their default route pointing at **vbourbon**, and all Brewery hosts route to **vlager** by default. If this is not the case, your only option is usually to use a routing daemon like *gated*. After creating the network route on **vlager**, the routing daemon broadcasts the new route to all hosts on the attached subnets.

Link Control Options

We already encountered the Link Control Protocol (LCP), which is used to negotiate link characteristics and test the link.

The two most important options negotiated by LCP are the *Asynchronous Control Character Map* and the *Maximum Receive Unit*. There are a number of other LCP configuration options, but they are far too specialized to discuss here.

The Asynchronous Control Character Map, colloquially called the *async map*, is used on asynchronous links, such as telephone lines, to identify control characters that must be escaped (replaced by a specific two-character sequence) to avoid them being interpreted by equipment used to establish the link. For instance, you may want to avoid the XON and XOFF characters used for software handshake because a misconfigured modem might choke upon receipt of an XOFF. Other candidates include Ctrl-l (the *telnet* escape character). PPP allows you to escape any of the characters with ASCII codes 0 through 31 by specifying them in the async map.

The async map is a 32-bit-wide bitmap expressed in hexadecimal. The least significant bit corresponds to the ASCII NULL character, and the most significant bit corresponds to ASCII 31 decimal. These 32 ASCII characters are the control

---

* If we wanted to have routes for other sites created when they dial in, we'd add appropriate case statements to cover those in which the . . . appears in the example.

characters. If a bit is set in the bitmap, it signals that the corresponding character must be escaped before it is transmitted across the link.

To tell your peer that it doesn't have to escape all control characters, but only a few of them, you can specify an async map to *pppd* using the *asyncmap* option. For example, if only ^S and ^Q (ASCII 17 and 19, commonly used for XON and XOFF) must be escaped, use the following option:

```
asyncmap 0x000A0000
```

The conversion is simple as long as you can convert binary to hex. Lay out 32 bits in front of you. The right-most bit corresponds to ASCII 00 (NULL), and the left-most bit corresponds to ASCII 32 decimal. Set the bits corresponding to the characters you want escaped to one, and all others to zero. To convert that into the hexadecimal number *pppd* expects, simply take each set of 4 bits and convert them into hex. You should end up with eight hexadecimal figures. String them all together and preprend "0x" to signify it is a hexadecimal number, and you are done.

Initially, the async map is set to 0xffffffff—that is, all control characters will be escaped. This is a safe default, but is usually much more than you need. Each character that appears in the async map results in two characters being transmitted across the link, so escaping comes at the cost of increased link utilization and a corresponding performance reduction.

In most circumstances, an async map of 0x0 works fine. No escaping is performed.

The Maximum Receive Unit (MRU), signals to the peer the maximum size of HDLC frames we want to receive. Although this may remind you of the Maximum Transfer Unit (MTU) value, these two have little in common. The MTU is a parameter of the kernel networking device and describes the maximum frame size the interface is able to transmit. The MRU is more of an advice to the remote end not to generate frames larger than the MRU; the interface must nevertheless be able to receive frames of up to 1,500 bytes.

Choosing an MRU is therefore not so much a question of what the link is capable of transferring, but of what gives you the best throughput. If you intend to run interactive applications over the link, setting the MRU to values as low as 296 is a good idea, so that an occasional larger packet (say, from an FTP session) doesn't make your cursor "jump." To tell *pppd* to request an MRU of 296, you give it the option mru 296. Small MRUs, however, make sense only if you have VJ header compression (it is enabled by default), because otherwise you'd waste a large amount of your bandwidth just carrying the IP header for each datagram.

pppd also understands a couple of LCP options that configure the overall behavior of the negotiation process, such as the maximum number of configuration requests that may be exchanged before the link is terminated. Unless you know exactly what you are doing, you should leave these options alone.

Finally, there are two options that apply to LCP echo messages. PPP defines two messages, *Echo Request* and *Echo Response*. *pppd* uses this feature to check if a link is still operating. You can enable this by using the *lcp-echo-interval* option together with a time in seconds. If no frames are received from the remote host within this interval, *pppd* generates an Echo Request and expects the peer to return an Echo Response. If the peer does not produce a response, the link is terminated after a certain number of requests are sent. This number can be set using the *lcp-echo-failure* option. By default, this feature is disabled altogether.

General Security Considerations

A misconfigured PPP daemon can be a devastating security breach. It can be as bad as letting anyone plug their machine into your Ethernet (and that can be very bad). In this section, we discuss a few measures that should make your PPP configuration safe.

> Root privilege is required to configure the network device and routing table. You will usually solve this by running *pppd* setuid **root**. However, *pppd* allows users to set various security-relevant options.

To protect against any attacks a user may launch by manipulating *pppd* options, you should set a couple of default values in the global */etc/ppp/options* file, like those shown in the sample file in "Using Options Files," earlier in this chapter. Some of them, such as the authentication options, cannot be overridden by the user, and thus provide reasonable protection against manipulations. An important option to protect is the `connect` option. If you intend to allow non-root users to invoke *pppd* to connect to the Internet, you should always add the `connect` and `noauth` options to the global options file */etc/ppp/options*. If you fail to do this, users will be able to execute arbitrary commands with `root` privileges by specifying the command as their `connect` command on the *pppd* line or in their personal options file.

Another good idea is to restrict which users may execute *pppd* by creating a group in */etc/group* and adding only those users who you wish to have the ability to execute the PPP daemon. You should then change group ownership of the *pppd* daemon to that group and remove the world execute privileges. To do this, assuming you've called your group **dialout**, you could use something like:

```
# chown root /usr/sbin/pppd
# chgrp dialout /usr/sbin/pppd
# chmod 4750 /usr/sbin/pppd
```

Of course, you have to protect yourself from the systems you speak PPP with, too. To fend off hosts posing as someone else, you should always require some sort of authentication from your peer. Additionally, you should not allow foreign hosts to use any IP address they choose, but restrict them to at most a few. The following section will deal with these topics in detail.

Authentication with PPP

With PPP, each system may require its peer to authenticate itself using one of two authentication protocols: the *Password Authentication Protocol* (PAP), and the *Challenge Handshake Authentication Protocol* (CHAP). When a connection is established, each end can request the other to authenticate itself, regardless of whether it is the caller or the callee. In the description that follows, we will loosely talk of "client" and "server" when we want to distinguish between the system sending authentication requests and the system responding to them. A PPP daemon can ask its peer for authentication by sending yet another LCP configuration request identifying the desired authentication protocol.

PAP Versus CHAP

PAP, which is offered by many Internet Service Providers, works basically the same way as the normal login procedure. The client authenticates itself by sending a username and a (optionally encrypted) password to the server, which the server compares to its secrets database.* This technique is vulnerable to eavesdroppers, who may try to obtain the password by listening in on the serial line, and to repeated trial and error attacks.

CHAP does not have these deficiencies. With CHAP, the server sends a randomly generated "challenge" string to the client, along with its hostname. The client uses the hostname to look up the appropriate secret, combines it with the challenge, and encrypts the string using a one-way hashing function. The result is returned to the server along with the client's hostname. The server now performs the same computation, and acknowledges the client if it arrives at the same result.

CHAP also doesn't require the client to authenticate itself only at startup time, but sends challenges at regular intervals to make sure the client hasn't been replaced by an intruder, for instance by switching phone lines, or because of a modem configuration error that causes the PPP daemon not to notice that the original phone call has dropped out and someone else has dialed in.

pppd keeps the secret keys for PAP and CHAP in two separate files called */etc/ppp/pap-secrets* and */etc/ppp/chap-secrets*. By entering a remote host in one or the other file, you have fine control over whether PAP or CHAP is used to authenticate yourself with your peer, and vice versa.

---

* "Secret" is just the PPP name for passwords. PPP secrets don't have the same length limitation as Linux login passwords.

By default, *pppd* doesn't require authentication from the remote host, but it will agree to authenticate itself when requested by the remote host. Since CHAP is so much stronger than PAP, *pppd* tries to use the former whenever possible. If the peer does not support it, or if *pppd* can't find a CHAP secret for the remote system in its *chap-secrets* file, it reverts to PAP. If it doesn't have a PAP secret for its peer either, it refuses to authenticate altogether. As a consequence, the connection is shut down.

You can modify this behavior in several ways. When given the *auth* keyword, *pppd* requires the peer to authenticate itself. *pppd* agrees to use either CHAP or PAP as long as it has a secret for the peer in its CHAP or PAP database. There are other options to turn a particular authentication protocol on or off, but I won't describe them here.

If all systems you talk to with PPP agree to authenticate themselves with you, you should put the *auth* option in the global */etc/ppp/options* file and define passwords for each system in the *chap-secrets* file. If a system doesn't support CHAP, add an entry for it to the *pap-secrets* file. That way, you can make sure no unauthenticated system connects to your host.

The next two sections discuss the two PPP secrets files, *pap-secrets* and *chap-secrets*. They are located in */etc/ppp* and contain triplets of clients, servers, and passwords, optionally followed by a list of IP addresses. The interpretation of the client and server fields is different for CHAP and PAP, and also depends on whether we authenticate ourselves with the peer, or whether we require the server to authenticate itself with us.

The CHAP Secrets File

When it has to authenticate itself with a server using CHAP, *pppd* searches the *chap-secrets* file for an entry with the client field equal to the local hostname, and the server field equal to the remote hostname sent in the CHAP challenge. When requiring the peer to authenticate itself, the roles are simply reversed: *pppd* then looks for an entry with the client field equal to the remote hostname (sent in the client's CHAP response), and the server field equal to the local hostname.

The following is a sample *chap-secrets* file for **vlager**:*

```
# CHAP secrets for vlager.vbrew.com
#
# client          server          secret              addrs
#-------------------------------------------------------------------
vlager.vbrew.com  c3po.lucas.com  "Use The Source Luke" vlager.vbrew.com
c3po.lucas.com    vlager.vbrew.com "arttoo! arttoo!"    c3po.lucas.com
*                 vlager.vbrew.com "TuXdrinksVicBitter"  pub.vbrew.com
```

---

* The double quotes are not part of the secret; they merely serve to protect the whitespace within it.

When **vlager** establishes a PPP connection with **c3po**, **c3po** asks **vlager** to authenticate itself by sending a CHAP challenge. *pppd* on **vlager** then scans *chap-secrets* for an entry with the client field equal to **vlager.vbrew.com** and the server field equal to **c3po.lucas.com**, and finds the first line shown in the example.* It then produces the CHAP response from the challenge string and the secret (Use The Source Luke), and sends it off to **c3po**.

pppd also composes a CHAP challenge for **c3po** containing a unique challenge string and its fully qualified hostname, **vlager.vbrew.com**. **c3po** constructs a CHAP response in the way we discussed, and returns it to **vlager**. *pppd* then extracts the client hostname (**c3po.vbrew.com**) from the response and searches the *chap-secrets* file for a line matching **c3po** as a client and **vlager** as the server. The second line does this, so *pppd* combines the CHAP challenge and the secret arttoo! arttoo!, encrypts them, and compares the result to **c3po**'s CHAP response.

The optional fourth field lists the IP addresses that are acceptable for the client named in the first field. The addresses can be given in dotted quad notation or as hostnames that are looked up with the resolver. For instance, if **c3po** asks to use an IP address during IPCP negotiation that is not in this list, the request is rejected, and IPCP is shut down. In the sample file shown above, **c3po** is therefore limited to using its own IP address. If the address field is empty, any addresses are allowed; a value of "-" prevents the use of IP with that client altogether.

The third line of the sample *chap-secrets* file allows any host to establish a PPP link with **vlager** because a client or server field of * is a wildcard matching any hostname. The only requirements are that the connecting host must know the secret and that it must use the IP address associated with **pub.vbrew.com**. Entries with wildcard hostnames may appear anywhere in the secrets file, since *pppd* will always use the best match it can find for the server/client pair.

pppd may need some help forming hostnames. As explained before, the remote hostname is always provided by the peer in the CHAP challenge or response packet. The local hostname is obtained by calling the *gethostname(2)* function by default. If you have set the system name to your unqualified hostname, you also have to provide *pppd* with the domain name using the *domain* option:

```
# pppd ... domain vbrew.com
```

This provision appends the Brewery's domain name to **vlager** for all authentication related activities. Other options that modify *pppd*'s idea of the local hostname are *usehostname* and *name*. When you give the local IP address on the command line using `local:remote` and `local` as a name instead of a dotted quad, *pppd* uses this as the local hostname.

---

* This hostname is taken from the CHAP challenge.

The PAP Secrets File

The PAP secrets file is very similar to CHAP's. The first two fields always contain a username and a server name; the third holds the PAP secret. When the remote host sends its authentication information, *pppd* uses the entry that has a server field equal to the local hostname, and a user field equal to the username sent in the request. When it is necessary for us to send our credentials to the peer, *pppd* uses the secret that has a user field equal to the local username and the server field equal to the remote hostname.

A sample PAP secrets file might look like this:

```
# /etc/ppp/pap-secrets
#
# user          server          secret          addrs
vlager-pap      c3po            cresspahl       vlager.vbrew.com
c3po            vlager          DonaldGNUth     c3po.lucas.com
```

The first line is used to authenticate ourselves when talking to **c3po**. The second line describes how a user named **c3po** has to authenticate itself with us.

The name `vlager-pap` in the first column is the username we send to **c3po**. By default, *pppd* picks the local hostname as the username, but you can also specify a different name by giving the *user* option followed by that name.

When picking an entry from the *pap-secrets* file to identify us to a remote host, *pppd* must know the remote host's name. As it has no way of finding that out, you must specify it on the command line using the *remotename* keyword followed by the peer's hostname. To use the above entry for authentication with **c3po**, for example, we must add the following option to *pppd*'s command line:

```
# pppd ... remotename c3po user vlager-pap
```

In the fourth field of the PAP secrets file (and all following fields), you can specify what IP addresses are allowed for that particular host, just as in the CHAP secrets file. The peer will be allowed to request only addresses from that list. In the sample file, the entry that **c3po** will use when it dials in—the line where **c3po** is the client—allows it to use its real IP address and no other.

Note that PAP is a rather weak authentication method, you should use CHAP instead whenever possible. We will therefore not cover PAP in greater detail here; if you are interested in using it, you will find more PAP features in the *pppd(8)* manual page.

Debugging Your PPP Setup

By default, *pppd* logs any warnings and error messages to *syslog*'s `daemon` facility. You have to add an entry to *syslog.conf* that redirects these messages to a file or even the console; otherwise, *syslog* simply discards them. The following entry sends all messages to */var/log/ppp-log*:

```
daemon.*                    /var/log/ppp-log
```

If your PPP setup doesn't work right away, you should look in this log file. If the log messages don't help, you can also turn on extra debugging output using the *debug* option. This output makes *pppd* log the contents of all control packets sent or received to *syslog*. All messages then go to the `daemon` facility.

Finally, the most drastic way to check a problem is to enable kernel-level debugging by invoking *pppd* with the *kdebug* option. It is followed by a numeric argument that is the sum of the following values: 1 for general debug messages, 2 for printing the contents of all incoming HDLC frames, and 4 to make the driver print all outgoing HDLC frames. To capture kernel debugging messages, you must either run a *syslogd* daemon that reads the */proc/kmsg* file, or the *klogd* daemon. Either of them directs kernel debugging to the *syslog* `kernel` facility.

More Advanced PPP Configurations

While configuring PPP to dial in to a network like the Internet is the most common application, there are those of you who have more advanced requirements. In this section we'll talk about a few of the more advanced configurations possible with PPP under Linux.

PPP Server

Running *pppd* as a server is just a matter of configuring a serial tty device to invoke *pppd* with appropriate options when an incoming data call has been received. One way to do this is to create a special account, say **ppp**, and give it a script or program as a login shell that invokes *pppd* with these options. Alternatively, if you intend to support PAP or CHAP authentication, you can use the *mgetty* program to support your modem and exploit its "/AutoPPP/" feature.

To build a server using the login method, you add a line similar to the following to your */etc/passwd* file:*

```
ppp:x:500:200:Public PPP Account:/tmp:/etc/ppp/ppplogin
```

If your system supports shadow passwords, you also need to add an entry to the */etc/shadow* file:

```
ppp:!:10913:0:99999:7:::
```

---

* The *useradd* or *adduser* utility, if you have it, will simplify this task.

Of course, the UID and GID you use depends on which user you wish to own the connection, and how you've created it. You also have to set the password for the mentioned account using the *passwd* command.

The *ppplogin* script might look like this:

```
#!/bin/sh
# ppplogin - script to fire up pppd on login
mesg n
stty -echo
exec pppd -detach silent modem crtscts
```

The *mesg* command disables other users from writing to the tty by using, for instance, the *write* command. The *stty* command turns off character echoing. This command is necessary; otherwise, everything the peer sends would be echoed back to it. The most important *pppd* option given is `-detach` because it prevents *pppd* from detaching from the controlling tty. If we didn't specify this option, it would go to the background, making the shell script exit. This in turn would cause the serial line to hang up and the connection to be dropped. The *silent* option causes *pppd* to wait until it receives a packet from the calling system before it starts sending. This option prevents transmit timeouts from occurring when the calling system is slow in firing up its PPP client. The `modem` option makes *pppd* drive the modem control lines of the serial port. You should always turn this option on when using *pppd* with a modem. The *crtscts* option turns on hardware handshake.

Besides these options, you might want to force some sort of authentication, for example, by specifying *auth* on *pppd*'s command line or in the global options file. The manual page also discusses more specific options for turning individual authentication protocols on and off.

If you wish to use *mgetty*, all you need to do is configure *mgetty* to support the serial device your modem is connected to (see "Configuring the mgetty Daemon" for details), configure *pppd* for either PAP or CHAP authentication with appropriate options in its *options* file, and finally, add a section similar to the following to your */etc/mgetty/login.config* file:

```
# Configure mgetty to automatically detect incoming PPP calls and invoke
# the pppd daemon to handle the connection.
#
/AutoPPP/ -    ppp    /usr/sbin/pppd auth -chap +pap login
```

The first field is a special piece of magic used to detect that an incoming call is a PPP one. You must not change the case of this string; it is case sensitive. The third column is the username that appears in *who* listings when someone has logged in. The rest of the line is the command to invoke. In our example, we've ensured that PAP authentication is required, disabled CHAP, and specified that the system *passwd* file should be used for authenticating users. This is probably similar to what you'll want. Remember, you can specify the options in the *options* file or on the command line if you prefer.

Here is a small checklist of tasks to perform and the sequence you should perform them to get PPP dial in working on your machine. Make sure each step works before moving on to the next:

1. Configure the modem for auto-answer mode. On Hayes-compatible modems, this is performed using a command like `ATS0=3`. If you're going to be using the *mgetty* daemon, this isn't necessary.

2. Configure the serial device with a *getty* type of command to answer incoming calls. A commonly used *getty* variant is *mgetty*.

3. Consider authentication. Will your callers authenticate using PAP, CHAP, or system login?

4. Configure *pppd* as server as described in this section.

5. Consider routing. Will you need to provide a network route to callers? Routing can be performed using the *ip-up* script.

Demand Dialing

When there is IP traffic to be carried across the link, *demand dialing* causes your telephone modem to dial and to establish a connection to a remote host. Demand dialing is most useful when you can't leave your telephone line permanently switched to your Internet provider. For example, you might have to pay timed local calls, so it might be cheaper to have the telephone line switched on only when you need it and disconnected when you aren't using the Internet.

Traditional Linux solutions have used the *diald* command, which worked well but was fairly tricky to configure. Versions 2.3.0 and later of the PPP daemon have built-in support for demand dialing and make it very simple to configure. You must use a modern kernel for this to work, too. Any of the later 2.0 kernels will work just fine.

To configure *pppd* for demand dialing, all you need to do is add options to your *options* file or the *pppd* command line. The following table summarizes the options related to demand dialing:

Option	Description
demand	This option specifies that the PPP link should be placed in demand dial mode. The PPP network device will be created, but the `connect` command will not be used until a datagram is transmitted by the local host. This option is mandatory for demand dialing to work.
active-filter *expression*	This option allows you to specify which data packets are to be considered active traffic. Any traffic matching the specified rule will restart the demand dial idle timer, ensuring that *pppd* waits again before closing the link. The filter syntax has been borrowed from the *tcpdump* command. The default filter matches all datagrams.
holdoff *n*	This option allows you to specify the minimum amount of time, in seconds, to wait before reconnecting this link if it terminates. If the connection fails while *pppd* believes it is in active use, it will be re-established after this timer has expired. This timer does not apply to reconnections after an idle timeout.
idle *n*	If this option is configured, *pppd* will disconnect the link whenever this timer expires. Idle times are specified in seconds. Each new active data packet will reset the timer.

A simple demand dialing configuration would therefore look something like this:

```
demand
holdoff 60
idle 180
```

This configuration would enable demand dialing, wait 60 seconds before re-establishing a failed connection, and drop the link if 180 seconds pass without any active data on the link.

Persistent Dialing

Persistent dialing is what people who have permanent dialup connections to a network will want to use. There is a subtle difference between demand dialing and persistent dialing. With persistent dialing, the connection is automatically established as soon as the PPP daemon is started, and the persistent aspect comes into play whenever the telephone call supporting the link fails. Persistent dialing ensures that the link is always available by automatically rebuilding the connection if it fails.

You might be fortunate to not have to pay for your telephone calls; perhaps they are local and free, or perhaps they're paid by your company. The persistent dialing option is extremely useful in this situation. If you do have to pay for your telephone calls, then you have to be a little careful. If you pay for your telephone calls on a time-charged basis, persistent dialing is almost certainly not what you want, unless you're very sure you'll be using the connection fairly steadily twenty-four hours a day. If you do pay for calls, but they are not time charged, you need to be careful to protect yourself against situations that might cause the modem to endlessly redial. The *pppd* daemon provides an option that can help reduce the effects of this problem.

To enable persistent dialing, you must include the `persist` option in one of your *pppd* options files. Including this option alone is all you need to have *pppd* automatically invoke the command specified by the `connect` option to rebuild the connection when the link fails. If you are concerned about the modem redialing too rapidly (in the case of modem or server fault at the other end of the connection), you can use the `holdoff` option to set the minimum amount of time that *pppd* will wait before attempting to reconnect. This option won't solve the problem of a fault costing you money in wasted phone calls, but it will at least serve to reduce the impact of one.

A typical configuration might have persistent dialing options that look like this:

```
persist
holdoff 600
```

The holdoff time is specified in seconds. In our example, *pppd* waits a full five minutes before redialing after the call drops out.

It is possible to combine persistent dialing with demand dialing, using `idle` to drop the link if it has been idle for a specified period of time. We doubt many users would want to do so, but this scenario is described briefly in the *pppd* manual page, if you'd like to pursue it.

## CHAPTER NINE

TCP/IP FIREWALL

Security is increasingly important for companies and individuals alike. The Internet has provided them with a powerful tool to distribute information about themselves and obtain information from others, but it has also exposed them to dangers that they have previously been exempt from. Computer crime, information theft, and malicious damage are all potential dangers.

An unauthorized and unscrupulous person who gains access to a computer system may guess system passwords or exploit the bugs and idiosyncratic behavior of certain programs to obtain a working account on that machine. Once they are able to log in to the machine, they may have access to information that may be damaging, such as commercially sensitive information like marketing plans, new project details, or customer information databases. Damaging or modifying this type of data can cause severe setbacks to the company.

The safest way to avoid such widespread damage is to prevent unauthorized people from gaining network access to the machine. This is where firewalls come in.

 Constructing secure firewalls is an art. It involves a good understanding of technology, but equally important, it requires an understanding of the philosophy behind firewall designs. We won't cover everything you need to know in this book; we strongly recommend you do some additional research before trusting any particular firewall design, including any we present here.

There is enough material on firewall configuration and design to fill a whole book, and indeed there are some good resources that you might like to read to expand your knowledge on the subject. Two of these are:

Building Internet Firewalls

by D. Chapman and E. Zwicky (O'Reilly). A guide explaining how to design and install firewalls for Unix, Linux, and Windows NT, and how to configure Internet services to work with the firewalls.

Firewalls and Internet Security

by W. Cheswick and S. Bellovin (Addison Wesley). This book covers the philosophy of firewall design and implementation.

We will focus on the Linux-specific technical issues in this chapter. Later we will present a sample firewall configuration that should serve as a useful starting point in your own configuration, but as with all security-related matters, trust no one. Double check the design, make sure you understand it, and then modify it to suit your requirements. To be safe, be sure.

Methods of Attack

As a network administrator, it is important that you understand the nature of potential attacks on computer security. We'll briefly describe the most important types of attacks so that you can better understand precisely what the Linux IP firewall will protect you against. You should do some additional reading to ensure that you are able to protect your network against other types of attacks. Here are some of the more important methods of attack and ways of protecting yourself against them:

Unauthorized access

This simply means that people who shouldn't use your computer services are able to connect and use them. For example, people outside your company might try to connect to your company accounting machine or to your NFS server.

There are various ways to avoid this attack by carefully specifying who can gain access through these services. You can prevent network access to all except the intended users.

Exploitation of known weaknesses in programs

Some programs and network services were not originally designed with strong security in mind and are inherently vulnerable to attack. The BSD remote services (rlogin, rexec, etc.) are an example.

The best way to protect yourself against this type of attack is to disable any vulnerable services or find alternatives. With Open Source, it is sometimes possible to repair the weaknesses in the software.

Denial of service

Denial of service attacks cause the service or program to cease functioning or prevent others from making use of the service or program. These may be performed at the network layer by sending carefully crafted and malicious datagrams that cause network connections to fail. They may also be performed at the application layer, where carefully crafted application commands are given to a program that cause it to become extremely busy or stop functioning.

Preventing suspicious network traffic from reaching your hosts and preventing suspicious program commands and requests are the best ways of minimizing the risk of a denial of service attack. It's useful to know the details of the attack method, so you should educate yourself about each new attack as it gets publicized.

Spoofing

This type of attack causes a host or application to mimic the actions of another. Typically the attacker pretends to be an innocent host by following IP addresses in network packets. For example, a well-documented exploit of the BSD rlogin service can use this method to mimic a TCP connection from another host by guessing TCP sequence numbers.

To protect against this type of attack, verify the authenticity of datagrams and commands. Prevent datagram routing with invalid source addresses. Introduce unpredictablility into connection control mechanisms, such as TCP sequence numbers and the allocation of dynamic port addresses.

Eavesdropping

This is the simplest type of attack. A host is configured to "listen" to and capture data not belonging to it. Carefully written eavesdropping programs can take usernames and passwords from user login network connections. Broadcast networks like Ethernet are especially vulnerable to this type of attack.

To protect against this type of threat, avoid use of broadcast network technologies and enforce the use of data encryption.

IP firewalling is very useful in preventing or reducing unauthorized access, network layer denial of service, and IP spoofing attacks. It not very useful in avoiding exploitation of weaknesses in network services or programs and eavesdropping.

What Is a Firewall?

A firewall is a secure and trusted machine that sits between a private network and a public network.* The firewall machine is configured with a set of rules that determine which network traffic will be allowed to pass and which will be

---

* The term *firewall* comes from a device used to protect people from fire. The firewall is a shield of material resistant to fire that is placed between a potential fire and the people it is protecting.

blocked or refused. In some large organizations, you may even find a firewall located inside their corporate network to segregate sensitive areas of the organization from other employees. Many cases of computer crime occur from within an organization, not just from outside.

Firewalls can be constructed in quite a variety of ways. The most sophisticated arrangement involves a number of separate machines and is known as a *perimeter network*. Two machines act as "filters" called chokes to allow only certain types of network traffic to pass, and between these chokes reside network servers such as a mail gateway or a World Wide Web proxy server. This configuration can be very safe and easily allows quite a great range of control over who can connect both from the inside to the outside, and from the outside to the inside. This sort of configuration might be used by large organizations.

Typically though, firewalls are single machines that serve all of these functions. These are a little less secure, because if there is some weakness in the firewall machine itself that allows people to gain access to it, the whole network security has been breached. Nevertheless, these types of firewalls are cheaper and easier to manage than the more sophisticated arrangement just described. Figure 9-1 illustrates the two most common firewall configurations.

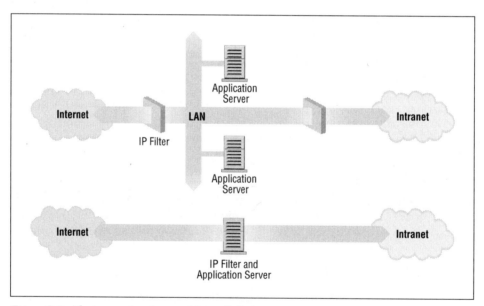

Figure 9-1. The two major classes of firewall design

The Linux kernel provides a range of built-in features that allow it to function quite nicely as an IP firewall. The network implementation includes code to do IP filtering in a number of different ways, and provides a mechanism to quite accurately configure what sort of rules you'd like to put in place. The Linux firewall is flexible enough to make it very useful in either of the configurations illustrated in Figure 9-1. Linux firewall software provides two other useful features that we'll discuss in separate chapters: IP Accounting (Chapter 10, *IP Accounting*) and IP masquerade (Chapter 11, *IP Masquerade and Network Address Translation*).

What Is IP Filtering?

IP filtering is simply a mechanism that decides which types of IP datagrams will be processed normally and which will be discarded. By *discarded* we mean that the datagram is deleted and completely ignored, as if it had never been received. You can apply many different sorts of criteria to determine which datagrams you wish to filter; some examples of these are:

- Protocol type: TCP, UDP, ICMP, etc.

- Socket number (for TCP/UPD)

- Datagram type: SYN/ACK, data, ICMP Echo Request, etc.

- Datagram source address: where it came from

- Datagram destination address: where it is going to

It is important to understand at this point that IP filtering is a network layer facility. This means it doesn't understand anything about the application using the network connections, only about the connections themselves. For example, you may deny users access to your internal network on the default telnet port, but if you rely on IP filtering alone, you can't stop them from using the telnet program with a port that you do allow to pass trhough your firewall. You can prevent this sort of problem by using proxy servers for each service that you allow across your firewall. The proxy servers understand the application they were designed to proxy and can therefore prevent abuses, such as using the telnet program to get past a firewall by using the World Wide Web port. If your firewall supports a World Wide Web proxy, their telnet connection will always be answered by the proxy and will allow only HTTP requests to pass. A large number of proxy-server programs exist. Some are free software and many others are commercial products. The Firewall-HOWTO discusses one popular set of these, but they are beyond the scope of this book.

The IP filtering ruleset is made up of many combinations of the criteria listed previously. For example, let's imagine that you wanted to allow World Wide Web users within the Virtual Brewery network to have no access to the Internet except to use other sites' web servers. You would configure your firewall to allow forwarding of:

- datagrams with a source address on Virtual Brewery network, a destination address of anywhere, and with a destination port of 80 (WWW)

- datagrams with a destination address of Virtual Brewery network and a source port of 80 (WWW) from a source address of anywhere

Note that we've used two rules here. We have to allow our data to go out, but also the corresponding reply data to come back in. In practice, as we'll see shortly, Linux simplifies this and allows us to specify this in one command.

Setting Up Linux for Firewalling

To build a Linux IP firewall, it is necessary to have a kernel built with IP firewall support and the appropriate configuration utility. In all production kernels prior to the 2.2 series, you would use the *ipfwadm* utility. The 2.2.x kernels marked the release of the third generation of IP firewall for Linux called *IP Chains*. IP chains use a program similar to *ipfwadm* called *ipchains*. Linux kernels 2.3.15 and later support the fourth generation of Linux IP firewall called *netfilter*. The *netfilter* code is the result of a large redesign of the packet handling flow in Linux. The *netfilter* is a multifaceted creature, providing direct backward-compatible support for both *ipfwadm* and *ipchains* as well as a new alternative command called *iptables*. We'll talk about the differences between the three in the next few sections.

Kernel Configured with IP Firewall

The Linux kernel must be configured to support IP firewalling. There isn't much more to it than selecting the appropriate options when performing a `make menu-config` of your kernel.* We described how to do this is in Chapter 3, *Configuring the Networking Hardware*". In 2.2 kernels you should select the following options:

```
Networking options  --->
        [*] Network firewalls
        [*] TCP/IP networking
        [*] IP: firewalling
        [*] IP: firewall packet logging
```

In kernels 2.4.0 and later you should select this option instead:

```
  Networking options  --->
    [*] Network packet filtering (replaces ipchains)
        IP: Netfilter Configuration  --->
              .
              <M> Userspace queueing via NETLINK (EXPERIMENTAL)
              <M> IP tables support (required for filtering/masq/NAT)
```

---

* Firewall packet logging is a special feature that writes a line of information about each datagram that matches a particular firewall rule out to a special device so you can see them.

```
<M>    limit match support
<M>    MAC address match support
<M>    netfilter MARK match support
<M>    Multiple port match support
<M>    TOS match support
<M>    Connection state match support
<M>    Unclean match support (EXPERIMENTAL)
<M>    Owner match support (EXPERIMENTAL)
<M>    Packet filtering
<M>       REJECT target support
<M>       MIRROR target support (EXPERIMENTAL)
 .
<M>    Packet mangling
<M>       TOS target support
<M>       MARK target support
<M>    LOG target support
<M> ipchains (2.2-style) support
<M> ipfwadm (2.0-style) support
```

The ipfwadm Utility

The *ipfwadm* (IP Firewall Administration) utility is the tool used to build the firewall rules for all kernels prior to 2.2.0. Its command syntax can be very confusing because it can do such a complicated range of things, but we'll provide some common examples that will illustrate the most important variations of these.

The *ipfwadm* utility is included in most modern Linux distributions, but perhaps not by default. There may be a specific software package for it that you have to install. If your distribution does not include it, you can obtain the source package from **ftp.xos.nl** in the */pub/linux/ipfwadm/* directory, and compile it yourself.

The ipchains Utility

Just as for the *ipfwadm* utility, the *ipchains* utility can be somewhat baffling to use at first. It provides all of the flexibility of *ipfwadm* with a simplified command syntax, and additionally provides a "chaining" mechanism that allows you to manage multiple rulesets and link them together. We'll cover rule chaining in a separate section near the end of the chapter, because for most situations it is an advanced concept.

The *ipchains* command appears in most Linux distributions based on the 2.2 kernels. If you want to compile it yourself, you can find the source package from its developer's site at *http://www.rustcorp.com/linux/ipchains/*. Included in the source package is a wrapper script called *ipfwadm-wrapper* that mimics the *ipfwadm* command, but actually invokes the *ipchains* command. Migration of an existing firewall configuration is much more painless with this addition.

The iptables Utility

The syntax of the *iptables* utility is quite similar to that of the *ipchains* syntax. The changes are improvements and a result of the tool being redesigned to be extensible through shared libraries. Just as for *ipchains*, we'll present *iptables* equivalents of the examples so you can compare and contrast its syntax with the others.

The *iptables* utility is included in the *netfilter* source package available at *http://www.samba.org/netfilter/*. It will also be included in any Linux distribution based on the 2.4 series kernels.

We'll talk a bit about *netfilter*'s huge step forward in a section of its own later in this chapter.

Three Ways We Can Do Filtering

Consider how a Unix machine, or in fact any machine capable of IP routing, processes IP datagrams. The basic steps, shown in Figure 9-2 are:

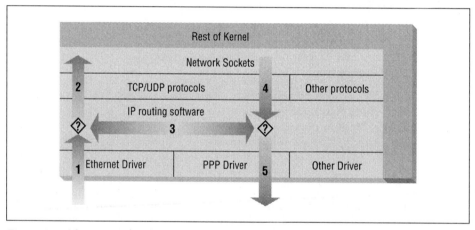

Figure 9-2. The stages of IP datagram processing

- The IP datagram is received. (1)

- The incoming IP datagram is examined to determine if it is destined for a process on this machine.

- If the datagram is for this machine, it is processed locally. (2)

- If it is not destined for this machine, a search is made of the routing table for an appropriate route and the datagram is forwarded to the appropriate interface or dropped if no route can be found. (3)

- Datagrams from local processes are sent to the routing software for forwarding to the appropriate interface. (4)

- The outgoing IP datagram is examined to determine if there is a valid route for it to take, if not, it is dropped.

- The IP datagram is transmitted. (5)

In our diagram, the flow 1→3→5 represents our machine routing data between a host on our Ethernet network to a host reachable via our PPP link. The flows 1→2 and 4→5 represent the data input and output flows of a network program running on our local host. The flow 4→3→2 would represent data flow via a loopback connection. Naturally data flows both into and out of network devices. The question marks on the diagram represent the points where the IP layer makes routing decisions.

The Linux kernel IP firewall is capable of applying filtering at various stages in this process. That is, you can filter the IP datagrams that come in to your machine, filter those datagrams being forwarded across your machine, and filter those datagrams that are ready to be transmitted.

In *ipfwadm* and *ipchains*, an Input rule applies to flow 1 on the diagram, a Forwarding rule to flow 3, and an Output rule to flow 5. We'll see when we discuss *netfilter* later that the points of interception have changed so that an Input rule is applied at flow 2, and an Output rule is applied at flow 4. This has important implications for how you structure your rulesets, but the general principle holds true for all versions of Linux firewalling.

This may seem unnecessarily complicated at first, but it provides flexibility that allows some very sophisticated and powerful configurations to be built.

Original IP Firewall (2.0 Kernels)

The first generation IP firewall support for Linux appeared in the 1.1 series kernel. It was a port of the BSD ipfw firewall support to Linux by Alan Cox. The firewall support that appeared in the 2.0 series kernels and is the second generation was enhanced by Jos Vos, Pauline Middelink, and others.

Using ipfwadm

The *ipfwadm* command was the configuration tool for the second generation Linux IP firewall. Perhaps the simplest way to describe the use of the *ipfwadm* command is by example. To begin, let's code the example we presented earlier.

A naïve example

Let's suppose that we have a network in our organization and that we are using a Linux-based firewall machine to connect our network to the Internet. Additionally, let's suppose that we wish the users of that network to be able to access web servers on the Internet, but to allow no other traffic to be passed.

We will put in place a forwarding rule to allow datagrams with a source address on our network and a destination socket of port 80 to be forwarded out, and for the corresponding reply datagrams to be forwarded back via the firewall.

Assume our network has a 24-bit network mask (Class C) and an address of 172.16.1.0. The rules we might use are:

```
# ipfwadm -F -f
# ipfwadm -F -p deny
# ipfwadm -F -a accept -P tcp -S 172.16.1.0/24 -D 0/0 80
# ipfwadm -F -a accept -P tcp -S 0/0 80 -D 172.16.1.0/24
```

The *-F* command-line argument tells *ipfwadm* that this is a forwarding rule. The first command instructs *ipfwadm* to "flush" all of the forwarding rules. This ensures we are working from a known state before we begin adding specific rules.

The second rule sets our default forwarding policy. We tell the kernel to deny or disallow forwarding of IP datagrams. It is very important to set the default policy, because this describes what will happen to any datagrams that are not specifically handled by any other rule. In most firewall configurations, you will want to set your default policy to "deny," as shown, to be sure that only the traffic you specifically allow past your firewall is forwarded.

The third and fourth rules are the ones that implement our requirement. The third command allows our datagrams out, and the fourth rule allows the responses back.

Let's review each of the arguments:

-F   This is a Forwarding rule.

-a accept
> Append this rule with the policy set to "accept," meaning we will forward any datagrams that match this rule.

-P tcp
> This rule applies to tcp datagrams (as opposed to UDP or ICMP).

-S 172.16.1.0/24
> The Source address must have the first 24 bits matching those of the network address 172.16.1.0.

-D 0/0 80

> The destination address must have zero bits matching the address 0.0.0.0. This is really a shorthand notation for "anything." The 80 is the destination port, in this case WWW. You may also use any entry that appears in the */etc/services* file to describe the port, so -D 0/0 www would have worked just as well.

ipfwadm accepts network masks in a form with which you may not be familiar. The /nn notation is a means of describing how many bits of the supplied address are significant, or the size of the mask. The bits are always counted from left to right; some common examples are listed in Table 9-1.

Table 9-1. Common Netmask Bit Values

Netmask	Bits
255.0.0.0	8
255.255.0.0	16
255.255.255.0	24
255.255.255.128	25
255.255.255.192	26
255.255.255.224	27
255.255.255.240	28
255.255.255.248	29
255.255.255.252	30

We mentioned earlier that *ipfwadm* implements a small trick that makes adding these sorts of rules easier. This trick is an option called *-b*, which makes the command a bidirectional rule.

The bidirectional flag allows us to collapse our two rules into one as follows:

```
# ipfwadm -F -a accept -P tcp -S 172.16.1.0/24 -D 0/0 80 -b
```

An important refinement

Take a closer look at our ruleset. Can you see that there is still one method of attack that someone outside could use to defeat our firewall?

Our ruleset allows all datagrams from outside our network with a source port of 80 to pass. This will include those datagrams with the SYN bit set! The SYN bit is what declares a TCP datagram to be a connection request. If a person on the outside had privileged access to a host, they could make a connection through our firewall to any of our hosts, provided they use port 80 at their end. This is not what we intended.

Fortunately there is a solution to this problem. The *ipfwadm* command provides another flag that allows us to build rules that will match datagrams with the SYN bit set. Let's change our example to include such a rule:

```
# ipfwadm -F -a deny -P tcp -S 0/0 80 -D 172.16.10.0/24 -y
# ipfwadm -F -a accept -P tcp -S 172.16.1.0/24 -D 0/0 80 -b
```

The *-y* flag causes the rule to match only if the SYN flag is set in the datagram. So our new rule says: "Deny any TCP datagrams destined for our network from anywhere with a source port of 80 and the SYN bit set," or "Deny any connection requests from hosts using port 80."

Why have we placed this special rule *before* the main rule? IP firewall rules operate so that the first match is the rule that is used. Both rules would match the datagrams we want to stop, so we must be sure to put the `deny` rule before the `accept` rule.

Listing our rules

After we've entered our rules, we ask *ipfwadm* to list them for us using the command:

```
# ipfwadm -F -l
```

This command will list all of the configured forwarding rules. The output should look something like this:

```
# ipfwadm -F -l
IP firewall forward rules, default policy: accept
type  prot source            destination          ports
deny  tcp  anywhere          172.16.10.0/24       www -> any
acc   tcp  172.16.1.0/24     anywhere             any -> www
```

The *ipfwadm* command will attempt to translate the port number into a service name using the */etc/services* if an entry exists there.

The default output is lacking in some important detail for us. In the default listing output, we can't see the effect of the −y argument. The *ipfwadm* command is able to produce a more detailed listing output if you specify the −e (extended output) argument too. We won't show the whole output here because it is too wide for the page, but it includes an `opt` (options) column that shows the *-y* option controlling SYN packets:

```
# ipfwadm -F -l -e
P firewall forward rules, default policy: accept
 pkts bytes type  prot opt  tosa tosx ifname ifaddress  source     ...
    0     0 deny  tcp  --y- 0xFF 0x00 any    any        anywhere   ...
    0     0 acc   tcp  b--- 0xFF 0x00 any    any        172.16.1.0/24 ...
```

A More Complex Example

The previous example was a simple one. Not all network services are as simple as the WWW service to configure; in practice, a typical firewall configuration would be much more complex. Let's look at another common example, this time FTP. We want our internal network users to be able to log into FTP servers on the Internet to read and write files. But we don't want people on the Internet to be able to log into our FTP servers.

We know that FTP uses two TCP ports: port 20 (ftp-data) and port 21 (ftp), so:

```
# ipfwadm -a deny -P tcp -S 0/0 20 -D 172.16.1.0/24 -y
# ipfwadm -a accept -P tcp -S 172.16.1.0/24 -D 0/0 20 -b
#
# ipfwadm -a deny -P tcp -S 0/0 21 -D 172.16.1.0/24 -y
# ipfwadm -a accept -P tcp -S 172.16.1.0/24 -D 0/0 21 -b
```

Right? Well, not necessarily. FTP servers can operate in two different modes: passive mode and active mode.* In passive mode, the FTP server listens for a connection from the client. In active mode, the server actually makes the connection to the client. Active mode is usually the default. The differences are illustrated in Figure 9-3.

Many FTP servers make their data connection from port 20 when operating in active mode, which simplifies things for us a little, but unfortunately not all do.†

But how does this affect us? Take a look at our rule for port 20, the FTP-data port. The rule as we have it now assumes that the connection will be made by our client to the server. This will work if we use passive mode. But it is very difficult for us to configure a satisfactory rule to allow FTP active mode, because we may not know in advance what ports will be used. If we open up our firewall to allow incoming connections on any port, we are exposing our network to attack on all services that accept connections.

The dilemna is most safely resolved by insisting that our users operate in passive mode. Most FTP servers and many FTP clients will operate this way. The popular *ncftp* client also supports passive mode, but it may require a small configuration change to make it default to passive mode. Many World Wide Web browsers such as the Netscape browser also support passive mode FTP, so it shouldn't be too hard to find appropriate software to use. Alternatively, you can avoid the issue entirely by using an FTP proxy server that accepts a connection from the internal network and establishes connections to the outside network.

---

* FTP active mode is somewhat nonintuitively enabled using the *PORT* command. FTP passive mode is enabled using the *PASV* command.

† The ProFTPd daemon is a good example of an FTP server that doesn't, at least in older versions.

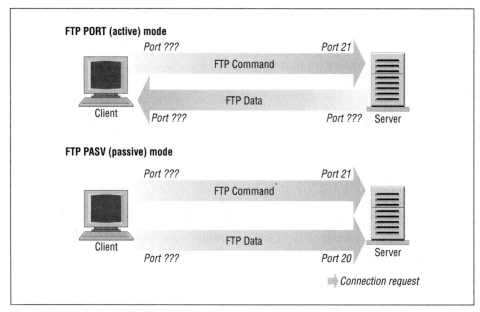

Figure 9-3. FTP server modes

In building your firewall, you will probably find a number of these sorts of problems. You should always give careful thought to how a service actually operates to be sure you have put in place an appropriate ruleset for it. A real firewall configuration can be quite complex.

Summary of ipfwadm Arguments

The *ipfwadm* has many different arguments that relate to IP firewall configuration. The general syntax is:

```
ipfwadm category command parameters [options]
```

Let's take a look at each of these.

Categories

One and only one of the following must be supplied. The category tells the firewall what sort of firewall rule you are configuring:

-I   Input rule

-O   Output rule

-F   Forwarding rule

Commands

At least one of the following must be supplied and applies only to those rules that relate to the supplied category. The command tells the firewall what action to take.

-a [policy]
>   Append a new rule

-i [policy]
>   Insert a new rule

-d [policy]
>   Delete an existing rule

-p policy
>   Set the default policy

-l   List all existing rules

-f   Flush all existing rules

The policies relevant to IP firewall and their meanings are:

accept
>   Allows matching datagrams to be received, forwarded, or transmitted

deny
>   Blocks matching datagrams from being received, forwarded, or transmitted

reject
>   Blocks matching datagrams from being received, forwarded, or transmitted, and sends the host that sent the datagram and ICMP error message

Parameters

At least one of the following must be supplied. Use the parameters to specify to which datagrams this rule applies:

-P protocol
>   Can be TCP, UDP, ICMP, or all. Example:

```
-P tcp
```

-S address[/mask] [port]

> Source IP address that this rule will match. A netmask of "/32" will be assumed if you don't supply one. You may optionally specify which ports this rule will apply to. You must also specify the protocol using the *-P* argument described above for this to work. If you don't specify a port or port range, "all" ports will be assumed to match. Ports may be specified by name, using their */etc/services* entry if you wish. In the case of the ICMP protocol, the port field is used to indicate the ICMP datagram types. Port ranges may be described; use the general syntax: `lowport:highport`. Here is an example:

> `-S 172.29.16.1/24 ftp:ftp-data`

-D address[/mask] [port]

> Specify the destination IP address that this rule will match. The destination address is coded with the same rules as the source address described previously. Here is an example:

> `-D 172.29.16.1/24 smtp`

-V address

> Specify the address of the network interface on which the packet is received (*-I*) or is being sent (*-O*). This allows us to create rules that apply only to certain network interfaces on our machine. Here is an example:

> `-V 172.29.16.1`

-W name

> Specify the name of the network interface. This argument works in the same way as the *-V* argument, except you supply the device name instead of its address. Here is an example:

> `-W ppp0`

Optional arguments

These arguments are sometimes very useful:

-b This is used for bidirectional mode. This flag matches traffic flowing in either direction between the specified source and destination. This saves you from having to create two rules: one for the forward direction of a connection and one for the reverse.

-o This enables logging of matching datagrams to the kernel log. Any datagram that matches this rule will be logged as a kernel message. This is useful to enable you to detect unauthorized access.

-*y*   This is used to match TCP connect datagrams. The option causes the rule to match only datagrams that attempt to establish TCP connections. Only datagrams that have their SYN bit set, but their ACK bit unset, will match. This is useful to filter TCP connection attempts and is ignored for other protocols.

-*k*   This is used to match TCP acknowledgement datagrams. This option causes the rule to match only datagrams that are acknowledgements to packets attempting to establish TCP connections. Only datagrams that have their ACK bit set will match. This is useful to filter TCP connection attempts and is ignored for all other protocols.

ICMP datagram types

Each of the firewall configuration commands allows you to specify ICMP datagram types. Unlike TCP and UDP ports, there is no convenient configuration file that lists the datagram types and their meanings. The ICMP datagram types are defined in RFC-1700, the Assigned Numbers RFC. The ICMP datagram types are also listed in one of the standard C library header files. The */usr/include/netinet/ip_icmp.h* file, which belongs to the GNU standard library package and is used by C programmers when writing network software that uses the ICMP protocol, also defines the ICMP datagram types. For your convenience, we've listed them in Table 9-2. The *iptables* command interface allows you to specify ICMP types by name, so we've listed the mnemonics it uses, as well.

Table 9-2. ICMP Datagram Types

Type Number	iptables Mnemonic	Type Description
0	echo-reply	Echo Reply
3	destination-unreachable	Destination Unreachable
4	source-quench	Source Quench
5	redirect	Redirect
8	echo-request	Echo Request
11	time-exceeded	Time Exceeded
12	parameter-problem	Parameter Problem
13	timestamp-request	Timestamp Request
14	timestamp-reply	Timestamp Reply
15	none	Information Request
16	none	Information Reply
17	address-mask-request	Address Mask Request
18	address-mask-reply	Address Mask Reply

IP Firewall Chains (2.2 Kernels)

Most aspects of Linux are evolving to meet the increasing demands of its users; IP firewall is no exception. The traditional IP firewall implementation is fine for most applications, but can be clumsy and inefficient to configure for complex environments. To solve this problem, a new method of configuring IP firewall and related features was developed. This new method was called "IP Firewall Chains" and was first released for general use in the 2.2.0 Linux kernel.

The IP Firewall Chains support was developed by Paul Russell and Michael Neuling.* Paul has documented the IP Firewall Chains software in the IPCHAINS-HOWTO.

IP Firewall Chains allows you to develop classes of firewall rules to which you may then add and remove hosts or networks. An artifact of firewall rule chaining is that it may improve firewall performance in configurations in which there are lots of rules.

IP Firewall Chains are supported by the 2.2 series kernels and are also available as a patch against the 2.0.* kernels. The HOWTO describes where to obtain the patch and provides lots of useful hints about how to effectively use the *ipchains* configuration utility.

Using ipchains

There are two ways you can use the *ipchains* utility. The first way is to make use of the *ipfwadm-wrapper* shell script, which is mostly a drop-in replacement for *ipfwadm* that drives the *ipchains* program in the background. If you want to do this, then read no further. Instead, reread the previous sections describing *ipfwadm*, and substitute *ipfwadm-wrapper* in its place. This will work, but there is no guarantee that the script will be maintained, and you will not be taking advantage of any of the advanced features that the IP Firewall Chains have to offer.

The second way to use *ipchains* is to learn its new syntax and modify any existing configurations you have to use the new syntax instead of the old. With some careful consideration, you may find you can optimize your configuration as you convert. The *ipchains* syntax is easier to learn than the *ipfwadm*, so this is a good option.

The *ipfwadm* manipulated three rulesets for the purpose of configuring firewalling. With IP Firewall Chains you can create arbitrary numbers of rulesets, each linked to one another, but there are three rulesets related to firewalling that are always present. The standard rulesets are direct equivalents of those used with *ipfwadm*, except they have names: `input`, `forward` and `output`.

---

* Paul can be reached at *Paul.Russell@rustcorp.com.au.*

Let's first look at the general syntax of the *ipchains* command, then we'll look at how we'd use *ipchains* instead of *ipfwadm* without worrying about any of the advanced chaining features. We'll do this by revisiting our previous examples.

ipchains Command Syntax

The *ipchains* command syntax is straightforward. We'll now look at the most important of those. The general syntax of most *ipchains* commands is:

```
ipchains command rule-specification options
```

Commands

There are a number of ways we can manipulate rules and rulesets with the *ipchains* command. Those relevant to IP firewalling are:

-A chain

Append one or more rules to the end of the nominated chain. If a hostname is supplied as either source or destination and it resolves to more than one IP address, a rule will be added for each address.

-I chain rulenum

Insert one or more rules to the start of the nominated chain. Again, if a hostname is supplied in the rule specification, a rule will be added for each of the addresses it resolves to.

-D chain

Delete one or more rules from the specified chain that matches the rule specification.

-D chain rulenum

Delete the rule residing at position `rulenum` in the specified chain. Rule positions start at one for the first rule in the chain.

-R chain rulenum

Replace the rule residing at position `rulenum` in the specific chain with the supplied rule specification.

-C chain

Check the datagram described by the rule specification against the specific chain. This command will return a message describing how the datagram was processed by the chain. This is very useful for testing your firewall configuration, and we look at it in detail a little later.

-L [chain]

List the rules of the specified chain, or for all chains if no chain is specified.

-F [chain]

Flush the rules of the specified chain, or for all chains if no chain is specified.

-Z [chain]

Zero the datagram and byte counters for all rules of the specified chain, or for all chains if no chain is specified.

-N chain

Create a new chain with the specified name. A chain of the same name must not already exist. This is how user-defined chains are created.

-X [chain]

Delete the specified user-defined chain, or all user-defined chains if no chain is specified. For this command to be successful, there must be no references to the specified chain from any other rules chain.

-P chain policy

Set the default policy of the specified chain to the specified policy. Valid fire-walling policies are `ACCEPT`, `DENY`, `REJECT`, `REDIR`, or `RETURN`. `ACCEPT`, `DENY`, and `REJECT` have the same meanings as those for the tradition IP fire-wall implementation. `REDIR` specifies that the datagram should be transparently redirected to a port on the firewall host. The `RETURN` target causes the IP firewall code to return to the Firewall Chain that called the one containing this rule and continues starting at the rule after the calling rule.

Rule specification parameters

A number of *ipchains* parameters create a rule specification by determining what types of packets match. If any of these parameters is omitted from a rule specification, its default is assumed:

-p [!]protocol

Specifies the protocol of the datagram that will match this rule. Valid protocol names are `tcp`, `udp`, `icmp`, or `all`. You may also specify a protocol number here to match other protocols. For example, you might use `4` to match the `ipip` encapsulation protocol. If the `!` is supplied, the rule is negated and the datagram will match any protocol other than the protocol specified. If this parameter isn't supplied, it will default to `all`.

-s [!]address[/mask] [!] [port]

Specifies the source address and port of the datagram that will match this rule. The address may be supplied as a hostname, a network name, or an IP address. The optional `mask` is the netmask to use and may be supplied either in the traditional form (e.g., /255.255.255.0) or the modern form (e.g., /24).

The optional `port` specifies the TCP or UDP port, or the ICMP datagram type that will match. You may supply a port specification only if you've supplied the *-p* parameter with one of the `tcp`, `udp`, or `icmp` protocols. Ports may be specified as a range by specifying the upper and lower limits of the range with a colon as a delimiter. For example, `20:25` described all of the ports numbered from 20 up to and including 25. Again, the `!` character may be used to negate the values.

-d [!]address[/mask] [!] [port]

Specifies the destination address and port of the datagram that will match this rule. The coding of this parameter is the same as that of the *-s* parameter.

-j target

Specifies the action to take when this rule matches. You can think of this parameter as meaning "jump to." Valid targets are ACCEPT, DENY, REJECT, REDIR, and RETURN. We described the meanings of each of these targets earlier. However, you may also specify the name of a user-defined chain where processing will continue. If this parameter is omitted, no action is taken on matching rule datagrams at all other than to update the datagram and byte counters.

-i [!]interface-name

Specifies the interface on which the datagram was received or is to be transmitted. Again, the `!` inverts the result of the match. If the interface name ends with +, then any interface that begins with the supplied string will match. For example, `-i ppp+` would match any PPP network device and `-i ! eth+` would match all interfaces except Ethernet devices.

[!] -f

Specifies that this rule applies to everything but the first fragment of a fragmented datagram.

Options

The following *ipchains* options are more general in nature. Some of them control rather esoteric features of the IP chains software:

-b Causes the command to generate two rules. One rule matches the parameters supplied, and the other rule added matches the corresponding parameters in the reverse direction.

-v Causes *ipchains* to be verbose in its output. It will supply more information.

-n Causes *ipchains* to display IP address and ports as numbers without attempting to resolve them to their corresponding names.

-l   Enables kernel logging of matching datagrams. Any datagram that matches the rule will be logged by the kernel using its *printk( )* function, which is usually handled by the *syslogd* program and written to a log file. This is useful for making unusual datagrams visible.

-o[maxsize]

Causes the IP chains software to copy any datagrams matching the rule to the userspace "netlink" device. The maxsize argument limits the number of bytes from each datagram that are passed to the netlink device. This option is of most use to software developers, but may be exploited by software packages in the future.

-m markvalue

Causes matching datagrams to be *marked* with a value. Mark values are unsigned 32-bit numbers. In existing implementations this does nothing, but at some point in the future, it may determine how the datagram is handled by other software such as the routing code. If a markvalue begins with a + or −, the value is added or subtracted from the existing markvalue.

-t andmask xormask

Enables you to manipulate the "type of service" bits in the IP header of any datagram that matches this rule. The type of service bits are used by intelligent routers to prioritize datagrams before forwarding them. The Linux routing software is capable of this sort prioritization. The **andmask** and **xormask** represent bit masks that will be logically ANDed and ORed with the type of service bits of the datagram respectively. This is an advanced feature that is discussed in more detail in the IPCHAINS-HOWTO.

-x   Causes any numbers in the *ipchains* output to be expanded to their exact values with no rounding.

-y   Causes the rule to match any TCP datagram with the SYN bit set and the ACK and FIN bits clear. This is used to filter TCP connection requests.

Our Naïve Example Revisited

Let's again suppose that we have a network in our organization and that we are using a Linux-based firewall machine to allow our users access to WWW servers on the Internet, but to allow no other traffic to be passed.

If our network has a 24-bit network mask (class C) and has an address of 172.16.1.0, we'd use the following *ipchains* rules:

```
# ipchains -F forward
# ipchains -P forward DENY
# ipchains -A forward -s 0/0 80 -d 172.16.1.0/24 -p tcp -y -j DENY
# ipchains -A forward -s 172.16.1.0/24 -d 0/0 80 -p tcp -b -j ACCEPT
```

The first of the commands flushes all of the rules from the forward rulesets and the second set of commands sets the default policy of the forward ruleset to DENY. Finally, the third and fourth commands do the specific filtering we want. The fourth command allows datagrams to and from web servers on the outside of our network to pass, and the third prevents incoming TCP connections with a source port of 80.

If we now wanted to add rules that allowed passive mode only access to FTP servers in the outside network, we'd add these rules:

```
# ipchains -A forward -s 0/0 20 -d 172.16.1.0/24 -p tcp -y -j DENY
# ipchains -A forward -s 172.16.1.0/24 -d 0/0 20 -p tcp -b -j ACCEPT
# ipchains -A forward -s 0/0 21 -d 172.16.1.0/24 -p tcp -y -j DENY
# ipchains -A forward -s 172.16.1.0/24 -d 0/0 21 -p tcp -b -j ACCEPT
```

Listing Our Rules with ipchains

To list our rules with *ipchains*, we use its *-L* argument. Just as with *ipfwadm*, there are arguments that control the amount of detail in the output. In its simplest form, *ipchains* produces output that looks like:

```
# ipchains -L -n
Chain input (policy ACCEPT):
Chain forward (policy DENY):
target     prot opt     source              destination         ports
DENY       tcp  -y----  0.0.0.0/0           172.16.1.0/24       80 ->    *
ACCEPT     tcp  ------  172.16.1.0/24       0.0.0.0/0           * ->     80
ACCEPT     tcp  ------  0.0.0.0/0           172.16.1.0/24       80 ->    *
ACCEPT     tcp  ------  172.16.1.0/24       0.0.0.0/0           * ->     20
ACCEPT     tcp  ------  0.0.0.0/0           172.16.1.0/24       20 ->    *
ACCEPT     tcp  ------  172.16.1.0/24       0.0.0.0/0           * ->     21
ACCEPT     tcp  ------  0.0.0.0/0           172.16.1.0/24       21 ->    *

Chain output (policy ACCEPT):
```

If you don't supply the name of a chain to list, *ipchains* will list all rules in all chains. The −n argument in our example tells *ipchains* not to attempt to convert any address or ports into names. The information presented should be self-explanatory.

A verbose form, invoked by the *-u* option, provides much more detail. Its output adds fields for the datagram and byte counters, Type of Service *AND* and *XOR* flags, the interface name, the mark, and the outsize.

All rules created with *ipchains* have datagram and byte counters associated with them. This is how IP Accounting is implemented and will be discussed in detail in Chapter 10. By default these counters are presented in a rounded form using the suffixes K and M to represent units of one thousand and one million, respectively. If the −x argument is supplied, the counters are expanded to their full unrounded form.

Making Good Use of Chains

You now know that the *ipchains* command is a replacement for the *ipfwadm* with a simpler command-line syntax and some interesting enhancements, but you're no doubt wanting to know where you'd use the user-defined chains and why. You'll also probably want to know how to use the support scripts that accompany the *ipchains* command in its software package. We'll now explore these subjects and address the questions.

User-defined chains

The three rulesets of the traditional IP firewall code provided a mechanism for building firewall configurations that were fairly simple to understand and manage for small networks with simple firewalling requirements. When the configuration requirements are not simple, a number of problems become apparent. Firstly, large networks often require much more than the small number of firewalling rules we've seen so far; inevitably needs arise that require firewalling rules added to cover special case scenarios. As the number of rules grows, the performance of the firewall deteriorates as more and more tests are conducted on each datagram and managability becomes an issue. Secondly, it is not possible to enable and disable sets of rules atomically; instead, you are forced to expose yourself to attack while you are in the middle of rebuilding your ruleset.

The design of IP Firewall Chains helps to alleviate these problems by allowing the network administrator to create arbitrary sets of firwewall rules that we can link to the three inbuilt rulesets. We can use the *-N* option of *ipchains* to create a new chain with any name we please of eight characters or less. (Restricting the name to lowercase letters only is probably a good idea.) The *-j* option configures the action to take when a datagram matches the rule specification. The *-j* option specifies that if a datagram matches a rule, further testing should be performed against a user-defined chain. We'll illustrate this with a diagram.

Consider the following *ipchains* commands:

```
ipchains -P input DENY
ipchains -N tcpin
ipchains -A tcpin -s ! 172.16.0.0/16
ipchains -A tcpin -p tcp -d 172.16.0.0/16 ssh -j ACCEPT
ipchains -A tcpin -p tcp -d 172.16.0.0/16 www -j ACCEPT
ipchains -A input -p tcp -j tcpin
ipchains -A input -p all
```

We set the default input chain policy to deny. The second command creates a user-defined chain called "tcpin." The third command adds a rule to the tcpin chain that matches any datagram that was sourced from outside our local network; the rule takes no action. This rule is an accounting rule and will be discussed in more detail in Chapter 10. The next two rules match any datagram that is destined for our local network and either of the **ssh** or **www** ports; datagrams matching these rules are accepted. The next rule is when the real *ipchains* magic begins. It causes the firewall software to check any datagram of protocol TCP against the tcpin user-defined chain. Lastly, we add a rule to our **input** chain that matches any datagram; this is another accounting rule. They will produce the following Firewall Chains shown in Figure 9-4.

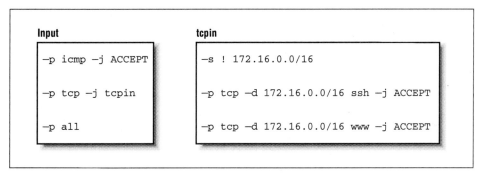

Figure 9-4. A simple IP chain ruleset

Our **input** and **tcpin** chains are populated with our rules. Datagram processing always beings at one of the inbuilt chains. We'll see how our user-defined chain is called into play by following the processing path of different types of datagrams.

First, let's look at what happens when a UDP datagram for one of our hosts is received. Figure 9-5 illustrates the flow through the rules.

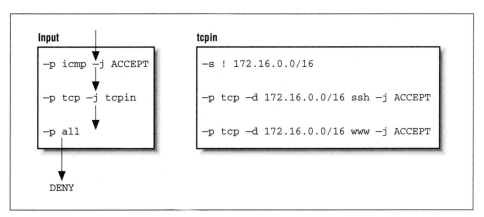

Figure 9-5. The sequence of rules tested for a received UDP datagram

The datagram is received by the **input** chain and falls through the first two rules because they match ICMP and TCP protocols, respectively. It matches the third rule in the input chain, but it doesn't specify a target, so its datagram and byte counters are updated, but no other action takes place. The datagram reaches the end of the input chain, meets with the default input chain policy, and is denied.

To see our user-defined chain in operation, let's now consider what happens when we receive a TCP datagram destined for the ssh port of one of our hosts. The sequence is shown in Figure 9-6.

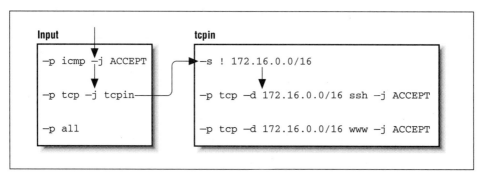

Figure 9-6. The rules flow for a received TCP datagram for ssh

This time the second rule in the input chain does match and it specifies a target of tcpin, our user-defined chain. Specifying a user-defined chain as a target causes the datagram to be tested against the rules in that chain, so the next rule tested is the first rule in the tcpin chain. The first rule matches any datagram that has a source address outside our local network and specifies no target, so it too is an accounting rule and testing falls through to the next rule. The second rule in our tcpin chain does match and specifies a target of ACCEPT. We have arrived at target, so no further firewall processing occurs. The datagram is accepted.

Finally, let's look at what happens when we reach the end of a user-defined chain. To see this, we'll map the flow for a TCP datagram destined for a port other than than the two we are handling specifically, as shown in Figure 9-7.

The user-defined chains do not have default policies. When all rules in a user-defined chain have been tested, and none have matched, the firewall code acts as though a RETURN rule were present, so if this isn't what you want, you should ensure you supply a rule at the end of the user-defined chain that takes whatever action you wish. In our example, our testing returns to the rule in the input rule-set immediately following the one that moved us to our user-defined chain. Eventually we reach the end of the input chain, which does have a default policy and our datagram is denied.

This example is very simple, but illustrates our point. A more practical use of IP chains would be much more complex. A slightly more sophisticated example is provided in the following list of commands:

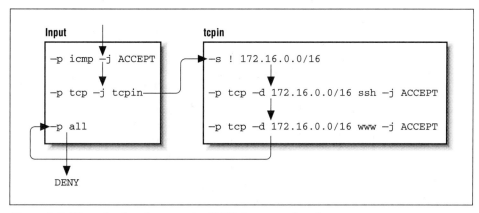

Figure 9-7. The rules flow for a received TCP datagram for telnet

```
#
# Set default forwarding policy to REJECT
ipchains -P forward REJECT
#
# create our user-defined chains
ipchains -N sshin
ipchains -N sshout
ipchains -N wwwin
ipchains -N wwwout
#
# Ensure we reject connections coming the wrong way
ipchains -A wwwin -p tcp -s 172.16.0.0/16 -y -j REJECT
ipchains -A wwwout -p tcp -d 172.16.0.0/16 -y -j REJECT
ipchains -A sshin -p tcp -s 172.16.0.0/16 -y -j REJECT
ipchains -A sshout -p tcp -d 172.16.0.0/16 -y -j REJECT
#
# Ensure that anything reaching the end of a user-defined chain is rejected.
ipchains -A sshin -j REJECT
ipchains -A sshout -j REJECT
ipchains -A wwwin -j REJECT
ipchains -A wwwout -j REJECT
#
# divert www and ssh services to the relevant user-defined chain
ipchains -A forward -p tcp -d 172.16.0.0/16 ssh -b -j sshin
ipchains -A forward -p tcp -s 172.16.0.0/16 -d 0/0 ssh -b -j sshout
ipchains -A forward -p tcp -d 172.16.0.0/16 www -b -j wwwin
ipchains -A forward -p tcp -s 172.16.0.0/16 -d 0/0 www -b -j wwwout
#
# Insert our rules to match hosts at position two in our user-defined chains.
ipchains -I wwwin 2 -d 172.16.1.2 -b -j ACCEPT
ipchains -I wwwout 2 -s 172.16.1.0/24 -b -j ACCEPT
ipchains -I sshin 2 -d 172.16.1.4 -b -j ACCEPT
```

```
ipchains -I sshout 2 -s 172.16.1.4 -b -j ACCEPT
ipchains -I sshout 2 -s 172.16.1.6 -b -j ACCEPT
#
```

In this example, we've used a selection of user-defined chains both to simplify management of our firewall configuration and improve the efficiency of our firewall as compared to a solution involving only the built-in chains.

Our example creates user-defined chains for each of the **ssh** and **www** services in each connection direction. The chain called **wwwout** is where we place rules for hosts that are allowed to make outgoing World Wide Web connections, and **sshin** is where we define rules for hosts to which we want to allow incoming ssh connections. We've assumed that we have a requirement to allow and deny individual hosts on our network the ability to make or receive **ssh** and **www** connections. The simplication occurs because the user-defined chains allow us to neatly group the rules for the host incoming and outgoing permissions rather than muddling them all together. The improvement in efficiency occurs because for any particular datagram, we have reduced the average number of tests required before a target is found. The efficiency gain increases as we add more hosts. If we hadn't used user-defined chains, we'd potentially have to search the whole list of rules to determine what action to take with each and every datagram received. Even if we assume that each of the rules in our list matches an equal proportion of the total number of datagrams processed, we'd still be searching half the list on average. User-defined chains allow us to avoid testing large numbers of rules if the datagram being tested doesn't match the simple rule in the built-in chain that jumps to them.

The ipchains support scripts

The *ipchains* software package is supplied with three support scripts. The first of these we've discussed briefly already, while the remaining two provide an easy and convenient means of saving and restoring your firewall configuration.

The *ipfwadm-wrapper* script emulates the command-line syntax of the *ipfwadm* command, but drives the *ipchains* command to build the firewall rules. This is a convenient way to migrate your existing firewall configuration to the kernel or an alternative to learning the *ipchains* syntax. The *ipfwadm-wrapper* script behaves differently from the *ipfwadm* command in two ways: firstly, because the *ipchains* command doesn't support specification of an interface by address, the *ipfwadm-wrapper* script accepts an argument of *-V* but attempts to convert it into the *ipchains* equivalent of a *-W* by searching for the interface name configured with the supplied address. The *ipfwadm-wrapper* script will always provide a warning when you use the *-V* option to remind you of this. Secondly, fragment accounting rules are not translated correctly.

The *ipchains-save* and *ipchains-restore* scripts make building and modifying a firewall configuration much simpler. The *ipchains-save* command reads the current firewall configuration and writes a simplified form to the standard output. The *ipchains-restore* command reads data in the output format of the *ipchains-save* command and configures the IP firewall with these rules. The advantage of using these scripts over directly modifying your firewall configuration script and testing the configuration is the ability to dynamically build your configuration once and then save it. You can then restore that configuration, modify it, and resave it as you please.

To use the scripts, you'd enter something like:

```
ipchains-save >/var/state/ipchains/firewall.state
```

to save your current firewall configuration. You'd restore it, perhaps at boot time, with:

```
ipchains-restore </var/state/ipchains/firewall.state
```

The *ipchains-restore* script checks if any user-defined chain listed in its input already exists. If you've supplied the `-f` argument, it will automatically flush the rules from the user-defined chain before configuring those in the input. The default behavior asks you whether to skip this chain or to flush it.

Netfilter and IP Tables (2.4 Kernels)

While developing IP Firewall Chains, Paul Russell decided that IP firewalling should be less difficult; he soon set about the task of simplifying aspects of datagram processing in the kernel firewalling code and produced a filtering framework that was both much cleaner and much more flexible. He called this new framework *netfilter*.

At the time of preparation of this book the *netfilter* design had not yet stabilized. We hope you'll forgive any errors in the description of *netfilter* or its associated configuration tools that result from changes that occurred after preparation of this material. We considered the *netfilter* work important enough to justify the inclusion of this material, despite parts of it being speculative in nature. If you're in any doubt, the relevant HOWTO documents will contain the most accurate and up-to-date information on the detailed issues associated with the *netfilter* configuration.

So what was wrong with IP chains? They vastly improved the efficiency and management of firewall rules. But the way they processed datagrams was still complex, especially in conjunction with firewall-related features like IP masquerade (discussed in Chapter 11) and other forms of address translation. Part of this complexity existed because IP masquerade and Network Address Translation were developed independently of the IP firewalling code and integrated later, rather than having been designed as a true part of the firewall code from the start. If a developer wanted to add yet more features in the datagram processing sequence, he would have had difficulty finding a place to insert the code and would have been forced to make changes in the kernel in order to do so.

Still, there were other problems. In particular, the "input" chain described input to the IP networking layer as a whole. The input chain affected both datagrams to be *destined for* this host and datagrams to be *routed by* this host. This was somewhat counterintuitive because it confused the function of the input chain with that of the forward chain, which applied only to datagrams to be forwarded, but which always followed the input chain. If you wanted to treat datagrams for this host differently from datagrams to be forwarded, it was necessary to build complex rules that excluded one or the other. The same problem applied to the output chain.

Inevitably some of this complexity spilled over into the system administrator's job because it was reflected in the way that rulesets had to be designed. Moreover, any extensions to filtering required direct modifications to the kernel, because all filtering policies were implemented there and there was no way of providing a transparent interface into it. *netfilter* addresses both the complexity and the rigidity of older solutions by implementing a generic framework in the kernel that streamlines the way datagrams are processed and provides a capability to extend filtering policy without having to modify the kernel.

Let's take a look at two of the key changes made. Figure 9-8 illustrates how datagrams are processed in the IP chains implementation, while Figure 9-9 illustrates how they are processed in the *netfilter* implementation. The key differences are the removal of the masquerading function from the core code and a change in the locations of the input and output chains. To accompany these changes, a new and extensible configuration tool called *iptables* was created.

In IP chains, the input chain applies to all datagrams received by the host, irrespective of whether they are destined for the local host or routed to some other host. In *netfilter*, the input chain applies *only* to datagrams destined for the local host, and the forward chain applies only to datagrams destined for *another* host. Similarly, in IP chains, the output chain applies to all datagrams leaving the local host, irrespective of whether the datagram is generated on the local host or routed from some other host. In *netfilter*, the output chain applies *only* to datagrams generated on this host and does not apply to datagrams being routed from another host. This change alone offers a huge simplification of many firewall configurations.

In Figure 9-8, the components labeled "demasq" and "masq" are separate kernel components responsible for the incoming and outgoing processing of masqueraded datagrams. These have been reimplemented as *netfilter* modules.

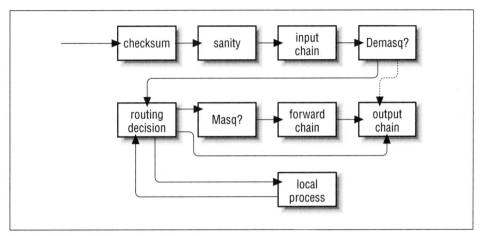

Figure 9-8. Datagram processing chain in IP chains

Consider the case of a configuration for which the default policy for each of the input, forward, and output chains is deny. In IP chains, six rules would be needed to allow any session through a firewall host: two each in the input, forward, and output chains (one would cover each forward path and one would cover each return path). You can imagine how this could easily become extremely complex and difficult to manage when you want to mix sessions that could be routed and sessions that could connect to the local host without being routed. IP chains allow you to create chains that would simplify this task a little, but the design isn't obvious and requires a certain level of expertise.

In the *netfilter* implementation with *iptables*, this complexity disappears completely. For a service to be routed across the firewall host, but not terminate on the local host, only two rules are required: one each for the forward and the reverse directions in the forward chain. This is the obvious way to design firewalling rules, and will serve to simplify the design of firewall configurations immensely.

The PACKET-FILTERING-HOWTO offers a detailed list of the changes that have been made, so let's focus on the more practical aspects here.

Backward Compatability with ipfwadm and ipchains

The remarkable flexibility of Linux *netfilter* is illustrated by its ability to emulate the *ipfwadm* and *ipchains* interfaces. Emulation makes transition to the new generation of firewall software a little easier.

The two *netfilter* kernel modules called *ipfwadm.o* and *ipchains.o* provide backward compatibility for *ipfwadm* and *ipchains*. You may load only one of these

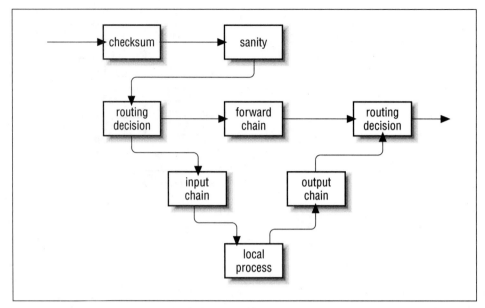

Figure 9-9. Datagram processing chain in netfilter

modules at a time, and use one only if the *ip_tables.o* module is not loaded. When the appropriate module is loaded, *netfilter* works exactly like the former firewall implementation.

netfilter mimics the *ipchains* interface with the following commands:

```
rmmod ip_tables
modprobe ipchains
ipchains ...
```

Using iptables

The *iptables* utility is used to configure *netfilter* filtering rules. Its syntax borrows heavily from the *ipchains* command, but differs in one very significant respect: it is *extensible*. What this means is that its functionality can be extended without recompiling it. It manages this trick by using shared libraries. There are standard extensions and we'll explore some of them in a moment.

Before you can use the *iptables* command, you must load the *netfilter* kernel module that provides support for it. The easiest way to do this is to use the *modprobe* command as follows:

```
modprobe ip_tables
```

The *iptables* command is used to configure both IP filtering and Network Address Translation. To facilitate this, there are two tables of rules called *filter* and *nat*. The filter table is assumed if you do not specify the *-t* option to override it. Five built-in chains are also provided. The `INPUT` and `FORWARD` chains are available for the `filter` table, the `PREROUTING` and `POSTROUTING` chains are available for the `nat` table, and the `OUTPUT` chain is available for both tables. In this chapter we'll discuss only the *filter* table. We'll look at the *nat* table in Chapter 11

The general syntax of most *iptables* commands is:

```
iptables command rule-specification extensions
```

Now we'll take a look at some options in detail, after which we'll review some examples.

Commands

There are a number of ways we can manipulate rules and rulesets with the *iptables* command. Those relevant to IP firewalling are:

-A chain

> Append one or more rules to the end of the nominated chain. If a hostname is supplied as either a source or destination and it resolves to more than one IP address, a rule will be added for each address.

-I chain rulenum

> Insert one or more rules to the start of the nominated chain. Again, if a hostname is supplied in the rule specification, a rule will be added for each of the addresses to which it resolves.

-D chain

> Delete one or more rules from the specified chain matching the rule specification.

-D chain rulenum

> Delete the rule residing at position `rulenum` in the specified chain. Rule positions start at 1 for the first rule in the chain.

-R chain rulenum

> Replace the rule residing at position `rulenum` in the specific chain with the supplied rule specification.

-C chain

> Check the datagram described by the rule specification against the specific chain. This command will return a message describing how the chain processed the datagram. This is very useful for testing your firewall configuration and we will look at it in detail later.

-L [chain]

> List the rules of the specified chain, or for all chains if no chain is specified.

-F [chain]

> Flush the rules of the specified chain, or for all chains if no chain is specified.

-Z [chain]

> Zero the datagram and byte counters for all rules of the specified chain, or for all chains if no chain is specified.

-N chain

> Create a new chain with the specified name. A chain of the same name must not already exist. This is how user-defined chains are created.

-X [chain]

> Delete the specified user-defined chain, or all user-defined chains if no chain is specified. For this command to be successful, there must be no references to the specified chain from any other rules chain.

-P chain policy

> Set the default policy of the specified chain to the specified policy. Valid firewalling policies are ACCEPT, DROP, QUEUE, and RETURN. ACCEPT allows the datagram to pass. DROP causes the datagram to be discarded. QUEUE causes the datagram to be passed to userspace for further processing. The RETURN target causes the IP firewall code to return to the Firewall Chain that called the one containing this rule, and continue starting at the rule after the calling rule.

Rule specification parameters

There are a number of *iptables* parameters that constitute a rule specification. Wherever a rule specification is required, each of these parameters must be supplied or their default will be assumed.

-p [!]protocol

> Specifies the protocol of the datagram that will match this rule. Valid protocol names are tcp, udp, icmp, or a number, if you know the IP protocol number.* For example, you might use 4 to match the ipip encapsulation protocol. If the ! character is supplied, the rule is negated and the datagram will match any protocol other than the specified protocol. If this parameter isn't supplied, it will default to match all protocols.

-s [!]address[/mask]

> Specifies the source address of the datagram that will match this rule. The address may be supplied as a hostname, a network name, or an IP address. The optional mask is the netmask to use and may be supplied either in the traditional form (e.g., /255.255.255.0) or in the modern form (e.g., /24).

---

* Take a look at */etc/protocols* for protocol names and numbers.

-d [!]address[/mask]

> Specifies the destination address and port of the datagram that will match this rule. The coding of this parameter is the same as that of the *-s* parameter.

-j target

> Specifies what action to take when this rule matches. You can think of this parameter as meaning "jump to." Valid targets are ACCEPT, DROP, QUEUE, and RETURN. We described the meanings of each of these previously in the "Commands" section. You may also specify the name of a user-defined chain where processing will continue. You may also supply the name of a target supplied by an extension. We'll talk about extensions shortly. If this parameter is omitted, no action is taken on matching datagrams at all, other than to update the datagram and byte counters of this rule.

-i [!]interface-name

> Specifies the interface on which the datagram was received. Again, the ! inverts the result of the match. If the interface name ends with "+" then any interface that begins with the supplied string will match. For example, -i ppp+ would match any PPP network device and -i ! eth+ would match all interfaces except ethernet devices.

-o [!]interface-name

> Specifies the interface on which the datagram is to be transmitted. This argument has the same coding as the *-i* argument.

[!] -f

> Specifies that this rule applies only to the second and later fragments of a fragmented datagram, not to the first fragment.

Options

The following *iptables* options are more general in nature. Some of them control rather esoteric features of the *netfilter* software.

-v   causes *iptables* to be verbose in its output; it will supply more information.

-n   causes *iptables* to display IP address and ports as numbers without attempting to resolve them to their corresponding names.

-x   causes any numbers in the *iptables* output to be expanded to their exact values with no rounding.

- -line-numbers

> causes line numbers to be displayed when listing rulesets. The line number will correspond to the rule's position within the chain.

Extensions

We said earlier that the *iptables* utility is extensible through optional shared library modules. There are some standard extensions that provide some of the features *ipchains* provided. To make use of an extension, you must specify its name through the *-m name* argument to *iptables*. The following list shows the *-m* and *-p* options that set up the extension's context, and the options provided by that extension.

TCP Extensions: used with -m tcp -p tcp

- -sport [!] [port[:port]]
> Specifies the port that the datagram source must be using to match this rule. Ports may be specified as a range by specifying the upper and lower limits of the range using the colon as a delimiter. For example, 20:25 described all of the ports numbered 20 up to and including 25. Again, the ! character may be used to negate the values.

- -dport [!] [port[:port]]
> Specifies the port that the datagram destination must be using to match this rule. The argument is coded identically to the - -sport option.

- -tcp-flags [!] mask comp
> Specifies that this rule should match when the TCP flags in the datagram match those specified by *mask* and *comp*. *mask* is a comma-separated list of flags that should be examined when making the test. *comp* is a comma-separated list of flags that must be set for the rule to match. Valid flags are: *SYN, ACK, FIN, RST, URG, PSH, ALL* or *NONE*. This is an advanced option: refer to a good description of the TCP protocol, such as RFC-793, for a description of the meaning and implication of each of these flags. The ! character negates the rule.

[!] - -syn
> Specifies the rule to match only datagrams with the SYN bit set and the ACK and FIN bits cleared. Datagrams with these options are used to open TCP connections, and this option can therefore be used to manage connection requests. This option is shorthand for:
>
> ```
> - -tcp-flags SYN,RST,ACK SYN
> ```
>
> When you use the negation operator, the rule will match all datagrams that do not have both the SYN and ACK bits set.

UDP Extensions: used with -m udp -p udp

- -sport [!] [port[:port]]
> Specifies the port that the datagram source must be using to match this rule. Ports may be specified as a range by specifying the upper and lower limits of

the range using the colon as a delimiter. For example, 20:25 describes all of the ports numbered 20 up to and including 25. Again, the ! character may be used to negate the values.

- *-dport [!] [port[:port]]*

    Specifies the port that the datagram destination must be using to match this rule. The argument is coded identically to the - *-sport* option.

ICMP Extensions: used with -m icmp -p icmp

- *-icmp-type [!] typename*

    Specifies the ICMP message type that this rule will match. The type may be specified by number or name. Some valid names are: echo-request, echo-reply, source-quench, time-exceeded, destination-unreachable, network-unreachable, host-unreachable, protocol-unreachable, and port-unreachable.

MAC Extensions: used with -m mac

- *-mac-source [!] address*

    Specifies the host's Ethernet address that transmitted the datagram that this rule will match. This only makes sense in a rule in the input or forward chains because we will be transmitting any datagram that passes the output chain.

Our Naïve Example Revisited, Yet Again

To implement our naïve example using the *netfilter*, you could simply load the *ipchains.o* module and pretend it is the *ipchains* version. Instead, we'll reimplement it using *iptables* to illustrate how similar it is.

Yet again, let's suppose that we have a network in our organization and that we are using a Linux-based firewall machine to allow our users to be able to access WWW servers on the Internet, but to allow no other traffic to be passed.

If our network has a 24-bit network mask (class C) and has an address of 172.16.1.0, then we'd use the following *iptables* rules:

```
# modprobe ip_tables
# iptables -F FORWARD
# iptables -P FORWARD DROP
# iptables -A FORWARD -m tcp -p tcp -s 0/0 --sport 80 -d 172.16.1.0/24 /
    --syn -j DROP
# iptables -A FORWARD -m tcp -p tcp -s 172.16.1.0/24 --sport /
    80 -d 0/0 -j ACCEPT
# iptables -A FORWARD -m tcp -p tcp -d 172.16.1.0/24 --dport 80 -s 0/0 -j /
    ACCEPT
```

In this example the *iptables* commands are interpreted exactly as the equivalent *ipchains* commands. The major exception that the *ip_tables.o* module must load. Note that *iptables* doesn't support the *-b* option, so we must supply a rule for each direction.

TOS Bit Manipulation

The Type Of Service (TOS) bits are a set of four-bit flags in the IP header. When any one of these bit flags is set, routers may handle the datagram differently than datagrams with no TOS bits set. Each of the four bits has a different purpose and only one of the TOS bits may be set at any time, so combinations are not allowed. The bit flags are called Type of Service bits because they enable the application transmitting the data to tell the network the type of network service it requires.

The classes of network service available are:

Minimum delay
> Used when the time it takes for a datagram to travel from the source host to destination host (latency) is most important. A network provider might, for example, use both optical fiber and satellite network connections. Data carried across satellite connections has farther to travel and their latency is generally therefore higher than for terrestrial-based network connections between the same endpoints. A network provider might choose to ensure that datagrams with this type of service set are not carried by satellite.

Maximum throughput
> Used when the volume of data transmitted in any period of time is important. There are many types of network applications for which latency is not particularly important but the network throughput is; for example, bulk-file transfers. A network provider might choose to route datagrams with this type of service set via high-latency, high-bandwidth routes, such as satellite connections.

Maximum reliability
> Used when it is important that you have some certainty that the data will arrive at the destination without retransmission being required. The IP protocol may be carried over any number of underlying transmission mediums. While SLIP and PPP are adequate datalink protocols, they are not as reliable as carrying IP over some other network, such as an X.25 network. A network provider might make an alternate network available, offering high reliability, to carry IP that would be used if this type of service is selected.

Minimum cost
> Used when it is important to minimize the cost of data transmission. Leasing bandwidth on a satellite for a transpacific crossing is generally less costly than leasing space on a fiber-optical cable over the same distance, so network

providers may choose to provide both and charge differently depending on which you use. In this scenario, your "minimum cost" type of service bit may cause your datagrams to be routed via the lower-cost satellite route.

Setting the TOS Bits Using ipfwadm or ipchains

The *ipfwadm* and *ipchains* commands deal with the TOS bits in much the same manner. In both cases you specify a rule that matches the datagrams with particular TOS bits set, and use the *-t* argument to specify the change you wish to make.

The changes are specified using two-bit masks. The first of these bit masks is logically ANDed with the IP options field of the datagram and the second is logically eXclusive-ORd with it. If this sounds complicated, we'll give you the recipes required to enable each of the types of service in a moment.

The bit masks are specified using eight-bit hexadecimal values. Both *ipfwadm* and *ipchains* use the same argument syntax:

```
-t andmask xormask
```

Fortunately the same mask arguments can be used each time you wish to set a particular type of service, to save you having to work them out. They are presented with some suggested uses in Table 9-3.

Table 9-3. Suggested Uses for TOS Bitmasks

TOS	ANDmask	XORmask	Suggested Use
Minimum Delay	0x01	0x10	ftp, telnet, ssh
Maximum Throughput	0x01	0x08	ftp-data, www
Maximum Reliability	0x01	0x04	snmp, dns
Minimum Cost	0x01	0x02	nntp, smtp

Setting the TOS Bits Using iptables

The *iptables* tool allows you to specify rules that capture only datagrams with TOS bits matching some predetermined value using the *-m tos* option, and for setting the TOS bits of IP datagrams matching a rule using the -j TOS target. You may set TOS bits only on the FORWARD and OUTPUT chains. The matching and the setting occur quite independently. You can configure all sort of interesting rules. For example, you can configure a rule that discads all datagrams with certain TOS bit combinations, or a rule that sets the TOS bits of datagrams only from certain hosts. Most often you will use rules that contain both matching and setting to perform TOS bit translations, just as you could for *ipfwadm* or *ipchains*.

Rather than the complicated two-mask configuration of *ipfwadm* and *ipchains*, *iptables* uses the simpler approach of plainly specifying what the TOS bits should match, or to what the TOS bits should be set. Additionally, rather than having to remember and use the hexadecimal value, you may specify the TOS bits using the more friendly mnemonics listed in the upcoming table.

The general syntax used to match TOS bits looks like:

```
-m tos --tos mnemonic [other-args] -j target
```

The general syntax used to set TOS bits looks like:

```
[other-args] -j TOS --set mnemonic
```

Remember that these would typically be used together, but they can be used quite independently if you have a configuration that requires it.

Mnemonic	Hexadecimal
Normal-Service	0x00
Minimize-Cost	0x02
Maximize-Reliability	0x04
Maximize-Throughput	0x08
Minimize-Delay	0x10

Testing a Firewall Configuration

After you've designed an appropriate firewall configuration, it's important to validate that it does in fact do what you want it to do. One way to do this is to use a test host outside your network to attempt to pierce your firewall: this can be quite clumsy and slow, though, and is limited to testing only those addresses that you can actually use.

A faster and easier method is available with the Linux firewall implementation. It allows you to manually generate tests and run them through the firewall configuration just as if you were testing with actual datagrams. All varieties of the Linux kernel firewall software, *ipfwadm, ipchains,* and *iptables,* provide support for this style of testing. The implementation involves use of the relevant *check* command.

The general test procedure is as follows:

1. Design and configure your firewall using *ipfwadm, ipchains,* or *iptables.*

2. Design a series of tests that will determine whether your firewall is actually working as you intend. For these tests you may use any source or destination address, so choose some address combinations that should be accepted and some others that should be dropped. If you're allowing or disallowing only

certain ranges of addresses, it is a good idea to test addresses on either side of the boundary of the range—one address just inside the boundary and one address just outside the boundary. This will help ensure that you have the correct boundaries configured, because it is sometimes easy to specify netmasks incorrectly in your configuration. If you're filtering by protocol and port number, your tests should also check all important combinations of these parameters. For example, if you intend to accept only TCP under certain circumstances, check that UDP datagrams are dropped.

3. Develop *ipfwadm*, *ipchains*, or *iptables* rules to implement each test. It is probably worthwhile to write all the rules into a script so you can test and retest easily as you correct mistakes or change your design. Tests use almost the same syntax as rule specifications, but the arguments take on slightly differing meanings. For example, the source address argument in a rule specification specifies the source address that datagrams matching this rule should have. The source address argument in test syntax, in contrast, specifies the source address of the test datagram that will be generated. For *ipfwadm*, you must use the *−c* option to specify that this command is a test, while for *ipchains* and *iptables*, you must use the *−C* option. In all cases you must *always* specify the source address, destination address, protocol, and interface to be used for the test. Other arguments, such as port numbers or TOS bit settings, are optional.

4. Execute each test command and note the output. The output of each test will be a single word indicating the final target of the datagram after running it through the firewall configuration—that is, where the processing ended. For *ipchains* and *iptables*, user-specified chains will be tested in addition to the built-in ones.

5. Compare the output of each test against the desired result. If there are any discrepancies, you will need to analyse your ruleset to determine where you've made the error. If you've written your test commands into a script file, you can easily rerun the test after correcting any errors in your firewall configuration. It's a good practice to flush your rulesets completely and rebuild them from scratch, rather than to make changes dynamically. This helps ensure that the active configuration you are testing actually reflects the set of commands in your configuration script.

Let's take a quick look at what a manual test transcript would look like for our naïve example with *ipchains*. You will remember that our local network in the example was 172.16.1.0 with a netmask of 255.255.255.0, and we were to allow TCP connections out to web servers on the net. Nothing else was to pass our forward chain. Start with a transmission that we know should work, a connection from a local host to a web server outside:

```
# ipchains -C forward -p tcp -s 172.16.1.0 1025 -d 44.136.8.2 80 -i eth0
accepted
```

Note the arguments had to be supplied and the way they've been used to describe a datagram. The output of the command indicates that that the datagram was accepted for forwarding, which is what we hoped for.

Now try another test, this time with a source address that doesn't belong to our network. This one should be denied:

```
# ipchains -C forward -p tcp -s 172.16.2.0 1025 -d 44.136.8.2 80 -i eth0
denied
```

Try some more tests, this time with the same details as the first test, but with different protocols. These should be denied, too:

```
# ipchains -C forward -p udp -s 172.16.1.0 1025 -d 44.136.8.2 80 -i eth0
denied
# ipchains -C forward -p icmp -s 172.16.1.0 1025 -d 44.136.8.2 80 -i eth0
denied
```

Try another destination port, again expecting it to be denied:

```
# ipchains -C forward -p tcp -s 172.16.1.0 1025 -d 44.136.8.2 23 -i eth0
denied
```

You'll go a long way toward achieving peace of mind if you design a series of exhaustive tests. While this can sometimes be as difficult as designing the firewall configuration, it's also the best way of knowing that your design is providing the security you expect of it.

A Sample Firewall Configuration

We've discussed the fundamentals of firewall configuration. Let's now look at what a firewall configuration might actually look like.

The configuration in this example has been designed to be easily extended and customized. We've provided three versions. The first version is implemented using the *ipfwadm* command (or the *ipfwadm-wrapper* script), the second uses *ipchains*, and the third uses *iptables*. The example doesn't attempt to exploit user-defined chains, but it will show you the similarities and differences between the old and new firewall configuration tool syntaxes:

```
#!/bin/bash
######################################################################
# IPFWADM VERSION
# This sample configuration is for a single host firewall configuration
# with no services supported by the firewall machine itself.
######################################################################

# USER CONFIGURABLE SECTION

# The name and location of the ipfwadm utility. Use ipfwadm-wrapper for
# 2.2.* kernels.
```

```
IPFWADM=ipfwadm

# The path to the ipfwadm executable.
PATH="/sbin"

# Our internal network address space and its supporting network device.
OURNET="172.29.16.0/24"
OURBCAST="172.29.16.255"
OURDEV="eth0"

# The outside address and the network device that supports it.
ANYADDR="0/0"
ANYDEV="eth1"

# The TCP services we wish to allow to pass - "" empty means all ports
# note: space separated
TCPIN="smtp www"
TCPOUT="smtp www ftp ftp-data irc"

# The UDP services we wish to allow to pass - "" empty means all ports
# note: space separated
UDPIN="domain"
UDPOUT="domain"

# The ICMP services we wish to allow to pass - "" empty means all types
# ref: /usr/include/netinet/ip_icmp.h for type numbers
# note: space separated
ICMPIN="0 3 11"
ICMPOUT="8 3 11"

# Logging; uncomment the following line to enable logging of datagrams
# that are blocked by the firewall.
# LOGGING=1

# END USER CONFIGURABLE SECTION
###########################################################################
# Flush the Incoming table rules
$IPFWADM -I -f

# We want to deny incoming access by default.
$IPFWADM -I -p deny

# SPOOFING
# We should not accept any datagrams with a source address matching ours
# from the outside, so we deny them.
$IPFWADM -I -a deny -S $OURNET -W $ANYDEV

# SMURF
# Disallow ICMP to our broadcast address to prevent "Smurf" style attack.
$IPFWADM -I -a deny -P icmp -W $ANYDEV -D $OURBCAST

# TCP
```

```
# We will accept all TCP datagrams belonging to an existing connection
# (i.e. having the ACK bit set) for the TCP ports we're allowing through.
# This should catch more than 95 % of all valid TCP packets.
$IPFWADM -I -a accept -P tcp -D $OURNET $TCPIN -k -b

# TCP - INCOMING CONNECTIONS
# We will accept connection requests from the outside only on the
# allowed TCP ports.
$IPFWADM -I -a accept -P tcp -W $ANYDEV -D $OURNET $TCPIN -y

# TCP - OUTGOING CONNECTIONS
# We accept all outgoing tcp connection requests on allowed TCP ports.
$IPFWADM -I -a accept -P tcp -W $OURDEV -D $ANYADDR $TCPOUT -y

# UDP - INCOMING
# We will allow UDP datagrams in on the allowed ports.
$IPFWADM -I -a accept -P udp -W $ANYDEV -D $OURNET $UDPIN

# UDP - OUTGOING
# We will allow UDP datagrams out on the allowed ports.
$IPFWADM -I -a accept -P udp -W $OURDEV -D $ANYADDR $UDPOUT

# ICMP - INCOMING
# We will allow ICMP datagrams in of the allowed types.
$IPFWADM -I -a accept -P icmp -W $ANYDEV -D $OURNET $UDPIN

# ICMP - OUTGOING
# We will allow ICMP datagrams out of the allowed types.
$IPFWADM -I -a accept -P icmp -W $OURDEV -D $ANYADDR $UDPOUT

# DEFAULT and LOGGING
# All remaining datagrams fall through to the default
# rule and are dropped. They will be logged if you've
# configured the LOGGING variable above.
#
if [ "$LOGGING" ]
then
        # Log barred TCP
        $IPFWADM -I -a reject -P tcp -o

        # Log barred UDP
        $IPFWADM -I -a reject -P udp -o

        # Log barred ICMP
        $IPFWADM -I -a reject -P icmp -o
fi
#
# end.
```

Now we'll reimplement it using the *ipchains* command:

```
#!/bin/bash
##########################################################################
# IPCHAINS VERSION
# This sample configuration is for a single host firewall configuration
# with no services supported by the firewall machine itself.
##########################################################################

# USER CONFIGURABLE SECTION

# The name and location of the ipchains utility.
IPCHAINS=ipchains

# The path to the ipchains executable.
PATH="/sbin"

# Our internal network address space and its supporting network device.
OURNET="172.29.16.0/24"
OURBCAST="172.29.16.255"
OURDEV="eth0"

# The outside address and the network device that supports it.
ANYADDR="0/0"
ANYDEV="eth1"

# The TCP services we wish to allow to pass - "" empty means all ports
# note: space separated
TCPIN="smtp www"
TCPOUT="smtp www ftp ftp-data irc"

# The UDP services we wish to allow to pass - "" empty means all ports
# note: space separated
UDPIN="domain"
UDPOUT="domain"

# The ICMP services we wish to allow to pass - "" empty means all types
# ref: /usr/include/netinet/ip_icmp.h for type numbers
# note: space separated
ICMPIN="0 3 11"
ICMPOUT="8 3 11"

# Logging; uncomment the following line to enable logging of datagrams
# that are blocked by the firewall.
# LOGGING=1

# END USER CONFIGURABLE SECTION
##########################################################################
# Flush the Input table rules
$IPCHAINS -F input

# We want to deny incoming access by default.
```

```
$IPCHAINS -P input deny

# SPOOFING
# We should not accept any datagrams with a source address matching ours
# from the outside, so we deny them.
$IPCHAINS -A input -s $OURNET -i $ANYDEV -j deny

# SMURF
# Disallow ICMP to our broadcast address to prevent "Smurf" style attack.
$IPCHAINS -A input -p icmp -w $ANYDEV -d $OURBCAST -j deny

# We should accept fragments, in ipchains we must do this explicitly.
$IPCHAINS -A input -f -j accept

# TCP
# We will accept all TCP datagrams belonging to an existing connection
# (i.e. having the ACK bit set) for the TCP ports we're allowing through.
# This should catch more than 95 % of all valid TCP packets.
$IPCHAINS -A input -p tcp -d $OURNET $TCPIN ! -y -b -j accept

# TCP - INCOMING CONNECTIONS
# We will accept connection requests from the outside only on the
# allowed TCP ports.
$IPCHAINS -A input -p tcp -i $ANYDEV -d $OURNET $TCPIN -y -j accept

# TCP - OUTGOING CONNECTIONS
# We accept all outgoing TCP connection requests on allowed TCP ports.
$IPCHAINS -A input -p tcp -i $OURDEV -d $ANYADDR $TCPOUT -y -j accept

# UDP - INCOMING
# We will allow UDP datagrams in on the allowed ports.
$IPCHAINS -A input -p udp -i $ANYDEV -d $OURNET $UDPIN -j accept

# UDP - OUTGOING
# We will allow UDP datagrams out on the allowed ports.
$IPCHAINS -A input -p udp -i $OURDEV -d $ANYADDR $UDPOUT -j accept

# ICMP - INCOMING
# We will allow ICMP datagrams in of the allowed types.
$IPCHAINS -A input -p icmp -w $ANYDEV -d $OURNET $UDPIN -j accept

# ICMP - OUTGOING
# We will allow ICMP datagrams out of the allowed types.
$IPCHAINS -A input -p icmp -i $OURDEV -d $ANYADDR $UDPOUT -j accept

# DEFAULT and LOGGING
# All remaining datagrams fall through to the default
# rule and are dropped. They will be logged if you've
# configured the LOGGING variable above.
#
if [ "$LOGGING" ]
then
```

```
        # Log barred TCP
        $IPCHAINS -A input -p tcp -l -j reject

        # Log barred UDP
        $IPCHAINS -A input -p udp -l -j reject

        # Log barred ICMP
        $IPCHAINS -A input -p icmp -l -j reject
fi
#
# end.
```

In our *iptables* example, we've switched to using the FORWARD ruleset because of the difference in meaning of the INPUT ruleset in the *netfilter* implementation. This has implications for us; it means that none of the rules protect the firewall host itself. To accurately mimic our *ipchains* example, we would replicate each of our rules in the INPUT chain. For clarity, we've dropped all incoming datagrams received from our outside interface instead.

```
#!/bin/bash
#########################################################################
# IPTABLES VERSION
# This sample configuration is for a single host firewall configuration
# with no services supported by the firewall machine itself.
#########################################################################

# USER CONFIGURABLE SECTION

# The name and location of the ipchains utility.
IPTABLES=iptables

# The path to the ipchains executable.
PATH="/sbin"

# Our internal network address space and its supporting network device.
OURNET="172.29.16.0/24"
OURBCAST="172.29.16.255"
OURDEV="eth0"

# The outside address and the network device that supports it.
ANYADDR="0/0"
ANYDEV="eth1"

# The TCP services we wish to allow to pass - "" empty means all ports
# note: comma separated
TCPIN="smtp,www"
TCPOUT="smtp,www,ftp,ftp-data,irc"

# The UDP services we wish to allow to pass - "" empty means all ports
# note: comma separated
UDPIN="domain"
UDPOUT="domain"
```

```
# The ICMP services we wish to allow to pass - "" empty means all types
# ref: /usr/include/netinet/ip_icmp.h for type numbers
# note: comma separated
ICMPIN="0,3,11"
ICMPOUT="8,3,11"

# Logging; uncomment the following line to enable logging of datagrams
# that are blocked by the firewall.
# LOGGING=1

# END USER CONFIGURABLE SECTION
##########################################################################
# Flush the Input table rules
$IPTABLES -F FORWARD

# We want to deny incoming access by default.
$IPTABLES -P FORWARD deny

# Drop all datagrams destined for this host received from outside.
$IPTABLES -A INPUT -i $ANYDEV -j DROP

# SPOOFING
# We should not accept any datagrams with a source address matching ours
# from the outside, so we deny them.
$IPTABLES -A FORWARD -s $OURNET -i $ANYDEV -j DROP

# SMURF
# Disallow ICMP to our broadcast address to prevent "Smurf" style attack.
$IPTABLES -A FORWARD -m multiport -p icmp -i $ANYDEV -d $OURNET -j DENY

# We should accept fragments, in iptables we must do this explicitly.
$IPTABLES -A FORWARD -f -j ACCEPT

# TCP
# We will accept all TCP datagrams belonging to an existing connection
# (i.e. having the ACK bit set) for the TCP ports we're allowing through.
# This should catch more than 95 % of all valid TCP packets.
$IPTABLES -A FORWARD -m multiport -p tcp -d $OURNET --dports $TCPIN /
    ! --tcp-flags SYN,ACK ACK -j ACCEPT
$IPTABLES -A FORWARD -m multiport -p tcp -s $OURNET --sports $TCPIN /
    ! --tcp-flags SYN,ACK ACK -j ACCEPT


# TCP - INCOMING CONNECTIONS
# We will accept connection requests from the outside only on the
# allowed TCP ports.
$IPTABLES -A FORWARD -m multiport -p tcp -i $ANYDEV -d $OURNET $TCPIN /
    --syn -j ACCEPT

# TCP - OUTGOING CONNECTIONS
# We will accept all outgoing tcp connection requests on the allowed /
    TCP ports.
```

```
$IPTABLES -A FORWARD -m multiport -p tcp -i $OURDEV -d $ANYADDR /
    --dports $TCPOUT --syn -j ACCEPT

# UDP - INCOMING
# We will allow UDP datagrams in on the allowed ports and back.
$IPTABLES -A FORWARD -m multiport -p udp -i $ANYDEV -d $OURNET /
    --dports $UDPIN -j ACCEPT
$IPTABLES -A FORWARD -m multiport -p udp -i $ANYDEV -s $OURNET /
    --sports $UDPIN -j ACCEPT

# UDP - OUTGOING
# We will allow UDP datagrams out to the allowed ports and back.
$IPTABLES -A FORWARD -m multiport -p udp -i $OURDEV -d $ANYADDR /
    --dports $UDPOUT -j ACCEPT
$IPTABLES -A FORWARD -m multiport -p udp -i $OURDEV -s $ANYADDR /
    --sports $UDPOUT -j ACCEPT

# ICMP - INCOMING
# We will allow ICMP datagrams in of the allowed types.
$IPTABLES -A FORWARD -m multiport -p icmp -i $ANYDEV -d $OURNET /
    --dports $ICMPIN -j ACCEPT

# ICMP - OUTGOING
# We will allow ICMP datagrams out of the allowed types.
$IPTABLES -A FORWARD -m multiport -p icmp -i $OURDEV -d $ANYADDR /
    --dports $ICMPOUT -j ACCEPT

# DEFAULT and LOGGING
# All remaining datagrams fall through to the default
# rule and are dropped. They will be logged if you've
# configured the LOGGING variable above.
#
if [ "$LOGGING" ]
then
        # Log barred TCP
        $IPTABLES -A FORWARD -m tcp -p tcp -j LOG

        # Log barred UDP
        $IPTABLES -A FORWARD -m udp -p udp -j LOG

        # Log barred ICMP
        $IPTABLES -A FORWARD -m udp -p icmp -j LOG
fi
#
# end.
```

In many simple situations, to use the sample all you have to do is edit the top section of the file labeled "USER CONFIGURABLE section" to specify which protocols and datagrams type you wish to allow in and out. For more complex configurations, you will need to edit the section at the bottom, as well. Remember, this is a simple example, so scrutinize it very carefully to ensure it does what you want while implementing it.

## CHAPTER TEN

IP ACCOUNTING

In today's world of commercial Internet service, it is becoming increasingly important to know how much data you are transmitting and receiving on your network connections. If you are an Internet Service Provider and you charge your customers by volume, this will be essential to your business. If you are a customer of an Internet Service Provider that charges by data volume, you will find it useful to collect your own data to ensure the accuracy of your Internet charges.

There are other uses for network accounting that have nothing to do with dollars and bills. If you manage a server that offers a number of different types of network services, it might be useful to you to know exactly how much data is being generated by each one. This sort of information could assist you in making decisions, such as what hardware to buy or how many servers to run.

The Linux kernel provides a facility that allows you to collect all sorts of useful information about the network traffic it sees. This facility is called *IP accounting*.

Configuring the Kernel for IP Accounting

The Linux IP accounting feature is very closely related to the Linux firewall software. The places you want to collect accounting data are the same places that you would be interested in performing firewall filtering: into and out of a network host, and in the software that does the routing of datagrams. If you haven't read the section on firewalls, now is probably a good time to do so, as we will be using some of the concepts described in Chapter 9, *TCP/IP Firewall*.

To activate the Linux IP accounting feature, you should first see if your Linux kernel is configured for it. Check to see if the */proc/net/ip_acct* file exists. If it does, your kernel already supports IP accounting. If it doesn't, you must build a new kernel, ensuring that you answer "Y" to the options in 2.0 and 2.2 series kernels:

```
Networking options  --->
        [*] Network firewalls
        [*] TCP/IP networking
        ...
        [*] IP: accounting
```

or in 2.4 series kernels:

```
Networking options  --->
    [*] Network packet filtering (replaces ipchains)
```

Configuring IP Accounting

Because IP accounting is closely related to IP firewall, the same tool was designated to configure it, so *ipfwadm, ipchains* or *iptables* are used to configure IP accounting. The command syntax is very similar to that of the firewall rules, so we won't focus on it, but we will discuss what you can discover about the nature of your network traffic using this feature.

The general syntax for IP accounting with *ipfwadm* is:

```
# ipfwadm -A [direction] [command] [parameters]
```

The direction argument is new. This is simply coded as in, out, or both. These directions are from the perspective of the linux machine itself, so in means data coming into the machine from a network connection and out means data that is being transmitted by this host on a network connection. The both direction is the sum of both the incoming and outgoing directions.

The general command syntax for *ipchains* and *iptables* is:

```
# ipchains -A chain rule-specification
# iptables -A chain rule-specification
```

The *ipchains* and *iptables* commands allow you to specify direction in a manner more consistent with the firewall rules. IP Firewall Chains doesn't allow you to configure a rule that aggregates both directions, but it does allow you to configure rules in the forward chain that the older implementation did not. We'll see the difference that makes in some examples a little later.

The commands are much the same as firewall rules, except that the policy rules do not apply here. We can add, insert, delete, and list accounting rules. In the case of *ipchains* and *iptables*, all valid rules are accounting rules, and any command that doesn't specify the *-j* option performs accounting only.

The rule specification parameters for IP accounting are the same as those used for IP firewall. These are what we use to define precisely what network traffic we wish to count and total.

Accounting by Address

Let's work with an example to illustrate how we'd use IP accounting.

Imagine we have a Linux-based router that serves two departments at the Virtual Brewery. The router has two Ethernet devices, *eth0* and *eth1*, each of which services a department; and a PPP device, *ppp0*, that connects us via a high-speed serial link to the main campus of the Groucho Marx University.

Let's also imagine that for billing purposes we want to know the total traffic generated by each of the departments across the serial link, and for management purposes we want to know the total traffic generated between the two departments.

The following table shows the interface addresses we will use in our example:

iface	address	netmask
eth0	172.16.3.0	255.255.255.0
eth1	172.16.4.0	255.255.255.0

To answer the question, "How much data does each department generate on the PPP link?", we could use a rule that looks like this:

```
# ipfwadm -A both -a -W ppp0 -S 172.16.3.0/24 -b
# ipfwadm -A both -a -W ppp0 -S 172.16.4.0/24 -b
```

or:

```
# ipchains -A input -i ppp0 -d 172.16.3.0/24
# ipchains -A output -i ppp0 -s 172.16.3.0/24
# ipchains -A input -i ppp0 -d 172.16.4.0/24
# ipchains -A output -i ppp0 -s 172.16.4.0/24
```

and with *iptables*:

```
# iptables -A FORWARD -i ppp0 -d 172.16.3.0/24
# iptables -A FORWARD -o ppp0 -s 172.16.3.0/24
# iptables -A FORWARD -i ppp0 -d 172.16.4.0/24
# iptables -A FORWARD -o ppp0 -s 172.16.4.0/24
```

The first half of each of these set of rules say, "Count all data traveling in either direction across the interface named ppp0 with a source or destination (remember the function of the *-b* flag in *ipfwadm* and *iptables*) address of 172.16.3.0/24." The second half of each ruleset is the same, but for the second Ethernet network at our site.

To answer the second question, "How much data travels between the two departments?", we need a rule that looks like this:

```
# ipfwadm -A both -a -S 172.16.3.0/24 -D 172.16.4.0/24 -b
```

or:

```
# ipchains -A forward -s 172.16.3.0/24 -d 172.16.4.0/24 -b
```

or:

```
# iptables -A FORWARD -s 172.16.3.0/24 -d 172.16.4.0/24
# iptables -A FORWARD -s 172.16.4.0/24 -d 172.16.3.0/24
```

These rules will count all datagrams with a source address belonging to one of the department networks and a destination address belonging to the other.

Accounting by Service Port

Okay, let's suppose we also want a better idea of exactly what sort of traffic is being carried across our PPP link. We might, for example, want to know how much of the link the FTP, smtp, and World Wide Web services are consuming.

A script of rules to enable us to collect this information might look like:

```
#!/bin/sh
# Collect FTP, smtp and www volume statistics for data carried on our
# PPP link using ipfwadm
#
ipfwadm -A both -a -W ppp0 -P tcp -S 0/0 ftp ftp-data
ipfwadm -A both -a -W ppp0 -P tcp -S 0/0 smtp
ipfwadm -A both -a -W ppp0 -P tcp -S 0/0 www
```

or:

```
#!/bin/sh
# Collect ftp, smtp and www volume statistics for data carried on our
# PPP link using ipchains
#
ipchains -A input -i ppp0 -p tcp -s 0/0 ftp-data:ftp
ipchains -A output -i ppp0 -p tcp -d 0/0 ftp-data:ftp
ipchains -A input -i ppp0 -p tcp -s 0/0 smtp
ipchains -A output -i ppp0 -p tcp -d 0/0 smtp
ipchains -A input -i ppp0 -p tcp -s 0/0 www
ipchains -A output -i ppp0 -p tcp -d 0/0 www
```

or:

```
#!/bin/sh
# Collect ftp, smtp and www volume statistics for data carried on our
# PPP link using iptables.
#
iptables -A FORWARD -i ppp0 -m tcp -p tcp --sport ftp-data:ftp
iptables -A FORWARD -o ppp0 -m tcp -p tcp --dport ftp-data:ftp
iptables -A FORWARD -i ppp0 -m tcp -p tcp --sport smtp
iptables -A FORWARD -o ppp0 -m tcp -p tcp --dport smtp
```

```
iptables -A FORWARD -i ppp0 -m tcp -p tcp --sport www
iptables -A FORWARD -o ppp0 -m tcp -p tcp --dport www
```

There are a couple of interesting features to this configuration. Firstly, we've specified the protocol. When we specify ports in our rules, we must also specify a protocol because TCP and UDP provide separate sets of ports. Since all of these services are TCB-based, we've specified it as the protocol. Secondly, we've specified the two services `ftp` and `ftp-data` in one command. *ipfwadm* allows you to specify single ports, ranges of ports, or arbitrary lists of ports. The *ipchains* command allows either single ports or ranges of ports, which is what we've used here. The syntax "`ftp-data:ftp`" means "ports ftp-data (20) through ftp (21)," and is how we encode ranges of ports in both *ipchains* and *iptables*. When you have a list of ports in an accounting rule, it means that any data received for any of the ports in the list will cause the data to be added to that entry's totals. Remembering that the FTP service uses two ports, the command port and the data transfer port, we've added them together to total the FTP traffic. Lastly, we've specified the source address as "`0/0`," which is special notation that matches all addresses and is required by both the *ipfwadm* and *ipchains* commands in order to specify ports.

We can expand on the second point a little to give us a different view of the data on our link. Let's now imagine that we class FTP, SMTP, and World Wide Web traffic as essential traffic, and all other traffic as nonessential. If we were interested in seeing the ratio of essential traffic to nonessential traffic, we could do something like:

```
# ipfwadm -A both -a -W ppp0 -P tcp -S 0/0 ftp ftp-data smtp www
# ipfwadm -A both -a -W ppp0 -P tcp -S 0/0 1:19 22:24 26:79 81:32767
```

If you have already examined your */etc/services* file, you will see that the second rule covers all ports except (`ftp`, `ftp-data`, `smtp`, and `www`).

How do we do this with the *ipchains* or *iptables* commands, since they allow only one argument in their port specification? We can exploit user-defined chains in accounting just as easily as in firewall rules. Consider the following approach:

```
# ipchains -N a-essent
# ipchains -N a-noness
# ipchains -A a-essent -j ACCEPT
# ipchains -A a-noness -j ACCEPT
# ipchains -A forward -i ppp0 -p tcp -s 0/0 ftp-data:ftp -j a-essent
# ipchains -A forward -i ppp0 -p tcp -s 0/0 smtp -j a-essent
# ipchains -A forward -i ppp0 -p tcp -s 0/0 www -j a-essent
# ipchains -A forward -j a-noness
```

Here we create two user-defined chains, one called `a-essent`, where we capture accounting data for essential services and another called `a-noness`, where we capture accounting data for nonessential services. We then add rules to our forward chain that match our essential services and jump to the `a-essent` chain, where we have just one rule that accepts all datagrams and counts them. The last rule in our forward chain is a rule that jumps to our `a-noness` chain, where again we have just one rule that accepts all datagrams and counts them. The rule that jumps to the `a-noness` chain will not be reached by any of our essential services, as they will have been accepted in their own chain. Our tallies for essential and nonessential services will therefore be available in the rules within those chains. This is just one approach you could take; there are others. Our *iptables* implementation of the same approach would look like:

```
# iptables -N a-essent
# iptables -N a-noness
# iptables -A a-essent -j ACCEPT
# iptables -A a-noness -j ACCEPT
# iptables -A FORWARD -i ppp0 -m tcp -p tcp --sport ftp-data:ftp -j a-essent
# iptables -A FORWARD -i ppp0 -m tcp -p tcp --sport smtp -j a-essent
# iptables -A FORWARD -i ppp0 -m tcp -p tcp --sport www -j a-essent
# iptables -A FORWARD -j a-noness
```

This looks simple enough. Unfortunately, there is a small but unavoidable problem when trying to do accounting by service type. You will remember that we discussed the role the MTU plays in TCP/IP networking in an earlier chapter. The MTU defines the largest datagram that will be transmitted on a network device. When a datagram is received by a router that is larger than the MTU of the interface that needs to retransmit it, the router performs a trick called *fragmentation*. The router breaks the large datagram into small pieces no longer than the MTU of the interface and then transmits these pieces. The router builds new headers to put in front of each of these pieces, and these are what the remote machine uses to reconstruct the original data. Unfortunately, during the fragmentation process the port is lost for all but the first fragment. This means that the IP accounting can't properly count fragmented datagrams. It can reliably count only the first fragment, or unfragmented datagrams. There is a small trick permitted by *ipfwadm* that ensures that while we won't be able to know exactly what port the second and later fragments were from, we can still count them. An early version of Linux accounting software assigned the fragments a fake port number, 0xFFFF, that we could count. To ensure that we capture the second and later fragments, we could use a rule like:

```
# ipfwadm -A both -a -W ppp0 -P tcp -S 0/0 0xFFFF
```

The IP chains implementation has a slightly more sophisticated solution, but the result is much the same. If using the *ipchains* command we'd instead use:

```
# ipchains -A forward -i ppp0 -p tcp -f
```

and with *iptables* we'd use:

```
# iptables -A FORWARD -i ppp0 -m tcp -p tcp -f
```

These won't tell us what the original port for this data was, but at least we are able to see how much of our data is fragments, and be able to account for the volume of traffic they consume.

In 2.2 kernels you can select a kernel compile-time option that negates this whole issue if your Linux machine is acting as the single access point for a network. If you enable the *IP: always defragment* option when you compile your kernel, all received datagrams will be reassembled by the Linux router before routing and retransmission. This operation is performed before the firewall and accounting software sees the datagram, and thus you will have no fragments to deal with. In 2.4 kernels you compile and load the *netfilter forward-fragment* module.

Accounting of ICMP Datagrams

The ICMP protocol does not use service port numbers and is therefore a little bit more difficult to collect details on. ICMP uses a number of different types of datagrams. Many of these are harmless and normal, while others should only be seen under special circumstances. Sometimes people with too much time on their hands attempt to maliciously disrupt the network access of a user by generating large numbers of ICMP messages. This is commonly called *ping flooding*. While IP accounting cannot do anything to prevent this problem (IP firewalling can help, though!) we can at least put accounting rules in place that will show us if anybody has been trying.

ICMP doesn't use ports as TCP and UDP do. Instead ICMP has ICMP message types. We can build rules to account for each ICMP message type. To do this, we place the ICMP message and type number in place of the port field in the *ipfwadm* accounting commands. We listed the ICMP message types in "ICMP datagram types," so refer to it if you need to remember what they are.

An IP accounting rule to collect information about the volume of ping data that is being sent to you or that you are generating might look like:

```
# ipfwadm -A both -a -P icmp -S 0/0 8
# ipfwadm -A both -a -P icmp -S 0/0 0
# ipfwadm -A both -a -P icmp -S 0/0 0xff
```

or, with *ipchains*:

```
# ipchains -A forward -p icmp -s 0/0 8
# ipchains -A forward -p icmp -s 0/0 0
# ipchains -A forward -p icmp -s 0/0 -f
```

or, with *iptables*:

```
# iptables -A FORWARD -m icmp -p icmp --sports echo-request
# iptables -A FORWARD -m icmp -p icmp --sports echo-reply
# iptables -A FORWARD -m icmp -p icmp -f
```

The first rule collects information about the "ICMP Echo Request" datagrams (ping requests), and the second rule collects information about the "ICMP Echo Reply" datagrams (ping replies). The third rule collects information about ICMP datagram fragments. This is a trick similar to that described for fragmented TCP and UDP datagrams.

If you specify source and/or destination addresses in your rules, you can keep track of where the pings are coming from, such as whether they originate inside or outside your network. Once you've determined where the rogue datagrams are coming from, you can decide whether you want to put firewall rules in place to prevent them or take some other action, such as contacting the owner of the offending network to advise them of the problem, or perhaps even legal action if the problem is a malicious act.

Accounting by Protocol

Let's now imagine that we are interested in knowing how much of the traffic on our link is TCP, UDP, and ICMP. We would use rules like the following:

```
# ipfwadm -A both -a -W ppp0 -P tcp -D 0/0
# ipfwadm -A both -a -W ppp0 -P udp -D 0/0
# ipfwadm -A both -a -W ppp0 -P icmp -D 0/0
```

or:

```
# ipchains -A forward -i ppp0 -p tcp -d 0/0
# ipchains -A forward -i ppp0 -p udp -d 0/0
# ipchains -A forward -i ppp0 -p icmp -d 0/0
```

or:

```
# iptables -A FORWARD -i ppp0 -m tcp -p tcp
# iptables -A FORWARD -o ppp0 -m tcp -p tcp
# iptables -A FORWARD -i ppp0 -m udp -p udp
# iptables -A FORWARD -o ppp0 -m udp -p udp
# iptables -A FORWARD -i ppp0 -m icmp -p icmp
# iptables -A FORWARD -o ppp0 -m icmp -p icmp
```

With these rules in place, all of the traffic flowing across the ppp0 interface will be analyzed to determine whether it is TCP, UDP, or IMCP traffic, and the appropriate counters will be updated for each. The *iptables* example splits incoming flow from outgoing flow as its syntax demands it.

Using IP Accounting Results

It is all very well to be collecting this information, but how do we actually get to see it? To view the collected accounting data and the configured accounting rules, we use our firewall configuration commands, asking them to list our rules. The packet and byte counters for each of our rules are listed in the output.

The *ipfwadm*, *ipchains*, and *iptables* commands differ in how accounting data is handled, so we will treat them independently.

Listing Accounting Data with *ipfwadm*

The most basic means of listing our accounting data with the *ipfwadm* command is to use it like this:

```
# ipfwadm -A -l
IP accounting rules
 pkts bytes dir prot source                destination         ports
 9833 2345K i/o all  172.16.3.0/24         anywhere            n/a
 56527   33M i/o all  172.16.4.0/24         anywhere            n/a
```

This will tell us the number of packets sent in each direction. If we use the extended output format with the *-e* option (not shown here because the output is too wide for the page), we are also supplied the options and applicable interface names. Most of the fields in the output will be self-explanatory, but the following may not:

dir The direction in which the rule applies. Expected values here are in, out, or i/o, meaning both ways.

prot
  The protocols to which the rule applies.

opt A coded form of the options we use when invoking *ipfwadm*.

ifname
  The name of the interface to which the rule applies.

ifaddress
  The address of the interface to which the rule applies.

By default, *ipfwadm* displays the packet and byte counts in a shortened form, rounded to the nearest thousand (K) or million (M). We can ask it to display the collected data in exact units by using the expanded option as follows:

```
# ipfwadm -A -l -e -x
```

Listing Accounting Data with *ipchains*

The *ipchains* command will not display our accounting data (packet and byte counters) unless we supply it the -v argument. The simplest means of listing our accounting data with the *ipchains* is to use it like this:

```
# ipchains -L -v
```

Again, just as with *ipfwadm*, we can display the packet and byte counters in units by using the expanded output mode. The *ipchains* uses the -x argument for this:

```
# ipchains -L -v -x
```

Listing Accounting Data with iptables

The *iptables* command behaves very similarly to the *ipchains* command. Again, we must use the -v when listing tour rules to see the accounting counters. To list our accounting data, we would use:

```
# iptables -L -v
```

Just as for the *ipchains* command, you can use the -x argument to show the output in expanded format with unit figures.

Resetting the Counters

The IP accounting counters will overflow if you leave them long enough. If they overflow, you will have difficulty determining the value they actually represent. To avoid this problem, you should read the accounting data periodically, record it, and then reset the counters back to zero to begin collecting accounting information for the next accounting interval.

The *ipfwadm* and *ipchains* commands provide you with a means of doing this quite simply:

```
# ipfwadm -A -z
```

or:

```
# ipchains -Z
```

or:

```
# iptables -Z
```

You can even combine the list and zeroing actions together to ensure that no accounting data is lost in between:

```
# ipfwadm -A -l -z
```

or:

```
# ipchains -L -Z
```

or:

```
# iptables -L -Z -v
```

These commands will first list the accounting data and then immediately zero the counters and begin counting again. If you are interested in collecting and using this information regularly, you would probably want to put this command into a script that recorded the output and stored it somewhere, and execute the script periodically using the *cron* command.

Flushing the Ruleset

One last command that might be useful allows you to flush all the IP accounting rules you have configured. This is most useful when you want to radically alter your ruleset without rebooting the machine.

The -f argument in combination with the *ipfwadm* command will flush all of the rules of the type you specify. *ipchains* supports the -F argument, which does the same:

```
# ipfwadm -A -f
```

or:

```
# ipchains -F
```

or:

```
# iptables -F
```

This flushes all of your configured IP accounting rules, removing them all and saving you having to remove each of them individually. Note that flushing the rules with *ipchains* does not cause any user-defined chains to be removed, only the rules within them.

Passive Collection of Accounting Data

One last trick you might like to consider: if your Linux machine is connected to an Ethernet, you can apply accounting rules to all of the data from the segment, not only that which it is transmitted by or destined for it. Your machine will passively listen to all of the data on the segment and count it.

You should first turn IP forwarding off on your Linux machine so that it doesn't try to route the datagrams it receives.* In the 2.0.36 and 2.2 kernels, this is a matter of:

```
# echo 0 >/proc/sys/net/ipv4/ip_forward
```

You should then enable promiscuous mode on your Ethernet interface using the *ifconfig* command. Now you can establish accounting rules that allow you to collect information about the datagrams flowing across your Ethernet without involving your Linux in the route at all.

---

* This isn't a good thing to do if your Linux machine serves as a router. If you disable IP forwarding, it will cease to route! Do this only on a machine with a single physical network interface.

CHAPTER ELEVEN
IP MASQUERADE AND NETWORK ADDRESS TRANSLATION

You don't have to have a good memory to remember a time when only large organizations could afford to have a number of computers networked together by a LAN. Today network technology has dropped so much in price that two things have happened. First, LANs are now commonplace, even in many household environments. Certainly many Linux users will have two or more computers connected by some Ethernet. Second, network resources, particularly IP addresses, are now a scarce resource and while they used to be free, they are now being bought and sold.

Most people with a LAN will probably also want an Internet connection that every computer on the LAN can use. The IP routing rules are quite strict in how they deal with this situation. Traditional solutions to this problem would have involved requesting an IP network address, perhaps a class C address for small sites, assigning each host on the LAN an address from this network and using a router to connect the LAN to the Internet.

In a commercialized Internet environment, this is quite an expensive proposition. First, you'd be required to pay for the network address that is assigned to you. Second, you'd probably have to pay your Internet Service Provider for the privilege of having a suitable route to your network put in place so that the rest of the Internet knows how to reach you. This might still be practical for companies, but domestic installations don't usually justify the cost.

Fortunately, Linux provides an answer to this dilemma. This answer involves a component of a group of advanced networking features called *Network Address Translation* (NAT). NAT describes the process of modifying the network addresses contained with datagram headers while they are in transit. This might sound odd at first, but we'll show that it is ideal for solving the problem we've just described and many have encountered. IP masquerade is the name given to one type of network address translation that allows all of the hosts on a private network to use the Internet at the price of a single IP address.

IP masquerading allows you to use a private (reserved) IP network address on your LAN and have your Linux-based router perform some clever, real-time translation of IP addresses and ports. When it receives a datagram from a computer on the LAN, it takes note of the type of datagram it is, "TCP," "UDP," "ICMP," etc., and modifies the datagram so that it looks like it was generated by the router machine itself (and remembers that it has done so). It then transmits the datagram onto the Internet with its single connected IP address. When the destination host receives this datagram, it believes the datagram has come from the routing host and sends any reply datagrams back to that address. When the Linux masquerade router receives a datagram from its Internet connection, it looks in its table of established masqueraded connections to see if this datagram actually belongs to a computer on the LAN, and if it does, it reverses the modification it did on the forward path and transmits the datagram to the LAN computer.

A simple example is illustrated in Figure 11-1.

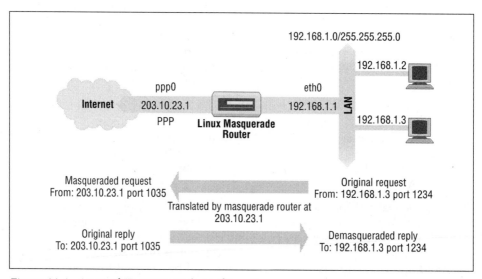

Figure 11-1. A typical IP masquerade configuration

We have a small Ethernet network using one of the reserved network addresses. The network has a Linux-based masquerade router providing access to the Internet. One of the workstations on the network (192.168.1.3) wishes to establish a connection to the remote host 209.1.106.178 on port 8888. The workstation routes its datagram to the masquerade router, which identifies this connection request as requiring masquerade services. It accepts the datagram and allocates a port number to use (1035), substitutes its own IP address and port number for those of the originating host, and transmits the datagram to the destination host. The destination host believes it has received a connection request from the Linux masquerade host and generates a reply datagram. The masquerade host, upon receiving this datagram, finds the association in its masquerade table and reverses the substution it performed on the outgoing datagram. It then transmits the reply datagram to the originating host.

The local host believes it is speaking directly to the remote host. The remote host knows nothing about the local host at all and believes it has received a connection from the Linux masquerade host. The Linux masquerade host knows these two hosts are speaking to each other, and on what ports, and performs the address and port translations necessary to allow communication.

This might all seem a little confusing, and it can be, but it works and is really quite simple to configure. So don't worry if you don't understand all the details yet.

Side Effects and Fringe Benefits

The IP masquerade facility comes with its own set of side effects, some of which are useful and some of which might become bothersome.

None of the hosts on the supported network behind the masquerade router are ever directly seen; consequently, you need only one valid and routable IP address to allow all hosts to make network connections out onto the Internet. This has a downside; none of those hosts are visible from the Internet and you can't directly connect to them from the Internet; the only host visible on a masqueraded network is the masquerade machine itself. This is important when you consider services such as mail or FTP. It helps determine what services should be provided by the masquerade host and what services it should proxy or otherwise treat specially.

Second, because none of the masqueraded hosts are visible, they are relatively protected from attacks from outside; this could simplify or even remove the need for firewall configuration on the masquerade host. You shouldn't rely too heavily on this, though. Your whole network will be only as safe as your masquerade host, so you should use firewall to protect it if security is a concern.

Third, IP masquerade will have some impact on the performance of your networking. In typical configurations this will probably be barely measurable. If you have large numbers of active masquerade sessions, though, you may find that the processing required at the masquerade machine begins to impact your network throughput. IP masquerade must do a good deal of work for each datagram compared to the process of conventional routing. That 386SX16 machine you have been planning on using as a masquerade machine supporting a dial-up link to the Internet might be fine, but don't expect too much if you decide you want to use it as a router in your corporate network at Ethernet speeds.

Last, some network services just won't work through masquerade, or at least not without a lot of help. Typically, these are services that rely on incoming sessions to work, such as some types of Direct Communications Channels (DCC), features in IRC, or certain types of video and audio multicasting services. Some of these services have specially developed kernel modules to provide solutions for these, and we'll talk about those in a moment. For others, it is possible that you will find no support, so be aware, it won't be suitable in all situations.

Configuring the Kernel for IP Masquerade

To use the IP masquerade facility, your kernel must be compiled with masquerade support. You must select the following options when configuring a 2.2 series kernel:

```
Networking options  --->
        [*] Network firewalls
        [*] TCP/IP networking
        [*] IP: firewalling
        [*] IP: masquerading
        --- Protocol-specific masquerading support will be built as modules.
        [*] IP: ipautofw masq support
        [*] IP: ICMP masquerading
```

Note that some of the masquerade support is available only as a kernel module. This means that you must ensure that you "make modules" in addition to the usual "make zImage" when building your kernel.

The 2.4 series kernels no longer offer IP masquerade support as a kernel compile time option. Instead, you should select the network packet filtering option:

```
Networking options  --->
    [M] Network packet filtering (replaces ipchains)
```

In the 2.2 series kernels, a number of protocol-specific helper modules are created during kernel compilation. Some protocols begin with an outgoing request on one port, and then expect an incoming connection on another. Normally these cannot be masqueraded, as there is no way of associating the second connection with the first without peering inside the protocols themselves. The helper modules do just that; they actually look inside the datagrams and allow masquerading to work for supported protocols that otherwise would be impossible to masquerade. The supported protocols are:

Module	Protocol
ip_masq_ftp	FTP
ip_masq_irc	IRC

Module	Protocol
ip_masq_raudio	RealAudio
ip_masq_cuseeme	CU-See-Me
ip_masq_vdolive	For VDO Live
ip_masq_quake	IdSoftware's Quake

You must load these modules manually using the *insmod* command to implement them. Note that these modules cannot be loaded using the *kerneld* daemon. Each of the modules takes an argument specifying what ports it will listen on. For the RealAudio™ module you might use:*

```
# insmod ip_masq_raudio.o ports=7070,7071,7072
```

The ports you need to specify depend on the protocol. An IP masquerade mini-HOWTO written by Ambrose Au explains more about the IP masquerade modules and how to configure them.†

The *netfilter* package includes modules that perform similar functions. For example, to provide connection tracking of FTP sessions, you'd load and use the *ip_conntrack_ftp* and *ip_nat_ftp.o* modules.

Configuring IP Masquerade

If you've already read the firewall and accounting chapters, it probably comes as no surprise that the *ipfwadm*, *ipchains*, and *iptables* commands are used to configure the IP masquerade rules as well.

Masquerade rules are a special class of filtering rule. You can masquerade only datagrams that are received on one interface that will be routed to another interface. To configure a masquerade rule you construct a rule very similar to a firewall forwarding rule, but with special options that tell the kernel to masquerade the datagram. The *ipfwadm* command uses the *-m* option, *ipchains* uses `-j MASQ`, and *iptables* uses `-j MASQUERADE` to indicate that datagrams matching the rule specification should be masqueraded.

Let's look at an example. A computing science student at Groucho Marx University has a number of computers at home internetworked onto a small Ethernet-based local area network. She has chosen to use one of the reserved private Internet network addresses for her network. She shares her accomodation with other students, all of whom have an interest in using the Internet. Because student living conditions are very frugal, they cannot afford to use a permanent Internet connection, so instead they use a simple dial-up PPP Internet connection. They would all like

---

* RealAudio is a trademark of the Progressive Networks Corporation.

† You can contact Ambrose at *ambrose@writeme.com*.

to be able to share the connection to chat on IRC, surf the Web, and retrieve files by FTP directly to each of their computers—IP masquerade is the answer.

The student first configures a Linux machine to support the dial-up link and to act as a router for the LAN. The IP address she is assigned when she dials up isn't important. She configures the Linux router with IP masquerade and uses one of the private network addresses for her LAN: 192.168.1.0. She ensures that each of the hosts on the LAN has a default route pointing at the Linux router.

The following *ipfwadm* commands are all that are required to make masquerading work in her configuration:

```
# ipfwadm -F -p deny
# ipfwadm -F -a accept -m -S 192.168.1.0/24 -D 0/0
```

or with *ipchains*:

```
# ipchains -P forward -j deny
# ipchains -A forward -s 192.168.1.0/24 -d 0/0 -j MASQ
```

or with *iptables*:

```
# iptables -t nat -P POSTROUTING DROP
# iptables -t nat -A POSTROUTING -o ppp0 -j MASQUERADE
```

Now whenever any of the LAN hosts try to connect to a service on a remote host, their datagrams will be automatically masqueraded by the Linux masquerade router. The first rule in each example prevents the Linux machine from routing any other datagrams and also adds some security.

To list the masquerade rules you have created, use the -1 argument to the *ipfwadm* command, as we described in earlier while discussing firewalls.

To list the rule we created earlier we use:

```
# ipfwadm -F -1 -e
```

which should display something like:

```
# ipfwadm -F -1 -e
IP firewall forward rules, default policy: accept
 pkts bytes type  prot opt  tosa tosx ifname  ifaddress  ...
    0     0 acc/m all  ----  0xFF 0x00 any     any        ...
```

The "/m" in the output indicates this is a masquerade rule.

To list the masquerade rules with the *ipchains* command, use the *-L* argument. If we list the rule we created earlier with *ipchains*, the output will look like:

```
# ipchains -L
Chain input (policy ACCEPT):
Chain forward (policy ACCEPT):
target     prot opt  source                destination        ports
MASQ       all  ------  192.168.1.0/24      anywhere           n/a
```

```
Chain output (policy ACCEPT):
```

Any rules with a target of MASQ are masquerade rules.

Finally, to list the rules using *iptables* you need to use:

```
# iptables -t nat -L
Chain PREROUTING (policy ACCEPT)
target     prot opt source                destination

Chain POSTROUTING (policy DROP)
target     prot opt source                destination
MASQUERADE  all  --  anywhere              anywhere             MASQUERADE

Chain OUTPUT (policy ACCEPT)
target     prot opt source                destination
```

Again, masquerade rules appear with a target of MASQUERADE.

Setting Timing Parameters for IP Masquerade

When each new connection is established, the IP masquerade software creates an association in memory between each of the hosts involved in the connection. You can view these associations at any time by looking at the */proc/net/ip_masquerade* file. These associations will timeout after a period of inactivity, though.

You can set the timeout values using the *ipfwadm* command. The general syntax for this is:

```
ipfwadm -M -s <tcp> <tcpfin> <udp>
```

and for the *ipchains* command it is:

```
ipchains -M -S <tcp> <tcpfin> <udp>
```

The *iptables* implementation uses much longer default timers and does not allow you to set them.

Each of these values represents a timer used by the IP masquerade software and are in units of seconds. The following table summarizes the timers and their meanings:

Name	Description
tcp	TCP session timeout. How long a TCP connection may remain idle before the association for it is removed.
tcpfin	TCP timeout after FIN. How long an association will remain after a TCP connection has been disconnected.
udp	UDP session timeout. How long a UDP connection may remain idle before the association for it is removed.

Handling Name Server Lookups

Handling domain name server lookups from the hosts on the LAN with IP masquerading has always presented a problem. There are two ways of accomodating DNS in a masquerade environment. You can tell each of the hosts that they use the same DNS that the Linux router machine does, and let IP masquerade do its magic on their DNS requests. Alternatively, you can run a caching name server on the Linux machine and have each of the hosts on the LAN use the Linux machine as their DNS. Although a more aggressive action, this is probably the better option because it reduces the volume of DNS traffic travelling on the Internet link and will be marginally faster for most requests, since they'll be served from the cache. The downside to this configuration is that it is more complex. "Caching-only named Configuration," in Chapter 6, describes how to configure a caching name server.

More About Network Address Translation

The *netfilter* software is capable of many different types of Network Address Translation. IP Masquerade is one simple application of it.

It is possible, for example, to build NAT rules that translate only certain addresses or ranges of addresses and leave all others untouched, or to translate addresses into pools of addresses rather than just a single address, as masquerade does. You can in fact use the *iptables* command to generate NAT rules that map just about anything, with combinations of matches using any of the standard attributes, such as source address, destination address, protocol type, port number, etc.

Translating the Source Address of a datagram is referred to as "Source NAT," or SNAT, in the *netfilter* documentation. Translating the Destination Address of a datagram is known as "Destination NAT," or DNAT. Translating the TCP or UDP port is known by the term REDIRECT. SNAT, DNAT, and REDIRECT are targets that you may use with the *iptables* command to build more complex and sophisticated rules.

The topic of Network Address Translation and its uses warrants at least a whole chapter of its own.* Unfortunately we don't have the space in this book to cover it in any greater depth. You should read the IPTABLES-HOWTO for more information, if you're interested in discovering more about how you might use Network Address Translation.

---

* ... and perhaps even a whole book!

## CHAPTER TWELVE

IMPORTANT NETWORK FEATURES

After successfully setting up IP and the resolver, you then must look at the services you want to provide over the network. This chapter covers the configuration of a few simple network applications, including the *inetd* server and the programs from the *rlogin* family. We'll also deal briefly with the Remote Procedure Call interface, upon which services like the Network File System (NFS) and the Network Information System (NIS) are based. The configuration of NFS and NIS, however, is more complex and are described in separate chapters, as are electronic mail and network news.

Of course, we can't cover all network applications in this book. If you want to install one that's not discussed here, like *talk*, *gopher*, or *http*, please refer to the manual pages of the server for details.

The inetd Super Server

Programs that provide application services via the network are called network *daemons*. A daemon is a program that opens a port, most commonly a well-known service port, and waits for incoming connections on it. If one occurs, the daemon creates a child process that accepts the connection, while the parent continues to listen for further requests. This mechanism works well, but has a few disadvantages; at least one instance of every possible service you wish to provide must be active in memory at all times. In addition, the software routines that do the listening and port handling must be replicated in every network daemon.

To overcome these inefficiencies, most Unix installations run a special network daemon, what you might consider a "super server." This daemon creates sockets on behalf of a number of services and listens on all of them simultaneously. When an incoming connection is received on any of these sockets, the super server accepts the connection and spawns the server specified for this port, passing the socket across to the child to manage. The server then returns to listening.

The most common super server is called *inetd*, the Internet Daemon. It is started at system boot time and takes the list of services it is to manage from a startup file named */etc/inetd.conf.* In addition to those servers, there are a number of trivial services performed by *inetd* itself called *internal services.* They include *chargen*, which simply generates a string of characters, and *daytime*, which returns the system's idea of the time of day.

An entry in this file consists of a single line made up of the following fields:

`service type protocol wait user server cmdline`

Each of the fields is described in the following list:

service

> Gives the service name. The service name has to be translated to a port number by looking it up in the */etc/services* file. This file will be described later in this chapter in the section "The Services and Protocols Files."

type

> Specifies a socket type, either `stream` (for connection-oriented protocols) or `dgram` (for datagram protocols). TCP-based services should therefore always use `stream`, while UDP-based services should always use `dgram`.

protocol

> Names the transport protocol used by the service. This must be a valid protocol name found in the *protocols* file, explained later.

wait

> This option applies only to `dgram` sockets. It can be either `wait` or `nowait`. If `wait` is specified, *inetd* executes only one server for the specified port at any time. Otherwise, it immediately continues to listen on the port after executing the server.

> This is useful for "single-threaded" servers that read all incoming datagrams until no more arrive, and then exit. Most RPC servers are of this type and should therefore specify `wait`. The opposite type, "multi-threaded" servers, allow an unlimited number of instances to run concurrently. These servers should specify `nowait`.

> `stream` sockets should always use `nowait`.

user

> This is the login ID of the user who will own the process when it is executing. This will frequently be the **root** user, but some services may use different accounts. It is a very good idea to apply the principle of least privilege here, which states that you shouldn't run a command under a privileged account if the program doesn't require this for proper functioning. For example, the NNTP news server runs as **news**, while services that may pose a security risk (such as *tftp* or *finger*) are often run as **nobody**.

server
> Gives the full pathname of the server program to be executed. Internal services are marked by the keyword `internal`.

cmdline
> This is the command line to be passed to the server. It starts with the name of the server to be executed and can include any arguments that need to be passed to it. If you are using the TCP wrapper, you specify the full pathname to the server here. If not, then you just specify the server name as you'd like it to appear in a process list. We'll talk about the TCP wrapper shortly.
>
> This field is empty for internal services.

A sample *inetd.conf* file is shown in Example 12-1. The *finger* service is commented out so that it is not available. This is often done for security reasons, because it can be used by attackers to obtain names and other details of users on your system.

Example 12-1: A Sample /etc/inetd.conf File

```
#
# inetd services
ftp       stream tcp nowait root   /usr/sbin/ftpd     in.ftpd -1
telnet    stream tcp nowait root   /usr/sbin/telnetd  in.telnetd -b/etc/issue
#finger   stream tcp nowait bin    /usr/sbin/fingerd  in.fingerd
#tftp     dgram  udp wait  nobody  /usr/sbin/tftpd    in.tftpd
#tftp     dgram  udp wait  nobody  /usr/sbin/tftpd    in.tftpd /boot/diskless
#login    stream tcp nowait root   /usr/sbin/rlogind  in.rlogind
#shell    stream tcp nowait root   /usr/sbin/rshd     in.rshd
#exec     stream tcp nowait root   /usr/sbin/rexecd   in.rexecd
#
#         inetd internal services
#
daytime   stream tcp nowait root internal
daytime   dgram  udp nowait root internal
time      stream tcp nowait root internal
time      dgram  udp nowait root internal
echo      stream tcp nowait root internal
echo      dgram  udp nowait root internal
discard   stream tcp nowait root internal
discard   dgram  udp nowait root internal
chargen   stream tcp nowait root internal
chargen   dgram  udp nowait root internal
```

The *tftp* daemon is shown commented out as well. *tftp* implements the *Trivial File Transfer Protocol* (TFTP), which allows someone to transfer any world-readable files from your system without password checking. This is especially harmful with the */etc/passwd* file, and even more so when you don't use shadow passwords.

TFTP is commonly used by diskless clients and Xterminals to download their code from a boot server. If you need to run *tftpd* for this reason, make sure to limit its scope to those directories from which clients will retrieve files; you will need to add those directory names to *tftpd's* command line. This is shown in the second *tftp* line in the example.

The tcpd Access Control Facility

Since opening a computer to network access involves many security risks, applications are designed to guard against several types of attacks. Some security features, however, may be flawed (most drastically demonstrated by the RTM Internet worm, which exploited a hole in a number of programs, including old versions of the sendmail mail daemon), or do not distinguish between secure hosts from which requests for a particular service will be accepted and insecure hosts whose requests should be rejected. We've already briefly discussed the *finger* and *tftp* services. Network Administrator would want to limit access to these services to "trusted hosts" only, which is impossible with the usual setup, for which *inetd* provides this service either to all clients or not at all.

A useful tool for managing host-specific access is *tcpd*, often called the daemon "wrapper."* For TCP services you want to monitor or protect, it is invoked instead of the server program. *tcpd* checks if the remote host is allowed to use that service, and only if this succeeds will it execute the real server program. *tcpd* also logs the request to the *syslog* daemon. Note that this does not work with UDP-based services.

For example, to wrap the *finger* daemon, you have to change the corresponding line in *inetd.conf* from this:

```
# unwrapped finger daemon
finger    stream tcp nowait bin    /usr/sbin/fingerd in.fingerd
```

to this:

```
# wrap finger daemon
finger   stream tcp    nowait   root    /usr/sbin/tcpd   in.fingerd
```

Without adding any access control, this will appear to the client as the usual *finger* setup, except that any requests are logged to *syslog's* *auth* facility.

Two files called */etc/hosts.allow* and */etc/hosts.deny* implement access control. They contain entries that allow and deny access to certain services and hosts. When *tcpd* handles a request for a service such as *finger* from a client host named **biff.foobar.com**, it scans *hosts.allow* and *hosts.deny* (in this order) for an entry matching both the service and client host. If a matching entry is found in *hosts.allow*, access is granted and *tcpd* doesn't consult the *hosts.deny* file. If no

---

* Written by Wietse Venema, *wietse@wzv.win.tue.nl.*

match is found in the *hosts.allow* file, but a match is found in *hosts.deny*, the request is rejected by closing down the connection. The request is accepted if no match is found at all.

Entries in the access files look like this:

```
servicelist: hostlist [:shellcmd]
```

servicelist is a list of service names from */etc/services*, or the keyword ALL. To match all services except *finger* and *tftp*, use ALL EXCEPT finger, tftp.

hostlist is a list of hostnames, IP addresses, or the keywords ALL, LOCAL, UNKNOWN or PARANOID. ALL matches any host, while LOCAL matches hostnames that don't contain a dot.* UNKNOWN matches any hosts whose name or address lookup failed. PARANOID matches any host whose hostname does not resolve back to its IP address.† A name starting with a dot matches all hosts whose domain is equal to this name. For example, .foobar.com matches biff.foobar.com, but not nurks.fredsville.com. A pattern that ends with a dot matches any host whose IP address begins with the supplied pattern, so 172.16. matches 172.16.32.0, but not 172.15.9.1. A pattern of the form *n.n.n.n/m.m.m.m* is treated as an IP address and network mask, so we could specify our previous example as 172.16.0.0/255.255.0.0 instead. Lastly, any pattern beginning with a "/" character allows you to specify a file that is presumed to contain a list of hostname or IP address patterns, any of which are allowed to match. So a pattern that looked like */var/access/trustedhosts* would cause the *tcpd* daemon to read that file, testing if any of the lines in it matched the connecting host.

To deny access to the *finger* and *tftp* services to all but the local hosts, put the following in */etc/hosts.deny* and leave */etc/hosts.allow* empty:

```
in.tftpd, in.fingerd: ALL EXCEPT LOCAL, .your.domain
```

The optional *shellcmd* field may contain a shell command to be invoked when the entry is matched. This is useful to set up traps that may expose potential attackers. The following example creates a log file listing the user and host connecting, and if the host is not **vlager.vbrew.com** it will append the output of a *finger* to that host:

```
in.ftpd: ALL EXCEPT LOCAL, .vbrew.com : \
    echo "request from %d@%h: >> /var/log/finger.log; \
    if [ %h != "vlager.vbrew.com:" ]; then \
        finger -l @%h >> /var/log/finger.log \
    fi
```

---

* Usually only local hostnames obtained from lookups in */etc/hosts* contain no dots.

† While its name suggests it is an extreme measure, the PARANOID keyword is a good default, as it protects you against mailicious hosts pretending to be someone they are not. Not all *tcpd* are supplied with PARANOID compiled in; if yours is not, you need to recompile *tcpd* to use it.

The %h and %d arguments are expanded by *tcpd* to the client hostname and service name, respectively. Please refer to the *hosts_access(5)* manual page for details.

The Services and Protocols Files

The port numbers on which certain "standard" services are offered are defined in the Assigned Numbers RFC. To enable server and client programs to convert service names to these numbers, at least part of the list is kept on each host; it is stored in a file called */etc/services*. An entry is made up like this:

```
service port/protocol    [aliases]
```

Here, `service` specifies the service name, `port` defines the port the service is offered on, and `protocol` defines which transport protocol is used. Commonly, the latter field is either *udp* or *tcp*. It is possible for a service to be offered for more than one protocol, as well as offering different services on the same port as long as the protocols are different. The `aliases` field allows you to specify alternative names for the same service.

Usually, you don't have to change the services file that comes along with the network software on your Linux system. Nevertheless, we give a small excerpt from that file in Example 12-2.

Example 12-2: A Sample /etc/services File

```
# The services file:
#
# well-known services
echo            7/tcp                   # Echo
echo            7/udp                   #
discard         9/tcp      sink null    # Discard
discard         9/udp      sink null    #
daytime        13/tcp                   # Daytime
daytime        13/udp                   #
chargen        19/tcp      ttytst source # Character Generator
chargen        19/udp      ttytst source #
ftp-data       20/tcp                   # File Transfer Protocol (Data)
ftp            21/tcp                   # File Transfer Protocol (Control)
telnet         23/tcp                   # Virtual Terminal Protocol
smtp           25/tcp                   # Simple Mail Transfer Protocol
nntp          119/tcp      readnews     # Network News Transfer Protocol
#
# UNIX services
exec          512/tcp                   # BSD rexecd
biff          512/udp      comsat       # mail notification
login         513/tcp                   # remote login
who           513/udp      whod         # remote who and uptime
shell         514/tcp      cmd          # remote command, no passwd used
syslog        514/udp                   # remote system logging
```

Example 12-2: A Sample /etc/services File (continued)

```
printer      515/tcp  spooler        # remote print spooling
route        520/udp  router routed  # routing information protocol
```

Note that the *echo* service is offered on port 7 for both TCP and UDP, and that port 512 is used for two different services: remote execution (*rexec*) using TCP, and the *COMSAT* daemon, which notifies users of new mail, over UDP (see *xbiff(1x)*).

Like the services file, the networking library needs a way to translate protocol names—for example, those used in the services file—to protocol numbers understood by the IP layer on other hosts. This is done by looking up the name in the */etc/protocols* file. It contains one entry per line, each containing a protocol name, and the associated number. Having to touch this file is even more unlikely than having to meddle with */etc/services*. A sample file is given in Example 12-3.

Example 12-3: A Sample /etc/protocols File

```
#
# Internet (IP) protocols
#
ip      0      IP      # internet protocol, pseudo protocol number
icmp    1      ICMP    # internet control message protocol
igmp    2      IGMP    # internet group multicast protocol
tcp     6      TCP     # transmission control protocol
udp     17     UDP     # user datagram protocol
raw     255    RAW     # RAW IP interface
```

Remote Procedure Call

The general mechanism for client-server applications is provided by the *Remote Procedure Call* (RPC) package. RPC was developed by Sun Microsystems and is a collection of tools and library functions. Important applications built on top of RPC are NIS, the Network Information System (described in Chapter 13, *The Network Information System*), and NFS, the Network File System (described in Chapter 14, *The Network File System*), which are both described in this book.

An RPC server consists of a collection of procedures that a client can call by sending an RPC request to the server along with the procedure parameters. The server will invoke the indicated procedure on behalf of the client, handing back the return value, if there is any. In order to be machine-independent, all data exchanged between client and server is converted to the *External Data Representation* format (XDR) by the sender, and converted back to the machine-local representation by the receiver. RPC relies on standard UDP and TCP sockets to transport the XDR formatted data to the remote host. Sun has graciously placed RPC in the public domain; it is described in a series of RFCs.

Sometimes improvements to an RPC application introduce incompatible changes in the procedure call interface. Of course, simply changing the server would crash all applications that still expect the original behavior. Therefore, RPC programs have version numbers assigned to them, usually starting with 1, and with each new version of the RPC interface, this counter will be bumped up. Often, a server may offer several versions simultaneously; clients then indicate by the version number in their requests which implementation of the service they want to use.

The communication between RPC servers and clients is somewhat peculiar. An RPC server offers one or more collections of procedures; each set is called a *program* and is uniquely identified by a *program number*. A list that maps service names to program numbers is usually kept in */etc/rpc*, an excerpt of which is shown in Example 12-4.

Example 12-4: A Sample /etc/rpc File

```
#
# /etc/rpc - miscellaneous RPC-based services
#
portmapper      100000   portmap sunrpc
rstatd          100001   rstat rstat_svc rup perfmeter
rusersd         100002   rusers
nfs             100003   nfsprog
ypserv          100004   ypprog
mountd          100005   mount showmount
ypbind          100007
walld           100008   rwall shutdown
yppasswdd       100009   yppasswd
bootparam       100026
ypupdated       100028   ypupdate
```

In TCP/IP networks, the authors of RPC faced the problem of mapping program numbers to generic network services. They designed each server to provide both a TCP and a UDP port for each program and each version. Generally, RPC applications use UDP when sending data, and fall back to TCP only when the data to be transferred doesn't fit into a single UDP datagram.

Of course, client programs need to find out to which port a program number maps. Using a configuration file for this would be too unflexible; since RPC applications don't use reserved ports, there's no guarantee that a port originally meant to be used by our database application hasn't been taken by some other process. Therefore, RPC applications pick any port they can get and register it with a special program called the *portmapper daemon*. The portmapper acts as a service broker for all RPC servers running on its machine. A client that wishes to contact a service with a given program number first queries the portmapper on the server's host, which returns the TCP and UDP port numbers the service can be reached at.

This method introduces a single point of failure, much like the *inetd* daemon does for the standard Berkeley services. However, this case is even a little worse because when the portmapper dies, all RPC port information is lost; this usually means you have to restart all RPC servers manually or reboot the entire machine.

On Linux, the portmapper is called */sbin/portmap*, or sometimes */usr/sbin/rpc.portmap*. Other than making sure it is started from your network boot scripts, the portmapper doesn't require any configuration.

Configuring Remote Login and Execution

It's often very useful to execute a command on a remote host and have input or output from that command be read from, or written to, a network connection.

The traditional commands used for executing commands on remote hosts are *rlogin*, *rsh* and *rcp*. We saw an example of the *rlogin* command in Chapter 1, *Introduction to Networking* in the section "Introduction to TCP/IP Networks." We briefly discussed the security issues associated with it in "System Security" and suggested *ssh* as a replacement. The *ssh* package provides replacements called *slogin*, *ssh*, and *scp*.

Each of these commands spawns a shell on the remote host and allows the user to execute commands. Of course, the client needs to have an account on the remote host where the command is to be executed. Thus, all these commands use an authentication process. The *r* commands use a simple username and password exchange between the hosts with no encryption, so anyone listening could easily intercept the passwords. The *ssh* command suite provides a higher level of security: it uses a technique called *Public Key Cryptography*, which provides authentication and encryption between the hosts to ensure that neither passwords nor session data are easily intercepted by other hosts.

It is possible to relax authentication checks for certain users even further. For instance, if you frequently have to log into other machines on your LAN, you might want to be admitted without having to type your password every time. This was always possible with the *r* commands, but the *ssh* suite allows you to do this a little more easily. It's still not a great idea because it means that if an account on one machine is breached, access can be gained to all other accounts that user has configured for password-less login, but it is very convenient and people will use it.

Let's talk about removing the *r* commands and getting *ssh* to work instead.

Disabling the r; Commands

Start by removing the *r* commands if they're installed. The easiest way to disable the old *r* commands is to comment out (or remove) their entries in the */etc/*

inetd.conf file. The relevant entries will look something like this:

```
# Shell, login, exec and talk are BSD protocols.
shell    stream  tcp     nowait  root  /usr/sbin/tcpd /usr/sbin/in.rshd
login    stream  tcp     nowait  root  /usr/sbin/tcpd /usr/sbin/in.rlogind
exec     stream  tcp     nowait  root  /usr/sbin/tcpd /usr/sbin/in.rexecd
```

You can comment them by placing a # character at the start of each line, or delete the lines completely. Remember, you need to restart the *inetd* daemon for this change to take effect. Ideally, you should remove the daemon programs themselves, too.

Installing and Configuring ssh

OpenSSH is a free version of the ssh suite of programs; the Linux port can be found at *http://violet.ibs.com.au/openssh/* and in most modern Linux distributions.* We won't describe compilation here; good instructions are included in the source. If you can install it from a precompiled package, then it's probably wise to do so.

There are two parts to an *ssh* session. There is an *ssh* client that you need to configure and run on the local host and an *ssh* daemon that must be running on the remote host.

The ssh daemon

The *sshd* daemon is the program that listens for network connections from *ssh* clients, manages authentication, and executes the requested command. It has one main configuration file called */etc/ssh/sshd_config* and a special file containing a key used by the authentication and encryption processes to represent the host end. Each host and each client has its own key.

A utility called *ssh-keygen* is supplied to generate a random key. This is usually used once at installation time to generate the host key, which the system administrator usually stores in a file called */etc/ssh/ssh_host_key*. Keys can be of any length of 512 bits or greater. By default, *ssh-keygen* generates keys of 1024 bits in length, and most people use the default. To generate a random key, you would invoke the *ssh-keygen* command like this:

```
# ssh-keygen -f /etc/ssh/ssh_host_key
```

You will be prompted to enter a passphrase. However, host keys must not use a passphrase, so just press the return key to leave it blank. The program output will look something like:

---

* OpenSSH was developed by the OpenBSD project and is a fine example of the benefit of free software.

```
Generating RSA keys:  ......oooooO.............................oooooO
Key generation complete.
Enter passphrase (empty for no passphrase):
Enter same passphrase again:
Your identification has been saved in /etc/ssh/ssh_host_key
Your public key has been saved in /etc/ssh/ssh_host_key.pub
The key fingerprint is:
1024 3a:14:78:8e:5a:a3:6b:bc:b0:69:10:23:b7:d8:56:82 root@moria
```

You will find at the end that two files have been created. The first is called the private key, which must be kept secret and will be in */etc/ssh/ssh_host_key*. The second is called the public key and is one that you can share; it will be in */etc/ssh/ ssh_host_key.pub*.

Armed with the keys for *ssh* communication, you need to create a configuration file. The *ssh* suite is very powerful and the configuration file may contain many options. We'll present a simple example to get you started; you should refer to the *ssh* documentation to enable other features. The following code shows a safe and minimal *sshd* configuration file. The rest of the configuration options are detailed in the *sshd*(8) manpage:

```
# /etc/ssh/sshd_config
#

# The IP adddresses to listen for connections on. 0.0.0.0 means all
# local addresses.
ListenAddress 0.0.0.0

# The TCP port to listen for connections on. The default is 22.
Port 22

# The name of the host key file.
HostKey /etc/ssh/ssh_host_key

# The length of the key in bits.
ServerKeyBits 1024

# Should we allow root logins via ssh?
PermitRootLogin no

# Should the ssh daemon check users' home directory and files permissions?
# are safe before allowing login?
StrictModes yes

# Should we allow old ~/.rhosts and /etc/hosts.equiv authentication method?
RhostsAuthentication no
# Should we allow pure RSA authentication?
RSAAuthentication yes
# Should we allow password authentication?
PasswordAuthentication yes

# Should we allow /etc/hosts.equiv combined with RSA host authentication?
```

```
RhostsRSAAuthentication no
# Should we ignore ~/.rhosts files?
IgnoreRhosts yes

# Should we allow logins to accounts with empty passwords?
PermitEmptyPasswords no
```

It's important to make sure the permissions of the configuration files are correct to ensure that system security is maintained. Use the following commands:

```
# chown -R root:root /etc/ssh
# chmod 755 /etc/ssh
# chmod 600 /etc/ssh/ssh_host_key
# chmod 644 /etc/ssh/ssh_host_key.pub
# chmod 644 /etc/ssh/sshd_config
```

The final stage of *sshd* administration daemon is to run it. Normally you'd create an *rc* file for it or add it to an existing one, so that it is automatically executed at boot time. The daemon runs standalone and doesn't require any entry in the */etc/inetd.conf* file. The daemon must be run as the **root** user. The syntax is very simple:

```
/usr/sbin/sshd
```

The *sshd* daemon will automatically place itself into the background when being run. You are now ready to accept *ssh* connections.

The ssh client

There are a number of *ssh* client programs: *slogin, scp* and *ssh.* They each read the same configuration file, usually called */etc/ssh/ssh_config.* They each also read configuration files from the *.ssh* directory in the home directory of the user executing them. The most important of these files is the *.ssh/config* file, which may contain options that override those specified in the */etc/ssh/ssh_config* file, the *.ssh/identity* file, which contains the user's own private key, and the corresponding *.ssh/identity.pub* file, containing the user's public key. Other important files are *.ssh/known_hosts* and *.ssh/authorized_keys;* we'll talk about those later in "Using ssh." First, let's create the global configuration file and the user key file.

/etc/ssh/ssh_config is very similar to the server configuration file. Again, there are lots of features you can configure, but a minimal configuration looks like that presented in Example 12-5. The rest of the configuration options are detailed in the *sshd(8)* manpage. You can add sections that match specific hosts or groups of hosts. The parameter to the "Host" statement may be either the full name of a host or a wildcard specification, as we've used in our example, to match all hosts. We could create an entry that used, for example, Host *.vbrew.com to match any host in the vbrew.com domain.

Example 12-5: Example ssh Client Configuration File

```
# /etc/ssh/ssh_config

# Default options to use when connecting to a remote host
Host *
  # Compress the session data?
  Compression yes
  # .. using which compression level? (1 - fast/poor, 9 - slow/good)
  CompressionLevel 6

  # Fall back to rsh if the secure connection fails?
  FallBackToRsh no

  # Should we send keep-alive messages? Useful if you use IP masquerade
  KeepAlive yes

  # Try RSA authentication?
  RSAAuthentication yes
  # Try RSA authentication in combination with .rhosts authentication?
  RhostsRSAAuthentication yes
```

We mentioned in the server configuration section that every host and user has a key. The user's key is stored in his or her ~/.ssh/indentity file. To generate the key, use the same *ssh-keygen* command as we used to generate the host key, except this time you do not need to specify the name of the file in which you save the key. The *ssh-keygen* defaults to the correct location, but it prompts you to enter a filename in case you'd like to save it elsewhere. It is sometimes useful to have multiple identity files, so *ssh* allows this. Just as before, *ssh-keygen* will prompt you to entry a passphrase. Passphrases add yet another level of security and are a good idea. Your passphrase won't be echoed on the screen when you type it.

 There is no way to recover a passphrase if you forget it. Make sure it is something you will remember, but as with all passwords, make it something that isn't obvious, like a proper noun or your name. For a passphrase to be truly effective, it should be between 10 and 30 characters long and not be plain English prose. Try to throw in some unusual characters. If you forget your passphrase, you will be forced to generate a new key.

You should ask each of your users to run the *ssh-keygen* command just once to ensure their key file is created correctly. The *ssh-keygen* will create their ~/.ssh/ directories for them with appropriate permissions and create their private and public keys in .ssh/identity and .ssh/identity.pub, respectively. A sample session should look like:

```
$ ssh-keygen
Generating RSA keys:  .......oooooO.............................
Key generation complete.
Enter file in which to save the key (/home/maggie/.ssh/identity):
Enter passphrase (empty for no passphrase):
Enter same passphrase again:
Your identification has been saved in /home/maggie/.ssh/identity.
Your public key has been saved in /home/maggie/.ssh/identity.pub.
The key fingerprint is:
1024 85:49:53:f4:8a:d6:d9:05:d0:1f:23:c4:d7:2a:11:67 maggie@moria
$
```

Now *ssh* is ready to run.

Using ssh

We should now have the *ssh* command and it's associated programs installed and ready to run. Let's now take a quick look at how to run them.

First, we'll try a remote login to a host. We can use the *slogin* program in much the same way as we used the *rlogin* program in our example earlier in the book. The first time you attempt a connection to a host, the *ssh* client will retrieve the public key of the host and ask you to confirm its identity by prompting you with a shortened version of the public key called a *fingerprint.*

The administrator at the remote host should have supplied you in advance with its public key fingerprint, which you should add to your *.ssh/known_hosts* file. If the remote administrator has not supplied you the appropriate key, you can connect to the remote host, but *ssh* will warn you that it does have a key and prompt you whether you wish to accept the one offered by the remote host. Assuming that you're sure no one is engaging in DNS spoofing and you are in fact talking to the correct host, answer yes to the prompt. The relevant key is then stored automatically in your *.ssh/known_hosts* and you will not be prompted for it again. If, on a future connection attempt, the public key retrieved from that host does not match the one that is stored, you will be warned, because this represents a potential security breach.

A first-time login to a remote host will look something like:

```
$ slogin vchianti.vbrew.com
The authenticity of host 'vchianti.vbrew.com' can't be established.
Key fingerprint is 1024 7b:d4:a8:28:c5:19:52:53:3a:fe:8d:95:dd:14:93:f5.
Are you sure you want to continue connecting (yes/no)? yes
Warning: Permanently added 'vchianti.vbrew.com,172.16.2.3' to the list of/
    known hosts.
maggie@vchianti.vbrew.com's password:
Last login: Tue Feb  1 23:28:58 2000 from vstout.vbrew.com
$
```

You will be prompted for a password, which you should answer with the password belonging to the remote account, not the local one. This password is not echoed when you type it.

Without any special arguments, *slogin* will attempt to log in with the same userid used on the local machine. You can override this using the −1 argument, supplying an alternate login name on the remote host. This is what we did in our example earlier in the book.

We can copy files to and from the remote host using the *scp* program. Its syntax is similar to the conventional *cp* with the exception that you may specify a hostname before a filename, meaning that the file path is on the specified host. The following example illustrates *scp* syntax by copying a local file called */tmp/fred* to the */home/maggie/* of the remote host **chianti.vbrew.com**:

```
$ scp /tmp/fred vchianti.vbrew.com:/home/maggie/
maggie@vchianti.vbrew.com's password:
fred                     100% |*****************************| 50165     00:01 ETA
```

Again, you'll be prompted for a password. The *scp* command displays useful progress messages by default. You can copy a file from a remote host with the same ease; simply specify its hostname and filepath as the source and the local path as the destination. It's even possible to copy a file from a remote host to some other remote host, but it is something you wouldn't normally want to do, because all of the data travels via your host.

You can execute commands on remote hosts using the *ssh* command. Again, its syntax is very simple. Let's have our user **maggie** retrieve the root directory of the remote host **vchianti.vbrew.com**. She'd do this with:

```
$ ssh vchianti.vbrew.com ls -CF /
maggie@vchianti.vbrew.com's password:
bin/    console@ dos/     home/    lost+found/  pub@    tmp/   vmlinuz@
boot/   dev/     etc/     initrd/  mnt/         root/   usr/   vmlinuz.old@
cdrom/  disk/    floppy/  lib/     proc/        sbin/   var/
```

You can place *ssh* in a command pipeline and pipe program input/output to or from it just like any other command, except that the input or output is directed to or from the remote host via the *ssh* connection. Here is an example of how you might use this capability in combination with the *tar* command to copy a whole directory with subdirectories and files from a remote host to the local host:

```
$ ssh vchianti.vbrew.com "tar cf - /etc/" | tar xvf -
maggie@vchianti.vbrew.com's password:
etc/GNUstep
etc/Muttrc
etc/Net
etc/X11
etc/adduser.conf
..
..
```

Here we surrounded the command we will execute with quotation marks to make it clear what is passed as an argument to *ssh* and what is used by the local shell. This command executes the *tar* command on the remote host to archive the */etc/* directory and write the output to standard output. We've piped to an instance of the *tar* command running on our local host in extract mode reading from standard input.

Again, we were prompted for the password. Now you can see why we encouraged you to configure *ssh* so that it doesn't prompt you for passwords all the time! Let's now configure our local *ssh* client so that it won't prompt for a password when connecting to the vchianti.vbrew.com host. We mentioned the *.ssh/authorized_keys* file earlier; this is where it is used. The *.ssh/authorized_keys* file contains the *public* keys on any remote user accounts that we wish to automatically log in to. You can set up automatic logins by copying the contents of the *.ssh/identity.pub* from the *remote* account into our local *.ssh/authorized_keys* file. It is vital that the file permissions of *.ssh/authorized_keys* allow only that you read and write it; anyone may steal and use the keys to log in to that remote account. To ensure the permissions are correct, change *.ssh/authorized_keys*, as shown:

```
$ chmod 600 ~/.ssh/authorized_keys
```

The public keys are a long *single* line of plain text. If you use copy and paste to duplicate the key into your local file, be sure to remove any end of line characters that might have been introduced along the way. The *.ssh/authorized_keys* file may contain many such keys, each on a line of its own.

The *ssh* suite of tools is very powerful and there are many other useful features and options that you will be interested in exploring. Please refer to the manual pages and other documentation that is supplied with the package for more information.

CHAPTER THIRTEEN
THE NETWORK INFORMATION SYSTEM

When you're running a local area network, your overall goal is usually to provide an environment for your users that makes the network transparent. An important stepping stone is keeping vital data such as user account information synchronized among all hosts. This provides users with the freedom to move from machine to machine without the inconvenience of having to remember different passwords and copy data from one machine to another. Data that is centrally stored doesn't need to be replicated, so long as there is some convenient means of accessing it from a network-connected host. By storing important administrative information centrally, you can make ensure consistency of that data, increase flexibility for the users by allowing them to move from host to host in a transparent way, and make the system administrator's life much easier by maintaining a single copy of information to maintain when required.

We previously discussed an important example of this concept that is used on the Internet—the Domain Name System (DNS). DNS serves a limited range of information, the most important being the mapping between hostname and IP address. For other types of information, there is no such specialized service. Moreover, if you manage only a small LAN with no Internet connectivity, setting up DNS may not seem to be worth the trouble.

This is why Sun developed the *Network Information System* (NIS). NIS provides generic database access facilities that can be used to distribute, for example, information contained in the *passwd* and *groups* files to all hosts on your network. This makes the network appear as a single system, with the same accounts on all hosts. Similarly, you can use NIS to distribute the hostname information from */etc/hosts* to all machines on the network.

NIS is based on RPC, and comprises a server, a client-side library, and several administrative tools. Originally, NIS was called *Yellow Pages*, or YP, which is still used to refer to it. Unfortunately, the name is a trademark of British Telecom, which required Sun to drop that name. As things go, some names stick with people, and so YP lives on as a prefix to the names of most NIS-related commands such as *ypserv* and *ypbind*.

Today, NIS is available for virtually all Unixes, and there are even free implementations. BSD Net-2 released one that has been derived from a public domain reference implementation donated by Sun. The library client code from this release had been in the Linux *libc* for a long time, and the administrative programs were ported to Linux by Swen Thümmler.* An NIS server is missing from the reference implementation, though.

Peter Eriksson developed a new implementation called NYS.† It supports both plain NIS and Sun's much enhanced NIS+. NYS not only provides a set of NIS tools and a server, but also adds a whole new set of library functions that need to be compiled into your *libc* if you wish to use it. This includes a new configuration scheme for hostname resolution that replaces the current scheme using *host.conf*.

The GNU libc, known as *libc6* in the Linux community, includes an updated version of the traditional NIS support developed by Thorsten Kukuk.‡ It supports all of the library functions that NYS provided and also uses the enhanced configuration scheme of NYS. You still need the tools and server, but using GNU *libc* saves you the trouble of having to meddle with patching and recompiling the library.

This chapter focuses on the NIS support included in the GNU *libc* rather than the other two packages. If you do want to run any of these packages, the instructions in this chapter may or may not be enough. For additional information, refer to the NIS-HOWTO or a book such as *Managing NFS and NIS* by Hal Stern (O'Reilly).

Getting Acquainted with NIS

NIS keeps database information in files called *maps*, which contain key-value pairs. An example of a key-value pair is a user's login name and the encrypted form of their login password. Maps are stored on a central host running the NIS server, from which clients may retrieve the information through various RPC calls. Quite frequently, maps are stored in DBM files.§

---

* Swen can be reached at *swen@uni-paderborn.de*. The NIS clients are available as *yp-linux.tar.gz* from **metalab.unc.edu** in *system/Network*.

† Peter may be reached at *pen@lysator.liu.se*. The current version of NYS is 1.2.8.

‡ Thorsten may be reached at *kukuk@uni-paderborn.de*.

§ DBM is a simple database management library that uses hashing techniques to speed up search operations. There's a free DBM implementation from the GNU project called *gdbm*, which is part of most Linux distributions.

The maps themselves are usually generated from master text files such as */etc/hosts* or */etc/passwd*. For some files, several maps are created, one for each search key type. For instance, you may search the *hosts* file for a hostname as well as for an IP address. Accordingly, two NIS maps are derived from it, called *hosts.byname* and *hosts.byaddr*. Table 13-1 lists common maps and the files from which they are generated.

Table 13-1. Some Standard NIS Maps and Corresponding Files

Master File	Map(s)	Description
/etc/hosts	*hosts.byname, hosts.byaddr*	Maps IP addresses to host names
/etc/networks	*networks.byname, networks.byaddr*	Maps IP network addresses to network names
/etc/passwd	*passwd.byname, passwd.byuid*	Maps encrypted passwords to user login names
/etc/group	*group.byname, group.bygid*	Maps Group IDs to group names
/etc/services	*services.byname, services.bynumber*	Maps service descriptions to service names
/etc/rpc	*rpc.byname, rpc.bynumber*	Maps Sun RPC service numbers to RPC service names
/etc/protocols	*protocols.byname, protocols.bynumber*	Maps protocol numbers to protocol names
/usr/lib/aliases	*mail.aliases*	Maps mail aliases to mail alias names

You may find support for other files and maps in other NIS packages. These usually contain information for applications not discussed in this book, such as the *bootparams* map that is used by Sun's *bootparamd* server.

For some maps, people commonly use *nicknames*, which are shorter and therefore easier to type. Note that these nicknames are understood only by *ypcat* and *ypmatch*, two tools for checking your NIS configuration. To obtain a full list of nicknames understood by these tools, run the following command:

```
$ ypcat -x
Use "passwd" for "passwd.byname"
Use "group" for "group.byname"
Use "networks" for "networks.byaddr"
Use "hosts" for "hosts.byaddr"
Use "protocols" for "protocols.bynumber"
Use "services" for "services.byname"
Use "aliases" for "mail.aliases"
Use "ethers" for "ethers.byname"
```

The NIS server program is traditionally called *ypserv*. For an average network, a single server usually suffices; large networks may choose to run several of these on different machines and different segments of the network to relieve the load on the server machines and routers. These servers are synchronized by making one of them the *master server*, and the others *slave servers*. Maps are created only on the master server's host. From there, they are distributed to all slaves.

We have been talking very vaguely about "networks." There's a distinctive term in NIS that refers to a collection of all hosts that share part of their system configuration data through NIS: the *NIS domain*. Unfortunately, NIS domains have absolutely nothing in common with the domains we encountered in DNS. To avoid any ambiguity throughout this chapter, we will therefore always specify which type of domain we mean.

NIS domains have a purely administrative function. They are mostly invisible to users, except for the sharing of passwords between all machines in the domain. Therefore, the name given to an NIS domain is relevant only to the administrators. Usually, any name will do, as long as it is different from any other NIS domain name on your local network. For instance, the administrator at the Virtual Brewery may choose to create two NIS domains, one for the Brewery itself, and one for the Winery, which she names **brewery** and **winery** respectively. Another quite common scheme is to simply use the DNS domain name for NIS as well.

To set and display the NIS domain name of your host, you can use the *domainname* command. When invoked without any argument, it prints the current NIS domain name; to set the domain name, you must become the superuser:

```
# domainname brewery
```

NIS domains determine which NIS server an application will query. For instance, the *login* program on a host at the Winery should, of course, query only the Winery's NIS server (or one of them, if there are several) for a user's password information, while an application on a Brewery host should stick with the Brewery's server.

One mystery now remains to be solved: how does a client find out which server to connect to? The simplest approach would use a configuration file that names the host on which to find the server. However, this approach is rather inflexible because it doesn't allow clients to use different servers (from the same domain, of course) depending on their availability. Therefore, NIS implementations rely on a special daemon called *ypbind* to detect a suitable NIS server in their NIS domain. Before performing any NIS queries, an application first finds out from *ypbind* which server to use.

ypbind probes for servers by broadcasting to the local IP network; the first to respond is assumed to be the fastest one and is used in all subsequent NIS queries. After a certain interval has elapsed, or if the server becomes unavailable, *ypbind* probes for active servers again.

Dynamic binding is useful only when your network provides more than one NIS server. Dynamic binding also introduces a security problem. *ypbind* blindly believes whoever answers, whether it be a humble NIS server or a malicious intruder. Needless to say, this becomes especially troublesome if you manage your password databases over NIS. To guard against this, the Linux *ypbind* program provides you with the option of probing the local network to find the local NIS server, or configuring the NIS server hostname in a configuration file.

NIS Versus NIS+

NIS and NIS+ share little more than their name and a common goal. NIS+ is structured entirely differently from NIS. Instead of a flat namespace with disjoint NIS domains, NIS+ uses a hierarchical namespace similar to that of DNS. Instead of maps, so-called *tables* are used that are made up of rows and columns, in which each row represents an object in the NIS+ database and the columns cover properties of the objects that NIS+ knows and cares about. Each table for a given NIS+ domain comprises those of its parent domains. In addition, an entry in a table may contain a link to another table. These features make it possible to structure information in many ways.

NIS+ additionally supports secure and encrypted RPC, which helps greatly to solve the security problems of NIS.

Traditional NIS has an RPC Version number of 2, while NIS+ is Version 3. At the time we're writing, there isn't yet a good working implementation of NIS+ for Linux, so it isn't covered here.

The Client Side of NIS

If you are familiar with writing or porting network applications, you may notice that most of the NIS maps listed previously correspond to library functions in the C library. For instance, to obtain *passwd* information, you generally use the *getpwnam* and *getpwuid* functions, which return the account information associated with the given username or numerical user ID, respectively. Under normal circumstances, these functions perform the requested lookup on the standard file, such as */etc/passwd*.

An NIS-aware implementation of these functions, however, modifies this behavior and places an RPC call to the NIS server, which looks up the username or user ID. This happens transparently to the application. The function may treat the NIS data as though it has been appended to the original *passwd* file so both sets of information are available to the application and used, or as though it has completely replaced it so that the information in the local *passwd* is ignored and only the NIS data is used.

For traditional NIS implementations, there were certain conventions for which maps were replaced and which were appended to the original information. Some, like the *passwd* maps, required kludgy modifications of the *passwd* file which, when done incorrectly, would open up security holes. To avoid these pitfalls, NYS and the GNU *libc* use a general configuration scheme that determines whether a particular set of client functions uses the original files, NIS, or NIS+, and in which order. This scheme will be described later in this chapter.

Running an NIS Server

After so much theoretical techno-babble, it's time to get our hands dirty with actual configuration work. In this section, we will cover the configuration of an NIS server. If an NIS server is running on your network, you won't have to set up your own; in this case, you may safely skip this section.

Note that if you are just going to experiment with the server, make sure you don't set it up for an NIS domain name that is already in use on your network. This may disrupt the entire network service and make a lot of people very unhappy and very angry.

There are two possible NIS server configurations: master and slave. The slave configuration provides a live backup machine, should your master server fail. We will cover the configuration only for a master server here. The server documentation will explain the differences, should you wish to configure a slave server.

There are currently two NIS servers freely available for Linux: one contained in Tobias Reber's *yps* package, and the other in Peter Eriksson's *ypserv* package. It doesn't matter which one you run.

After installing the server program (*ypserv*) in */usr/sbin*, you should create the directory that is going to hold the map files your server is to distribute. When setting up an NIS domain for the **brewery** domain, the maps would go to */var/yp/brewery*. The server determines whether it is serving a particular NIS domain by checking if the map directory is present. If you are disabling service for some NIS domain, make sure to remove the directory as well.

Maps are usually stored in DBM files to speed up lookups. They are created from the master files using a program called *makedbm* (for Tobias's server) or *dbmload* (for Peter's server).

Transforming a master file into a form that *dbmload* can parse usually requires some *awk* or *sed* magic, which tends to be a little tedious to type and hard to remember. Therefore, Peter Eriksson's *ypserv* package contains a Makefile (called *ypMakefile*) that manages the conversion of the most common master files for you. You should install it as *Makefile* in your map directory and edit it to reflect the maps you want the NIS server to share. Towards the top of the file, you'll find the `all` target that lists the services *ypserv* offers. By default, the line looks something like this:

```
all: ethers hosts networks protocols rpc services passwd group netid
```

If you don't want to produce, for example, the *ethers.byname* and *ethers.byaddr* maps, simply remove the `ethers` prerequisite from this rule. To test your setup, you can start with just one or two maps, like the *services.** maps.

After editing the *Makefile*, while in the map directory, type **make**. This will automatically generate and install the maps. You have to make sure to update the maps whenever you change the master files, otherwise the changes will remain invisible to the network.

The section "Setting Up an NIS Client with GNU libc" will explain how to configure the NIS client code. If your setup doesn't work, you should try to find out whether requests are arriving at your server. If you specify the *—debug* command-line flag to *ypserv*, it prints debugging messages to the console about all incoming NIS queries and the results returned. These should give you a hint as to where the problem lies. Tobias's server doesn't have this option.

NIS Server Security

NIS used to have a major security flaw: it left your password file readable by virtually anyone in the entire Internet, which made for quite a number of possible intruders. As long as an intruder knew your NIS domain name and the address of your server, he could simply send it a request for the *passwd.byname* map and instantly receive all your system's encrypted passwords. With a fast password-cracking program like *crack* and a good dictionary, guessing at least a few of your users' passwords is rarely a problem.

This is what the *securenets* option is all about. It simply restricts access to your NIS server to certain hosts, based on their IP addresses or network numbers. The latest version of *ypserv* implements this feature in two ways. The first relies on a special configuration file called */etc/ypserv.securenets* and the second conveniently uses the */etc/hosts.allow* and */etc/hosts.deny* files we already encountered in Chapter 12, *Important Network Features.** Thus, to restrict access to hosts from within the Brewery, their network manager would add the following line to *hosts.allow*:

```
ypserv: 172.16.2.
```

---

* To enable use of the */etc/hosts.allow* method, you may have to recompile the server. Please read the instructions in the *README* included in the distribution.

This would let all hosts from IP network **172.16.2.0** access the NIS server. To shut out all other hosts, a corresponding entry in *hosts.deny* would have to read:

```
ypserv: ALL
```

IP numbers are not the only way you can specify hosts or networks in *hosts.allow* and *hosts.deny*. Please refer to the *hosts_access(5)* manual page on your system for details. However, be warned that you *cannot* use host or domain names for the **ypserv** entry. If you specify a hostname, the server tries to resolve this hostname—but the resolver in turn calls *ypserv*, and you fall into an endless loop.

To configure **securenets** security using the */etc/ypserv.securenets* method, you need to create its configuration file, */etc/ypserv.securenets*. This configuration file is simple in structure. Each line describes a host or network of hosts that will be allowed access to the server. Any address not described by an entry in this file will be refused access. A line beginning with a # will be treated as a comment. Example 13-1 shows what a simple */etc/ypserv.securenets* would look like:

Example 13-1: Sample ypserv.securenets File

```
# allow connections from local host -- necessary
host 127.0.0.1
# same as 255.255.255.255 127.0.0.1
#
# allow connections from any host on the Virtual Brewery network
255.255.255.0    172.16.1.0
#
```

The first entry on each line is the netmask to use for the entry, with **host** being treated as a special keyword meaning "netmask 255.255.255.255." The second entry on each line is the IP address to which to apply the netmask.

A third option is to use the secure portmapper instead of the *securenets* option in *ypserv*. The secure portmapper (*portmap-5.0*) uses the *hosts.allow* scheme as well, but offers this for all RPC servers, not just *ypserv*.* However, you should not use both the *securenets* option and the secure portmapper at the same time, because of the overhead this authorization incurs.

Setting Up an NIS Client with GNU libc

We will now describe and discuss the configuration of an NIS client using the GNU libc library support.

---

* The secure portmapper is available via anonymous FTP from **ftp.win.tue.nl** below the */pub/security/* directory.

Your first step should be to tell the GNU libc NIS client which server to use for NIS service. We mentioned earlier that the Linux *ypbind* allows you to configure the NIS server to use. The default behavior is to query the server on the local network. If the host you are configuring is likely to move from one domain to another, such as a laptop, you would leave the */etc/yp.conf* file empty and it would query on the local network for the local NIS server wherever it happens to be.

A more secure configuration for most hosts is to set the server name in the */etc/yp.conf* configuration file. A very simple file for a host on the Winery's network may look like this:

```
# yp.conf - YP configuration for GNU libc library.
#
ypserver vbardolino
```

The **ypserver** statement tells your host to use the host supplied as the NIS server for the local domain. In this example we've specified the NIS server as **vbardolino**. Of course, the IP address corresponding to **vbardolino** must be set in the *hosts* file; alternatively, you may use the IP address itself with the **server** argument.

In the form shown in the example, the *ypserver* command tells *ypbind* to use the named server regardless of what the current NIS domain may be. If, however, you are moving your machine between different NIS domains frequently, you may want to keep information for several domains in the *yp.conf* file. You can have information on the servers for various NIS domains in *yp.conf* by specifying the information using the **domain** statement. For instance, you might change the previous sample file to look like this for a laptop:

```
# yp.conf - YP configuration for GNU libc library.
#
domain winery server vbardolino
domain brewery server vstout
```

This lets you bring up the laptop in either of the two domains by simply setting the desired NIS domain at boot time using the *domainname* command. The NIS client then uses whichever server is relevant for the current domain.

There is a third option you may want to use. It covers the case when you don't know the name or IP address of the server to use in a particular domain, but still want the ability use a fixed server on certain domains. Imagine we want to insist on using a specified server while operating within the Winery domain, but want to probe for the server to use while in the Brewery domain. We would modify our *yp.conf* file again to look like this instead:

```
# yp.conf - YP configuration for GNU libc library.
#
domain winery server vbardolino
domain brewery broadcast
```

The `broadcast` keyword tells *ypbind* to use whichever NIS server it finds for the domain.

After creating this basic configuration file and making sure it is world-readable, you should run your first test to connect to your server. Make sure to choose a map your server distributes, like *hosts.byname*, and try to retrieve it by using the *ypcat* utility:

```
# ypcat hosts.byname
172.16.2.2      vbeaujolais.vbrew.com     vbeaujolais
172.16.2.3      vbardolino.vbrew.com      vbardolino
172.16.1.1      vlager.vbrew.com          vlager
172.16.2.1      vlager.vbrew.com          vlager
172.16.1.2      vstout.vbrew.com          vstout
172.16.1.3      vale.vbrew.com            vale
172.16.2.4      vchianti.vbrew.com        vchianti
```

The output you get should resemble that just shown. If you get an error message instead that says: `Can't bind to server which serves domain`, then either the NIS domain name you've set doesn't have a matching server defined in *yp.conf*, or the server is unreachable for some reason. In the latter case, make sure that a *ping* to the host yields a positive result, and that it is indeed running an NIS server. You can verify the latter by using *rpcinfo*, which should produce the following output:

```
# rpcinfo -u serverhost ypserv
program 100004 version 1 ready and waiting
program 100004 version 2 ready and waiting
```

Choosing the Right Maps

Having made sure you can reach the NIS server, you have to decide which configuration files to replace or augment with NIS maps. Commonly, you will want to use NIS maps for the host and password lookup functions. The former is especially useful if you do not have the BIND name service. The password lookup lets all users log into their accounts from any system in the NIS domain; this usually goes along with sharing a central */home* directory among all hosts via NFS. The password map is explained detail in the next section.

Other maps, like *services.byname*, don't provide such dramatic gains, but do save you some editing work. The *services.byname* map is valuable if you install any network applications that use a service name not in the standard *services* file.

Generally, you want to have some choice of when a lookup function uses the local files, when it queries the NIS server, and when it uses other servers such as DNS. GNU libc allows you to configure the order in which a function accesses these services. This is controlled through the */etc/nsswitch.conf* file, which stands for *Name Service Switch*, but of course isn't limited to the name service. For any of the data lookup functions supported by GNU libc, the file contains a line naming the services to use.

The right order of services depends on the type of data each service is offering. It is unlikely that the *services.byname* map will contain entries differing from those in the local *services* file; it will only contain additional entries. So it appears reasonable to query the local files first and check NIS only if the service name isn't found. Hostname information, on the other hand, may change very frequently, so DNS or the NIS server should always have the most accurate account, while the local *hosts* file is only kept as a backup if DNS and NIS should fail. For hostnames, therefore, you normally want to check the local file last.

The following example shows how to force *gethostbyname* and *gethostbyaddr* to look in NIS and DNS before the *hosts* file and how to have the *getservbyname* function look in the local files before querying NIS. These resolver functions will try each of the listed services in turn; if a lookup succeeds, the result is returned; otherwise, they will try the next service in the list. The file setting for these priorities is:

```
# small sample /etc/nsswitch.conf
#
hosts:     nis dns files
services:  files nis
```

The following is a complete list of services and locations that may be used with an entry in the *nsswitch.conf* file. The actual maps, files, servers, and objects queried depend on the entry name. The following can appear to the right of a colon:

nis

Use the current domain NIS server. The location of the server queried is configured in the *yp.conf* file, as shown in the previous section. For the hosts entry, the *hosts.byname* and *hosts.byaddr* maps are queried.

nisplus *or* nis+

Use the NIS+ server for this domain. The location of the server is obtained from the */etc/nis.conf* file.

dns

Use the DNS name server. This service type is useful only with the hosts entry. The name servers queried are still determined by the standard *resolv.conf* file.

files

Use the local file, such as the */etc/hosts* file for the hosts entry.

`compat`

> Be compatible with older file formats. This option can be used when either NYS or glibc 2.x is used for NIS or NIS+ lookups. While these versions normally can't interpret older NIS entries in *passwd* and *group* files, `compat` option allows them to work with those formats.

`db` Look up the information from DBM files located in the */var/db* directory. The corresponding NIS map name is used for that file.

Currently, the NIS support in GNU libc caters to the following *nsswitch.conf* databases: `aliases, ethers.group, hosts, netgroup, network, passwd, protocols, publickey, rpc, services`, and `shadow`. More entries are likely to be added.

Example 13-2 shows a more complete example that introduces another feature of *nsswitch.conf*. The `[NOTFOUND=return]` keyword in the `hosts` entry tells the NIS client to return if the desired item couldn't be found in the NIS or DNS database. That is, the NIS client will continue searching the local files *only* if calls to the NIS and DNS servers fail for some other reason. The local files will then be used only at boot time and as a backup when the NIS server is down.

Example 13-2: Sample nsswitch.conf File

```
# /etc/nsswitch.conf
#
hosts:      nis dns [NOTFOUND=return] files
networks:   nis [NOTFOUND=return] files
services:   files nis
protocols:  files nis
rpc:        files nis
```

GNU libc provides some other actions that are described in the *nsswitch* manpage.

Using the passwd and group Maps

One of the major applications of NIS is synchronizing user and account information on all hosts in an NIS domain. Consequently, you usually keep only a small local */etc/passwd* file, to which site-wide information from the NIS maps is appended. However, simply enabling NIS lookups for this service in *nsswitch.conf* is not nearly enough.

When relying on the password information distributed by NIS, you first have to make sure that the numeric user IDs of any users you have in your local *passwd* file match the NIS server's idea of user IDs. Consistency in user IDs is important for other purposes as well, like mounting NFS volumes from other hosts in your network.

If any of the numeric IDs in */etc/passwd* or */etc/group* differ from those in the maps, you have to adjust file ownerships for all files that belong to that user. First, you should change all uids and gids in *passwd* and *group* to the new values, then find that all files that belong to the users just changed and change their ownership. Assume **news** used to have a user ID of 9 and **okir** had a user ID of 103, which were changed to some other value; you could then issue the following commands as root:

```
# find / -uid   9 -print >/tmp/uid.9
# find / -uid 103 -print >/tmp/uid.103
# cat /tmp/uid.9   | xargs chown news
# cat /tmp/uid.103 | xargs chown okir
```

It is important that you execute these commands with the new *passwd* file installed, and that you collect all filenames before you change the ownership of any of them. To update the group ownerships of files, use a similar method with the gid instead of the uid, and chgrp instead of chown.

Once you do this, the numerical uids and gids on your system will agree with those on all other hosts in your NIS domain. The next step is to add configuration lines to *nsswitch.conf* that enable NIS lookups for user and group information:

```
# /etc/nsswitch.conf - passwd and group treatment
passwd: nis files
group:  nis files
```

This affects where the *login* command and all its friends look for user information. When a user tries to log in, *login* queries the NIS maps first, and if this lookup fails, falls back to the local files. Usually, you will remove almost all users from your local files, and only leave entries for **root** and generic accounts like **mail** in it. This is because some vital system tasks may have to map uids to usernames or vice versa. For example, administrative *cron* jobs may execute the *su* command to temporarily become **news**, or the UUCP subsystem may mail a status report. If **news** and **uucp** don't have entries in the local *passwd* file, these jobs will fail miserably during an NIS brownout.

Lastly, if you are using either the old NIS implementation (supported by the `compat` mode for the *passwd* and *group* files in the NYS or glibc implementations), you must insert the unwieldy special entries into them. These entries represent where the NIS derived records will be inserted into the database of information. The entries can be added anywhere, but are usually just added to the end. The entries to add for the */etc/passwd* file are:

```
+:::::::
```

and for the */etc/groups* file:

```
+:::
```

With both glibc 2.x and NYS you can override parameters in a user's record received from the NIS server by creating entries with a "+" prepended to the login name, and exclude specified users by creating entries with a "-" prepended to the login name. For example the entries:

```
+stuart::::::/bin/jacl
-jedd::::::
```

would override the shell specified for the user **stuart** supplied by the NIS server, and would disallow the user **jedd** from logging in on this machine. Any fields left blank use the information supplied by the NIS server.

There are two big caveats in order here. First, the setup as described up to here works only for login suites that don't use shadow passwords. The intricacies of using shadow passwords with NIS will be discussed in the next section. Second, the login commands are not the only ones that access the *passwd* file—look at the *ls* command, which most people use almost constantly. Whenever compiling a long listing, *ls* displays the symbolic names for user and group owners of a file; that is, for each uid and gid it encounters, it has to query the NIS server. An NIS query takes slightly longer to perform than the equivalent lookup in a local file. You may find that sharing your *passwd* and *group* information using NIS causes a noticable reduction in the performance of some programs that use this information frequently.

Still, this is not the whole story. Imagine what happens if a user wants to change her password. Usually, she will invoke *passwd*, which reads the new password and updates the local *passwd* file. This is impossible with NIS, since that file isn't available locally anymore, but having users log into the NIS server whenever they want to change their passwords is not an option, either. Therefore, NIS provides a drop-in replacement for *passwd* called *yppasswd*, which handles password changes under NIS. To change the password on the server host, it contacts the *yppasswdd* daemon on that host via RPC, and provides it with the updated password information. Usually you install *yppasswd* over the normal program by doing something like this:

```
# cd /bin
# mv passwd passwd.old
# ln yppasswd passwd
```

At the same time, you have to install *rpc.yppasswdd* on the server and start it from a network script. This will effectively hide any of the contortions of NIS from your users.

Using NIS with Shadow Support

Using NIS in conjunction with shadow password files is somewhat problematic. First we have some bad news: using NIS defeats the goals of shadow passwords. The *shadow* password scheme was designed to prevent nonroot users from having access to the encrypted form of the login passwords. Using NIS to share *shadow* data by necessity makes the encrypted passwords available to any user who can listen to the NIS server replies on the network. A policy to enforce users to choose "good" passwords is arguably better than trying to shadow passwords in an NIS environment. Let's take a quick look at how you do it, should you decide to forge on ahead.

In libc5 there is no real solution to sharing *shadow* data using NIS. The only way to distribute password and user information by NIS is through the standard *passwd.** maps. If you do have shadow passwords installed, the easiest way to share them is to generate a proper *passwd* file from */etc/shadow* using tools like *pwuncov*, and create the NIS maps from that file.

Of course, there are some hacks necessary to use NIS and shadow passwords at the same time, for instance, by installing an */etc/shadow* file on each host in the network, while distributing user information, through NIS. However, this hack is really crude and defies the goal of NIS, which is to ease system administration.

The NIS support in the GNU libc library (libc6) provides support for shadow password databases. It does not provide any real solution to making your passwords accessible, but it does simplify password management in environments in which you do want to use NIS with shadow passwords. To use it, you must create a *shadow.byname* database and add the following line to your */etc/nsswitch.conf*:

```
# Shadow password support
shadow:         compat
```

If you use shadow passwords along with NIS, you must try to maintain some security by restricting access to your NIS database. See "NIS Server Security" earlier in this chapter.

CHAPTER FOURTEEN

THE NETWORK FILE SYSTEM

The Network File System (NFS) is probably the most prominent network service using RPC. It allows you to access files on remote hosts in exactly the same way you would access local files. A mixture of kernel support and user-space daemons on the client side, along with an NFS server on the server side, makes this possible. This file access is completely transparent to the client and works across a variety of server and host architectures.

NFS offers a number of useful features:

- Data accessed by all users can be kept on a central host, with clients mounting this directory at boot time. For example, you can keep all user accounts on one host and have all hosts on your network mount */home* from that host. If NFS is installed beside NIS, users can log into any system and still work on one set of files.

- Data consuming large amounts of disk space can be kept on a single host. For example, all files and programs relating to LaTeX and METAFONT can be kept and maintained in one place.

- Administrative data can be kept on a single host. There is no need to use *rcp* to install the same stupid file on 20 different machines.

It's not too hard to set up basic NFS operation on both the client and server; this chapter tells you how.

Linux NFS is largely the work of Rick Sladkey, who wrote the NFS kernel code and large parts of the NFS server.* The latter is derived from the **unfsd** user space NFS server, originally written by Mark Shand, and the **hnfs** Harris NFS server, written by Donald Becker.

---

* Rick can be reached at *jrs@world.std.com*.

Let's have a look at how NFS works. First, a client tries to mount a directory from a remote host on a local directory just the same way it does a physical device. However, the syntax used to specify the remote directory is different. For example, to mount */home* from host **vlager** to */users* on **vale**, the administrator issues the following command on **vale**:*

```
# mount -t nfs vlager:/home /users
```

mount will try to connect to the *rpc.mountd* mount daemon on **vlager** via RPC. The server will check if **vale** is permitted to mount the directory in question, and if so, return it a file handle. This file handle will be used in all subsequent requests to files below */users*.

When someone accesses a file over NFS, the kernel places an RPC call to *rpc.nfsd* (the NFS daemon) on the server machine. This call takes the file handle, the name of the file to be accessed, and the user and group IDs of the user as parameters. These are used in determining access rights to the specified file. In order to prevent unauthorized users from reading or modifying files, user and group IDs must be the same on both hosts.

On most Unix implementations, the NFS functionality of both client and server is implemented as kernel-level daemons that are started from user space at system boot. These are the *NFS Daemon* (*rpc.nfsd*) on the server host, and the *Block I/O Daemon* (*biod*) on the client host. To improve throughput, *biod* performs asynchronous I/O using read-ahead and write-behind; also, several *rpc.nfsd* daemons are usually run concurrently.

The current NFS implementation of Linux is a little different from the classic NFS in that the server code runs entirely in user space, so running multiple copies simultaneously is more complicated. The current *rpc.nfsd* implementation offers an experimental feature that allows limited support for multiple servers. Olaf Kirch developed kernel-based NFS server support featured in 2.2 Version Linux kernels. Its performance is significantly better than the existing userspace implementation. We'll describe it later in this chapter.

Preparing NFS

Before you can use NFS, be it as server or client, you must make sure your kernel has NFS support compiled in. Newer kernels have a simple interface on the *proc* filesystem for this, the */proc/filesystems* file, which you can display using *cat*:

```
$ cat /proc/filesystems
        minix
        ext2
        msdos
```

---

* Actually, you can omit the -t nfs argument because *mount* sees from the colon that this specifies an NFS volume.

```
nodev   proc
nodev   nfs
```

If `nfs` is missing from this list, you have to compile your own kernel with NFS enabled, or perhaps you will need to load the kernel module if your NFS support was compiled as a module. Configuring the kernel network options is explained in the "Kernel Configuration" section of Chapter 3, *Configuring the Networking Hardware*.

Mounting an NFS Volume

The mounting of NFS volumes closely resembles regular file systems. Invoke *mount* using the following syntax:*

```
# mount -t nfs nfs_volume local_dir options
```

nfs_volume is given as *remote_host:remote_dir*. Since this notation is unique to NFS filesystems, you can leave out the *–t nfs* option.

There are a number of additional options that you can specify to *mount* upon mounting an NFS volume. These may be given either following the *–o* switch on the command line or in the options field of the */etc/fstab* entry for the volume. In both cases, multiple options are separated by commas and must not contain any whitespace characters. Options specified on the command line always override those given in the *fstab* file.

Here is a sample entry from */etc/fstab*:

```
# volume                 mount point       type   options
news:/var/spool/news  /var/spool/news    nfs    timeo=14,intr
```

This volume can then be mounted using this command:

```
# mount news:/var/spool/news
```

In the absence of an *fstab* entry, NFS *mount* invocations look a lot uglier. For instance, suppose you mount your users' home directories from a machine named **moonshot**, which uses a default block size of 4 K for read/write operations. You might increase the block size to 8 K to obtain better performance by issuing the command:

```
# mount moonshot:/home /home -o rsize=8192,wsize=8192
```

The list of all valid options is described in its entirety in the *nfs(5)* manual page. The following is a partial list of options you would probably want to use:

---

* One doesn't say filesystem because these are not proper filesystems.

rsize=n and *wsize=n*

These specify the datagram size used by the NFS clients on read and write requests, respectively. The default depends on the version of kernel, but is normally 1,024 bytes.

timeo=n

This sets the time (in tenths of a second) the NFS client will wait for a request to complete. The default value is 7 (0.7 seconds). What happens after a time-out depends on whether you use the *hard* or *soft* option.

hard

Explicitly mark this volume as hard-mounted. This is on by default. This option causes the server to report a message to the console when a major timeout occurs and continues trying indefinitely.

soft

Soft-mount (as opposed to hard-mount) the driver. This option causes an I/O error to be reported to the process attempting a file operation when a major timeout occurs.

intr

Allow signals to interrupt an NFS call. Useful for aborting when the server doesn't respond.

Except for *rsize* and *wsize*, all of these options apply to the client's behavior if the server should become temporarily inaccessible. They work together in the following way: Whenever the client sends a request to the NFS server, it expects the operation to have finished after a given interval (specified in the *timeout* option). If no confirmation is received within this time, a so-called *minor timeout* occurs, and the operation is retried with the timeout interval doubled. After reaching a maximum timeout of 60 seconds, a *major timeout* occurs.

By default, a major timeout causes the client to print a message to the console and start all over again, this time with an initial timeout interval twice that of the previous cascade. Potentially, this may go on forever. Volumes that stubbornly retry an operation until the server becomes available again are called *hard-mounted*. The opposite variety, called *soft-mounted*, generate an I/O error for the calling process whenever a major timeout occurs. Because of the write-behind introduced by the buffer cache, this error condition is not propagated to the process itself before it calls the *write* function the next time, so a program can never be sure that a write operation to a soft-mounted volume has succeeded at all.

Whether you hard- or soft-mount a volume depends partly on taste but also on the type of information you want to access from a volume. For example, if you mount your X programs by NFS, you certainly would not want your X session to go berserk just because someone brought the network to a grinding halt by firing up seven copies of Doom at the same time or by pulling the Ethernet plug for a

moment. By hard-mounting the directory containing these programs, you make
sure that your computer waits until it is able to re-establish contact with your NFS
server. On the other hand, non-critical data such as NFS-mounted news partitions
or FTP archives may also be soft-mounted, so if the remote machine is temporarily
unreachable or down, it doesn't hang your session. If your network connection to
the server is flaky or goes through a loaded router, you may either increase the
initial timeout using the *timeo* option or hard-mount the volumes. NFS volumes
are hard-mounted by default.

Hard mounts present a problem because, by default, the file operations are not
interruptible. Thus, if a process attempts, for example, a write to a remote server
and that server is unreachable, the user's application hangs and the user can't do
anything to abort the operation. If you use the *intr* option in conjuction with a
hard mount, any signals received by the process interrupt the NFS call so that
users can still abort hanging file accesses and resume work (although without saving the file).

Usually, the *rpc.mountd* daemon in some way or other keeps track of which directories have been mounted by what hosts. This information can be displayed using
the *showmount* program, which is also included in the NFS server package:

```
# showmount -e moonshot
Export list for localhost:
/home <anon clnt>

# showmount -d moonshot
Directories on localhost:
/home

# showmount -a moonshot
All mount points on localhost:
localhost:/home
```

The NFS Daemons

If you want to provide NFS service to other hosts, you have to run the *rpc.nfsd*
and *rpc.mountd* daemons on your machine. As RPC-based programs, they are not
managed by *inetd*, but are started up at boot time and register themselves with the
portmapper; therefore, you have to make sure to start them only after *rpc.portmap*
is running. Usually, you'd use something like the following example in one of
your network boot scripts:

```
if [ -x /usr/sbin/rpc.mountd ]; then
        /usr/sbin/rpc.mountd; echo -n " mountd"
fi
if [ -x /usr/sbin/rpc.nfsd ]; then
        /usr/sbin/rpc.nfsd; echo -n " nfsd"
fi
```

The ownership information of the files an NFS daemon provides to its clients usually contains only numerical user and group IDs. If both client and server associate the same user and group names with these numerical IDs, they are said to their share uid/gid space. For example, this is the case when you use NIS to distribute the *passwd* information to all hosts on your LAN.

On some occasions, however, the IDs on different hosts do not match. Rather than updating the uids and gids of the client to match those of the server, you can use the *rpc.ugidd* mapping daemon to work around the disparity. Using the *map_daemon* option explained a little later, you can tell *rpc.nfsd* to map the server's uid/gid space to the client's uid/gid space with the aid of the *rpc.ugidd* on the client. Unfortunately, the *rpc.ugidd* daemon isn't supplied on all modern Linux distributions, so if you need it and yours doesn't have it, you will need to compile it from source.

rpc.ugidd is an RPC-based server that is started from your network boot scripts, just like *rpc.nfsd* and *rpc.mountd*:

```
if [ -x /usr/sbin/rpc.ugidd ]; then
        /usr/sbin/rpc.ugidd; echo -n " ugidd"
fi
```

The exports File

Now we'll look at how we configure the NFS server. Specifically, we'll look at how we tell the NFS server what filesystems it should make available for mounting, and the various parameters that control the access clients will have to the filesystem. The server determines the type of access that is allowed to the server's files. The */etc/exports* file lists the filesystems that the server will make available for clients to mount and use.

By default, *rpc.mountd* disallows all directory mounts, which is a rather sensible attitude. If you wish to permit one or more hosts to NFS-mount a directory, you must *export* it, that is, specify it in the *exports* file. A sample file may look like this:

```
# exports file for vlager
/home           vale(rw) vstout(rw) vlight(rw)
/usr/X11R6      vale(ro) vstout(ro) vlight(ro)
/usr/TeX        vale(ro) vstout(ro) vlight(ro)
/               vale(rw,no_root_squash)
/home/ftp       (ro)
```

Each line defines a directory and the hosts that are allowed to mount it. A hostname is usually a fully qualified domain name but may additionally contain the * and ? wildcards, which act the way they do with the Bourne shell. For instance, `lab*.foo.com` matches lab01.foo.com as well as laboratory.foo.com. The host may also be specified using an IP address range in the form *address/netmask*. If no hostname is given, as with the */home/ftp* directory in the previous example, any host matches and is allowed to mount the directory.

When checking a client host against the *exports* file, *rpx.mountd* looks up the client's hostname using the *gethostbyaddr* call. With DNS, this call returns the client's canonical hostname, so you must make sure not to use aliases in *exports*. In an NIS environment the returned name is the first match from the hosts database, and with neither DNS or NIS, the returned name is the first hostname found in the *hosts* file that matches the client's address.

The hostname is followed by an optional comma-separated list of flags, enclosed in parentheses. Some of the values these flags may take are:

secure

>   This flag insists that requests be made from a reserved source port, i.e., one that is less than 1,024. This flag is set by default.

insecure

>   This flag reverses the effect of the *secure* flag.

ro   This flag causes the NFS mount to be read-only. This flag is enabled by default.

rw   This option mounts file hierarchy read-write.

root_squash

>   This security feature denies the superusers on the specified hosts any special access rights by mapping requests from uid 0 on the client to the uid 65534 (that is, -2) on the server. This uid should be associated with the user **nobody**.

no_root_squash

>   Don't map requests from uid 0. This option is on by default, so superusers have superuser access to your system's exported directories.

link_relative

>   This option converts absolute symbolic links (where the link contents start with a slash) into relative links. This option makes sense only when a host's entire filesystem is mounted; otherwise, some of the links might point to nowhere, or even worse, to files they were never meant to point to. This option is on by default.

link_absolute

>   This option leaves all symbolic links as they are (the normal behavior for Sun-supplied NFS servers).

map_identity

>   This option tells the server to assume that the client uses the same uids and gids as the server. This option is on by default.

map_daemon

This option tells the NFS server to assume that client and server do not share the same uid/gid space. *rpc.nfsd* then builds a list that maps IDs between client and server by querying the client's *rpc.ugidd* daemon.

map_static

This option allows you to specify the name of a file that contains a static map of uids and gids. For example, `map_static=/etc/nfs/vlight.map` would specify the */etc/nfs/vlight.map* file as a uid/gid map. The syntax of the map file is described in the *exports(5)* manual page.

map_nis

This option causes the NIS server to do the uid and gid mapping.

anonuid and *anongid*

These options allow you to specify the uid and gid of the anonymous account. This is useful if you have a volume exported for public mounts.

Any error in parsing the *exports* file is reported to *syslogd*'s `daemon` facility at level `notice` whenever *rpc.nfsd* or *rpc.mountd* is started up.

Note that hostnames are obtained from the client's IP address by reverse mapping, so the resolver must be configured properly. If you use BIND and are very security conscious, you should enable spoof checking in your *host.conf* file. We discuss these topics in Chapter 6, *Name Service and Resolver Configuration.*

Kernel-Based NFSv2 Server Support

The user-space NFS server traditionally used in Linux works reliably but suffers performance problems when overworked. This is primarily because of the overhead the system call interface adds to its operation, and because it must compete for time with other, potentially less important, user-space processes.

The 2.2.0 kernel supports an experimental kernel-based NFS server developed by Olaf Kirch and further developed by H.J. Lu, G. Allan Morris, and Trond Myklebust. The kernel-based NFS support provides a significant boost in server performance.

In current release distributions, you may find the server tools available in prepackaged form. If not, you can locate them at *http://csua.berkeley.edu/~gam3/knfsd/*. You need to build a 2.2.0 kernel with the kernel-based NFS daemon included in order to make use of the tools. You can check if your kernel has the NFS daemon included by looking to see if the */proc/sys/sunrpc/nfsd_debug* file exists. If it's not there, you may have to load the *rpc.nfsd* module using the *modprobe* utility.

The kernel-based NFS daemon uses a standard */etc/exports* configuration file. The package supplies replacement versions of the *rpc.mountd* and *rpc.nfsd* daemons that you start much the same way as their userspace daemon counterparts.

Kernel-Based NFSv3 Server Support

The version of NFS that has been most commonly used is NFS Version 2. Technology has rolled on ahead and it has begun to show weaknesses that only a revision of the protocol could overcome. Version 3 of the Network File System supports larger files and filesystems, adds significantly enhanced security, and offers a number of performance improvements that most users will find useful.

Olaf Kirch and Trond Myklebust are developing an experimental NFSv3 server. It is featured in the developer Version 2.3 kernels and a patch is available against the 2.2 kernel source. It builds on the Version 2 kernel-based NFS daemon.

The patches are available from the Linux Kernel based NFS server home page at *http://csua.berkeley.edu/~gam3/knfsd/*.

## CHAPTER FIFTEEN

IPX AND THE NCP FILESYSTEM

Long before Microsoft learned about networking, and even before the Internet was known outside academic circles, corporate environments shared files and printers using file and print servers based on the Novell NetWare operating system and associated protocols.* Many of these corporate users still have legacy networks using these protocols and want to integrate this support with their new TCP/IP support.

Linux supports not only the TCP/IP protocols, but also the suite of protocols used by the Novell Corporation's NetWare operating system. These protocols are distant cousins of TCP/IP, and while they perform similar sorts of functions, they differ in a number of ways and are unfortunately incompatible.

Linux has both free and commercial software offerings to provide support for integration with the Novell products.

We'll provide a brief description of the protocols themselves in this chapter, but we focus on how to configure and use free software to allow Linux to interoperate with Novell products.

Xerox, Novell, and History

First, let's look at where the protocols came from and what they look like. In the late 1970s, the Xerox Corporation developed and published an open standard called the Xerox Network Specification (XNS). The Xerox Network Specification described a series of protocols designed for general purpose internetworking, with a strong emphasis on the use of local area networks. There were two primary networking protocols involved: the Internet Datagram Protocol (IDP), which provided a connectionless and unreliable transport of datagrams from one host to another, and the Sequenced Packet Protocol (SPP), which was a modified form of IDP that was connection-based and reliable. The datagrams of an XNS network were individually addressed. The addressing scheme used a combination of a 4-byte IDP

---

* Novell and NetWare are trademarks of the Novell Corporation.

network address (which was uniquely assigned to each Ethernet LAN segment), and the 6-byte node address (the address of the NIC card). Routers were devices that switched datagrams between two or more separate IDP networks. IDP has no notion of subnetworks; any new collection of hosts requires another network address to be assigned. Network addresses are chosen such that they are unique on the internetwork in question. Sometimes administrators develop conventions by having each byte encode some other information, such as geographic location, so that network addresses are allocated in a systemic way; it isn't a protocol requirement, however.

The Novell Corporation chose to base their own networking suite on the XNS suite. Novell made small enhancements to IDP and SPP and renamed them IPX (Internet Packet eXchange) and SPX (Sequenced Packet eXchange). Novell added new protocols, such as the NetWare Core Protocol (NCP), which provided file and printer sharing features that ran over IPX, and the Service Advertisement Protocol (SAP), which enabled hosts on a Novell network to know which hosts provided which services.

Table 15-1 maps the relationship between the XNS, Novell, and TCP/IP suites in terms of function. The relationships are an approximation only, but should help you understand what is happening when we refer to these protocols later on.

Table 15-1. XNS, Novell, and TCP/IP Protocol Relationships

XNS	Novell	TCP/IP	Features
IDP	IPX	UDP/IP	Connectionless, unreliable transport
SPP	SPX	TCP	Connection-based, reliable transport
	NCP	NFS	File services
	RIP	RIP	Routing information exchange
	SAP		Service availability information exchange

IPX and Linux

Alan Cox first developed IPX support for the Linux kernel in 1985.* Initially it was useful for little more than routing IPX datagrams. Since then, other people, notably Greg Page, have provided additional support.† Greg developed the IPX configuration utilities that we'll use in this chapter to configure our interfaces. Volker Lendecke developed support for the NCP filesystem to allow Linux to mount

---

* Alan can be reached at *alan@lxorguk.ukuu.org.uk.*

† Greg can be reached at *gpage@sovereign.org.*

volumes on network-connected NetWare fileservers.* He also created tools that allow printing to and from Linux. Ales Dryak and Martin Stover each independently developed NCP fileserver daemons for Linux that allow network-connected NetWare clients to mount Linux directories exported as NCP volumes, just as the NFS daemon allows Linux to serve filesystems to clients using the NFS protocol.† Caldera Systems, Inc. offers a commercial and fully licensed NetWare client and server that supports the latest Novell standards, including support for the NetWare Directory Service (NDS).‡

Today, therefore, Linux supports a wide range of services that allow systems to be integrated with existing Novell-based networks.

Caldera Support

Although we don't detail the Caldera NetWare support in this chapter, it is important that we talk about it. Caldera was founded by Ray Noorda, the former CEO of Novell. The Caldera NetWare support is a commercial product and fully supported by Caldera. Caldera provides the NetWare support as a component of their own Linux distribution called Caldera OpenLinux. The Caldera solution is an ideal way of introducing Linux into environments that demand both commercial support and the ability to integrate into existing or new Novell networks.

The Caldera NetWare support is fully licensed by Novell, providing a high degree of certainty that the two companies' products will be interoperable. The two exceptions to this certainty are "pure IP" operation for the client, and NDS server, though neither of these were available at the time of writing. NetWare client and NetWare server are both available. A suite of management tools is also provided that can simplify management of not only your Linux-based NetWare machines, but your Novell NetWare machines, too, by bringing the power of Unix scripting languages to the task. More information on Caldera can be found at their web site.

More on NDS Support

Along with Version 4 of NetWare, Novell introduced a feature called the NetWare Directory Service (NDS). The NDS specifications are not available without a nondisclosure agreement, a restriction that hampers development of free support. Only Version 2.2.0 or later of the *ncpfs* package, which we'll discuss later, has any support for NDS. This support was developed by reverse engineering the NDS protocol. The support seems to work, but is still officially considered experimental. You can use the non-NDS tools with NetWare 4 servers, provided they have "bindery emulation mode" enabled.

---

* Volker can be reached at *lendecke@namu01.gwdg.de.*

† Ales can be reached at *A.Dryak@sh.cvut.cz.* Martin can be reached at *mstover@freeway.de.*

‡ Information on Caldera can be found at *http://www.caldera.com/.*

The Caldera software has full support for NDS because their implementation is licensed from Novell. This implementation is not free, however. So you will not have access to the source code and will not be able to freely copy and distribute the software.

Configuring the Kernel for IPX and NCPFS

Configuring the kernel for IPX and the NCP filesystem is simply a matter of selecting the appropriate kernel options at kernel build time. As with many other parts of the kernel, IPX and NCPFS kernel components can be built into the kernel, or compiled as modules and loaded using the *insmod* command when you need them.

The following options must be selected if you want to have Linux support and route the IPX protocol:

```
General setup  --->
    [*] Networking support

Networking options  --->
    <*> The IPX protocol

Network device support  --->
    [*] Ethernet (10 or 100Mbit)
        ... and appropriate Ethernet device drivers
```

If you want Linux to support the NCP filesystem so it can mount remote NetWare volumes, you must additionally select these options:

```
Filesystems  --->
    [*] /proc filesystem support
    <*> NCP filesystem support (to mount NetWare volumes)
```

When you've compiled and installed your new kernel, you're ready to run IPX.

Configuring IPX Interfaces

Just as with TCP/IP, you must configure your IPX interfaces before you can use them. The IPX protocol has some unique requirements; consequently, a special set of configuration tools was developed. We will use these tools to configure our IPX interfaces and routes.

Network Devices Supporting IPX

The IPX protocol assumes that any collection of hosts that can transmit datagrams to each other without routing belong to the same IPX network. All hosts belonging to a single Ethernet segment would all belong to the same IPX network. Similarly (but less intuitively), both hosts supporting a PPP-based serial link must belong to the IPX network that is the serial link itself. In an Ethernet environment, there are a number of different frame types that may be used to carry IPX datagrams. The frame types represent different Ethernet protocols and describe differing ways of carrying multiple protocols on the same Ethernet network. The most common frame types you will encounter are `802.2` and `ethernet_II`. We'll talk more about frame types in the next section.

The Linux network devices that currently support the IPX protocol are the Ethernet and PPP drivers. The Ethernet or PPP interface must be active before it can be configured for IPX use. Typically, you configure an Ethernet device with both IP and IPX, so the device already exists, but if your network is IPX only, you need to use the *ifconfig* to change the Ethernet device status to the following:

```
# ifconfig eth0 up
```

IPX Interface Configuration Tools

Greg Page developed a set of configuration tools for IPX interfaces, which is a precompiled package in modern distributions and may also be obtained in source form by anonymous FTP from *http://metalab.unc.edu/* in the */pub/Linux/system/ filesystems/ncpfs/ipx.tgz* file.

An *rc* script file usually runs the IPX tools at boot time. Your distribution may already do this for you if you have installed the prepackaged software.

The ipx_configure Command

Each IPX interface must know which IPX network it belongs to and which frame type to use for IPX. Each host supporting IPX has at least one interface that the rest of the network will use to refer to it, known as the *primary* interface. The Linux kernel IPX support provides a means of automatically configuring these parameters; the *ipx_configure* command enables or disables this automatic configuration feature.

With no arguments, the *ipx_configure* command displays the current setting of the automatic configuration flags:

```
# ipx_configure
Auto Primary Select is OFF
Auto Interface Create is OFF
```

Both the Auto Primary and Auto Interface flags are off by default. To set them and enable automatic configuration, you simply supply arguments like these:

```
# ipx_configure --auto_interface=on --auto_primary=on
```

When the `--auto_primary` argument is set to on, the kernel will automatically ensure that at least one active interface operates as the primary interface for the host.

When the `--auto_interface` argument is set to on, the kernel IPX driver will listen to all of the frames received on the active network interfaces and attempt to determine the IPX network address and frame type used.

The auto-detection mechanism works well on properly managed networks. Sometimes network administrators take shortcuts and break rules, and this can cause problems for the Linux auto-detection code. The most common example of this is when one IPX network is configured to run over the same Ethernet with multiple frame types. This is technically an invalid configuration, as an **802.2** host cannot directly communicate with an Ethernet-II host and therefore they cannot be on the same IPX network. The Linux IPX network software listens on the segment to IPX datagrams transmitted on it. From these, it attempts to identify which network addresses are in use and which frame type is associated with each. If the same network address is in use with multiple frame types or on multiple interfaces, the Linux code detects this as a network address collision and is unable to determine which is the correct frame type. You will know this is occurring if you see messages in your system log that look like:

```
IPX: Network number collision 0x3901ab00
eth0 etherII and eth0 802.3
```

If you see this problem, disable the auto-detection feature and configure the interfaces manually using the *ipx_interface* command described in the next section.

The ipx_interface Command

The *ipx_interface* command is used to manually add, modify, and delete IPX capability from an existing network device. You should use *ipx_interface* when the automatic configuration method just described does not work for you, or if you don't want to leave your interface configuration to chance. *ipx_interface* allows you to specify the IPX network address, primary interface status, and IPX frame type that a network device will use. If you are creating multiple IPX interfaces, you need one *ipx_interface* for each.

The command syntax to add IPX to an existing device is straightforward and best explained with an example. Let's add IPX to an existing Ethernet device:

```
# ipx_interface add -p eth0 etherII 0x32a10103
```

The parameters in turn mean:

-p This parameter specifies that this interface should be a primary interface. This parameter is optional.

eth0
> This is the name of the network device to which we are adding IPX support.

etherII
> This parameter is the frame type, in this case Ethernet-II. This value may also be coded as `802.2`, `802.3`, or `SNAP`.

0x32a10103
> This is the IPX network address to which this interface belongs.

The following command removes IPX from an interface:

```
# ipx_interface del eth0 etherII
```

Lastly, to display the current IPX configuration of a network device, use:

```
# ipx_interface check eth0 etherII
```

The *ipx_interface* command is explained more fully in its manual page.

Configuring an IPX Router

You will recall from our short discussion of the protocols used in an IPX environment that IPX is a routable protocol and that the Routing Information Protocol (RIP) is used to propagate routing information. The IPX version of RIP is quite similar to the IP version. They operate in essentially the same way; routers periodically broadcast the contents of their routing tables and other routers learn of them by listening and integrating the information they receive. Hosts need only know who their local network is and be sure to send datagrams for all other destinations via their local router. The router is responsible for carrying these datagrams and forwarding them on to the next hop in the route.

In an IPX environment, a second class of information must be propagated around the network. The Service Advertisement Protocol (SAP) carries information relating to which services are available at which hosts around the network. It is the SAP protocol, for example, that allows users to obtain lists of file or print servers on the network. The SAP protocol works by having hosts that provide services periodically broadcast the list of services they offer. The IPX network routers collect this information and propagate it throughout the network alongside the network routing information. To be a compliant IPX router, you must propagate both RIP and SAP information.

Just like IP, IPX on Linux provides a routing daemon named *ipxd* to perform the tasks associated with managing routing. Again, just as with IP, it is actually the kernel that manages the forwarding of datagrams between IPX network interfaces, but it performs this according to a set of rules called the IPX routing table. The *ipxd* daemon keeps that set of rules up to date by listening on each of the active network interfaces and analyzing when a routing change is necessary. The *ipxd* daemon also answers requests from hosts on a directly connected network that ask for routing information.

The *ipxd* command is available prepackaged in some distributions, and in source form by anonymous FTP from *http://metalab.unc.edu/* in the */pub/Linux/system/filesystems/ncpfs/ipxripd-x.xx.tgz* file.

No configuration is necessary for the *ipxd* daemon. When it starts, it automatically manages routing among the IPX devices that have been configured. The key is to ensure that you have your IPX devices configured correctly using the *ipx_interface* command before you start *ipxd*. While auto-detection may work, when you're performing a routing function it's best not to take chances, so manually configure the interfaces and save yourself the pain of nasty routing problems. Every 30 seconds, *ipxd* rediscovers all of the locally attached IPX networks and automatically manages them. This provides a means of managing networks on interfaces that may not be active all of the time, such as PPP interfaces.

The *ipxd* would normally be started at boot time from an *rc* boot script like this:

```
# /usr/sbin/ipxd
```

No & character is necessary because *ipxd* will move itself into the background by default. While the *ipxd* daemon is most useful on machines acting as IPX routers, it is also useful to hosts on segments where there are multiple routers present. When you specify the –p argument, *ipxd* will act passively, listening to routing information from the segment and updating the routing tables, but it will not transmit any routing information. This way, a host can keep its routing tables up to date without having to request routes each time it wants to contact a remote host.

Static IPX Routing Using the ipx_route Command

There are occasions when we might want to hardcode an IPX route. Just as with IP, we can do this with IPX. The *ipx_route* command writes a route into the IPX routing table without it needing to have been learned by the *ipxd* routing daemon. The routing syntax is very simple (since IPX does not support subnetworking) and looks like:

```
# ipx_route add 203a41bc 31a10103 00002a02b102
```

The command shown would add a route to the remote IPX network **203a41bc** via the router on our local network **31a10103** with node address **00002a02b102**.

You can find the node address of a router by making judicious use of the *tcpdump* command with the **−e** argument to display link level headers and look for traffic from the router. If the router is a Linux machine, you can more simply use the *ifconfig* command to display it.

You can delete a route using the *ipx_route* command:

```
# ipx_route del 203a41bc
```

You can list the routes that are active in the kernel by looking at the */proc/net/ipx_route* file. Our routing table so far looks like this:

```
# cat ipx_route
Network     Router_Net     Router_Node
203A41BC    31A10103       00002a02b102
31A10103    Directly       Connected
```

The route to the **31A10103** network was automatically created when we configured the IPX interface. Each of our local networks will be represented by an */proc/net/ipx_route* entry like this one. Naturally, if our machine is to act as a router, it will need at least one other interface.

Internal IPX Networks and Routing

IPX hosts with more than one IPX interface have a unique network/node address combination for each of their interfaces. To connect to such a host, you may use any of these network/node address combinations. When SAP advertizes services, it supplies the network/node address associated with the service that is offered. On hosts with multiple interfaces, this means that one of the interfaces must be chosen as the one to propagate; this is the function of the primary interface flag we talked about earlier. But this presents a problem: the route to this interface may not always be the optimal one, and if a network failure occurs that isolates that network from the rest of the network, the host will become unreachable even though there are other *possible* routes to the other interfaces. The other routes are never known to other hosts because they are never propagated, and the kernel has no way of knowing that it should choose another primary interface. To avoid this problem, a device was developed that allows an IPX host to be known by a single route-independent network/node address for the purposes of SAP propagation. This solves our problem because this new network/node address is reachable via all of the host interfaces, and is the one that is advertised by SAP.

To illustrate the problem and its solution, Figure 15-1 shows a server attached to two IPX networks. The first network has no internal network, but the second does. The host in diagram Figure 15-1 would choose one of its interfaces as its primary interface, let's assume **0000001a:0800000010aa**, and that is what would be advertised as its service access point. This works well for hosts on the **0000001a** network, but means that users on the 0000002c network will route via the network to reach that port, despite the server having a port directly on that network if they've discovered this server from the SAP broadcasts.

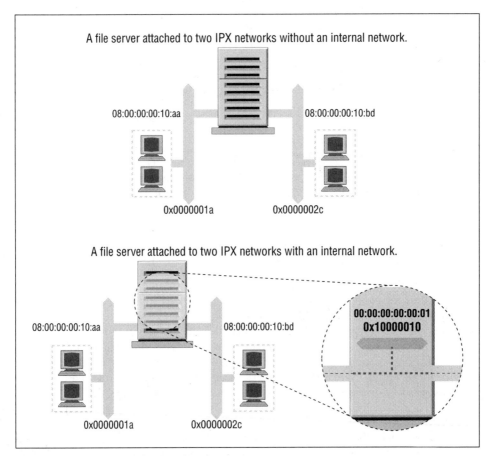

Figure 15-1. IPX internal network

Allowing such hosts to have a virtual network with virtual host addresses that are entirely a software construct solves this problem. This virtual network is best thought of as being *inside* the IPX host. The SAP information then needs only to be propagated for this virtual network/node address combination. This virtual network is known as an *internal network*. But how do other hosts know how to reach this internal network? Remote hosts route to the internal network via the directly connected networks of the host. This means that you see routing entries that refer to the internal network of hosts supporting multiple IPX interfaces.

Those routes should choose the optimal route available at the time, and should one fail, the routing is automatically updated to the next best interface and route. In Figure 15-1, we've configured an internal IPX network of address **0x10000010** and used a host address of **00:00:00:00:00:01**. It is this address that will be our primary interface and will be advertised via SAP. Our routing will reflect this network as being reachable via *either* of our real network ports, so hosts will always use the best network route to connect to our server.

To create this internal network, use the *ipx_internal_net* command included in Greg Page's IPX tools package. Again, a simple example demonstrates its use:

```
# ipx_internal_net add 10000010 000000000001
```

This command would create an IPX internal network with address **10000010** and a node address of **000000000001**. The network address, just like any other IPX network address, must be unique on your network. The node address is completely arbitrary, as there will normally be only one node on the network. Each host may have only one IPX Internal Network, and if configured, the Internal Network will always be the primary network.

To delete an IPX Internal Network, use:

```
# ipx_internal_net del
```

An internal IPX network is of absolutely no use to you unless your host both provides a service and has more than one IPX interface active.

Mounting a Remote NetWare Volume

IPX is commonly used to mount NetWare volumes in the Linux filesystem. This allows file-based data sharing between other operating systems and Linux. Volker Lendecke developed the NCP client for Linux and a suite of associated tools that make data sharing possible.

In an NFS environment, we'd use the Linux *mount* command to mount the remote filesystem. Unfortunately, the NCP filesystem has unique requirements that make it impractical to build it into the normal *mount*. Linux has an *ncpmount* command that we will use instead. The *ncpmount* command is one of the tools in Volker's *ncpfs* package, which is available prepackaged in most modern distributions or in source form from **ftp.gwdg.de** in the */pub/linux/misc/ncpfs/* directory. The version current at the time of writing is 2.2.0.

Before you can mount remote NetWare volumes, you must ensure your IPX network interface is configured correctly (as described earlier). Next, you must know your login details on the NetWare server you wish to mount; this includes the user ID and password. Lastly, you need to know which volume you wish to mount and what local directory you wish to mount it under.

A Simple ncpmount Example

A simple example of *ncpmount* usage looks like this:

```
# ncpmount -S ALES_F1 -U rick -P d00-b-gud /mnt/brewery
```

This command mounts all volumes of the `ALES_F1` fileserver under the */mnt/ brewery* directory, using the NetWare login `rick` with the password `d00-b-gud`.

The *ncpmount* command is normally setuid to **root** and may therefore be used by any Linux user. By default, that user owns the connection and only he or the **root** user will be able to unmount it.

NetWare embodies the notion of a *volume*, which is analogous to a filesystem in Linux. A NetWare volume is the logical representation of a NetWare filesystem, which might be a single disk partition be spread across many partitions. By default, the Linux NCPFS support treats volumes as subdirectories of a larger logical filesystem represented by the whole fileserver. The *ncpmount* command causes each of the NetWare volumes of the mounted fileserver to appear as a subdirectory under the mount point. This is convenient if you want access to the whole server, but for complex technical reasons you will be unable to re-export these directories using NFS, should you wish to do so. We'll discuss a more complex alternative that works around this problem in a moment.

The ncpmount Command in Detail

The *ncpmount* has a large number of command line options that allow you quite a lot of flexibility in how you manage your NCP mounts. The most important of these are described in Table 15-2.

Table 15-2. ncpmount Command Arguments

Argument	Description
–S *server*	The name of the fileserver to mount.
–U *user_name*	The NetWare user ID to use when logging in to the fileserver.
–P *password*	The password to use for the NetWare login.
–n	This option must be used for NetWare logins that don't have a password associated with them.
–C	This argument disables automatic conversion of passwords to uppercase.
–c *client_name*	This option allows you to specify who owns the connection to the fileserver. This is useful for NetWare printing, which we will discuss in more detail later.

Table 15-2. ncpmount Command Arguments (continued)

Argument	Description
–u *uid*	The Linux user ID that should be shown as the owner of files in the mounted directory. If this is not specified, it defaults to the user ID of the user who invokes the *ncpmount* command.
–g *gid*	The Linux group ID that should be shown as the owner of files in the mounted directory. If this is not specified, it will default to the group ID of the user who invokes the *ncpmount* command.
–f *file_mode*	This option allows you to specify the file mode (permissions) that files in the mounted directory should have. The value should be specified in octal, e.g., 0664. The permissions that you will actually have are the file mode permissions specified with this option masked with the permissions that your NetWare login ID has for the files on the fileserver. You must have rights on the server and rights specified by this option in order to access a file. The default value is derived from the current umask.
–d *dir_mode*	This option allows you to specify the directory permissions in the mounted directory. It behaves in the same way as the *–f* option, except that the default permissions are derived from the current umask. Execute permissions are granted where read access is granted.
–V *volume*	This option allows you to specify the name of a single NetWare volume to mount under the mount point, rather than mounting all volumes of the target server. This option is necessary if you wish to re-export a mounted NetWare volume using NFS.
–t *time_out*	This option allows you to specify the time that the NCPFS client will wait for a response from a server. The default value is 60mS and the timeout is specified in hundredths of a second. If you experience any stability problems with NCP mounts, you should try increasing this value.
–r *retry_count*	The NCP client code attempts to resend datagrams to the server a number of times before deciding the connection is dead. This option allows you to change the retry count from the default of 5.

Hiding Your NetWare Login Password

It is somewhat of a security risk to be putting a password on the command line, as we did with the *ncpmount* command. Other active, concurrent users could see the password if they happen to be running a program like *top* or *ps*. To reduce the risk of others seeing and stealing NetWare login passwords, *ncpmount* is able to read certain details from a file in a user's home directory. In this file, the user keeps the login name and password associated with each of the fileservers he or she intends to mount. The file is called ˜/.*nwclient* and it must have permissions of 0600 to ensure that others cannot read it. If the permissions are not correct, the *ncpmount* command will refuse to use it.

The file has a very simple syntax. Any lines beginning with a # character are treated as comments and ignored. The remainder of the lines have the syntax:

```
fileserver/userid password
```

The *fileserver* is the name of the fileserver supporting the volumes you wish to mount. The *userid* is the login name of your account on that server. The *password* field is optional. If it is not supplied, the *ncpmount* command prompts users for the password when they attempt the mount. If the *password* field is specified as the – character, no password is used; this is equivalent to the –n command-line argument.

You can supply any number of entries, but the fileserver field must be unique. The first fileserver entry has special significance. The *ncpmount* command uses the –S command-line argument to determine which of the entries in ˜/.*nwclient* to use. If no server is specified using the –S argument, the first server entry in ˜/.*nwclient* is assumed, and is treated as your preferred server. You should place the fileserver you mount most frequently in the first position in the file.

A More Complex ncpmount Example

Let's look at a more complex *ncpmount* example involving a number of the features we've described. First, let's build a simple ˜/.*nwclient* file:

```
# NetWare login details for the Virtual Brewery and Winery
#
# Brewery Login
ALES_F1/MATT staoic1
#
# Winery Login
REDS01/MATT staoic1
#
```

Make sure its permissions are correct:

```
$ chmod 600 ~/.nwclient
```

Let's mount one volume of the Winery's server under a subdirectory of a shared directory, specifying the file and directory permissions such that others may share the data from there:

```
$ ncpmount -S REDS01 -V RESEARCH -f 0664 -d 0775 /usr/share/winery/data/
```

This command, in combination with the *~/.nwclient* file shown, would mount the **RESEARCH** volume of the **REDS01** server onto the */usr/share/winery/data/* directory using the NetWare login ID of **MATT** and the password retrieved from the *~/.nwclient* file. The permissions of the mounted files are **0664** and the directory permissions are **0775**.

Exploring Some of the Other IPX Tools

The *ncpfs* package contains a number of useful tools that we haven't described yet. Many of these tools emulate the tools that are supplied with NetWare. We'll look at the most useful ones in this section.

Server List

The *slist* command lists all of the fileservers accessible to the host. The information is actually retrieved from the nearest IPX router. This command was probably originally intended to allow users to see what fileservers were available to mount. But it has become useful as a network diagnosis tool, allowing network admins to see where SAP information is being propagated:

```
$ slist
NPPWR-31-CD01                    23A91330   000000000001
V242X-14-F02                     A3062DB0   000000000001
QITG_284ELI05_F4                 78A20430   000000000001
QRWMA-04-F16                     B2030D6A   000000000001
VWPDE-02-F08                     35540430   000000000001
NMCS_33PARK08_F2                 248B0530   000000000001
NCCRD-00-CD01                    21790430   000000000001
NWGNG-F07                        53171D02   000000000001
QCON_7TOMLI04_F7                 72760630   000000000001
W639W-F04                        D1014D0E   000000000001
QCON_481GYM0G_F1                 77690130   000000000001
VITG_SOE-MAIL_F4R                33200C30   000000000001
```

slist accepts no arguments. The output displays the fileserver name, the IPX network address, and the host address.

Send Messages to NetWare Users

NetWare supports a mechanism to send messages to logged-in users. The *nsend* command implements this feature in Linux. You must be logged in to the server to send messages, so you need to supply the fileserver name and login details on the command line with the destination user and the message to send:

```
# nsend -S vbrew_f1 -U gary -P j0yj0y supervisor
      "Join me for a lager before we do the print queues!"
```

Here a user with login name `gary` sends a tempting invitation to the person using the `supervisor` account on the `ALES_F1` fileserver. Our default fileserver and login credentials will be used if we don't supply them.

Browsing and Manipulating Bindery Data

Each NetWare fileserver maintains a database of information about its users and configuration. This database is called the *bindery*. Linux supports a set of tools that allow you to read it, and if you have supervisor permissions on the server, to set and remove it. A summary of these tools is listed in Table 15-3.

Table 15-3. Linux Bindery Manipulation Tools

Command Name	Command Description
nwfstime	Display or set a NetWare server's date and time
nwuserlist	List users logged in at a NetWare server
nwvolinfo	Display info about NetWare volumes
nwbocreate	Create a NetWare bindery object
nwbols	List NetWare bindery objects
nwboprops	List properties of a NetWare bindery object
nwborm	Remove a NetWare bindery object
nwbpcreate	Create a NetWare bindery property
nwbpvalues	Print a NetWare bindery property's contents
nwbpadd	Set the value of a NetWare bindery property
nwbprm	Remove a NetWare bindery property

Printing to a NetWare Print Queue

The *ncpfs* package contains a small utility called *nprint* that sends print jobs across an NCP connection to a NetWare print queue. This command creates the connection if it doesn't currently exist and uses the *˜/.nwclient* file that we described earlier to hide the username and password from prying eyes. The command-line arguments used to manage the login process are the same as those used by the *ncpmount*, so we won't go through those again here. We will cover the most important command-line options in our examples; refer to the *nprint(1)* manual page for details.

The only required option for *nprint* is the name of the file to print. If the filename specified is – or if no filename is specified at all, *nprint* will accept the print job from `stdin`. The most important *nprint* options specify the fileserver and print queue to which you wish the job to be sent. Table 15-4 lists the most important options.

Table 15-4. nprint Command-Line Options

Option	Description
-S `server_name`	The name of the NetWare fileserver supporting the print queue to which you wish to print. Usually it is convenient for the server to have an entry in ˜/.*nwclient*. This option is mandatory.
-q `queue_name`	The print queue to which to send the print job. This option is mandatory.
-d `job_description`	Text that will appear in the print console utility when displaying the list of queued jobs.
-l `lines`	The number of lines per printed page. This defaults to 66.
-r `columns`	The number of columns per printed page. This defaults to 80.
-c `copies`	The number of copies of the job that will be printed. The default is 1.

A simple example using *nprint* would look like:

```
$ nprint -S REDS01 -q PSLASER -c 2 /home/matt/ethylene.ps
```

This command would print two copies of the file */home/matt/ethylene.ps* to the printer named `PSLASER` on the `REDS01` fileserver using a username and password obtained from the ˜/.*nwclient* file.

Using nprint with the Line Printer Daemon

You will recall we previously mentioned that the *–c* option for the *ncpmount* is useful for printing. At last we'll explain why and how.

Linux usually uses BSD-style line printer software. The line printer daemon (*lpd*) is a daemon that checks a local spool directory for queued jobs that are to be printed. *lpd* reads the printer name and some other parameters from the specially formatted spool file and writes the data to the printer, optionally passing the data through a filter to transform or manipulate it in some way.

The *lpd* daemon uses a simple database called */etc/printcap* to store printer configuration information, including what filters are to be run. *lpd* usually runs with the
permissions of a special system user called **lp**.

You could configure *nprint* as a filter for the *lpd* to use, which allows users of
your Linux machine to output directly to remote printers hosted by a NetWare fileserver. To do this, the **lp** user must be able to write NCP requests to the NCP connection to the server.

An easy way to achieve this without requiring the **lp** user to establish its own connection and login is to specify **lp** as the owner of a connection established by
another user. A complete example of how to set up the Linux printing system to
handle print jobs from clients over NetWare is listed in three steps:

1. Write a wrapper script.

    The */etc/printcap* file doesn't permit options to be supplied to filters. There-
    fore, you need to write a short script that invokes the command you want
    along with its options. The wrapper script could be as simple as:

    ```
    #!/bin/sh
    # p2pslaser - simple script to redirect stdin to the
    # PSLASER queue on the REDS01 server
    #
    /usr/bin/nprint -S REDS01 -U stuart -q PSLASER
    #
    ```

    Store the script in the file */usr/local/bin/p2pslaser.*

2. Write the */etc/printcap* entry.

    We'll need to configure the *p2pslaser* script we created as the output filter in
    the */etc/printcap.* This would look something like:

    ```
    pslaser|Postscript Laser Printer hosted by NetWare server:\
    :lp=/dev/null:\
    :sd=/var/spool/lpd/pslaser:\
    :if=/usr/local/bin/p2pslaser:\
    :af=/var/log/lp-acct:\
    :lf=/var/log/lp-errs:\
    :pl#66:\
    :pw#80:\
    :pc#150:\
    :mx#0:\
    :sh:
    ```

3. Add the *−c* option to the *ncpmount.*

    ```
    ncpmount -S REDS01 .... -c lp ....
    ```

Our local user **stuart** must specify the **lp** user as the owner of the connection when he mounts the remote NetWare server.

Now any Linux user may choose to specify `pslaser` as the printer name when invoking **lp**. The print job will be sent to the specified NetWare server and spooled for printing.

Managing Print Queues

The *pqlist* command lists all of the print queues available to you on the specified server. If you do not specify a fileserver on the command line using the *-S* option, or a login name and password, these will be taken from the default entry in your ˜/.nwclient file:

```
# pqlist -S vbrew_f1 -U guest -n
Server: ALES_F1
Print queue name                                              Queue ID
-------------------------------------------------------------
TEST                                                          AA02009E
Q2                                                            EF0200D9
NPI223761_P1                                                  DA03007C
Q1                                                            F1060004
I-DATA                                                        0D0A003B
NPI223761_P3                                                  D80A0031
```

Our example shows a list of the print queues available to the `guest` user on the `ALES_F1` fileserver.*

To view the print jobs on a print queue, use the *pqstat* command. It takes the print queue name as an argument and lists all of the jobs in that queue. You may optionally supply another argument indicating how many of the jobs in the queue you'd like to list. The following sample output has been compressed a bit to fit the width of this book's page:

```
$ pqstat -S ALES_F1 NPI223761_P1

Server: ALES_F1       Queue: NPI223761_P1        Queue ID: 6A0E000C
   Seq  Name      Description                    Status   Form  Job ID
-------------------------------------------------------------------
     1  TOTRAN    LyX document - proposal.lyx    Active      0  02660001
```

We can see just one print job in the queue, owned by user `TOTRAN`. The rest of the options include a description of the job, its status, and its job identifier.

---

* It looks like the system administrators had been sampling some of the Virtual Brewery's wares before they chose some of those print queue names. Hopefully your print queue names are more meaningful!

The *pqrm* command is used to remove print jobs from a specified print queue. To remove the job in the queue we've just obtained the status of, we'd use:

```
$ pqrm -S ALES_F1 NPI223761_P1 02660001
```

The command is pretty straightforward but is clumsy to use in a hurry. It would be a worthwhile project to write a basic script to simplify this operation.

NetWare Server Emulation

There are two free software emulators for NetWare fileservers under Linux. *lwared* was developed by Ales Dryak and *mars_nwe* was developed by Martin Stover. Both of these packages provide elementary NetWare fileserver emulation under Linux, allowing NetWare clients to mount Linux directories exported as NetWare volumes. While the *lwared* server is simpler to configure, the *mars_nwe* server is more fully featured. The installation and configuration of these packages is beyond the scope of this chapter, but both are described in the IPX-HOWTO.

CHAPTER SIXTEEN
MANAGING TAYLOR UUCP

UUCP was designed in the late seventies by Mike Lesk at AT&T Bell Laboratories to provide a simple dialup network over public telephone lines. Despite the popularity of dialup PPP and SLIP connections to the Internet, many people who want to have email and Usenet News on their home machine still use UUCP because it is often cheaper, especially in countries where Internet users have to pay by the minute for local telephone calls, or where they do not have a local ISP and must pay long distance toll rates to connect. Although there are many implementations of UUCP running on a wide variety of hardware platforms and operating systems, overall, they are highly compatible.

However, as with most software that has somehow become "standard" over the years, there is no UUCP that one would call *the* UUCP. It has undergone a steady evolution since the first version was implemented in 1976. Currently, there are two major species that differ mainly in their hardware support and configuration. Of these two, various implementations exist, each varying slightly from its siblings.

One species is known as Version 2 UUCP, which dates back to a 1977 implementation by Mike Lesk, David A. Novitz, and Greg Chesson. Although it is fairly old, it is still frequently used. Recent implementations of Version 2 provide much of the comfort that the newer UUCP species do.

The second species was developed in 1983 and is commonly referred to as BNU (Basic Networking Utilities) or HoneyDanBer UUCP. The latter name is derived from the authors' names (P. Honeyman, D. A. Novitz, and B. E. Redman) and is often shortened further to HDB, which is the term we'll use in this chapter. HDB was conceived to eliminate some of Version 2 UUCP's deficiencies. For example, new transfer protocols were added, and the spool directory was split so that now there is one directory for each site with which you have UUCP traffic.

The implementation of UUCP currently distributed with Linux is Taylor UUCP 1.06, which is the version this chapter is based upon.* Taylor UUCP Version 1.06 was released in August 1995. Apart from traditional configuration files, Taylor UUCP can also be compiled to understand the newstyle—a.k.a. Taylor—configuration files.

Taylor UUCP is usually compiled for HDB compatibility, the Taylor configuration scheme, or both. Because the Taylor scheme is much more flexible and probably easier to understand than the often obscure HDB configuration files, we will describe the Taylor scheme below.

This chapter is not designed to exhaustively describe the command-line options for the UUCP commands and what they do, but to give you an introduction to how to set up a working UUCP node. The first section gives a gentle introduction about how UUCP implements remote execution and file transfers. If you are not entirely new to UUCP, you might want to skip to the section "UUCP Configuration Files" later in this chapter, which explains the various files used to set up UUCP.

We will, however, assume that you are familiar with the user programs of the UUCP suite, *uucp* and *uux*. For a description, refer to the online manual pages.

Besides the publicly accessible programs *uucp* and *uux*, the UUCP suite contains a number of commands used for administrative purposes only. They are used to monitor UUCP traffic across your node, remove old log files, or compile statistics. None of these will be described here because they are peripheral to the main tasks of UUCP. Besides, they're well documented and fairly easy to understand; refer to the manual pages for more information. However, there is a third category, which comprise the actual UUCP "work horses." They are called *uucico* (where *cico* stands for copy-in copy-out), and *uuxqt*, which executes jobs sent from remote systems. We concentrate on these two important programs in this chapter.

If you're not satisfied with our coverage of these topics, you should read the documentation that comes with the UUCP package. This is a set of Texinfo files that describe the setup using the Taylor configuration scheme. You can convert the Texinfo files into a *dvi* file using the *texi2dvi* (found in the Texinfo package in your distribution) and view the *dvi* file using the *xdvi* command.

Guylhem Aznar's UUCP-HOWTO is another good source for information about UUCP in a Linux environment. It is available at any Linux Documentation Project mirror and is posted regularly to *comp.os.linux.answers*.

---

* Written and copyrighted by Ian Taylor, 1995.

There's also a newsgroup for the discussion of UUCP called *comp.mail.uucp*. If you have questions specific to Taylor UUCP, you may be better off asking them there, rather than on the *comp.os.linux.** groups.

UUCP Transfers and Remote Execution

The concept of jobs is vital to understanding UUCP. Every transfer that a user initiates with *uucp* or *uux* is called a *job*. It is made up of a command to be executed on a remote system, a collection of files to be transferred between sites, or both.

As an example, the following command makes UUCP copy the file *netguide.ps* to a remote host named **pablo** and execute the *lpr* command on **pablo** to print the file:

```
$ uux -r pablo!lpr !netguide.ps
```

UUCP does not generally call the remote system immediately to execute a job (or else you could make do with *kermit*). Instead, it temporarily stores the job description away. This is called *spooling*. The directory tree under which jobs are stored is therefore called the *spool directory* and is generally located in */var/spool/uucp*. In our example, the job description would contain information about the remote command to be executed (*lpr*), the user who requested the execution, and a couple of other items. In addition to the job description, UUCP has to store the input file *netguide.ps*.

The exact location and naming of spool files may vary, depending on some compile-time options. HDB-compatible UUCPs generally store spool files in a */var/spool/uucp* subdirectory with the name of the remote site. When compiled for Taylor configuration, UUCP creates subdirectories below the site-specific spool directory for different types of spool files.

At regular intervals, UUCP dials up the remote system. When a connection to the remote machine is established, UUCP transfers the files describing the job, plus any input files. The incoming jobs will not be executed immediately, but only after the connection terminates. Execution is handled by *uuxqt*, which also takes care of forwarding any jobs that are designated for another site.

To distinguish between more and less important jobs, UUCP associates a *grade* with each job. This is a single digit ranging from 0 through 9, A through Z, and a through z, in decreasing precedence. Mail is customarily spooled with grade B or C, while news is spooled with grade N. Jobs with higher grades are transferred earlier. Grades may be assigned using the *–g* flag when invoking *uucp* or *uux*.

You can also prohibit the transfer of jobs below a given grade at certain times. To do this we set the *maximum spool grade* that will be prohibited during a conversation. The maximum spool grade defaults to z, meaning all grades will be transferred every time. Note the semantic ambiguity here: a file is transferred only if it has a grade *equal to* or *above* the maximum spool grade threshold.

The Inner Workings of uucico

To understand why *uucico* needs to know particular information, a quick description of how it actually connects to a remote system is helpful.

When you execute *uucico -s* `system` from the command line, *uucico* first has to connect physically. The actions taken depend on the type of connection to open. Thus, when using a telephone line, it has to find a modem and dial out. Over TCP, it has to call *gethostbyname* to convert the name to a network address, find out which port to open, and bind the address to the corresponding socket.

A successful connection is followed by authorization. This procedure generally consists of the remote system asking for a login name and possibly a password. This exchange is commonly called the *login chat*. The authorization procedure is performed either by the usual *getty/login* suite, or on TCP sockets by *uucico* itself. If authorization succeeds, the remote end fires up *uucico*. The local copy of *uucico* that initiated the connection is referred to as *master*, and the remote copy as *slave*.

Next follows the *handshake phase*: the master sends its hostname plus several flags. The slave checks this hostname for permission to log in, send, and receive files, etc. The flags describe (among other things) the maximum grade of spool files to transfer. If enabled, a conversation count or *call sequence number* check takes place here. With this feature, both sites maintain a count of successful connections, which are compared. If they do not match, the handshake fails. This is useful to protect yourself against impostors.

Finally, the two *uucico*s try to agree on a common *transfer protocol*. This protocol governs the way data is transferred, checked for consistency, and retransmitted in case of an error. There is a need for different protocols because of the differing types of connections supported. For example, telephone lines require a "safe" protocol, which is pessimistic about errors, while TCP transmission is inherently reliable and can use a more efficient protocol that foregoes most extra error checking.

After the handshake is complete, the actual transmission phase begins. Both ends turn on the selected protocol driver. At this point, the drivers possibly perform a protocol-specific initialization sequence.

The master then sends all files queued for the remote system whose spool grade is high enough. When it has finished, it informs the slave that it is done and that the slave may now hang up. The slave now can either agree to hang up or take over the conversation. This is a change of roles: now the remote system becomes master, and the local one becomes slave. The new master now sends its files. When done, both *uucico*s exchange termination messages and close the connection.

If you need additional information on UUCP, please refer to the source code. There is also a really antique article floating around the Net, written by David A.

Novitz, which gives a detailed description of the UUCP protocol.* The Taylor UUCP FAQ also discusses some details UUCP's implementation. It is posted to *comp.mail.uucp* regularly.

uucico Command-line Options

In this section, we describe the most important command-line options for *uucico*:

—— system, —s `system`
> Calls the named `system` unless prohibited by call-time restrictions.

—S `system`
> Calls the named `system` unconditionally.

——master, —r1
> Starts *uucico* in master mode. This is the default when *—s* or *—S* is given. All by itself, the *—r1* option causes *uucico* to try to call all systems in the *sys* file described in the next section of this chapter, unless prohibited by call or retry time restrictions.

——slave, —r0
> Starts *uucico* in slave mode. This is the default when no *—s* or *—S* is given. In slave mode, either standard input/output are assumed to be connected to a serial port, or the TCP port specified by the *—p* option is used.

——ifwork, —C
> This option supplements *—s* or *—S* and tells *uucico* to call the named system only if there are jobs spooled for it.

——debug `type`*, —x* `type`*, —X* `type`
> Turns on debugging of the specified type. Several types can be given as a comma-separated list. The following types are valid: `abnormal`, `chat`, `handshake`, `uucp-proto`, `proto`, `port`, `config`, `spooldir`, `execute`, `incoming`, and `outgoing`. Using `all` turns on all options. For compatibility with other UUCP implementations, a number may be specified instead, which turns on debugging for the first *n* items from the above list.

> Debugging messages will be logged to the *Debug* file below */var/spool/uucp*.

UUCP Configuration Files

In contrast to simpler file transfer programs, UUCP was designed to be able to handle all transfers automatically. Once it is set up properly, interference by the administrator should not be necessary on a day-to-day basis. The information required for automated transfer is kept in a couple of configuration files that reside in the */usr/lib/uucp* directory. Most of these files are used only when dialing out.

---

* It's also included in the 4.4BSD *System Manager's Manual.*

A Gentle Introduction to Taylor UUCP

To say that UUCP configuration is difficult would be an understatement. It is really a hairy subject, and the sometimes terse format of the configuration files doesn't make things easier (although the Taylor format is almost easy reading compared to the older formats in HDB or Version 2).

To give you a feel for how all the configuration files interact, we will introduce you to the most important ones and have a look at sample entries from these files. We won't explain everything in detail now; a more accurate account is given in separate sections that follow. If you want to set up your machine for UUCP, you had best start with some sample files and adapt them gradually. You can pick either those shown below or those included in your favorite Linux distribution.

All files described in this section are kept in */etc/uucp* or a subdirectory thereof. Some Linux distributions contain UUCP binaries that have support for both HDB and Taylor configuration enabled, and use different subdirectories for each configuration file set. There will usually be a *README* file in */usr/lib/uucp*.

For UUCP to work properly, these files must be owned by the **uucp** user. Some of them contain passwords and telephone numbers, and therefore should have permissions of 600. Note that although most UUCP commands must be setuid to **uucp**, you must make sure the *uuchk* program is *not*. Otherwise, users will be able to display system passwords even though the files have mode 600.

The central UUCP configuration file is */etc/uucp/config*, which is used to set general parameters. The most important of them (and for now, the only one) is your host's UUCP name. At the Virtual Brewery, they use **vstout** as their UUCP gateway:

```
# /etc/uucp/config - UUCP main configuration file
nodename        vstout
```

The *sys* file is the next important configuration file. It contains all the system-specific information of sites to which you are linked. This includes the site's name and information on the link itself, such as the telephone number when using a modem link. A typical entry for a modem-connected site called **pablo** would look like this:

```
# /usr/lib/uucp/sys - name UUCP neighbors
# system: pablo
system          pablo
time            Any
phone           555-22112
port            serial1
speed           38400
chat            ogin: vstout ssword: lorca
```

time specifies the times at which the remote system may be called. chat describes the login chat scripts—the sequence of strings that must be exchanged to allow *uucico* to log into **pablo**. We will get back to chat scripts later. The port keyword simply names an entry in the *port* file. (Refer to Figure 16-1.) You can assign whatever name you like as long as it refers to a valid entry in *port*.

The *port* file holds information specific to the link itself. For modem links, it describes the device special file to be used, the range of speeds supported, and the type of dialing equipment connected to the port. The following entry describes */dev/ttyS1* (a.k.a. COM 2), to which the administrator has connected a NakWell modem capable of running at speeds up to 38,400 bps. The port's name is chosen to match the port name given in the *sys* file:

```
# /etc/uucp/port - UUCP ports
# /dev/ttyS1 (COM2)
port            serial1
type            modem
device          /dev/ttyS1
speed           38400
dialer          nakwell
```

The information pertaining to the dialers is kept in yet another file called—you guessed it—*dial*. For each dialer type, it basically contains the sequence of commands that are issued to dial up a remote site, given the telephone number. Again, this is specified as a chat script. For example, the entry for NakWell might look like this:

```
# /etc/uucp/dial - per-dialer information
# NakWell modems
dialer          nakwell
chat            "" AT&F OK ATDT\T CONNECT
```

The line starting with chat specifies the modem chat, which is the sequence of commands sent to and received from the modem to initialize it and make it dial the desired number. The \T sequence will be replaced with the phone number by *uucico*.

To give you a rough idea how *uucico* deals with these configuration files, assume you issue the following command:

$ **uucico -s pablo**

The first thing *uucico* does is look up **pablo** in the *sys* file. From the *sys* file entry for **pablo**, it sees that it should use the serial1 port to establish the connection. The *port* file tells *uucico* that this is a modem port, and that it has a NakWell modem attached.

uucico now searches *dial* for the entry describing the NakWell modem, and having found one, opens the serial port */dev/cua1* and executes the dialer chat. That is, it sends *AT&F*, waits for the *OK* response, etc. When encountering the string \T, it substitutes the phone number (555-22112) extracted from the *sys* file.

After the modem returns *CONNECT*, the connection has been established, and the modem chat is complete. *uucico* now returns to the *sys* file and executes the login chat. In our example, it would wait for the *login:* prompt, then send its username (**vstout**), wait for the *password:* prompt, and send its password (*lorca*).

After completing authorization, the remote end is assumed to fire up its own *uucico*. The two then enter the handshake phase described in the previous section.

Figure 16-1 illustrates the dependencies among configuration files.

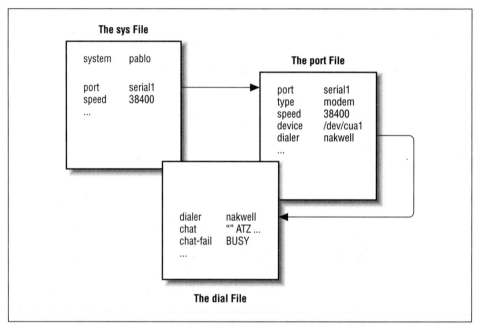

Figure 16-1. Interaction of Taylor UUCP configuration files

What UUCP Needs to Know

Before you start writing the UUCP configuration files, you have to gather some information that UUCP requires.

First, you have to figure out what serial device your modem is attached to. Usually, the (DOS) ports COM1: through COM4: map to the device special files */dev/ttyS0* through */dev/ttyS3*. Some distributions, such as Slackware, create a link called */dev/modem* to the appropriate *ttyS** device file, and configure *kermit, seyon,* and any other communication programs to use this generic file. In this case, you should use */dev/modem* in your UUCP configuration, too.

The reason for using a symbolic link is that all dial-out programs use so-called *lock files* to signal when a serial port is in use. The names of these lock files are a concatenation of the string *LCK..* and the device filename, for instance *LCK..ttyS1*. If programs use different names for the same device, they will fail to recognize each other's lock files. As a consequence, they will disrupt each other's session when started at the same time. This is quite possible when you schedule your UUCP calls using a *crontab* entry. For details on serial port setup, please refer to Chapter 4, *Configuring the Serial Hardware*.

Next, you must find out at what speed your modem and Linux will communicate. You have to set this speed to the maximum effective transfer rate you expect to get. The effective transfer rate may be much higher than the raw physical transfer rate your modem is capable of. For instance, many modems send and receive data at 56 kbps. Using compression protocols such as V.42bis, the actual transfer rate may climb over 100 kbps.

Of course, if UUCP is to do anything at all, you need the phone number of a system to call. Also, you need a valid login ID and possibly a password for the remote machine.*

You also have to know *exactly* how to log into the system. Do you have to press the Enter key before the login prompt appears? Does it display `login:` or `user:`? This is necessary for composing the *chat script*. If you don't know, or if the usual chat script fails, try to call the system with a terminal program like *kermit* or *minicom* and record exactly what you have to do.

Site Naming

As with TCP/IP-based networking, your host has to have a name for UUCP networking. As long as you simply want to use UUCP for file transfers to or from sites you dial up directly, or on a local network, this name does not have to meet any standards.†

However, if you use UUCP for a mail or news link, you should think about having the name registered with the UUCP Mapping Project.‡ The UUCP Mapping Project is described in Chapter 17, *Electronic Mail*. Even if you participate in a domain, you might consider having an official UUCP name for your site.

---

* If you're just going to try out UUCP, get the number of an archive site near you. Write down the login and password—they're public to make anonymous downloads possible. In most cases, they're something like **uucp/uucp** or **nuucp/uucp**.

† The only limitation is that it shouldn't be longer than seven characters, so as to not confuse UUCP implementations that run on an operating system that imposes a narrow limit on filenames. Names that are longer than seven characters are often truncated by UUCP. Some versions even limit the name to six characters.

‡ The UUCP Mapping Project registers all UUCP hostnames worldwide and makes sure they are unique.

Frequently, people choose their UUCP name to match the first component of their fully qualified domain name. Suppose your site's domain address is **swim.twobirds.com**; then your UUCP hostname would be **swim**. Think of UUCP sites as knowing each other on a first-name basis. Of course, you can also use a UUCP name completely unrelated to your fully qualified domain name.

However, make sure not to use the unqualified site name in mail addresses unless you have registered it as your official UUCP name. At the very best, mail to an unregistered UUCP host will vanish in some big black bit bucket. If you use a name already held by some other site, this mail will be routed to that site and cause its postmaster a lot of headaches.

By default, the UUCP suite uses the name set by *hostname* as the site's UUCP name. This name is commonly set by a command on the boot time *rc* scripts, and is usually stored in the */etc/hostname*. If your UUCP name is different from what you set your hostname to, you have to use the *hostname* option in the *config* file to tell *uucico* about your UUCP name. This is described next.

Taylor Configuration Files

We now return to the configuration files. Taylor UUCP gets its information from the following files:

config
> This is the main configuration file. You can define your site's UUCP name here.

sys This file describes all known sites. For each site, it specifies its name, what times to call it, which number to dial (if any), what type of device to use, and how to log on.

port
> This file contains entries describing each available port, together with the line speed supported and the dialer to be used.

dial
> This file describes dialers used to establish a telephone connection.

dialcode
> This file contains expansions for symbolic dial codes.

call
> This file contains the login name and password to be used when calling a system. Rarely used.

passwd

> This file contains login names and passwords that systems may use when logging in. It is used only when *uucico* does its own password checking.

Taylor configuration files are generally made up of lines containing keyword-value pairs. A hash sign introduces a comment that extends to the end of the line. To use a hash sign to mean itself, escape it with a backslash like this: \#.

There are quite a number of options you can tune with these configuration files. We can't go into all the parameters, but we will cover the most important ones here. Then you should be able to configure a modem-based UUCP link. Additional sections describe the modifications necessary if you want to use UUCP over TCP/IP or over a direct serial line. A complete reference is given in the Texinfo documents that accompany the Taylor UUCP sources.

When you think you have configured your UUCP system completely, you can check your configuration using the *uuchk* tool (located in */usr/lib/uucp*). *uuchk* reads your configuration files and prints out a detailed report of the configuration values used for each system.

General Configuration Options Using the config File

You won't generally use this file to describe much beside your UUCP hostname. By default, UUCP will use the name you set with the *hostname* command, but it is generally a good idea to set the UUCP name explicitly. Here's a sample *config* file:

```
# /usr/lib/uucp/config - UUCP main configuration file
hostname        vstout
```

A number of miscellaneous parameters can be set here too, such as the name of the spool directory or access rights for anonymous UUCP. The latter will be described later in this chapter in the section "Anonymous UUCP."

How to Tell UUCP About Other Systems Using the sys File

The *sys* file describes the systems that your machine knows about. An entry is introduced by the `system` keyword; the subsequent lines up to the next `system` directive detail the parameters specific to that site. Commonly, a system entry defines parameters such as the telephone number and login chat.

Parameters before the very first `system` line set default values used for all systems. Usually, you set protocol parameters and the like in the defaults section.

The most prominent fields are discussed in detail in the following sections.

System name

The *system* command names the remote system. You must specify the correct name of the remote system, not an alias you invented, because *uucico* will check it against what the remote system says it is called when you log on.*

Each system name can appear only once. If you want to use several sets of configurations for the same system (such as different telephone numbers *uucico* should try in turn), you can specify *alternates*, which we'll describe after the basic configuration options.

Telephone number

If the remote system is to be reached over a telephone line, the `phone` field specifies the number the modem should dial. It may contain several tokens interpreted by *uucico*'s dialing procedure. An equal sign (=) means wait for a secondary dial tone, and a dash (-) generates a one-second pause. Some telephone installations choke when you don't pause between dialing a special access code and the telephone number.†

It is often convenient to use names instead of numbers to describe area dialing codes. The *dialcode* file allows you to associate a name with a code that you may subsequently use when specifying telephone numbers for remote hosts. Suppose you have the following *dialcode* file:

```
# /usr/lib/uucp/dialcode - dialcode translation
Bogoham          024881
Coxton           035119
```

With these translations, you can use a phone number such as `Bogoham7732` in the *sys* file, which will probably make things a little more legible and a whole lot easier to update should the dialing code for Bogoham ever change.

port and speed

The `port` and `speed` options are used to select the device used for calling the remote system and the maximum speed to which the device should be set.‡ A `system` entry may use either option alone or both options in conjunction. When looking up a suitable device in the *port* file, only ports that have a matching port name and/or speed range are selected.

---

* Older Version 2 UUCPs don't broadcast their name when being called; however, newer implementations often do, and so does Taylor UUCP.

† For instance, most companies' private installations require you to dial a 0 or 9 to get a line to the outside.

‡ The bit rate of the *tty* must be at least as high as the maximum transfer speed.

Generally, using the `speed` option only should suffice. If you have only one serial device defined in *port*, *uucico* always picks the right one anyway, so you only have to give it the desired speed. If you have several modems attached to your systems, you still often don't want to name a particular port, because if *uucico* finds that there are several matches, it tries each device in turn until it finds an unused one.

The login chat

We already encountered the login chat script, which tells *uucico* how to log in to the remote system. It consists of a list of tokens specifying strings expected and sent by the local *uucico* process. *uucico* waits until the remote machine sends a login prompt, then returns the login name, waits for the remote system to send the password prompt, and sends the password. Expect and send strings appear in alternation in the script. *uucico* automatically appends a carriage return character (\r) to any send string. Thus, a simple chat script would look like:

```
ogin: vstout ssword: catch22
```

You will probably notice that the expect fields don't contain the whole prompts. This ensures that the login succeeds, even if the remote system transmits *Login:* instead of *login:*. If the string you are expecting or sending contains spaces or other white-space characters, you must use quotes to surround the text.

uucico also allows for some sort of conditional execution. Let's say the remote machine's *getty* needs to be reset before sending a prompt. For this, you can attach a subchat to an expect string, set off by a dash. The subchat is executed only if the main expect fails, i.e., a timeout occurs. One way to use this feature is to send a BREAK if the remote site doesn't display a login prompt. The following example gives a general-purpose chat script that should also work in case you have to press Enter before the login appears. The empty first argument, `""`, tells UUCP to not wait for anything, but to continue with the next send string:

```
"" \n\r\d\r\n\c ogin:-BREAK-ogin: vstout ssword: catch22
```

A couple of special strings and escape characters can occur in the chat script. The following is a partial list of characters legal in expect strings:

`""` The empty string. It tells *uucico* to not wait for anything, but to proceed with the next send string immediately.

`\t` Tab character.

`\r` Carriage return character.

`\s` Space character. You need this to embed spaces in a chat string.

\n Newline character.

\\ Backslash character.

On send strings, the following escape characters and strings are legal in addition to the above:

EOT

   End of transmission character (^D).

BREAK

   Break character.

\c Suppress sending of carriage return at end of string.

\d Delay sending for 1 second.

\E Enable echo checking. This requires *uucico* to wait for the echo of everything it writes to be read back from the device before it can continue with the chat. It is primarily useful when used in modem chats (which we will encounter later). Echo checking is off by default.

\e Disable echo checking.

\K Same as BREAK.

\p Pause for fraction of a second.

Alternates

Sometimes you want to have multiple entries for a single system, for instance if the system can be reached on different modem lines. With Taylor UUCP, you can do this by defining a so-called *alternate*.

An alternate entry retains all settings from the main system entry and specifies only those values that should be overridden in the default system entry or added to it. An alternate is offset from the system entry by a line containing the keyword `alternate`.

To use two phone numbers for **pablo**, you would modify its *sys* entry in the following way:

```
system      pablo
phone       123-456
.. entries as above ...
alternate
phone       123-455
```

When calling **pablo**, *uucico* will first dial 123-456, and if this fails, it will try the alternate. The alternate entry retains all settings from the main system entry and overrides the telephone number only.

Restricting call times

Taylor UUCP provides a number of ways you may restrict the times when calls can be placed to a remote system. You might do this either because of limitations the remote host places on its services during business hours, or simply to avoid times with high call rates. Note that it is always possible to override call-time restrictions by giving *uucico* the *−S* or *−f* option.

By default, Taylor UUCP disallows connections at any time, so you *have* to use some sort of time specification in the *sys* file. If you don't care about call time restrictions, you can specify the *time* option with a value of Any in your *sys* file.

The simplest way to restrict call time is to include a time entry, followed by a string made up of a day and a time subfield. Day may be any combination of Mo, Tu, We, Th, Fr, Sa, and Su. You can also specify Any, Never, or Wk for weekdays. The time consists of two 24-hour clock values, separated by a dash. They specify the range during which calls may be placed. The combination of these tokens is written without white space in between. Any number of day and time specifications may be grouped together with commas, as this line shows:

```
time          MoWe0300-0730,Fr1805-2200
```

This example allows calls on Mondays and Wednesdays from 3:00 a.m. to 7:30 a.m., and on Fridays between 6:05 p.m. and 10:00 p.m. When a time field spans midnight, say Mo1830-0600, it actually means Monday, between midnight and 6:00 a.m. and between 6:30 p.m. and midnight.

The special time strings Any and Never mean what they say: calls may be placed at any or no time, respectively.

Taylor UUCP also has a number of special tokens you may use in time strings, such as NonPeak and Night. These special tokens are shorthand for Any2300-0800, SaSu0800-1700 and Any1800-0700, SaSu, respectively.

The *time* command takes an optional second argument that describes a retry time in minutes. When an attempt to establish a connection fails, *uucico* will not allow another attempt to dial up the remote host within a certain interval. For instance, when you specify a retry time of 5 minutes, *uucico* will refuse to call the remote system within 5 minutes after the last failure. By default, *uucico* uses an exponential backoff scheme, where the retry interval increases with each repeated failure.

The *timegrade* command allows you to attach a maximum spool grade to a schedule. For instance, assume you have the following *timegrade* commands in a **system** entry:

```
timegrade     N Wk1900-0700,SaSu
timegrade     C Any
```

This allows jobs with a spool grade of C or higher (usually mail is queued with grade B or C) to be transferred whenever a call is established, while news (usually queued with grade N) are transferred only during the night and at weekends.

Just like *time*, the *timegrade* command takes a retry interval in minutes as an optional third argument.

However, a caveat about spool grades is in order here. First, the *timegrade* option applies only to what *your* systems sends; the remote system may still transfer anything it likes. You can use the *call-timegrade* option to explicitly request it to send only jobs above some given spool grade; but there's no guarantee it will obey this request.*

Similarly, the `timegrade` field is not checked when a remote system calls in, so any jobs queued for the calling system will be sent. However, the remote system can explicitly request your *uucico* to restrict itself to a certain spool grade.

Identifying Available Devices Through the port File

The *port* file tells *uucico* about the available ports. These are usually modem ports, but other types, such as direct serial lines and TCP sockets, are supported as well.

Like the *sys* file, *port* consists of separate entries starting with the keyword `port` followed by the port name. This name may be used in the *sys* file's `port` statement. The name need not be unique; if there are several ports with the same name, *uucico* will try each in turn until it finds one that is not currently being used.

The *port* command should be followed immediately by the `type` statement, which indicates what type of port is described. Valid types are `modem`, `direct` for direct connections, and `tcp` for TCP sockets. If the *port* command is missing, the port type defaults to modem.

In this section, we cover only modem ports; TCP ports and direct lines are discussed in a later section.

For modem and direct ports, you have to specify the device for calling out using the `device` directive. Usually, this is the name of a device special file in the */dev* directory, like */dev/ttyS1*.

In the case of a modem device, the port entry also determines what type of modem is connected to the port. Different types of modems have to be configured differently. Even modems that claim to be Hayes-compatible aren't always really compatible with one another. Therefore, you have to tell *uucico* how to initialize the modem and make it dial the desired number. Taylor UUCP keeps the descrip-

---

* If the remote system runs Taylor UUCP, it will obey.

tions of all dialers in a file named *dial*. To use any of these, you have to specify the dialer's name using the *dialer* command.

Sometimes, you will want to use a modem in different ways, depending on which system you call. For instance, some older modems don't understand when a high-speed modem attempts to connect at 56 kbps; they simply drop the line instead of negotiating a connect at 9,600 bps, for instance. When you know site **drop** uses such a dumb modem, you have to set up your modem differently when calling them. For this, you need an additional port entry in the *port* file that specifies a different dialer. Now you can give the new port a different name, such as `serial1-slow`, and use the **port** directive in the **drop** system entry in *sys*.

A better to distinguish the ports is by the speeds they support. For instance, the two port entries for the above situation may look like this:

```
# NakWell modem; connect at high speed
port            serial1          # port name
type            modem            # modem port
device          /dev/ttyS1       # this is COM2
speed           115200           # supported speed
dialer          nakwell          # normal dialer
# NakWell modem; connect at low speed
port            serial1          # port name
type            modem            # modem port
device          /dev/ttyS1       # this is COM2
speed           9600             # supported speed
dialer          nakwell-slow     # don't attempt fast connect
```

The system entry for site **drop** would now give `serial1` as the port name, but request to use it at only 9,600 bps. *uucico* then automatically uses the second port entry. All remaining sites that have a speed of 115,200 bps in the system entry will be called using the first port entry. By default, the first entry with a matching speed will be used.

How to Dial a Number Using the dial File

The *dial* file describes the way various dialers are used. Traditionally, UUCP talks of dialers rather than modems, because in earlier times, it was usual practice to have one (expensive) automatic dialing device serve a whole bank of modems. Today, most modems have dialing support built in, so this distinction gets a little blurred.

Nevertheless, different dialers or modems may require a different configuration. You can describe each of them in the *dial* file. Entries in *dial* start with the *dialer* command that gives the dialer's name.

The most important entry besides *dialer* is the modem chat, specified by the *chat* command. Similar to the login chat, it consists of a sequence of strings *uucico* sends to the dialer and the responses it expects in return. It is commonly used to reset the modem to some known state and dial the number. The following sample `dialer` entry shows a typical modem chat for a Hayes-compatible modem:

```
# NakWell modem; connect at high speed
dialer          nakwell         # dialer name
chat            "" AT&F OK\r ATH1E0Q0 OK\r ATDT\T CONNECT
chat-fail       BUSY
chat-fail       ERROR
chat-fail       NO\sCARRIER
dtr-toggle      true
```

The modem chat begins with `" "`, the empty expect string. *uucico* therefore sends the first command *AT&F* right away. *AT&F* is the Hayes command to reset the modem to factory default configuration. *uucico* then waits until the modem has sent `OK` and sends the next command, which turns off local echo and the like. After the modem returns `OK` again, *uucico* sends the dialing command *ATDT*. The escape sequence `\T` in this string is replaced with the phone number taken from the system entry *sys* file. *uucico* then waits for the modem to return the string `CONNECT`, which signals that a connection with the remote modem has been established successfully.

Sometimes the modem fails to connect to the remote system; for instance, if the other system is talking to someone else and the line is busy. In this case, the modem returns an error message indicating the reason. Modem chats are not capable of detecting such messages; *uucico* continues to wait for the expected string until it times out. The UUCP log file therefore only shows a bland "timed out in chat script" instead of the specific reason.

However, Taylor UUCP allows you to tell *uucico* about these error messages using the *chat-fail* command as shown above. When *uucico* detects a chat-fail string while executing the modem chat, it aborts the call and logs the error message in the UUCP log file.

The last command in the example shown above tells UUCP to toggle the Data Terminal Ready (DTR) control line before starting the modem chat. Normally, the serial driver raises DTR when a process opens the device to tell the attached modem that someone wants to talk to it. The `dtr-toggle` feature then drops DTR, waits a moment, and raises it again. Many modems can be configured to react to a drop of DTR by going off-hook, entering command state, or resetting themselves.*

UUCP Over TCP

Absurd as it may sound, using UUCP to transfer data over TCP is not that bad an idea, especially when transferring large amounts of data such as Usenet news. On TCP-based links, news is generally exchanged using the NNTP protocol, through

---

* Some modems don't seem to like this and occasionally hang.

which articles are requested and sent individually without compression or any other optimization. Although adequate for large sites with several concurrent newsfeeds, this technique is very unfavorable for small sites that receive their news over a relatively slow connection such as ISDN. These sites will usually want to combine the qualities of TCP with the advantages of sending news in large batches, which can be compressed and thus transferred with very low overhead. A common way to transfer these batches is to use UUCP over TCP.

In *sys*, you would specify a system to be called via TCP like this:

```
system      gmu
address     news.groucho.edu
time        Any
port        tcp-conn
chat        ogin: vstout word: clouseau
```

The *address* command gives the IP address of the host or its fully qualified domain name. The corresponding *port* entry would read:

```
port        tcp-conn
type        tcp
service     540
```

The entry states that a TCP connection should be used when a *sys* entry references `tcp-conn`, and that *uucico* should attempt to connect to the TCP network port 540 on the remote host. This is the default port number of the UUCP service. Instead of the port number, you may also give a symbolic port name to the *service* command. The port number corresponding to this name will be looked up in */etc/services*. The common name for the UUCP service is `uucpd`.

Using a Direct Connection

Assume you use a direct line to connect your system **vstout** to **tiny**. Much like in the modem case, you have to write a system entry in the *sys* file. The *port* command identifies the serial port **tiny** is hooked up to:

```
system      tiny
time        Any
port        direct1
speed       38400
chat        ogin: cathcart word: catch22
```

In the *port* file, you have to describe the serial port for the direct connection. A `dialer` entry is not needed because there's no need for dialing:

```
port        direct1
type        direct
speed       38400
device         /dev/ttyS1
```

Controlling Access to UUCP Features

UUCP is quite a flexible system. With that flexibility comes a need to carefully control access to its features to prevent abuse, whether it be intentional or accidental. The primary features of concern to the UUCP administrator are remote command execution, file transfer, and forwarding. Taylor UUCP provides a means of limiting the freedom that remote UUCP hosts have in exercising each of these features. With careful selection of permissions, the UUCP administrator can ensure that the host's security is preserved.

Command Execution

UUCP's task is to copy files from one system to another and to request execution of certain commands on remote hosts. Of course, you as an administrator would want to control what rights you grant other systems—allowing them to execute any command they choose on your system is definitely not a good idea.

By default, the only commands Taylor UUCP allows other systems to execute on your machine are *rmail* and *rnews*, which are commonly used to exchange email and Usenet News over UUCP. To change the set of commands for a particular system, you can use the **commands** keyword in the *sys* file. Similarly, you may want to limit the search path to just those directories containing the allowed commands. You can change the search path allowed for a remote host with the **command-path** statement. For instance, you may want to allow system **pablo** to execute the *bsmtp* command in addition to *rmail* and *rnews:**

```
system          pablo
...
commands        rmail rnews bsmtp
```

File Transfers

Taylor UUCP also allows you to fine-tune file transfers in great detail. At one extreme, you can disable transfers to and from a particular system. Just set **request** to **no**, and the remote system will not be able to either retrieve files from your system or send it any files. Similarly, you can prohibit your users from transferring files to or from a system by setting **transfer** to **no**. By default, users on both the local and the remote system are allowed to upload and download files.

In addition, you can configure the directories that files may be copied to and from. Usually you will want to restrict access from remote systems to a single directory hierarchy, but still allow your users to send files from their home directory. Commonly, remote users are allowed to receive files only from the public UUCP

---

* *bsmtp* is used to deliver mail with batched SMTP.

directory */var/spool/uucppublic*. This is the traditional place to make files publicly available, very much like FTP servers on the Internet.*

Taylor UUCP provides four different commands to configure the directories for sending and receiving files. They are: *local-send*, which specifies the list of directories a user may ask UUCP to send files from; *local-receive*, which gives the list of directories a user may ask to receive files to; and *remote-send* and *remote-receive*, which do the analogous for requests from a foreign system. Consider the following example:

```
system          pablo
...
local-send      /home  ~
local-receive   /home  ~/receive
remote-send     ~  !~/incoming !~/receive
remote-receive  ~/incoming
```

The *local-send* command allows users on your host to send any files below */home* and from the public UUCP directory to **pablo**. The *local-receive* command allows them to receive files either to the world-writable *receive* directory in the *uucppublic*, or any world-writable directory below */home*. The *remote-send* directive allows **pablo** to request files from */var/spool/uucppublic*, except for files from the *incoming* and *receive* directories. This is signaled to *uucico* by preceding the directory names with exclamation marks. Finally, the last line allows **pablo** to upload files to **incoming**.

A major problem with file transfers using UUCP is that it receives files only to directories that are world-writable. This may tempt some users to set up traps for other users. However, there's no way to escape this problem outside of disabling UUCP file transfers altogether.

Forwarding

UUCP provides a mechanism to have other systems execute file transfers on your behalf. For instance, suppose your system has *uucp* access to a system called **seci**, but not to another system called **uchile**. This allows you to make **seci** retrieve a file from **uchile** for you and send it to your system. The following command would achieve this:

$ uucp -r seci!uchile!~/find-ls.gz ~/uchile.files.gz

This technique of passing a job through several systems is called *forwarding*. On your own UUCP system, you would want to limit the forwarding service to a few hosts you trust not to run up a horrendous phone bill by making you download the latest X11R6 source release for them.

---

* You may use a tilde (~) character to refer to the UUCP public directory, but only in UUCP configuration files; outside it usually translates to the user's home directory.

By default, Taylor UUCP prohibits forwarding altogether. To enable forwarding for a particular system, you can use the *forward* command. This command specifies a list of sites the system may request you to forward jobs to and from. For instance, the UUCP administrator of **seci** would have to add the following lines to the *sys* file to allow **pablo** to request files from **uchile**:

```
###################
# pablo
system          pablo
...
forward         uchile
###################
# uchile
system          uchile
...
forward-to      pablo
```

The `forward-to` entry for **uchile** is necessary so that any files returned by it are actually passed on to **pablo**. Otherwise UUCP would drop them. This entry uses a variation of the *forward* command that permits **uchile** to send files only to **pablo** through **seci**, not the other way round.

To permit forwarding to any system, use the special keyword `ANY` (capital letters required).

Setting Up Your System for Dialing In

If you want to set up your site for dialing in, you have to permit logins on your serial port and customize some system files to provide UUCP accounts, which we will cover in this section.

Providing UUCP Accounts

To begin with, you have to set up user accounts that let remote sites log into your system and establish a UUCP connection. Generally, you will provide a separate login name to each system that polls you. When setting up an account for system **pablo**, you might give it the username **Upablo**. There is no enforced policy on login names; they can be just about anything, but it will be convenient for you if the login name is easily related to the remote host name.

For systems that dial in through the serial port, you usually have to add these accounts to the system password file */etc/passwd*. It is good practice to put all UUCP logins in a special group, such as **uuguest**. The account's home directory should be set to the public spool directory */var/spool/uucppublic*; its login shell must be *uucico*.

To serve UUCP systems that connect to your site over TCP, you have to set up *inetd* to handle incoming connections on the `uucp` port by adding the following line to */etc/inetd.conf*:*

```
uucp   stream  tcp   nowait  root  /usr/sbin/tcpd  /usr/lib/uucp/uucico -l
```

The *–l* option makes *uucico* perform its own login authorization. It prompts for a login name and a password just like the standard *login* program, but relies on its private password database instead of */etc/passwd*. This private password file is named */etc/uucp/passwd* and contains pairs of login names and passwords:

```
Upablo  IslaNegra
Ulorca  co'rdoba
```

This file must be owned by **uucp** and have permissions of 600.

Does this database sound like such a good idea that you would like to use it on normal serial logins, too? Well, in some cases you can. What you need is a *getty* program that you can tell to invoke *uucico* instead of */bin/login* for your UUCP users.† The invocation of *uucico* would look like this:

```
/usr/lib/uucp/uucico -l -u user
```

The *–u* option tells it to use the specified user name rather than prompting for it.‡

To protect your UUCP users from callers who might give a false system name and snarf all their mail, you should add *called-login* commands to each system entry in the *sys* file. This is described in the next section.

Protecting Yourself Against Swindlers

A major problem with UUCP is that the calling system can lie about its name; it announces its name to the called system after logging in, but the server doesn't have any way to check it. Thus, an attacker could log into his or her own UUCP account, pretend to be someone else, and pick up that other site's mail. This is particularly troublesome if you offer login via anonymous UUCP, where the password is made public.

---

* Note that *tcpd* usually has mode 700, so that you must invoke it as user **root**, not **uucp**. *tcpd* is discussed in more detail in Chapter 12, *Important Network Features*.

† Gert Doering's *mgetty* is such a beast. It runs on a variety of platforms, including SCO Unix, AIX, SunOS, HP-UX, and Linux.

‡ This option is not present in Version 1.04.

You *must* guard against this sort of impostor. The cure for this disease is to require each system to use a particular login name by specifying a `called-login` in *sys*. A sample system entry may look like this:

```
system          pablo
... usual options ...
called-login    Upablo
```

The upshot is that whenever a system logs in and pretends it is **pablo**, *uucico* checks whether it has logged in as **Upablo**. If it hasn't, the calling system is turned down, and the connection is dropped. You should make it a habit to add the *called-login* command to every system entry you add to your *sys* file. It is important that you do this for *all* systems in your *sys* file, regardless of whether they will ever call your site or not. For those sites that never call you, you should probably set `called-login` to some totally bogus user name, such as **neverlogsin**.

Be Paranoid: Call Sequence Checks

Another way to fend off and detect impostors is to use *call sequence checks*. These help you protect against intruders who somehow manage to find out the password with which you log into your UUCP system.

When using call sequence checks, both machines keep track of the number of connections established so far. The counter is incremented with each connection. After logging in, the caller sends its call sequence number, and the receiver checks it against its own number. If they don't match, the connection attempt is rejected. If the initial number is chosen at random, attackers will have a hard time guessing the correct call sequence number.

But call sequence checks do more for you. Even if some very clever person should detect your call sequence number as well as your password, you will find out. When the attacker calls your UUCP feed and steals your mail, this will increase the feeds call sequence number by one. The next time *you* call your feed and try to log in, the remote *uucico* will refuse you, because the numbers don't match anymore!

If you have enabled call sequence checks, you should check your log files regularly for error messages that hint at possible attacks. If your system rejects the call sequence number the calling system offers, *uucico* will put a message into the log file saying something like, "Out of sequence call rejected." If your system is rejected by its feed because the sequence numbers are out of sync, it will put a message in the log file saying, "Handshake failed (RBADSEQ)."

To enable call sequence checks, add the following command to the system entry:

```
# enable call sequence checks
sequence        true
```

In addition, you have to create the file containing the sequence number itself. Taylor UUCP keeps the sequence number in a file called *.Sequence* in the remote site's spool directory. It *must* be owned by **uucp** and must be mode 600 (i.e., readable and writeable only by **uucp**). It is best to initialize this file with an arbitrary, previously agreed-upon start value. A simple way to create this file is:

```
# cd /var/spool/uucp/pablo
# echo 94316 > .Sequence
# chmod 600 .Sequence
# chown uucp.uucp .Sequence
```

Of course, the remote site has to enable call sequence checks as well and start by using exactly the same sequence number as you.

Anonymous UUCP

If you want to provide anonymous UUCP access to your system, you first have to set up a special account for it as previously described. A common practice is to give the anonymous account a login name and a password of **uucp**.

In addition, you have to set a few of the security options for unknown systems. For instance, you may want to prohibit them from executing any commands on your system. However, you cannot set these parameters in a *sys* file entry because the *system* command requires the system's name, which you don't have. Taylor UUCP solves this dilemma through the *unknown* command. *unknown* can be used in the *config* file to specify any command that can usually appear in a system entry:

```
unknown          remote-receive ~/incoming
unknown          remote-send ~/pub
unknown          max-remote-debug none
unknown          command-path /usr/lib/uucp/anon-bin
unknown          commands rmail
```

This will restrict unknown systems to downloading files from below the *pub* directory and uploading files to the *incoming* directory below */var/spool/uucppublic*. The next line will make *uucico* ignore any requests from the remote system to turn on debugging locally. The last two lines permit unknown systems to execute *rmail*; but the command path specified makes *uucico* look for the *rmail* command in a private directory named *anon-bin* only. This restriction allows you to provide some special *rmail* that, for instance, forwards all mail to the superuser for examination. This allows anonymous users to reach the maintainer of the system, but at the same time prevents them from injecting any mail to other sites.

To enable anonymous UUCP, you must specify at least one `unknown` statement in *config*. Otherwise *uucico* will reject all unknown systems.

UUCP Low-Level Protocols

To negotiate session control and file transfers with the remote end, *uucico* uses a set of standardized messages. This is often referred to as the *high-level protocol*. During the initialization phase and the hangup phase these are simply sent across as strings. However, during the real transfer phase, an additional low-level protocol that is mostly transparent to the higher levels is employed. This protocol offers some added benefits, such as allowing error checks on data sent over unreliable links.

Protocol Overview

UUCP is used over different types of connections, such as serial lines, TCP, or sometimes even X.25; it is advantageous to transport UUCP within protocols designed specifically for the underlying network protocol. In addition, several implementations of UUCP have introduced different protocols that do roughly the same thing.

Protocols can be divided into two categories: *streaming* and *packet* protocols. Protocols of the streaming variety transfer a file as a whole, possibly computing a checksum over it. This is nearly free of overhead, but requires a reliable connection because any error will cause the whole file to be retransmitted. These protocols are commonly used over TCP connections but are not suitable for use over telephone lines. Although modern modems do quite a good job at error correction, they are not perfect, nor is there any error detection between your computer and the modem.

On the other hand, packet-oriented protocols split up the file into several chunks of equal size. Each packet is sent and received separately, a checksum is computed, and an acknowledgment is returned to the sender. To make this more efficient, sliding-window protocols have been invented, which allow for a limited number (a window) of outstanding acknowledgments at any time. This greatly reduces the amount of time *uucico* has to wait during a transmission. Still, the relatively large overhead compared to a streaming protocol makes packet protocols inefficient for TCP use, but ideal for telephone lines.

The width of the data path also makes a difference. Sometimes sending 8-bit characters over a serial connection is impossible; for instance, the connection could go through a stupid terminal server that strips off the eighth bit. When you transmit 8-bit characters over a 7-bit connection, they have to be quoted on transmission. In the worst-case scenerio, quoting doubles the amount of data to be transmitted, although compression done by the hardware may compensate. Lines that can transmit arbitrary 8-bit characters are usually called *8-bit clean*. This is the case for all TCP connections, as well as for most modem connections.

Taylor UUCP 1.06 supports a wide variety of UUCP protocols. The most common of these are:

g   This is the most common protocol and should be understood by virtually all *uucico*s. It does thorough error checking and is therefore well suited for noisy telephone links. *g* requires an 8-bit clean connection. It is a packet-oriented protocol that uses a sliding-window technique.

i   This is a bidirectional packet protocol, which can send and receive files at the same time. It requires a full-duplex connection and an 8-bit clean data path. It is currently understood by Taylor UUCP only.

t   This protocol is intended for use over a TCP connection or other truly error-free networks. It uses packets of 1,024 bytes and requires an 8-bit clean connection.

e   This should basically do the same as *t*. The main difference is that *e* is a streaming protocol and is thus suited only to reliable network connections.

f   This is intended for use with reliable X.25 connections. It is a streaming protocol and expects a 7-bit data path. 8-bit characters are quoted, which can make it very inefficient.

G   This is the System V Release 4 version of the *g* protocol. It is also understood by some other versions of UUCP.

a   This protocol is similiar to ZMODEM. It requires an 8-bit connection, but quotes certain control characters like XON and XOFF.

Tuning the Transmission Protocol

All protocols allow for some variation in packet sizes, timeouts, etc. Usually, the defaults work well under standard circumstances, but may not be optimal for your situation. The *g* protocol, for instance, uses window sizes from 1 to 7, and packet sizes in powers of 2 ranging from 64 through 4096. If your telephone line is usually so noisy that it drops more than 5 percent of all packets, you should probably lower the packet size and shrink the window. On the other hand, on very good telephone lines the protocol overhead of sending acknowledgments for every 128 bytes may prove wasteful, so you might increase the packet size to 512 or even 1,024. Most binaries included in Linux distributions default to a window size of 7 and 128-byte packets.

Taylor UUCP lets you tune parameters with the *protocol-parameter* command in the *sys* file. For instance, to set the *g* protocol's packet size to 512 when talking to **pablo**, you have to add:

```
system          pablo
...
protocol-parameter g  packet-size  512
```

The tunable parameters and their names vary from protocol to protocol. For a complete list of them, refer to the documentation enclosed in the Taylor UUCP source.

Selecting Specific Protocols

Not every implementation of *uucico* speaks and understands each protocol, so during the initial handshake phase, both processes have to agree on a common one. The master *uucico* offers the slave a list of supported protocols by sending P*protlist*, from which the slave may pick one.

Based on the type of port used (modem, TCP, or direct), *uucico* will compose a default list of protocols. For modem and direct connections, this list usually comprises *i*, *a*, *g*, *G*, and *j*. For TCP connections, the list is *t*, *e*, *i*, *a*, *g*, *G*, *j*, and *f*. You can override this default list with the *protocols* command, which may be specified in a system entry as well as a port entry. For instance, you might edit the *port* file entry for your modem port like this:

```
port            serial1
...
protocols       igG
```

This will require any incoming or outgoing connection through this port to use *i*, *g*, or *G*. If the remote system does not support any of these, the conversation will fail.

Troubleshooting

This section describes what may go wrong with your UUCP connection and makes location suggestions to fix the error. Although these problems are encountered on a regular basis, there is much more that can go wrong than what we have listed.

If you have a problem, enable debugging with *–xall*, and take a look at the output in *Debug* in the spool directory. The file should help you to quickly recognize the problem. It is often helpful to turn on the modem's speaker when it doesn't connect. With Hayes-compatible modems, you can turn on the speaker by adding ATL1M1 OK to the modem chat in the *dial* file.

The first check should always be whether all file permissions are set correctly. *uucico* should be setuid **uucp**, and all files in */usr/lib/uucp*, */var/spool/uucp*, and */var/spool/uucppublic* should be owned by **uucp**. There are also some hidden files in the spool directory which must be owned by **uucp** as well.*

When you're sure you have the permissions of all files set correctly, and you're still experiencing problems, you can then begin to take error messages more literally. We'll now look at some of the more common errors and problems.

---

* That is, files with names beginning with a dot. Such files aren't normally displayed by the *ls* command.

uucico Keeps Saying "Wrong Time to Call"

This probably means that in the system entry in *sys*, you didn't specify a *time* command that details when the remote system may be called, or you gave one that actually forbids calling at the current time. If no call schedule is given, *uucico* assumes the system can never be called.

uucico Complains That the Site Is Already Locked

This means that *uucico* detects a lock file for the remote system in */var/spool/uucp*. The lock file may be from an earlier call to the system that crashed or was killed. Another possible explanation is that there's another *uucico* process sitting around that is trying to dial the remote system and has gotten stuck in a chat script, or stalled for some other reason.

To correct this error, kill all *uucico* processes open for the site with a hangup signal, and remove all lock files that they have left lying around.

You Can Connect to the Remote Site, but the Chat Script Fails

Look at the text you receive from the remote site. If it's garbled, you might have a speed-related problem. Otherwise, confirm that it really agrees with what your chat script expects. Remember, the chat script starts with an expect string. If you receive the login prompt and send your name, but never get the password prompt, insert some delays before sending it, or even in between the letters. You might be too fast for your modem.

Your Modem Does Not Dial

If your modem doesn't indicate that the DTR line has been raised when *uucico* calls out, you might not have given the right device to *uucico*. If your modem recognizes DTR, check with a terminal program that you can write to the modem. If this works, turn on echoing with \E at the start of the modem chat. If the modem doesn't echo your commands during the modem chat, check if your line speed is too high or low. If you see the echo, check if you have disabled modem responses or set them to number codes. Verify that the chat script itself is correct. Remember that you have to write two backslashes to send one to the modem.

Your Modem Tries to Dial but Doesn't Get Out

Insert a delay into the phone number, especially if you have to dial a special sequence to gain an outside line from a corporate telephone network. Make sure you are using the correct dial type, as some telephone networks support only one type of dialing. Additionally, double check the telephone number to make sure it's correct.

Login Succeeds, but the Handshake Fails

Well, there can be a number of problems in this situation. The output in the log file should tell you a lot. Look at what protocols the remote site offers (it sends a string P *protlist* during the handshake). For the handshake to succeed, both ends must support at least one common protocol, so check that they do.

If the remote system sends *RLCK*, there is a stale lockfile for you on the remote system already connected to the remote system on a different line. Otherwise, ask the remote system administrator to remove the file.

If the remote system sends *RBADSEQ*, it has conversation count checks enabled for you, but the numbers didn't match. If it sends *RLOGIN*, you were not permitted to log in under this ID.

Log Files and Debugging

When compiling the UUCP suite to use Taylor-style logging, you have only three global log files, all of which reside in the spool directory. The main log file is named *Log* and contains all the information about established connections and transferred files. A typical excerpt looks like this (after a little reformatting to make it fit the page):

```
uucico pablo - (1994-05-28 17:15:01.66 539) Calling system pablo (port cua3)
uucico pablo - (1994-05-28 17:15:39.25 539) Login successful
uucico pablo - (1994-05-28 17:15:39.90 539) Handshake successful
               (protocol 'g' packet size 1024 window 7)
uucico pablo postmaster (1994-05-28 17:15:43.65 539) Receiving D.pabloB04aj
uucico pablo postmaster (1994-05-28 17:15:46.51 539) Receiving X.pabloX04ai
uucico pablo postmaster (1994-05-28 17:15:48.91 539) Receiving D.pabloB04at
uucico pablo postmaster (1994-05-28 17:15:51.52 539) Receiving X.pabloX04as
uucico pablo postmaster (1994-05-28 17:15:54.01 539) Receiving D.pabloB04c2
uucico pablo postmaster (1994-05-28 17:15:57.17 539) Receiving X.pabloX04c1
uucico pablo - (1994-05-28 17:15:59.05 539) Protocol 'g' packets: sent 15,
               resent 0, received 32
uucico pablo - (1994-05-28 17:16:02.50 539) Call complete (26 seconds)
uuxqt pablo postmaster (1994-05-28 17:16:11.41 546) Executing X.pabloX04ai
               (rmail okir)
uuxqt pablo postmaster (1994-05-28 17:16:13.30 546) Executing X.pabloX04as
               (rmail okir)
uuxqt pablo postmaster (1994-05-28 17:16:13.51 546) Executing X.pabloX04c1
               (rmail okir)
```

The next important log file is *Stats*, which lists file transfer statistics. The section of *Stats* corresponding to the above transfer looks like this (again, the lines have been split to fit the page):

```
postmaster pablo (1994-05-28 17:15:44.78)
                 received 1714 bytes in 1.802 seconds (951 bytes/sec)
postmaster pablo (1994-05-28 17:15:46.66)
                 received 57 bytes in 0.634 seconds (89 bytes/sec)
postmaster pablo (1994-05-28 17:15:49.91)
                 received 1898 bytes in 1.599 seconds (1186 bytes/sec)
postmaster pablo (1994-05-28 17:15:51.67)
                 received 65 bytes in 0.555 seconds (117 bytes/sec)
postmaster pablo (1994-05-28 17:15:55.71)
                 received 3217 bytes in 2.254 seconds (1427 bytes/sec)
postmaster pablo (1994-05-28 17:15:57.31)
                 received 65 bytes in 0.590 seconds (110 bytes/sec)
```

The third file is *Debug*. Debugging information is written here. If you use debugging, make sure this file has protection mode 600. Depending on the debug mode you select, it may contain the login and password you use to connect to the remote system.

If you have some tools around that expect your log files to be in the traditional format used by HDB-compatible UUCP implementations, you can also compile Taylor UUCP to produce HDB-style logs. This is simply a matter of enabling a compile-time option in *config.h*.

CHAPTER SEVENTEEN

ELECTRONIC MAIL

Electronic mail transport has been one of the most prominent uses of networking since the first networks were devised. Email started as a simple service that copied a file from one machine to another and appended it to the recipient's *mailbox* file. The concept remains the same, although an ever-growing net, with its complex routing requirements and its ever increasing load of messages, has made a more elaborate scheme necessary.

Various standards of mail exchange have been devised. Sites on the Internet adhere to one laid out in RFC-822, augmented by some RFCs that describe a machine-independent way of transferring just about *anything*, including graphics, sound files, and special characters sets, by email.* CCITT has defined another standard, X.400. It is still used in some large corporate and government environments, but is progressively being retired.

Quite a number of mail transport programs have been implemented for Unix systems. One of the best known is *sendmail*, which was developed by Eric Allman at the University of California at Berkeley. Eric Allman now offers *sendmail* through a commercial venture, but the program remains free software. *sendmail* is supplied as the standard mail agent in some Linux distributions. We describe *sendmail* configuration in Chapter 18, *Sendmail*.

Linux also uses *Exim*, written by Philip Hazel of the University of Cambridge. We describe *Exim* configuration in Chapter 19, *Getting Exim Up and Running*.

Compared to *sendmail*, *Exim* is rather young. For the vast bulk of sites with email requirements, their capabilities are pretty close.

Both *Exim* and *sendmail* support a set of configuration files that have to be customized for your system. Apart from the information that is required to make the

---

* Read RFC-1437 if you don't believe this statement!

mail subsystem run (such as the local hostname), there are many parameters that may be tuned. *sendmail*'s main configuration file is very hard to understand at first. It looks as if your cat has taken a nap on your keyboard with the shift key pressed. *Exim* configuration files are more structured and easier to understand than *sendmail*'s. *Exim*, however, does not provide direct support for UUCP and handles only domain addresses. Today that isn't as big a limitation as it once might have been; most sites stay within *Exim*'s limitations. However, for most sites, the work required in setting up either of them is roughly the same.

In this chapter, we deal with what email is and what issues administrators have to deal with. Chapter 18 and Chapter 19 provide instructions on setting up *sendmail* and *Exim* and for the first time. The included information should help smaller sites become operational, but there are several more options and you can spend many happy hours in front of your computer configuring the fanciest features.

Toward the end of this chapter we briefly cover setting up *elm*, a very common mail user agent on many Unix-like systems, including Linux.

For more information about issues specific to electronic mail on Linux, please refer to the Electronic Mail HOWTO by Guylhem Aznar,* which is posted to *comp.os.linux.answers* regularly. The source distributions of *elm*, *Exim*, and *sendmail* also contain extensive documentation that should answer most questions on setting them up, and we provide references to this documentation in their respective chapters. If you need general information on email, a number of RFCs deal with this topic. They are listed in the bibliography at the end of the book.

What Is a Mail Message?

A mail message generally consists of a message body, which is the text of the message, and special administrative data specifying recipients, transport medium, etc., like what you see when you look at a physical letter's envelope.

This administrative data falls into two categories. In the first category is any data that is specific to the transport medium, like the address of sender and recipient. It is therefore called the *envelope*. It may be transformed by the transport software as the message is passed along.

The second variety is any data necessary for handling the mail message, which is not particular to any transport mechanism, such as the message's subject line, a list of all recipients, and the date the message was sent. In many networks, it has become standard to prepend this data to the mail message, forming the so-called *mail header*. It is offset from the *mail body* by an empty line.†

---

* Guylhem can be reached at *guylhem@danmark.linux.eu.org*.

† It is customary to append a *signature* or *.sig* to a mail message, usually containing information on the author along with a joke or a motto. It is offset from the mail message by a line containing "−" followed by a space.

Most mail transport software in the Unix world use a header format outlined in RFC-822. Its original purpose was to specify a standard for use on the ARPANET, but since it was designed to be independent from any environment, it has been easily adapted to other networks, including many UUCP-based networks.

RFC-822 is only the lowest common denominator, however. More recent standards have been conceived to cope with growing needs such as data encryption, international character set support, and MIME (Multipurpose Internet Mail Extensions, described in RFC-1341 and other RFCs).

In all these standards, the header consists of several lines separated by an end-of-line sequence. A line is made up of a field name, beginning in column one, and the field itself, offset by a colon and white space. The format and semantics of each field vary depending on the field name. A header field can be continued across a newline if the next line begins with a whitespace character such as tab. Fields can appear in any order.

A typical mail header may look like this:

```
Return-Path: <ph10@cus.cam.ac.uk>
Received: ursa.cus.cam.ac.uk (cusexim@ursa.cus.cam.ac.uk [131.111.8.6])
    by al.animats.net (8.9.3/8.9.3/Debian 8.9.3-6) with ESMTP id WAA04654
    for <terry@animats.net>; Sun, 30 Jan 2000 22:30:01 +1100
Received: from ph10 (helo=localhost) by ursa.cus.cam.ac.uk with local-smtp
    (Exim 3.13 #1) id 12EsYC-0001eF-00; Sun, 30 Jan 2000 11:29:52 +0000
Date: Sun, 30 Jan 2000 11:29:52 +0000 (GMT)
From: Philip Hazel <ph10@cus.cam.ac.uk>
Reply-To: Philip Hazel <ph10@cus.cam.ac.uk>
To: Terry Dawson <terry@animats.net>, Andy Oram <andyo@oreilly.com>
Subject: Electronic mail chapter
In-Reply-To: <38921283.A58948F2@animats.net>
Message-ID: <Pine.SOL.3.96.1000130111515.5800A-200000@ursa.cus.cam.ac.uk>
```

Usually, all necessary header fields are generated by the mailer interface you use, like *elm*, *pine*, *mush*, or *mailx*. However, some are optional and may be added by the user. *elm*, for example, allows you to edit part of the message header. Others are added by the mail transport software. If you look into a local mailbox file, you may see each mail message preceded by a "From" line (note: no colon). This is *not* an RFC-822 header; it has been inserted by your mail software as a convenience to programs reading the mailbox. To avoid potential trouble with lines in the message body that also begin with "From," it has become standard procedure to escape any such occurrence by preceding it with a > character.

This list is a collection of common header fields and their meanings:

`From:`
>   This contains the sender's email address and possibly the "real name." A complete zoo of formats is used here.

`To:`

This is a list of recipient email addresses. Multiple recipient addresses are separated by a comma.

`Cc:`

This is a list of email addresses that will receive "carbon copies" of the message. Multiple recipient addresses are separated by a comma.

`Bcc:`

This is a list of email addresses that will receive "carbon copies" of the message. The key difference between a "Cc:" and a "Bcc:" is that the addresses listed in a "Bcc:" will not appear in the header of the mail messages delivered to any recipient. It's a way of alerting recipients that you've sent copies of the message to other people without telling them who those others are. Multiple recipient addresses are separated by a comma.

`Subject:`

Describes the content of the mail in a few words.

`Date:`

Supplies the date and time the mail was sent.

`Reply-To:`

Specifies the address the sender wants the recipient's reply directed to. This may be useful if you have several accounts, but want to receive the bulk of mail only on the one you use most frequently. This field is optional.

`Organization:`

The organization that owns the machine from which the mail originates. If your machine is owned by you privately, either leave this out, or insert "private" or some complete nonsense. This field is not described by any RFC and is completely optional. Some mail programs support it directly, many don't.

`Message-ID:`

A string generated by the mail transport on the originating system. It uniquely identifies this message.

`Received:`

Every site that processes your mail (including the machines of sender and recipient) inserts such a field into the header, giving its site name, a message ID, time and date it received the message, which site it is from, and which transport software was used. These lines allow you to trace which route the message took, and you can complain to the person responsible if something went wrong.

`X-anything:`
No mail-related programs should complain about any header that starts with `X-`. It is used to implement additional features that have not yet made it into an RFC, or never will. For example, there was once a very large Linux mailing list server that allowed you to specify which channel you wanted the mail to go to by adding the string **X-Mn-Key:** followed by the channel name.

How Is Mail Delivered?

Generally, you will compose mail using a mailer interface like *mail* or *mailx*, or more sophisticated ones like *mutt, tkrat,* or *pine.* These programs are called *mail user agents,* or MUAs. If you send a mail message, the interface program will in most cases hand it to another program for delivery. This is called the *mail transport agent,* or MTA. On most systems the same MTA is used for both local and remote delivery and is usually invoked as */usr/sbin/sendmail,* or on non-FSSTND compliant systems as */usr/lib/sendmail.* On UUCP systems it is not uncommon to see mail delivery handled by two separate programs: *rmail* for remote mail delivery and *lmail* for local mail delivery.

Local delivery of mail is, of course, more than just appending the incoming message to the recipient's mailbox. Usually, the local MTA understands aliasing (setting up local recipient addresses pointing to other addresses) and forwarding (redirecting a user's mail to some other destination). Also, messages that cannot be delivered must usually be *bounced,* that is, returned to the sender along with some error message.

For remote delivery, the transport software used depends on the nature of the link. Mail delivered over a network using TCP/IP commonly uses *Simple Mail Transfer Protocol* (SMTP), which is described in RFC-821. SMTP was designed to deliver mail directly to a recipient's machine, negotiating the message transfer with the remote side's SMTP daemon. Today it is common practice for organizations to establish special hosts that accept all mail for recipients in the organization and for that host to manage appropriate delivery to the intended recipient.

Mail is usually not delivered directly in UUCP networks, but rather is forwarded to the destination host by a number of intermediate systems. To send a message over a UUCP link, the sending MTA usually executes *rmail* on the forwarding system using *uux,* and feeds it the message on standard input.

Since *uux* is invoked for each message separately, it may produce a considerable workload on a major mail hub, as well as clutter the UUCP spool queues with hundreds of small files taking up a disproportionate amount of disk space.* Some MTAs therefore allow you to collect several messages for a remote system in a

---

* This is because disk space is usually allocated in blocks of 1,024 bytes. So even a message of a few dozen bytes will eat a full kilobyte.

single batch file. The batch file contains the SMTP commands that the local host would normally issue if a direct SMTP connection were used. This is called BSMTP, or *batched* SMTP. The batch is then fed to the *rsmtp* or *bsmtp* program on the remote system, which processes the input almost as if a normal SMTP connection has occurred.

Email Addresses

Email addresses are made up of at least two parts. One part is the name of a *mail domain* that will ultimately translate to either the recipient's host or some host that accepts mail on behalf of the recipient. The other part is some form of unique user identification that may be the login name of that user, the real name of that user in "Firstname.Lastname" format, or an arbitrary alias that will be translated into a user or list of users. Other mail addressing schemes, like X.400, use a more general set of "attributes" that are used to look up the recipient's host in an X.500 directory server.

How email addresses are interpreted depends greatly on what type of network you use. We'll concentrate on how TCP/IP and UUCP networks interpret email addresses.

RFC-822

Internet sites adhere to the RFC-822 standard, which requires the familiar notation of *user@host.domain*, for which *host.domain* is the host's fully qualified domain name. The character separating the two is properly called a "commercial at" sign, but it helps if you read it as "at." This notation does not specify a route to the destination host. Routing of the mail message is left to the mechanisms we'll describe shortly.

You will see a lot of RFC-822 if you run an Internet connected site. Its use extends not only to mail, but has also spilled over into other services, such as news. We discuss how RFC-822 is used for news in Chapter 20, *Netnews*.

Obsolete Mail Formats

In the original UUCP environment, the prevalent form was *path!host!user*, for which *path* described a sequence of hosts the message had to travel through before reaching the destination *host*. This construct is called the *bang path* notation, because an exclamation mark is colloquially called a "bang." Today, many UUCP-based networks have adopted RFC-822 and understand domain-based addresses.

Other networks have still different means of addressing. DECnet-based networks, for example, use two colons as an address separator, yielding an address of *host::user.** The X.400 standard uses an entirely different scheme, describing a recipient by a set of attribute-value pairs, like country and organization.

Lastly, on FidoNet, each user is identified by a code like **2:320/204.9**, consisting of four numbers denoting zone (2 is for Europe), net (320 being Paris and Banlieue), node (the local hub), and point (the individual user's PC). Fidonet addresses can be mapped to RFC-822; the above, for example, would be written as *Thomas.Quinot@p9.f204.n320.z2.fidonet.org*. Now didn't we say domain names were easy to remember?

Mixing Different Mail Formats

It is inevitable that when you bring together a number of different systems and a number of clever people, they will seek ways to interconnect the differing systems so they are capable of internetworking. Consequently, there are a number of different mail gateways that are able to link two different email systems together so that mail may be forwarded from one to another. Addressing is the critical question when linking two systems. We won't look at the gateways themselves in any detail, but let's take a look at some of the addressing complications that may arise when gateways of this sort are used.

Consider mixing the UUCP style bang-path notation and RFC-822. These two types of addressing don't mix too well. Assume there is an address of *domainA!user@domainB*. It is not clear whether the @ sign takes precedence over the path, or vice versa: do we have to send the message to *domainB*, which mails it to *domainA!user*, or should it be sent to *domainA*, which forwards it to *user@domainB*?

Addresses that mix different types of address operators are called *hybrid addresses*. The most common type, which we just illustrated, is usually resolved by giving the @ sign precedence over the path. In *domainA!user@domainB*, this means sending the message to *domainB* first.

However, there is a way to specify routes in RFC-822 conformant ways: *<@domainA,@domainB:user@domainC>* denotes the address of *user* on *domainC*, where *domainC* is to be reached through *domainA* and *domainB* (in that order). This type of address is frequently called a *source routed* address. It's not a good idea to rely on this behavior, as revisions to the RFCs describing mail routing recommend that source routing in a mail address be ignored and instead an attempt should be made to deliver directly to the remote destination.

---

* When trying to reach a DECnet address from an RFC-822 environment, you can use *"host::user"@relay*, for which *relay* is the name of a known Internet-DECnet relay.

Then there is the % address operator: *user%domainB@domainA* is first sent to *domainA*, which expands the rightmost (in this case, the only) percent sign to an @ sign. The address is now **user@domainB**, and the mailer happily forwards your message to *domainB*, which delivers it to *user*. This type of address is sometimes referred to as "Ye Olde ARPAnet Kludge," and its use is discouraged.

There are some implications to using these different types of addressing that will be described throughout the following sections. In an RFC-822 environment, you should avoid using anything other than absolute addresses, such as *user@host.domain*.

How Does Mail Routing Work?

The process of directing a message to the recipient's host is called *routing*. Apart from finding a path from the sending site to the destination, it involves error checking and may involve speed and cost optimization.

There is a big difference between the way a UUCP site handles routing and the way an Internet site does. On the Internet, the main job of directing data to the recipient host (once it is known by its IP address) is done by the IP networking layer, while in the UUCP zone, the route has to be supplied by the user or generated by the mail transfer agent.

Mail Routing on the Internet

On the Internet, the destination host's configuration determines whether any specific mail routing is performed. The default is to deliver the message to the destination by first determining what host the message should be sent to and then delivering it directly to that host. Most Internet sites want to direct all inbound mail to a highly available mail server that is capable of handling all this traffic and have it distribute the mail locally. To announce this service, the site publishes a so-called MX record for its local domain in its DNS database. MX stands for *Mail Exchanger* and basically states that the server host is willing to act as a mail forwarder for all mail addresses in the domain. MX records can also be used to handle traffic for hosts that are not connected to the Internet themselves, like UUCP networks or FidoNet hosts that must have their mail passed through a gateway.

MX records are always assigned a *preference*. This is a positive integer. If several mail exchangers exist for one host, the mail transport agent will try to transfer the message to the exchanger with the lowest preference value, and only if this fails will it try a host with a higher value. If the local host is itself a mail exchanger for the destination address, it is allowed to forward messages only to MX hosts with a lower preference than its own; this is a safe way of avoiding mail loops. If there is no MX record for a domain, or no MX records left that are suitable, the mail transport agent is permitted to see if the domain has an IP address associated with it and attempt delivery directly to that host.

Suppose that an organization, say Foobar, Inc., wants all its mail handled by its machine **mailhub**. It will then have MX records like this in the DNS database:

```
green.foobar.com.        IN   MX      5    mailhub.foobar.com.
```

This announces **mailhub.foobar.com** as a mail exchanger for **green.foobar.com** with a preference of 5. A host that wishes to deliver a message to *joe@green.foobar.com* checks DNS and finds the MX record pointing at **mailhub**. If there's no MX with a preference smaller than 5, the message is delivered to **mailhub**, which then dispatches it to **green**.

This is a very simple description of how MX records work. For more information on mail routing on the Internet, refer to RFC-821, RFC-974, and RFC-1123.

Mail Routing in the UUCP World

Mail routing on UUCP networks is much more complicated than on the Internet because the transport software does not perform any routing itself. In earlier times, all mail had to be addressed using bang paths. Bang paths specified a list of hosts through which to forward the message, separated by exclamation marks and followed by the user's name. To address a letter to a user called Janet on a machine named **moria**, you would use the path *eek!swim!moria!janet*. This would send the mail from your host to **eek**, from there on to **swim**, and finally to **moria**.

The obvious drawback of this technique is that it requires you to remember much more about network topology, fast links, etc. than Internet routing requires. Much worse than that, changes in the network topology—like links being deleted or hosts being removed—may cause messages to fail simply because you aren't aware of the change. And finally, in case you move to a different place, you will most likely have to update all these routes.

One thing, however, that made the use of source routing necessary was the presence of ambiguous hostnames. For instance, assume there are two sites named **moria**, one in the U.S. and one in France. Which site does *moria!janet* refer to now? This can be made clear by specifying what path to reach **moria** through.

The first step in disambiguating hostnames was the founding of the UUCP Mapping Project. It is located at Rutgers University and registers all official UUCP hostnames, along with information on their UUCP neighbors and their geographic location, making sure no hostname is used twice. The information gathered by the Mapping Project is published as the *Usenet Maps*, which are distributed regularly through Usenet. A typical system entry in a map (after removing the comments) looks like this:*

---

* Maps for sites registered with the UUCP Mapping Project are distributed through the newsgroup *comp.mail.maps*; other organizations may publish separate maps for their networks.

```
moria
        bert(DAILY/2),
        swim(WEEKLY)
```

This entry says **moria** has a link to **bert**, which it calls twice a day, and **swim**, which it calls weekly. We will return to the map file format in more detail later.

Using the connectivity information provided in the maps, you can automatically generate the full paths from your host to any destination site. This information is usually stored in the *paths* file, also called the *pathalias database*. Assume the maps state that you can reach **bert** through **ernie**; a pathalias entry for **moria** generated from the previous map snippet may then look like this:

```
moria           ernie!bert!moria!%s
```

If you now give a destination address of *janet@moria.uucp*, your MTA will pick the route shown above and send the message to **ernie** with an envelope address of *bert!moria!janet*.

Building a *paths* file from the full Usenet maps is not a very good idea, however. The information provided in them is usually rather distorted and occasionally out of date. Therefore, only a number of major hosts use the complete UUCP world maps to build their *paths* files. Most sites maintain routing information only for sites in their neighborhood and send any mail to sites they don't find in their databases to a smarter host with more complete routing information. This scheme is called *smart-host routing*. Hosts that have only one UUCP mail link (so-called *leaf sites*) don't do any routing of their own; they rely entirely on their smart host.

Mixing UUCP and RFC-822

The best cure for the problems of mail routing in UUCP networks so far is the adoption of the domain name system in UUCP networks. Of course, you can't query a name server over UUCP. Nevertheless, many UUCP sites have formed small domains that coordinate their routing internally. In the maps, these domains announce one or two hosts as their mail gateways so that there doesn't have to be a map entry for each host in the domain. The gateways handle all mail that flows into and out of the domain. The routing scheme inside the domain is completely invisible to the outside world.

This works very well with the smart-host routing scheme. Global routing information is maintained by the gateways only; minor hosts within a domain get along with only a small, handwritten *paths* file that lists the routes inside their domain and the route to the mail hub. Even the mail gateways do not need routing information for every single UUCP host in the world anymore. Besides the complete routing information for the domain they serve, they only need to have routes to entire domains in their databases now. For instance, this pathalias entry will route all mail for sites in the **sub.org** domain to **smurf**:

```
.sub.org        swim!smurf!%s
```

Mail addressed to *claire@jones.sub.org* will be sent to **swim** with an envelope address of *smurf!jones!claire*.

The hierarchical organization of the domain namespace allows mail servers to mix more specific routes with less specific ones. For instance, a system in France may have specific routes for subdomains of **fr**, but route any mail for hosts in the **us** domain toward some system in the U.S. In this way, domain-based routing (as this technique is called) greatly reduces the size of routing databases, as well as the administrative overhead needed.

The main benefit of using domain names in a UUCP environment, however, is that compliance with RFC-822 permits easy gatewaying between UUCP networks and the Internet. Many UUCP domains nowadays have a link with an Internet gateway that acts as their smart host. Sending messages across the Internet is faster, and routing information is much more reliable because Internet hosts can use DNS instead of the Usenet Maps.

In order to be reachable from the Internet, UUCP-based domains usually have their Internet gateway announce an MX record for them (MX records were described previously in the section "Mail Routing on the Internet"). For instance, assume that **moria** belongs to the **orcnet.org** domain. **gcc2.groucho.edu** acts as its Internet gateway. **moria** would therefore use **gcc2** as its smart host so that all mail for foreign domains is delivered across the Internet. On the other hand, **gcc2** would announce an MX record for **.orcnet.org** and deliver all incoming mail for **orcnet** sites to **moria**. The asterisk in **.orcnet.org** is a wildcard that matches all hosts in that domain that don't have any other record associated with them. This should normally be the case for UUCP-only domains.

The only remaining problem is that the UUCP transport programs can't deal with fully qualified domain names. Most UUCP suites were designed to cope with site names of up to eight characters, some even less, and using nonalphanumeric characters such as dots is completely out of the question for most.

Therefore, we need mapping between RFC-822 names and UUCP hostnames. This mapping is completely implementation-dependent. One common way of mapping FQDNs to UUCP names is to use the pathalias file:

```
moria.orcnet.org  ernie!bert!moria!%s
```

This will produce a pure UUCP-style bang path from an address that specifies a fully qualified domain name. Some mailers provide a special file for this; *sendmail*, for instance, uses the *uucpxtable*.

The reverse transformation (colloquially called *domainizing*) is sometimes required when sending mail from a UUCP network to the Internet. As long as the mail sender uses the fully qualified domain name in the destination address, this problem can be avoided by not removing the domain name from the envelope address when forwarding the message to the smart host. However, there are still some UUCP sites that are not part of any domain. They are usually domainized by appending the pseudo-domain **uucp**.

The pathalias database provides the main routing information in UUCP-based networks. A typical entry looks like this (site name and path are separated by tabs):

```
moria.orcnet.org   ernie!bert!moria!%s
moria              ernie!bert!moria!%s
```

This makes any message to **moria** be delivered via **ernie** and **bert**. Both **moria**'s fully qualified name and its UUCP name have to be given if the mailer does not have a separate way to map between these namespaces.

If you want to direct all messages to hosts inside a domain to its mail relay, you may also specify a path in the pathalias database, giving the domain name preceded by a dot as the target. For example, if all hosts in **sub.org** can be reached through **swim!smurf**, the pathalias entry might look like this:

```
.sub.org           swim!smurf!%s
```

Writing a pathalias file is acceptable only when you are running a site that does not have to do much routing. If you have to do routing for a large number of hosts, a better way is to use the *pathalias* command to create the file from map files. Maps can be maintained much more easily, because you may simply add or remove a system by editing the system's map entry and recreating the map file. Although the maps published by the Usenet Mapping Project aren't used for routing very much anymore, smaller UUCP networks may provide routing information in their own set of maps.

A map file mainly consists of a list of sites that each system polls or is polled by. The system name begins in the first column and is followed by a comma-separated list of links. The list may be continued across newlines if the next line begins with a tab. Each link consists of the name of the site followed by a cost given in brackets. The cost is an arithmetic expression made up of numbers and symbolic expressions like DAILY or WEEKLY. Lines beginning with a hash sign are ignored.

As an example, consider **moria**, which polls **swim.twobirds.com** twice a day and **bert.sesame.com** once per week. The link to **bert** uses a slow 2,400 bps modem. **moria** would publish the following maps entry:

```
moria.orcnet.org
        bert.sesame.com(DAILY/2),
        swim.twobirds.com(WEEKLY+LOW)
moria.orcnet.org = moria
```

The last line makes **moria** known under its UUCP name, as well. Note that its cost must be specified as DAILY/2 because calling twice a day actually halves the cost for this link.

Using the information from such map files, *pathalias* is able to calculate optimal routes to any destination site listed in the paths file and produce a pathalias database from this which can then be used for routing to these sites.

pathalias provides a couple of other features like site-hiding (i.e., making sites accessible only through a gateway). See the *pathalias* manual page for details and a complete list of link costs.

Comments in the map file generally contain additional information on the sites described in it. There is a rigid format in which to specify this information so that it can be retrieved from the maps. For instance, a program called *uuwho* uses a database created from the map files to display this information in a nicely formatted way. When you register your site with an organization that distributes map files to its members, you generally have to fill out such a map entry. Below is a sample map entry (in fact, it's the one for Olaf's site):

```
#N      monad, monad.swb.de, monad.swb.sub.org
#S      AT 486DX50; Linux 0.99
#O      private
#C      Olaf Kirch
#E      okir@monad.swb.de
#P      Kattreinstr. 38, D-64295 Darmstadt, FRG
#L      49 52 03 N / 08 38 40 E
#U      brewhq
#W      okir@monad.swb.de (Olaf Kirch); Sun Jul 25 16:59:32 MET DST 1993
#
monad   brewhq(DAILY/2)
# Domains
monad = monad.swb.de
monad = monad.swb.sub.org
```

The whitespace after the first two characters is a tab. The meaning of most of the fields is pretty obvious; you will receive a detailed description from whichever domain you register with. The L field is the most fun to find out: it gives your geographical position in latitude/longitude and is used to draw the PostScript maps that show all sites for each country, as well as worldwide.*

---

* They are posted regularly in *news.lists.ps-maps*. Beware. They're HUGE.

Configuring elm

elm stands for "electronic mail" and is one of the more reasonably named Unix tools. It provides a full-screen interface with a good help feature. We won't discuss how to use *elm* here, but only dwell on its configuration options.

Theoretically, you can run *elm* unconfigured, and everything works well—if you are lucky. But there are a few options that must be set, although they are required only on occasion.

When it starts, *elm* reads a set of configuration variables from the *elm.rc* file in */etc/elm*. Then it attempts to read the file *.elm/elmrc* in your home directory. You don't usually write this file yourself. It is created when you choose "Save new options" from *elm*'s options menu.

The set of options for the private *elmrc* file is also available in the global *elm.rc* file. Most settings in your private *elmrc* file override those of the global file.

Global elm Options

In the global *elm.rc* file, you must set the options that pertain to your host's name. For example, at the Virtual Brewery, the file for **vlager** contains the following:

```
#
# The local hostname
hostname = vlager
#
# Domain name
hostdomain = .vbrew.com
#
# Fully qualified domain name
hostfullname = vlager.vbrew.com
```

These options set *elm*'s idea of the local hostname. Although this information is rarely used, you should set the options. Note that these particular options only take effect when giving them in the global configuration file; when found in your private *elmrc*, they will be ignored.

National Character Sets

A set of standards and RFCs have been developed that amend the RFC-822 standard to support various types of messages, such as plain text, binary data, PostScript files, etc. These standards are commonly referred to as MIME, or Multipurpose Internet Mail Extensions. Among other things, MIME also lets the recipient know if a character set other than standard ASCII has been used when writing the message, for example, using French accents or German umlauts. *elm* supports these characters to some extent.

The character set used by Linux internally to represent characters is usually referred to as ISO-8859-1, which is the name of the standard it conforms to. It is also known as Latin-1. Any message using characters from this character set should have the following line in its header:

```
Content-Type: text/plain; charset=iso-8859-1
```

The receiving system should recognize this field and take appropriate measures when displaying the message. The default for `text/plain` messages is a `charset` value of `us-ascii`.

To be able to display messages with character sets other than ASCII, *elm* must know how to print these characters. By default, when *elm* receives a message with a *charset* field other than `us-ascii` (or a content type other than `text/plain`, for that matter), it tries to display the message using a command called *metamail*. Messages that require *metamail* to be displayed are shown with an *M* in the very first column in the overview screen.

Since Linux's native character set is ISO-8859-1, calling *metamail* is not necessary to display messages using this character set. If *elm* is told that the display understands ISO-8859-1, it will not use *metamail*, but will display the message directly instead. This can be enabled by setting the following option in the global *elm.rc*:

```
displaycharset = iso-8859-1
```

Note that you should set this option even when you are never going to send or receive any messages that actually contain characters other than ASCII. This is because people who do send such messages usually configure their mailer to put the proper `Content-Type:` field into the mail header by default, whether or not they are sending ASCII-only messages.

However, setting this option in *elm.rc* is not enough. When displaying the message with its built-in pager, *elm* calls a library function for each character to determine whether it is printable. By default, this function will only recognize ASCII characters as printable and display all other characters as `^?`. You may overcome this function by setting the environment variable `LC_CTYPE` to `ISO-8859-1`, which tells the library to accept Latin-1 characters as printable. Support for this and other features have been available since Version 4.5.8 of the Linux standard library.

When sending messages that contain special characters from ISO-8859-1, you should make sure to set two more variables in the *elm.rc* file:

```
charset = iso-8859-1
textencoding = 8bit
```

This makes *elm* report the character set as ISO-8859-1 in the mail header and send it as an 8-bit value (the default is to strip all characters to 7-bit).

Of course, all character set options we've discussed here may also be set in the private *elmrc* file instead of the global one so individual users can have their own default settings if the global one doesn't suit them.

## CHAPTER EIGHTEEN

SENDMAIL

Introduction to sendmail

It's been said that you aren't a *real* Unix system administrator until you've edited a *sendmail.cf* file. It's also been said that you're crazy if you've attempted to do so twice.

sendmail is an incredibly powerful mail program. It's also incredibly difficult to learn and understand. Any program whose definitive reference (*sendmail*, by Bryan Costales and Eric Allman, published by O'Reilly) is 1,050 pages long scares most people off. Information on the *sendmail* reference is contained in the bibliography at the end of this book.

Fortunately, new versions of sendmail are different. You no longer need to directly edit the cryptic *sendmail.cf* file; the new version provides a configuration utility that will create the *sendmail.cf* file for you based on much simpler macro files. You do not need to understand the complex syntax of the *sendmail.cf* file; the macro files don't require you to. Instead, you need only list items, such as the name of features you wish to include in your configuration, and specify some of the parameters that determine how that feature operates. A traditional Unix utility called *m4* then takes your macro configuration data and mixes it with the data it reads from template files containing the actual *sendmail.cf* syntax, to produce your *sendmail.cf* file.

In this chapter we introduce *sendmail* and describe how to install, configure and test it, using the Virtual Brewery as an example. If the information presented here helps make the task of configuring *sendmail* less daunting for you, we hope you'll gain the confidence to tackle more complex configurations on your own.

Installing sendmail

The *sendmail* mail transport agent is included in prepackaged form in most Linux distributions. Installation in this case is relatively simple. Despite this fact, there are some good reasons to install *sendmail* from source, especially if you are security conscious. The *sendmail* program is very complex and has earned a reputation over the years for containing bugs that allow security breaches. One of the best known examples is the RTM Internet worm that exploited a buffer overflow problem in early versions of *sendmail*. We touched on this briefly in Chapter 9, *TCP/IP Firewall*. Most security exploits involving buffer overflows rely on all copies of *sendmail* on different machines being identical, as the exploits rely on data being stored in specific locations. This, of course, is precisely what happens with *sendmail* installed from Linux distributions. Compiling *sendmail* from source yourself can help reduce this risk. Modern versions of *sendmail* are less vulnerable because they have come under exceedingly close scrutiny as security has become a more widespread concern throughout the Internet community.

The *sendmail* source code is available via anonymous FTP from **ftp.sendmail.org**.

Compilation is very simple bceause the *sendmail* source package directly supports Linux. The steps involved in compiling *sendmail* are:

```
# cd /usr/local/src
# tar xvfz sendmail.8.9.3.tar.gz
# cd src
# ./Build
```

You need `root` permissions to complete the installation of the resulting binary files using:

```
# cd obj.Linux.2.0.36.i586
# make install
```

You have now installed the *sendmail* binary into the */usr/sbin* directory. Several symbolic links to the *sendmail* binary will be installed into the */usr/bin/* directory. We'll talk about those links when we discuss common tasks in running *sendmail*.

Overview of Configuration Files

Traditionally, *sendmail* was set up through a system configuration file (typically called */etc/mail/sendmail.cf*, or in older distributions, */etc/sendmail.cf*, or even */usr/lib/sendmail.cf*) that is not anything close to any language you've seen before. Editing the *sendmail.cf* file to provide customized behavior can be a humbling experience.

Today *sendmail* makes all configuration options macro driven with an easy-to-understand syntax. The macro method generates configurations to cover most installations, but you always have the option of tuning the resultant *sendmail.cf* manually to work in a more complex environment.

The sendmail.cf and sendmail.mc Files

The *m4* macro processor program generates the *sendmail.df* file when it processes the macro configuration file provided by the local system administrator. Throughout the remainder of this chapter we will refer to this configuration file as the *sendmail.mc* file.

The configuration process is basically a matter of creating a suitable *sendmail.mc* file that includes macros that describe your desired configuration. The macros are expressions that the *m4* macro processor understands and expands into the complex *sendmail.cf* syntax. The macro expressions are made up of the macro name (the text in capital letters at the start), which can be likened to a function in a programming language, and some parameters (the text within brackets) that are used in the expansion. The parameters may be passed literally into the *sendmail.cf* output or may be used to govern the way the macro processing occurs.

A *sendmail.mc* file for a minimal configuration (UUCP or SMTP with all nonlocal mail being relayed to a directly connected smart host) can be as short as 10 or 15 lines, excluding comments.

Two Example sendmail.mc Files

If you're an administator of a number of different mail hosts, you might not want to name your configuration file *sendmail.mc*. Instead, it is common practice to name it after the host—*vstout.m4* in our case. The name doesn't really matter as long as the output is called *sendmail.cf*. Providing a unique name for the configuration file for each host allows you to keep all configuration files in the same directory and is just an administrative convenience. Let's look at two example macro configuration files so we know where we are heading.

Most *sendmail* configurations today use SMTP only. It is very simple to configure *sendmail* for SMTP. Example 18-1 expects a DNS name server to be available to resolve hosts and will attempt to accept and deliver all mail for hosts using just SMTP.

Example 18-1: Sample Configuration File vstout.smtp.m4

```
divert(-1)
#
# Sample configuration file for vstout - smtp only
#
divert(0)
```

Example 18-1: Sample Configuration File vstout.smtp.m4 (continued)

```
VERSIONID('@(#)sendmail.mc    8.7 (Linux) 3/5/96')
OSTYPE('linux')
#
# Include support for the local and smtp mail transport protocols.
MAILER('local')
MAILER('smtp')
#
FEATURE(rbl)
FEATURE(access_db)
# end
```

A *sendmail.mc* file for **vstout** at the Virtual Brewery is shown in Example 18-2. **vstout** uses SMTP to talk to all hosts on the Brewery's LAN, and you'll see the commonality with the generic SMTP-only configuration just presented. In addition, the **vstout** configuration sends all mail for other destinations to **moria**, its Internet relay host, via UUCP.

Example 18-2: Sample Configuration File vstout.uucpsmtp.m4

```
divert(-1)
#
# Sample configuration file for vstout
#
divert(0)
VERSIONID('@(#)sendmail.mc    8.7 (Linux) 3/5/96')
OSTYPE('linux')
dnl
# moria is our smart host, using the "uucp-new" transport.
define('SMART_HOST', 'uucp-new:moria')
dnl
# Support the local, smtp and uucp mail transport protocols.
MAILER('local')
MAILER('smtp')
MAILER('uucp')
LOCAL_NET_CONFIG
# This rule ensures that all local mail is delivered using the
# smtp transport, everything else will go via the smart host.
R$* < @ $* .$m. > $*    $#smtp $@ $2.$m. $: $1 < @ $2.$m. > $3
dnl
#
FEATURE(rbl)
FEATURE(access_db)
# end
```

If you compare and contrast the two configurations, you might be able to work out what each of the configuration parameters does. We'll explain them all in detail.

Typically Used sendmail.mc Parameters

A few of the items in the *sendmail.mc* file are required all the time; others can be ignored if you can get away with defaults. The general sequence of the definitions in the *sendmail.mc* is as follows:

1. VERSIONID

2. OSTYPE

3. DOMAIN

4. FEATURE

5. Local macro definitions

6. MAILER

7. LOCAL_* rulesets

We'll talk about each of these in turn in the following sections and refer to our examples in Example 18-1 and Example 18-2, when appropriate, to explain them.

Comments

Lines in the *sendmail.mc* file that begin with the # character are not parsed by *m4*, and will by default be output directly into the *sendmail.cf* file. This is useful if you want to comment on what your configuration is doing in both the input and output files.

To allow comments in your *sendmail.mc* that are *not* placed into the *sendmail.cf*, you can use the *m4* divert and dnl tokens. divert(-1) will cause all output to cease. divert(0) will cause output to be restored to the default. Any output generated by lines between these will be discarded. In our example, we've used this mechanism to provide a comment that appears only in the *sendmail.mc* file. To achieve the same result for a single line, you can use the dnl token that means, literally, "starting at the beginning of the next line, delete all characters up to and including the next newline." We've used this in our example, too.

These are standard *m4* features, and you can obtain more information on them from its manual page.

VERSIONID and OSTYPE

```
VERSIONID('@(#)sendmail.mc  8.9 (Linux) 01/10/98')
```

The VERSIONID macro is optional, but is useful to record the version of the sendmail configuration in the *sendmail.cf* file. So you'll often encounter it, and we recommend it. In any case, be sure to include:

```
OSTYPE('linux')
```

This is probably the most important definition. The OSTYPE macro causes a file of definitions to be included that are good defaults for your operating system. Most of the definitions in an OSTYPE macro file set the pathnames of various configuration files, mailer program paths and arguments, and the location of directories sendmail uses to store messages. The standard sendmail source code release includes such a file for Linux, which would be included by the previous example. Some Linux distributions, notably the Debian distribution, include their own definition file that is completely Linux-FHS compliant. When your distribution does this, you should probably use its definition instead of the Linux default one.

The OSTYPE definition should be one of the first definitions to appear in your *sendmail.mc* file, as many other definitions depend upon it.

DOMAIN

The DOMAIN macro is useful when you wish to configure a large number of machines on the same network in a standard way. It you're configuring a small number of hosts, it probably isn't worth bothering with. You typically configure items, such as the name of mail relay hosts or hubs that all hosts on your network will use.

The standard installation contains a directory of *m4* macro templates used to drive the configuration process. This directory is usually named */usr/share/sendmail.cf* or something similar. Here you will find a subdirectory called *domain* that contains domain-specific configuration templates. To make use of the DOMAIN macro, you must create your own macro file containing the standard definitions you require for your site, and write it into the *domain* subdirectory. You'd normally include only the macro definitions that were unique to your domain here, such as smart host definitions or relay hosts, but you are not limited to these.

The *sendmail* source distribution comes with a number of sample domain macro files that you can use to model your own.

If you saved your domain macro file as */usr/share/sendmail.cf/domain/vbrew.m4*, you'd include definitions in your *sendmail.mc* using:

```
DOMAIN('vbrew')
```

FEATURE

The `FEATURE` macro enables you to include predefined *sendmail* features in your configuration. These *sendmail* features make the supported configurations very simple to use. There are a large number, and throughout this chapter we'll talk about only a few of the more useful and important ones. You can find full details of the features available in the *CF* file included in the source package.

To use any of the features listed, you should include a line in your *sendmail.mc* that looks like:

`FEATURE(name)`

where *name* is substituted with the feature name. Some features take one optional parameter. If you wish to use something other than the default, you should use an entry that looks like:

`FEATURE(name, param)`

where *param* is the parameter to supply.

Local macro definitions

The standard *sendmail* macro configuration files provide lots of hooks and variables with which you can customize your configuration. These are called *local macro definitions*. Many of them are listed in the *CF* file in the *sendmail* source package.

The local macro definitions are usually invoked by supplying the name of the macro with an argument representing the value you wish to assign to the variable the macro manages. Again, we'll explore some of the more common local macro definitions in the examples we present later in the chapter.

Defining mail transport protocols

If you want *sendmail* to transport mail in any way other than by local delivery, you must tell it which transports to use. The `MAILER` macro makes this very easy. The current version of *sendmail* supports a variety of mail transport protocols; some of these are experimental, others are probably rarely used.

In our network we need the SMTP transport to send and receive mail among the hosts on our local area network, and the UUCP transport to send and receive mail from our smart host. To achieve this, we simply include both the `smtp` and `uucp` mail transports. The `local` mail transport is included by default, but may be defined for clarity, if you wish. If you are including both the `smtp` and the `uucp` mailers in your configuration, you must always be sure to define the `smtp` mailer first.

The more commonly used transports available to you using the `MAILER` macro are described in the following list:

local

> This transport includes both the local delivery agent used to send mail into the mailbox of users on this machine and the `prog` mailer used to send messages to local programs. This transport is included by default.

smtp

> This transport implements the Simple Mail Transport Protocol (SMTP), which is the most common means of transporting mail on the Internet. When you include this transport, four mailers are configured: `smtp` (basic SMTP), `esmtp` (Extended SMTP), `smtp8` (8bit binary clean SMTP), and `relay` (specifically designed for gatewaying messages between hosts).

uucp

> The `uucp` transport provides support for two mailers: `uucp-old`, which is the traditional UUCP, and `uucp-new`, which allows multiple recipients to be handled in one transfer.

usenet

> This mailer allows you to send mail messages directly into Usenet style news networks. Any local message directed to an address of *news.group.usenet* will be fed into the news network for the *news.group* newsgroup.

fax

> If you have the HylaFAX software installed, this mailer will allow you to direct email to it so that you may build an email-fax gateway. This feature is experimental at the time of writing and more information may be obtained from *http://www.vix.com/hylafax/*.

There are others, such as the `pop`, `procmail`, `mail11`, `phquery`, and `cyrus` that are useful, but less common. If your curiosity is piqued, you can read about these in the sendmail book or the documentation supplied in the source package.

Configure mail routing for local hosts

The Virtual Brewery's configuration is probably more complex than most sites require. Most sites today would use the SMTP transport only and do not have to deal with UUCP at all. In our configuration we've configured a "smart host" that is used to handle all outgoing mail. Since we are using the SMTP transport on our local network we must tell *sendmail* that it is not to send local mail via the smart host. The `LOCAL_NET_CONFIG` macro allows you to insert sendmail rules directly into the output *sendmail.cf* to modify the way that local mail is handled. We'll talk more about rewrite rules later on, but for the moment you should accept that the rule we've supplied in our example specifies that any mail destined for hosts in the **vbrew.com** domain should be delivered directly to the target hosts using the SMTP mail transport.

Generating the sendmail.cf File

When you have completed editing your *m4* configuration file, you must process it to produce the */etc/mail/sendmail.cf* file read by *sendmail*. This is straightforward, as illustrated by the following example:

```
# cd /etc/mail
# m4 /usr/share/sendmail.cf/m4/cf.m4 vstout.uucpsmtp.mc >sendmail.cf
```

This command invokes the *m4* macro processor, supplying it the name of two macro definition files to process. *m4* processes the files in the order given. The first file is a standard *sendmail* macro template supplied with the *sendmail* source package, the second, of course, is the file containing our own macro definitions. The output of the command is directed to the */etc/mail/sendmail.cf* file, which is our target file.

You may now start *sendmail* with the new configuration.

Interpreting and Writing Rewrite Rules

Arguably the most powerful feature of *sendmail* is the rewrite rule. Rewrite rules are used by *sendmail* to determine how to process a received mail message. *sendmail* passes the addresses from the *headers* of a mail message through collections of rewrite rules called *rulesets* The rewrite rules transform a mail address from one form to another and you can think of them as being similar to a command in your editor that replaces all text matching a specified pattern with another.

Each rule has a lefthand side and a righthand side, separated by at least one tab character. When *sendmail* is processing mail it scans through the rewriting rules looking for a match on the lefthand side. If an address matches the lefthand side of a rewrite rule, the address is replaced by the righthand side and processed again.

sendmail.cf R and S Commands

In the *sendmail.cf* file, the rulesets are defined using commands coded as `Sn`, where *n* specifies the ruleset that is considered the current one.

The rules themselves appear in commands coded as *R*. As each *R* command is read, it is added to the current ruleset.

If you're dealing only with the *sendmail.mc* file, you won't need to worry about *S* commands at all, as the macros will build those for you. You will need to manually code your *R* rules.

A *sendmail* ruleset therefore looks like:

```
Sn
Rlhs rhs
Rlhs2 rhs2
```

Some Useful Macro Definitions

sendmail uses a number of standard macro definitions internally. The most useful of these in writing rulesets are:

$j   The fully qualified domain name of this host.

$w The hostname component of the FQDN.

$m
>   The domain name component of the FQDN.

We can incorporate these macro definitions in our rewrite rules. Our Virtual Brewery configuration uses the $m macro.

The Lefthand Side

In the lefthand side of a rewriting rule, you specify a pattern that will match an address you wish to transform. Most characters are matched literally, but there are a number of characters that have special meaning; these are described in the following list. The rewrite rules for the lefthand side are:

$@ Match exactly zero tokens

$* Match zero or more tokens

$+ Match one or more tokens

$- Match exactly one token

$=x
>   Match any phrase in class *x*

$~x
>   Match any word not in class *x*

A token is a string of characters delimited by spaces. There is no way to include spaces in a token, nor is it necessary, as the expression patterns are flexible enough to work around this need. When a rule matches an address, the text matched by each of the patterns in the expression will be assigned to special variables that we'll use in the righthand side. The only exception to this is the $@, which matches no tokens and therefore will never generate text to be used on the righthand side.

The Righthand Side

When the lefthand side of a rewrite rule matches an address, the original text is deleted and replaced by the righthand side of the rule. All tokens in the righthand side are copied literally, unless they begin with a dollar sign. Just as for the left-hand side, a number of metasymbols may be used on the righthand side. These are described in the following list. The rewrite rules for the righthand side are:

$n This metasymbol is replaced with the n'th expression from the lefthand side.

$[*name*$]
> This metasymbol resolves hostname to canonical name. It is replaced by the canonical form of the host name supplied.

$(*map key* $@*arguments* $:*default* $)
> This is the more general form of lookup. The output is the result of looking up *key* in the map named *map* passing *arguments* as arguments. The *map* can be any of the maps that *sendmail* supports such as the `virtusertable` that we describe a little later. If the lookup is unsuccessful, *default* will be output. If a default is not supplied and lookup fails, the input is unchanged and *key* is output.

$>*n*
> This will cause the rest of this line to be parsed and then given to ruleset *n* to evaluate. The output of the called ruleset will be written as output to this rule. This is the mechanism that allows rules to call other rulesets.

$#*mailer*
> This metasymbol causes ruleset evaluation to halt and specifies the mailer that should be used to transport this message in the next step of its delivery. This metasymbol should be called only from ruleset 0 or one of its subroutines. This is the final stage of address parsing and should be accompanied by the next two metasymbols.

$@*host*
> This metasymbol specifies the host that this message will be forwarded to. If the destination host is the local host, it may be omitted. The *host* may be a colon-separated list of destination hosts that will be tried in sequence to deliver the message.

$:*user*
> This metasymbol specifies the target user for the mail message.

A rewrite rule that matches is normally tried repeatedly until it fails to match, then parsing moves on to the next rule. This behavior can be changed by preceding the righthand side with one of two special righthand side metaymbols described in the following list. The rewrite rules for a righthand side loop control metasymbols are:

$@ This metasymbol causes the ruleset to return with the remainder of the right-hand side as the value. No other rules in the ruleset are evaluated.

$: This metasymbol causes this rule to terminate immediately, but the rest of the current ruleset is evaluated.

A Simple Rule Pattern Example

To better see how the macro substitution patterns operate, consider the following rule lefthand side:

$* < $+ >

This rule matches "Zero or more tokens, followed by the < character, followed by one or more tokens, followed by the > character."

If this rule were applied to `brewer@vbrew.com` or `Head Brewer < >`, the rule would not match. The first string would not match because it does not include a < character, and the second would fail because $+ matches *one or more* tokens and there are no tokens between the <> characters. In any case in which a rule does not match, the righthand side of the rule is not used.

If the rule were applied to `Head Brewer < brewer@vbrew.com >`, the rule would match, and on the righthand side $1 would be substituted with `Head Brewer` and $2 would be substituted with `brewer@vbrew.com`.

If the rule were applied to `< brewer@vbrew.com >` the rule would match because $* matches *zero* or more tokens, and on the righthand side $1 would be substituted with the empty string.

Ruleset Semantics

Each of the *sendmail* rulesets is called upon to perform a different task in mail processing. When you are writing rules, it is important to understand what each of the rulesets are expected to do. We'll look at each of the rulesets that the *m4* configuration scripts allow us to modify:

LOCAL_RULE_3

Ruleset 3 is responsible for converting an address in an arbitrary format into a common format that *sendmail* will then process. The output format expected is the familiar looking *local-part@host-domain-spec*.

Ruleset 3 should place the hostname part of the converted address inside the < and > characters to make parsing by later rulesets easier. Ruleset 3 is applied before *sendmail* does any other processing of an email address, so if you want *sendmail* to gateway mail from some system that uses some unusual address format, you should add a rule using the LOCAL_RULE_3 macro to convert addresses into the common format.

LOCAL_RULE_0 and LOCAL_NET_CONFIG

Ruleset 0 is applied to recipient addresses by *sendmail* after Ruleset 3. The LOCAL_NET_CONFIG macro causes rules to be inserted into the *bottom half* of Ruleset 0.

Ruleset 0 is expected to perform the delivery of the message to the recipient, so it must resolve to a triple that specifies each of the mailer, host, and user. The rules will be placed before any smart host definition you may include, so if you add rules that resolve addresses appropriately, any address that matches a rule will not be handled by the smart host. This is how we handle the direct *smtp* for the users on our local LAN in our example.

LOCAL_RULE_1 and LOCAL_RULE_2

Ruleset 1 is applied to all sender addresses and Ruleset 2 is applied to all recipient addresses. They are both usually empty.

Interpreting the rule in our example

Our sample in Example 18-3 uses the LOCAL_NET_CONFIG macro to declare a local rule that ensures that any mail within our domain is delivered directly using the *smtp* mailer. Now that we've looked at how rewrite rules are constructed, we will be able to understand how this rule works. Let's take another look at it.

Example 18-3: Rewrite Rule from vstout.uucpsmtp.m4

```
LOCAL_NET_CONFIG
# This rule ensures that all local mail is delivered using the
# smtp transport, everything else will go via the smart host.
R$* < @ $* .$m. > $*   $#smtp $@ $2.$m. $: $1 < @ $2.$m. > $3
```

We know that the LOCAL_NET_CONFIG macro will cause the rule to be inserted somewhere near the end of ruleset 0, but before any smart host definition. We also know that ruleset 0 is the last ruleset to be executed and that it should resolve to a three-tuple specifying the mailer, user, and host.

We can ignore the two comment lines; they don't do anything useful. The rule itself is the line beginning with R. We know that the R is a *sendmail* command and that it adds this rule to the current ruleset, in this case ruleset 0. Let's look at the lefthand side and the righthand side in turn.

The lefthand side looks like: `$* < @ $* .$m. > $*`.

Ruleset 0 expects < and > characters because it is fed by ruleset 3. Ruleset 3 converts addresses into a common form and to make parsing easier, it also places the host part of the mail address inside <>s.

This rule matches any mail address that looks like: `'DestUser < @ some-host.ourdomain. > Some Text'`. That is, it matches mail for any user at any host within our domain.

You will remember that the text matched by metasymbols on the lefthand side of a rewrite rule is assigned to macro definitions for use on the righthand side. In our example, the first `$*` matches all text from the start of the address until the `<` character. All of this text is assigned to `$1` for use on the righthand side. Similarly the second `$*` in our rewrite rule is assigned to `$2`, and the last is assigned to `$3`.

We now have enough to understand the lefthand side. This rule matches mail for any user at any host within our domain. It assigns the username to `$1`, the hostname to `$2`, and any trailing text to `$3`. The righthand side is then invoked to process these.

Let's now look at what we're expecting to see outputed. The righthand side of our example rewrite rule looks like: `$#smtp $@ $2.$m. $: $1 < @ $2.$m. > $3`.

When the righthand side of our ruleset is processed, each of the metasymbols are interpreted and relevant substitutions are made.

The `$#` metasymbol causes this rule to resolve to a specific mailer, *smtp* in our case.

The `$@` resolves the target host. In our example, the target host is specified as `$2.$m.`, which is the fully qualified domain name of the host on in our domain. The FQDN is constructed of the hostname component assigned to `$2` from our lefthand side with our domain name (`.$m.`) appended.

The `$:` metasymbol specifies the target user, which we again captured from the lefthand side and had stored in `$1`.

We preserve the contents of the `<>` section, and any trailing text, using the data we collected from the lefthand side of the rule.

Since this rule resolves to a mailer, the message is forwarded to the mailer for delivery. In our example, the message would be forwarded to the destination host using the SMTP protocol.

Configuring sendmail Options

sendmail has a number of options that allow you to customize the way it performs certain tasks. There are a large number of these, so we've listed only a few of the more commonly used ones in the upcoming list.

To configure any of these options, you may either define them in the *m4* configuration file, which is the preferable method, or you may insert them directly into the *sendmail.cf* file. For example, if we wished to have *sendmail* fork a new job for each mail message to be delivered, we might add the following line to our *m4* configuration file:

```
define('confSEPARATE_PROC','true')
```

The corresponding *sendmail.cf* entry created is:

```
O ForkEachJob=true
```

The following list describes common *sendmail m4* options (and *sendmail.cf* equivalents):

confMIN_FREE_BLOCKS (MinFreeBlocks)
There are occasions when a problem might prevent the immediate delivery of mail messages, causing messages to be queued in the mail spool. If your mail host processes large volumes of mail, it is possible for the mail spool to grow to such a size that it fills the filesystem supporting the spool. To prevent this, *sendmail* provides this option to specify the minimum number of free disk blocks that must exist before a mail message will be accepted. This allows you to ensure that *sendmail* never causes your spool filesystem to be filled (Default: 100).

confME_TOO (MeToo)
When a mail target such as an email alias is expanded, it is sometimes possible for the sender to appear in the recipient list. This option determines whether the originators of an email message will receive a copy if they appear in the expanded recipient list. Valid values are "true" and "false" (Default: false).

confMAX_DAEMON_CHILDREN (MaxDaemonChildren)
Whenever *sendmail* receives an SMTP connection from a remote host, it spawns a new copy of itself to deal with the incoming mail message. This way, it is possible for *sendmail* to be processing multiple incoming mail messages simulatanenously. While this is useful, each new copy of *sendmail* consumes memory in the host computer. If an unusually large number of incoming connections are received, by chance, because of a problem or a malicious attack, it is possible for *sendmail* daemons to consume all system memory. This option provides you with a means of limiting the maximum number of daemon children that will be spawned. When this number is reached, new connections are rejected until some of the existing children have terminated (Default: undefined).

confSEPARATE_PROC (ForkEachJob)
When processing the mail queue and sending mail messages, *sendmail* processes one mail message at a time. When this option is enabled, *sendmail* will fork a new copy of itself for each message to be delivered. This is particularly useful when there are some mail messages that are stuck in the queue because of a problem with the target host (Default: false).

`confSMTP_LOGIN_MSG` (`SmtpGreetingMessage`)

> Whenever a connection is made to *sendmail*, a greeting message is sent. By default, this message contains the hostname, name of the mail transfer agent, the sendmail version number, the local version number, and the current date. RFC821 specifies that the first word of the greeting should be the fully qualified domain name of the host, but the rest of the greeting can be configured however you please. You can specify sendmail macros here and they will be expanded when used. The only people who will see this message are suffering system administrators diagnosing mail delivery problems or strongly curious people interested in discovering how your machine is configured. You can relieve some of the tedium of their task by customizing the welcome message with some witticisms; be nice. The word "EMSTP" will be inserted between the first and second words by *sendmail*, as this is the signal to remote hosts that we support the ESMTP protocol (Default: `$j Sendmail $v/$Z; $b`).

Some Useful sendmail Configurations

There are myriad possible *sendmail* configurations. In this space we'll illustrate just a few important types of configuration that will be useful in many *sendmail* installations.

Trusting Users to Set the From: Field

It is sometimes useful to overwrite the `From:` field of an outgoing mail message. Let's say you have a web-based program that generates email. Normally the mail message would appear to come from the user who owned the web server process. We might want to specify some other source address so that the mail appears to have originated from some other user or address on that machine. *sendmail* provides a means of specifying which systems users are to be entrusted with the ability to do this.

The `use_ct_file` feature enables the specification and use of a file that lists the names of trusted users. By default, a small number of system users are trusted by *sendmail* (`root`, for example). The default filename for this feature is */etc/mail/trusted-users* in systems exploiting the */etc/mail/* configuration directory and */etc/sendmail.ct* in those that don't. You can specify the name and location of the file by overriding the `confCT_FILE` definition.

Add FEATURE(use_ct_file) to your *sendmail.mc* file to enable the feature.

Managing Mail Aliases

Mail aliases are a powerful feature that enable mail to be directed to mailboxes that are alternate names for users or processes on a destination host. For example, it is common practice to have feedback or comments relating to a World Wide Web server to be directed to "webmaster." Often there isn't a user known as "webmaster" on the target machine, instead it is an alias of another system user. Another common use of mail aliases is exploited by mailing list server programs in which an alias directs incoming messages to the list server program for handling.

The */etc/aliases* file is where the aliases are stored. The *sendmail* program consults this file when determining how to handle an incoming mail message. If it finds an entry in this file matching the target user in the mail message, it redirects the message to wherever the entry describes.

Specifically there are three things that aliases allow to happen:

- They provide a shorthand or well-known name for mail to be addressed to in order to go to one or more persons.

- They can invoke a program with the mail message as the input to the program.

- They can send mail to a file.

All systems require aliases for **Postmaster** and **MAILER-DAEMON** to be RFC-compliant.

Always be extremely aware of security when defining aliases that invoke programs or write to programs, since *sendmail* generally runs with **root** permissions.

Details concerning mail aliases may be found in the *aliases(5)* manual page. A sample *aliases* file is shown in Example 18-4.

Example 18-4: Sample aliases File

```
#
# The following two aliases must be present to be RFC-compliant.
# It is important to resolve them to 'a person' who reads mail routinely.
#
postmaster:     root                         # required entry
MAILER-DAEMON: postmaster                     # required entry
#
#
# demonstrate the common types of aliases
#
usenet:         janet                        # alias for a person
admin:          joe,janet                    # alias for several people
newspak-users: :include:/usr/lib/lists/newspak # read recipients from file
changefeed:     |/usr/local/lib/gup          # alias that invokes program
complaints:     /var/log/complaints          # alias writes mail to file
#
```

Whenever you update the */etc/aliases* file, be sure to run the command:

```
# /usr/bin/newaliases
```

to rebuild the database that *sendmail* uses internally. The */usr/bin/newaliases* command is a symbolic link to the *sendmail* executable, and when invoked this way, behaves exactly as though it were invoked as:

```
# /usr/lib/sendmail -bi
```

The *newaliases* command is an alternative and more convenient way to do this.

Using a Smart Host

Sometimes a host finds mail that it is unable to deliver directly to the desired remote host. It is often convenient to have a single host on a network take on the role of managing transmission of mail to remote hosts that are difficult to reach, rather than have each local host try to do this independently.

There are a few good reasons to have a single host take on mail management. You can simplify management by having only one host with a comprehensive mail configuration that knows how to handle all of the different mail transport types, such as UUCP, Usenet, etc. All other hosts need only a single tranport protocol to send their mail to this central host. Hosts that fill this central mail routing and forwarding role are called *smart hosts*. If you have a smart host that will accept mail from you, you can send it mail of any sort and it will manage the routing and transmission of that mail to the desired remote destinations.

Another good application for smart host configurations is to manage transmission of mail across a private firewall. An organization may elect to install a private IP network and use their own, unregistered IP addresses. The private network may be connected to the Internet through a firewall. Sending mail to and from hosts in the private network to the outside world using SMTP would not be possible in a conventional configuration because the hosts are not able to accept or establish direct network connections to hosts on the Internet. Instead, the organization could elect to have the firewall provide a mail smart host function. The smart host running on the firewall is able to establish direct network connections with hosts both on the private network and on the Internet. The smart host would accept mail from both hosts on the private network and the Internet, store them in local storage and then manage the retransmission of that mail to the correct host directly.

Smart hosts are usually used when all other methods of delivery have failed. In the case of the organization with the private network, it would be perfectly reasonable to have the hosts attempt to deliver mail directly first, and if that fails then to send it to the smart host. This relieves the smart host of a lot of traffic because other hosts can directly send mail to other hosts on the private network.

sendmail provides a simple method of configuring a smart host using the SMART_HOST feature; when implementing it in the Virtual Brewery configuration, we do exactly this. The relevant portions of our configuration that define the smart host are:

```
define('SMART_HOST', 'uucp-new:moria')
LOCAL_NET_CONFIG
# This rule ensures that all local mail is delivered using the
# smtp transport, everything else will go via the smart host.
R$* < @ $* .$m. > $*    $#smtp $@ $2.$m. $: $1 < @ $2.$m. > $3
```

The SMART_HOST macro allows you to specify the host that should relay all outgoing mail that you are unable to deliver directly, and the mail transport protocol to use to talk to it.

In our configuration we are using the uucp-new transport to UUCP host **moria**. If we wanted to configure *sendmail* to use an SMTP-based Smart Host, we would instead use something like:

```
define('SMART_HOST', 'mail.isp.net')
```

We don't need to specify SMTP as the transport, as it is the default.

Can you guess what the LOCAL_NET_CONFIG macro and the rewrite rule might be doing?

The LOCAL_NET_CONFIG macro allows you to add raw *sendmail* rewrite rules to your configuration that define what mail should stay within the local mail system. In our example, we've used a rule that matches any email address where the host belongs to our domain (.$m.) and rewrite it so that it is sent directly to the SMTP mailer. This ensures that any message for a host on our local domain is directed immediately to the SMTP mailer and forwarded to that host, rather than falling through to our smart host, which is the default treatment.

Managing Unwanted or Unsolicited Mail (Spam)

If you've subscribed to a mailing list, published your email address on a web site, or posted an article to UseNet, you will most likely have begun to receive unsolicited advertising email. It is commonplace now for people to scour the net in search of email addresses to add to mailing lists that they then sell to companies seeking to advertise their products. This sort of mass-mailing behavior is commonly called spamming.

The Free On-line Dictionary of Computing offers a mail-specific definition of spam as:*

> 2. (A narrowing of sense 1, above) To indiscrimately send large amounts of unsolicited e-mail meant to promote a product or service. Spam in this sense is sort of like the electronic equivalent of junk mail sent to "Occupant."

> In the 1990s, with the rise in commercial awareness of the net, there are actually scumbags who offer spamming as a "service" to companies wishing to advertise on the net. They do this by mailing to collections of e-mail addresses, Usenet news, or mailing lists. Such practises have caused outrage and aggressive reaction by many net users against the individuals concerned.

Fortunately, *sendmail* includes some support for mechanisms that can help you deal with unsolicited mail.

The Real-time Blackhole List

The Real-time Blackhole List is a public facility provided to help reduce the volume of unsolicited advertising you have to contend with. Known email sources and hosts are listed in a queryable database on the Internet. They're entered there by people who have received unsolicited advertising from some email address. Major domains sometimes find themselves on the list because of slip-ups in shutting down spam. While some people complain about particular choices made by the maintainers of the list, it remains very popular and disagreements are usually worked out quickly. Full details on how the service is operated may be found from the home site of the Mail Abuse Protection System at *http://maps.vix.com/rbl/*.

If you enable this *sendmail* feature, it will test the source address of each incoming mail message against the Real-time Blackhole List to determine whether to accept the message. If you run a large site with many users, this feature could save a considerable volume of disk space. This feature accepts a parameter to specify the name of the server to use. The default is the main server at **rbl.maps.vix.com**.

To configure the Real-time Blackhole List feature, add the following macro declaration to your *sendmail.mc* file:

```
FEATURE(rbl)
```

Should you wish to specify some other RBL server, you would use a declaration that looks like:

```
FEATURE(rbl,`rbl.host.net')
```

---

* The Free On-Line Dictionary of Computing can be found packaged in many Linux distributions, or online at its home page at *http://wombat.doc.ic.ac.uk/foldoc/*.

The access database

An alternative system that offers greater flexibility and control at the cost of manual configuration is the *sendmail* `access_db` feature. The access database allows you to configure which hosts or users you will accept mail from and which you will relay mail for.

Managing who you will relay mail for is important, as it is another technique commonly employed by spamming hosts to circumvent systems such as the Real-time Blackhole List just described. Instead of sending the mail to you directly, spammers will relay the mail via some other unsuspecting host who allows it. The incoming SMTP connection then doesn't come from the known spamming host, it instead comes from the relay host. To ensure that your own mail hosts aren't used in this way, you should relay mail only for known hosts. Versions of *sendmail* that are 8.9.0 or newer have relaying disabled by default, so for those you'll need to use the access database to enable individual hosts to relay.

The general idea is simple. When a new incoming SMTP connection is received, *sendmail* retrieves the message header information and then consults the access database to see whether it should proceed to accept the body of the message itself.

The access database is a collection of rules that describe what action should be taken for messages received from nominated hosts. The default access control file is called */etc/mail/access*. The table has a simple format. Each line of the table contains an access rule. The lefthand side of each rule is a pattern used to match the sender of an incoming mail message. It may be a complete email address, a hostname, or an IP address. The righthand side is the action to take. There are five types of action you may configure. These are:

OK
> Accept the mail message.

RELAY
> Accept messages from this host or user even if they are not destined for our host; that is, accept messages for relaying to other hosts from this host.

REJECT
> Reject the mail with a generic message.

DISCARD
> Discard the message using the `$#discard` mailer.

any text
> Return an error message using `###` as the error code (which should be RFC-821 compliant) and "any text" as the message.

An example */etc/mail/access* might look like:

```
friends@cybermail.com    REJECT
aol.com                  REJECT
207.46.131.30            REJECT
postmaster@aol.com       OK
linux.org.au             RELAY
```

This example would reject any email received from *friends@cybermail.com*, any host in the domain **aol.com** and the host **207.46.131.30**. The next rule would accept email from *postmaster@aol.com* despite the fact that the domain itself has a reject rule. The last rule allows relaying of mail from any host in the **linux.org.au** domain.

To enable the access database feature, use the following declaration in your *sendmail.mc* file:

```
FEATURE(access_db)
```

The default definition builds the database using `hash -o /etc/mail/access`, which generates a simple hashed database from the plain text file. This is perfectly adequate in most installations. There are other options that you should consider if you intend to have a large access database. Consult the *sendmail* book or other *sendmail* documentation for details.

Barring users from receiving mail

If you have users or automated processes that send mail but will never need to receive it, it is sometimes useful to refuse to accept mail destined for them. This saves wasted disk-space storing mail that will never be read. The `blacklist_recipients` feature, when used in combination with the `access_db` feature, allows you to disable the receipt of mail for local users.

To enable the feature, you add the following lines to your *sendmail.mc* file, if they're not already there:

```
FEATURE(access_db)
FEATURE(blacklist_recipients)
```

To disable receipt of mail for a local user, simply add his details into the access database. Usually you would use the `###` entry style that would return a meaningful error message to the sender so they know why the mail is not being delivered. This feature applies equally well to users in virtual mail domains, and you must include the virtual mail domain in the access database specification. Some sample */etc/mail/access* entries might look like:

```
daemon          550 Daemon does not accept or read mail.
flacco          550 Mail for this user has been administratively disabled.
grump@dairy.org 550 Mail disabled for this recipient.
```

Configuring Virtual Email Hosting

Virtual email hosting provides a host the capability of accepting and delivering mail on behalf of a number of different domains as though it were a number of separate mail hosts. Most commonly, virtual hosting is exploited by Internet Application Providers in combination with virtual web hosting, but it's simple to configure and you never know when you might be in a position to virtual host a mailing list for your favorite Linux project, so we'll describe it here.

Accepting mail for other domains

When *sendmail* receives an email message, it compares the destination host in the message headers to the local host name. If they match, *sendmail* accepts the message for local delivery; if they differ, *sendmail* may decide to accept the message and attempt to forward it on to the final destination (See "The access database" earlier in this chapter for details on how to configure *sendmail* to accept mail for forwarding).

If we wish to configure virtual email hosting, the first thing we need to do is to convince *sendmail* that it should also accept mail for the domains that we are hosting. Fortunately, this is a very simple thing to do.

The *sendmail* `use_cw_file` feature allows us to specify the name of a file where we store domain names for which *sendmail* accepts mail. To configure the feature, add the feature declaration to your *sendmail.mc* file:

```
FEATURE(use_cw_file)
```

The default name of the file will be */etc/mail/local-host-names* for distributions using the */etc/mail/* configuration directory or */etc/sendmail.cw* for those that don't. Alternatively, you can specify the name and location of the file by overriding the `confCW_FILE` macro using a variation on:

```
define(`confCW_FILE','/etc/virtualnames')
```

To stick with the default filename, if we wished to offer virtual hosting to the **bovine.net**, **dairy.org**, and **artist.org** domains, we would create a */etc/mail/local-host-names* that looks like:

```
bovine.net
dairy.org
artist.org
```

When this is done, and assuming appropriate DNS records exist that point those domain names to our host, *sendmail* will accept mail messages for those domains as though they were destined for our real domain name.

Forwarding virtual-hosted mail to other destinations

The *sendmail* `virtusertable` feature configures support for the virtual user table, where we configure virtual email hosting. The virtual user table maps incoming mail destined for some *user@host* to some *otheruser@otherhost*. You can think of this as an advanced mail alias feature, one that operates using not just the destination user, but also the destination domain.

To configure the `virtusertable` feature, add the feature to your *sendmail.mc* configuration as shown:

```
FEATURE(virtusertable)
```

By default, the file containing the rules to perform translations will be */etc/mail/ virtusertable*. You can override this by supplying an argument to the macro definition; consult a detailed *sendmail* reference to learn about what options are available.

The format of the virtual user table is very simple. The lefthand side of each line contains a pattern representing the original destination mail address; the righthand side has a pattern representing the mail address the virtual hosted address will be mapped to.

The following example shows three possible types of entries:

```
samiam@bovine.net       colin
sunny@bovine.net        darkhorse@mystery.net
@dairy.org              mail@jhm.org
@artist.org             $1@red.firefly.com
```

In this example, we are virtual hosting three domains: **bovine.net**, **dairy.org**, and **artist.org**.

The first entry redirects mail sent to a user in the **bovine.net** virtual domain to a local user on the machine. The second entry redirects mail to a user in the same virtual domain to a user in another domain. The third example redirects all mail addressed to any user in the **dairly.org** virtual domain to a single remote mail address. Finally, the last entry redirects any mail to a user in the **artist.org** virtual domain to the same user in another domain; for example, *julie@artists.org* would be redirected to *julie@red.firefly.com*.

Testing Your Configuration

The *m4* command processes the macro definition files according to its own syntax rules without understanding anything about correct *sendmail* syntax; so there won't be any error messages if you've gotten anything wrong in your macro definition file. For this reason, it is very important that you thoroughly test your configuration. Fortunately, *sendmail* provides a relatively easy way of doing this.

sendmail supports an "address test" mode that allows us to test our configuration and identify any errors. In this mode of operation, we invoke *sendmail* from the command line, and it prompts us for a ruleset specification and a destination mail address. *sendmail* then processes that destination address using the rules specified, displaying the output of each rewrite rule as it proceeds. To place *sendmail* into this mode, we invoke it with the −bt argument:

```
# /usr/sbin/sendmail -bt
ADDRESS TEST MODE (ruleset 3 NOT automatically invoked)
Enter <ruleset> <address>
>
```

The default configuration file used is the */etc/mail/sendmail.cf* file; you can specify an alternate configuration file using the −C argument. To test our configuration, we need to select a number of addresses to process that will tell us that each of our mail-handing requirements are met. To illustrate this, we'll work through a test of our more complicated UUCP configuration shown in Example 18-2.

First we'll test that *sendmail* is able to deliver mail to local users on the system. In these tests we expect all addresses to be rewritten to the **local** mailer on this machine:

```
# /usr/sbin/sendmail -bt
ADDRESS TEST MODE (ruleset 3 NOT automatically invoked)
Enter <ruleset> <address>
> 3,0 isaac
rewrite: ruleset   3   input: isaac
rewrite: ruleset  96   input: isaac
rewrite: ruleset  96 returns: isaac
rewrite: ruleset   3 returns: isaac
rewrite: ruleset   0   input: isaac
rewrite: ruleset 199   input: isaac
rewrite: ruleset 199 returns: isaac
rewrite: ruleset  98   input: isaac
rewrite: ruleset  98 returns: isaac
rewrite: ruleset 198   input: isaac
rewrite: ruleset 198 returns: $# local $: isaac
rewrite: ruleset   0 returns: $# local $: isaac
```

This output shows us how *sendmail* processes mail addressed to **isaac** on this system. Each line shows us what information has been supplied to a ruleset or the result obtained from processing by a ruleset. We told *sendmail* we wished to use rulesets 3 and 0 to process the address. Ruleset 0 is what is normally invoked and we forced ruleset 3 because it is not tested by default. The last line shows us that the result of ruleset 0 does indeed direct mail to **isaac** to the **local** mailer.

Next we'll test mail addressed to our SMTP address: **isaac@vstout.vbrew.com**. We should be able to produce the same end result as our last example:

```
# /usr/sbin/sendmail -bt
ADDRESS TEST MODE (ruleset 3 NOT automatically invoked)
Enter <ruleset> <address>
> 3,0 isaac@vstout.vbrew.com
rewrite: ruleset   3   input: isaac @ vstout . vbrew . com
rewrite: ruleset  96   input: isaac < @ vstout . vbrew . com >
rewrite: ruleset  96 returns: isaac < @ vstout . vbrew . com . >
rewrite: ruleset   3 returns: isaac < @ vstout . vbrew . com . >
rewrite: ruleset   0   input: isaac < @ vstout . vbrew . com . >
rewrite: ruleset 199   input: isaac < @ vstout . vbrew . com . >
rewrite: ruleset 199 returns: isaac < @ vstout . vbrew . com . >
rewrite: ruleset  98   input: isaac < @ vstout . vbrew . com . >
rewrite: ruleset  98 returns: isaac < @ vstout . vbrew . com . >
rewrite: ruleset 198   input: isaac < @ vstout . vbrew . com . >
rewrite: ruleset 198 returns: $# local $: isaac
rewrite: ruleset   0 returns: $# local $: isaac
```

Again, this test passed. Next we'll test mail to our UUCP style address: **vstout!isaac**.

```
# /usr/sbin/sendmail -bt
ADDRESS TEST MODE (ruleset 3 NOT automatically invoked)
Enter <ruleset> <address>
> 3,0 vstout!isaac
rewrite: ruleset   3   input: vstout ! isaac
rewrite: ruleset  96   input: isaac < @ vstout . UUCP >
rewrite: ruleset  96 returns: isaac < @ vstout . vbrew . com . >
rewrite: ruleset   3 returns: isaac < @ vstout . vbrew . com . >
rewrite: ruleset   0   input: isaac < @ vstout . vbrew . com . >
rewrite: ruleset 199   input: isaac < @ vstout . vbrew . com . >
rewrite: ruleset 199 returns: isaac < @ vstout . vbrew . com . >
rewrite: ruleset  98   input: isaac < @ vstout . vbrew . com . >
rewrite: ruleset  98 returns: isaac < @ vstout . vbrew . com . >
rewrite: ruleset 198   input: isaac < @ vstout . vbrew . com . >
rewrite: ruleset 198 returns: $# local $: isaac
rewrite: ruleset   0 returns: $# local $: isaac
```

This test has also passed. These tests confirm that any mail received for local users on this machine will be properly delivered irrespective of how the address is formatted. If you've defined any aliases for your machine, such as virtual hosts, you should repeat these tests for each of the alternate names by which this host is known to ensure they also work correctly.

Next we will test that mail addressed to other hosts in the **vbrew.com** domain is delivered directly to that host using the SMTP mailer:

```
# /usr/sbin/sendmail -bt
ADDRESS TEST MODE (ruleset 3 NOT automatically invoked)
Enter <ruleset> <address>
> 3,0 isaac@vale.vbrew.com
```

```
rewrite: ruleset    3   input: isaac @ vale . vbrew . com
rewrite: ruleset   96   input: isaac < @ vale . vbrew . com >
rewrite: ruleset   96 returns: isaac < @ vale . vbrew . com . >
rewrite: ruleset    3 returns: isaac < @ vale . vbrew . com . >
rewrite: ruleset    0   input: isaac < @ vale . vbrew . com . >
rewrite: ruleset  199   input: isaac < @ vale . vbrew . com . >
rewrite: ruleset  199 returns: isaac < @ vale . vbrew . com . >
rewrite: ruleset   98   input: isaac < @ vale . vbrew . com . >
rewrite: ruleset   98 returns: isaac < @ vale . vbrew . com . >
rewrite: ruleset  198   input: isaac < @ vale . vbrew . com . >
rewrite: ruleset  198 returns: $# smtp $@ vale . vbrew . com . /
    $: isaac < @ vale . vbrew . com . >
rewrite: ruleset    0 returns: $# smtp $@ vale . vbrew . com . /
    $: isaac < @ vale . vbrew . com . >
```

We can see that this test has directed the message to the SMTP mailer to be forwarded directly to the **vale.vbrew.com** host and specifies the user **isaac**. This test confirms that our LOCAL_NET_CONFIG definition works correctly. For this test to succeed, the destination hostname must be able to be resolved correctly, so it must either have an entry in our */etc/hosts* file, or in our local DNS. We can see what happens if the destination hostname isn't able to be resolved by intentionally specifying an unknown host:

 # /usr/sbin/sendmail -bt
```
ADDRESS TEST MODE (ruleset 3 NOT automatically invoked)
Enter <ruleset> <address>
> 3,0 isaac@vXXXX.vbrew.com
rewrite: ruleset    3   input: isaac @ vXXXX . vbrew . com
rewrite: ruleset   96   input: isaac < @ vXXXX . vbrew . com >
vXXXX.vbrew.com: Name server timeout
rewrite: ruleset   96 returns: isaac < @ vXXXX . vbrew . com >
rewrite: ruleset    3 returns: isaac < @ vXXXX . vbrew . com >
== Ruleset 3,0 (3) status 75
rewrite: ruleset    0   input: isaac < @ vXXXX . vbrew . com >
rewrite: ruleset  199   input: isaac < @ vXXXX . vbrew . com >
rewrite: ruleset  199 returns: isaac < @ vXXXX . vbrew . com >
rewrite: ruleset   98   input: isaac < @ vXXXX . vbrew . com >
rewrite: ruleset   98 returns: isaac < @ vXXXX . vbrew . com >
rewrite: ruleset  198   input: isaac < @ vXXXX . vbrew . com >
rewrite: ruleset   95   input: < uucp-new : moria > isaac </
    @ vXXXX . vbrew . com >
rewrite: ruleset   95 returns: $# uucp-new $@ moria $: isaac </
    @ vXXXX . vbrew . com >
rewrite: ruleset  198 returns: $# uucp-new $@ moria $: isaac </
    @ vXXXX . vbrew . com >
rewrite: ruleset    0 returns: $# uucp-new $@ moria $: isaac </
    @ vXXXX . vbrew . com >
```

This result is very different. First, ruleset 3 returned an error message indicating the hostname could not be resolved. Second, we deal with this situation by relying on the other key feature of our configuration, the smart host. The smart host will is to handle any mail that is otherwise undeliverable. The hostname we specified in this test was unable to be resolved and the rulesets determined that the mail should be forwarded to our smart host **moria** using the **uucp-new** mailer. Our smart host might be better connected and know what to do with the address.

Our final test ensures that any mail addressed to a host not within our domain is delivered to our smart host. This should produce a result similar to our previous example:

```
# /usr/sbin/sendmail -bt
ADDRESS TEST MODE (ruleset 3 NOT automatically invoked)
Enter <ruleset> <address>
> 3,0 isaac@linux.org.au
rewrite: ruleset   3    input: isaac @ linux . org . au
rewrite: ruleset  96    input: isaac < @ linux . org . au >
rewrite: ruleset  96 returns: isaac < @ linux . org . au . >
rewrite: ruleset   3 returns: isaac < @ linux . org . au . >
rewrite: ruleset   0    input: isaac < @ linux . org . au . >
rewrite: ruleset 199    input: isaac < @ linux . org . au . >
rewrite: ruleset 199 returns: isaac < @ linux . org . au . >
rewrite: ruleset  98    input: isaac < @ linux . org . au . >
rewrite: ruleset  98 returns: isaac < @ linux . org . au . >
rewrite: ruleset 198    input: isaac < @ linux . org . au . >
rewrite: ruleset  95    input: < uucp-new : moria > isaac </
        @ linux . org . au . >
rewrite: ruleset  95 returns: $# uucp-new $@ moria $: isaac </
        @ linux . org . au . >
rewrite: ruleset 198 returns: $# uucp-new $@ moria $: isaac </
        @ linux . org . au . >
rewrite: ruleset   0 returns: $# uucp-new $@ moria $: isaac </
        @ linux . org . au . >
```

The results of this test indicate that the hostname was resolved, and that the message would still have been routed to our smart host. This proves that our LOCAL_NET_CONFIG definition works correctly and it handled both cases correctly. This test was also successful, so we can happily assume our configuration is correct and use it.

Running sendmail

The *sendmail* daemon can be run in either of two ways. One way is to have to have it run from the *inetd* daemon; the alternative, and more commonly used method is to run *sendmail* as a standalone daemon. It is also common for mailer programs to invoke *sendmail* as a user command to accept locally generated mail for delivery.

When running *sendmail* in standalone mode, place the command in an *rc* file so it starts at boot time. The syntax used is commonly:

```
/usr/sbin/sendmail -bd -q10m
```

The **-bd** argument tells *sendmail* to run as a daemon. It will fork and run in the background. The **-q10m** argument tells *sendmail* to check its queue every ten minutes. You may choose to use a different queue to check time.

To run *sendmail* from the *inetd* network daemon, you'd use an entry like:

```
smtp  stream  tcp nowait  nobody  /usr/sbin/sendmail -bs
```

The **-bs** argument here tells *sendmail* to use the SMTP protocol on stdin/stdout, which is required for use with *inetd*.

The *runq* command is usually a symlink to the *sendmail* binary and is a more convenient form of:

```
# sendmail -q
```

When *sendmail* is invoked this way, it processes any mail waiting in the queue to be transmitted. When running *sendmail* from *inetd* you must also create a *cron* job that runs the *runq* command periodically to ensure that the mail spool is serviced periodically.

A suitable *cron* table entry would be similar to:

```
# Run the mail spool every fifteen minutes
0,15,30,45    *    *    *    *      /usr/bin/runq
```

In most installations *sendmail* processes the queue every 15 minutes as shown in our *crontab* example, attempting to transmit any messages there.

Tips and Tricks

There are a number of things you can do to make managing a *sendmail* site efficient. A number of management tools are provided in the *sendmail* package; let's look at the most important of these.

Managing the Mail Spool

Mail is queued in the */var/spool/mqueue* directory before being transmitted. This directory is called the mail spool. The *sendmail* program provides a means of displaying a formatted list of all spooled mail messages and their status.

The */usr/bin/mailq* command is a symbolic link to the *sendmail* executable and behaves indentically to:

```
# sendmail -bp
```

The output displays the message ID, its size, the time it was placed in the queue, who sent it, and a message indicating its current status. The following example shows a mail message stuck in the queue with a problem:

```
$ mailq
                   Mail Queue (1 request)
--Q-ID-- --Size-- -----Q-Time----- -----------Sender/Recipient-----------
RAA00275       124 Wed Dec  9 17:47 root
                      (host map: lookup (tao.linux.org.au): deferred)
                                   terry@tao.linux.org.au
```

This message is still in the mail queue because the destination host IP address could not be resolved.

We can force *sendmail* to process the queue now by issuing the */usr/bin/runq* command.

The *runq* command produces no output. *sendmail* will begin processing the mail queue in the background.

Forcing a Remote Host to Process its Mail Queue

If you use a temporary dial-up Internet connection with a *fixed* IP address and rely on an MX host to collect your mail while you are disconnected, you will find it useful to force the MX host to process its mail queue soon after you establish your connection.

A small *perl* program is included with the *sendmail* distribution that makes this simple for mail hosts that support it. The *etrn* script has much the same effect on a remote host as the *runq* command has on our own. If we invoke the command as shown in this example:

```
# etrn vstout.vbrew.com
```

we will force the host **vstout.vbrew.com** to process any mail queued for our local machine.

Typically you'd add this command to your PPP *ip-up* script so that it is executed soon after your network connection is established.

Analyzing Mail Statistics

sendmail collects data on mail traffic volumes and some information on hosts to which it has delivered mail. There are two commands available to display this information, *mailstats*, and *hoststat*.

mailstats

The *mailstats* command displays statistics on the volume of mail processed by *sendmail*. The time at which data collection commenced is printed first, followed by a table with one row for each configured mailer and one showing a summary total of all mail. Each line presents eight items of information:

Field	Meaning
M	The mailer (transport protocol) number
msgsfr	The number of messages received from the mailer
bytes_from	The Kbytes of mail from the mailer
msgsto	The number of messages sent to the mailer
bytes_to	The Kbytes of mail sent to the mailer
msgsreg	The number of messages rejected
msgsdis	The number of messages discarded
Mailer	The name of the mailer

A sample of the output of the *mailstats* command is shown in Example 18-5.

Example 18-5: Sample Output of the mailstats Command

```
# /usr/sbin/mailstats
Statistics from Sun Dec 20 22:47:02 1998
 M    msgsfr  bytes_from    msgsto    bytes_to  msgsrej  msgsdis  Mailer
 0         0          0K        19        515K        0        0  prog
 3        33        545K         0          0K        0        0  local
 5        88        972K       139       1018K        0        0  esmtp
=================================================================
 T       121       1517K       158       1533K        0        0
```

This data is collected if the *StatusFile* option is enabled in the *sendmail.cf* file and the status file exists. Typically you'd add the following to your *sendmail.cf* file:

```
# status file
O StatusFile=/var/log/sendmail.st
```

To restart the statistics collection, you need to make the statistics file zero length:

```
> /var/log/sendmail.st
```

and restart *sendmail.*

hoststat

The *hoststat* command displays information about the status of hosts that *sendmail* has attempted to deliver mail to. The *hoststat* command is equivalent to invoking *sendmail* as:

```
sendmail -bh
```

The output presents each host on a line of its own, and for each the time since delivery was attempted to it, and the status message received at that time.

Example 18-6 shows the sort of output you can expect from the *hoststat* command. Note that most of the results indicate successful delivery. The result for **earthlink.net**, on the other hand, indicates that delivery was unsuccessful. The status message can sometimes help determine the cause of the failure. In this case, the connection timed out, probably because the host was down or unreachable at the time delivery was attempted.

Example 18-6: Sample Output of the oststat Command

```
# hoststat
-------------- Hostname ---------- How long ago ---------Results---------
mail.telstra.com.au                     04:05:41 250 Message accepted for
scooter.eye-net.com.au               81+08:32:42 250 OK id=0zTGai-0008S9-0
yarrina.connect.com.a                53+10:46:03 250 LAA09163 Message acce
happy.optus.com.au                   55+03:34:40 250 Mail accepted
mail.zip.com.au                         04:05:33 250 RAA23904 Message acce
kwanon.research.canon.com.au         44+04:39:10 250 ok 911542267 qp 21186
linux.org.au                         83+10:04:11 250 IAA31139 Message acce
albert.aapra.org.au                     00:00:12 250 VAA21968 Message acce
field.medicine.adelaide.edu.au       53+10:46:03 250 ok 910742814 qp 721
copper.fuller.net                    65+12:38:00 250 OAA14470 Message acce
amsat.org                             5+06:49:21 250 UAA07526 Message acce
mail.acm.org                         53+10:46:17 250 TAA25012 Message acce
extmail.bigpond.com                  11+04:06:20 250 ok
earthlink.net                        45+05:41:09 Deferred: Connection time
```

The *purgestat* command flushes the collected host data and is equivalent to invoking sendmail as:

```
# sendmail -bH
```

The statistics will continue to grow until you purge them. You might want to periodically run the *purgestat* command to make it easier to search and find recent entries, especially if you have a busy site. You could put the command into a *crontab* file so it runs automatically, or just do it yourself occasionally.

CHAPTER NINETEEN

GETTING EXIM UP AND RUNNING

This chapter gives you a quick introduction to setting up Exim and an overview of its functionality. Although Exim is largely compatible with *sendmail* in its behavior, its configuration files are completely different.

The main configuration file is usually called */etc/exim.conf* or */etc/exim/config* in most Linux distributions, or */usr/lib/exim/config* in older configurations. You can find out where the configuration file is by running the command:

```
$ exim -bP configure_file
```

You may have to edit the configuration file to reflect values specific to your site. In most common configurations there isn't a great deal to change, and a working configuration should rarely have to be modified.

By default, Exim processes and delivers all incoming mail immediately. If you have relatively high traffic, you may instead have Exim collect all messages in the so-called *queue*, and process them at regular intervals only.

When handling mail within a TCP/IP network, Exim is frequently run in daemon mode: at system boot time, it is invoked from */etc/init.d/exim** and puts itself in the background, where it waits for incoming TCP connections on the SMTP port (usually port 25). This is beneficial whenever you expect to have a significant amount of traffic because Exim doesn't have to start up for every incoming connection. Alternatively, *inetd* could manage the SMTP port and have it spawn Exim whenever there is a connection on this port. This configuration might be useful when you have limited memory and low mail traffic volumes.

Exim has a complicated set of command-line options, including many that match those of sendmail. Instead of trying to put together exactly the right options for

---

* Other possible locations are */etc/rc.d/init.d* and *rc.inet2*. The latter is common on systems using a BSD-style structure for system administration files in the */etc* directory.

your needs, you can implement the most common types of operation by invoking traditional commands like *rmail* or *rsmtp*. These are symbolic links to Exim (or if they're not, you can easily link them to it). When you run one of the commands, Exim checks the name you used to invoke it and sets the proper options itself.

There are two links to Exim that you should have under all circumstances: */usr/ bin/rmail* and */usr/sbin/sendmail.** When you compose and send a mail message with a user agent like *elm*, the message is piped to *sendmail* or *rmail* for delivery, which is why both */usr/sbin/sendmail* and */usr/bin/rmail* should point to Exim. The list of recipients for the message is passed to Exim on the command line.† The same happens with mail coming in via UUCP. You can set up the required path-names to point to Exim by typing the following at a shell prompt:

```
$ ln -s /usr/sbin/exim /usr/bin/rmail
$ ln -s /usr/sbin/exim /usr/sbin/sendmail
```

If you want to dig further into the details of configuring Exim, you should consult the full Exim specification. If this isn't included in your favorite Linux distribution, you can get it from the source to Exim, or read it online from Exim's web site at *http://www.exim.org.*

Running Exim

To run Exim, you must first decide whether you want it to handle incoming SMTP messages by running as a separate daemon, or whether to have *inetd* manage the SMTP port and invoke Exim only whenever an SMTP connection is requested from a client. Usually, you will prefer daemon operation on the mail server because it loads the machine far less than spawning Exim over and over again for each connection. As the mail server also delivers most incoming mail directly to the users, you should choose *inetd* operation on most other hosts.

Whatever mode of operation you choose for each individual host, you have to make sure you have the following entry in your */etc/services* file:

```
smtp            25/tcp          # Simple Mail Transfer Protocol
```

This defines the TCP port number that is used for SMTP conversations. Port number 25 is the standard defined by the "Assigned Numbers" RFC (RFC-1700).

---

* This is the new standard location of *sendmail* according to the Linux File System Standard. Another common location is */usr/lib/sendmail*, which is likely to be used by mail programs that are not specially configured for Linux. You can define both filenames as symbolic links to Exim so that programs and scripts invoking *sendmail* will instead invoke Exim to do the same things.

† Some user agents, however, use the SMTP protocol to pass messages to the transport agent, calling it with the *−bs* option.

When run in daemon mode, Exim puts itself in the background and waits for connections on the SMTP port. When a connection occurs, it forks, and the child process conducts an SMTP conversation with the peer process on the calling host. The Exim daemon is usually started by invoking it from the *rc* script at boot time using the following command:

```
/usr/sbin/exim -bd -q15m
```

The *—bd* flag turns on daemon mode, and *—q15m* makes it process whatever messages have accumulated in the message queue every 15 minutes.

If you want to use *inetd* instead, your */etc/inetd.conf* file should contain a line like this:

```
smtp    stream tcp nowait  root  /usr/sbin/exim  in.exim -bs
```

Remember you have to make *inetd* re-read *inetd.conf* by sending it an HUP signal after making any changes.*

Daemon and *inetd* modes are mutually exclusive. If you run Exim in daemon mode, you should make sure to comment out any line in *inetd.conf* for the smtp service. Equivalently, when having *inetd* manage Exim, make sure that no *rc* script starts the Exim daemon.

You can check that Exim is correctly set up for receiving incoming SMTP messages by telnetting to the SMTP port on your machine. This is what a successful connect to the SMTP server looks like:

```
$ telnet localhost smtp
Trying 127.0.0.1...
Connected to localhost.
Escape character is '^]'.
220 richard.vbrew.com ESMTP Exim 3.13 #1 Sun, 30 Jan 2000 16:23:55 +0600
quit
221 richard.brew.com closing connection
Connection closed by foreign host.
```

If this test doesn't produce the SMTP banner (the line starting with the 220 code), check that you are either running an Exim daemon process or have *inetd* correctly configured. If that doesn't reveal the problem, look in the Exim log files (described next) in case there is an error in Exim's configuration file.

---

* Use `kill HUP` *pid,* for which *pid* is the process ID of the *inetd* process retrieved from a *ps* listing.

If Your Mail Doesn't Get Through

A number of features are available for troubleshooting installation problems. The first place to check is Exim's log files. On Linux systems they are normally kept in */var/log/exim/log* and are named *exim_mainlog*, *exim_rejectlog*, and *exim_paniclog*. On other operating systems, they are often kept in */var/spool/exim/log*. You can find out where the log files are by running the command:

```
exim -bP log_file_path
```

The main log lists all transactions, the reject log contains details of messages that were rejected for policy reasons, and the panic log is for messages related to configuration errors and the like.

Typical entries in the main log are shown below. Each entry in the log itself is a single line of text, starting with a date and time. They have been split into several lines here in order to fit them on the page:

```
2000-01-30 15:46:37 12EwYe-0004WO-00 <= jack@vstout.vbrew.com
  H=vstout.vbrew.com [192.168.131.111] U=exim P=esmtp S=32100
  id=38690D72.286F@vstout.vbrew.com
2000-01-30 15:46:37 12EwYe-0004WO-00 => jill <jill@vbrew.com>
  D=localuser T=local_delivery
2000-01-30 15:46:37 12EwYe-0004WO-00 Completed
```

These entries show that a message from *jack@vstout.vbrew.com* to *jill@vbrew.com* was successfully delivered to a mailbox on the local host. Message arrivals are flagged with <=, and deliveries with =>.

There are two kinds of delivery errors: permanent and temporary. A permanent delivery error is recorded in a log entry like this, flagged with "**":

```
2000-01-30 14:48:28 12EvcH-0003rC-00 ** bill@lager.vbrew.com
  R=lookuphost T=smtp: SMTP error from remote mailer after RCPT TO:
  <bill@lager.vbrew.com>: host lager.vbrew.com [192.168.157.2]:
  550 <bill@lager.vbrew.com>... User unknown
```

After a failure like this, Exim sends a delivery failure report, often called a *bounce message* back to the sender.

Temporary errors are flagged with "==":

```
2000-01-30 12:50:50 12E9Un-0004Wq-00 == jim@bitter.vbrew.com
  T=smtp defer (145): Connection timed out
```

This error is typical for a situation in which Exim properly recognizes that the message should be delivered to a remote host, but is not able to connect to the SMTP service on that host. The host may be down or there could be a network problem. Whenever a message is *deferred* like this, it remains on Exim's queue and is retried at intervals. However, if it fails to be delivered for a sufficiently long time (usually several days), a permanent error occurs and the message is bounced.

If you are unable to locate your problem from the error message Exim generates, you may want to turn on debugging messages. You can do this using the *–d* flag, optionally followed by a number specifying the level of verbosity (a value of 9 gives maximum information). Exim then displays a report of its operation on the screen, which may give you more hints about what is going wrong.

Compiling Exim

Exim is still under active development; the version of Exim included in Linux distributions is probably not the latest release. If you need a feature or a bugfix found in a later release, you have to obtain a copy of the source code and compile it yourself. The latest release can be found via Exim's web page at *http://www.exim.org.*

Linux is one of the many operating systems supported by the Exim source. To compile Exim for Linux, you should edit the *src/EDITME* file and put the result in a file called *Local/Makefile.* There are comments in *src/EDITME* that tell you what the various settings are used for. Then run *make.* See the Exim manual for detailed information on building Exim from source.

Mail Delivery Modes

As noted previously, Exim is able to deliver messages immediately or queue them for later processing. All incoming mail is stored in the *input* directory below */var/ spool/exim.* When queueing is not in operation, a delivery process is started for each message as soon as it arrives. Otherwise, it is left on the queue until a *queue-runner* process picks it up. Queueing can be made unconditional by setting *queue_only* in the configuration file, or it can be conditional on the 1-minute system load by a setting such as:

```
queue_only_load = 4
```

which causes messages to be queued if the system load exceeds 4.*

If your host is not permanently connected to the Internet, you may want to turn on queueing for remote addresses, while allowing Exim to perform local deliveries immediately. You can do this by setting:

```
queue_remote_domains = *
```

in the configuration file.

---

* The system load is a standard Unix measure of the average number of processes that are queued up, waiting to run. The *uptime* shows load averages taken over the previous 1, 5, and 15 minutes.

If you turn on any form of queuing, you have to make sure the queues are checked regularly, probably every 10 or 15 minutes. Even without any explicit queueing options, the queues need to be checked for messages that have been deferred because of temporary delivery failures. If you run Exim in daemon mode, you must add the *–q15m* option on the command line to process the queue every 15 minutes. You can also invoke *exim –q* from *cron* at these intervals.

You can display the current mail queue by invoking Exim with the *–bp* option. Equivalently, you can make *mailq* a link to Exim, and invoke *mailq*:

```
$ mailq
 2h    52K 12EwGE-0005jD-00 <sam@vbrew.com>
          D bob@vbrew.com
            harry@example.net
```

This shows a single message from *sam@vbrew.com* to two recipients sitting in the message queue. It has been successfully delivered to *bob@vbrew.com*, but has not yet been delivered to *harry@example.net*, though it has been on the queue for two hours. The size of the message is 52K, and the ID by which Exim identifies this message is 12EwGE-0005jD-00. You can find out why the delivery is not yet complete by looking at the message's individual log file, which is kept in the *msglog* directory in Exim's spool directory. The *–Mvl* option is an easy way of doing this:

```
$ exim –Mvl 12EwGE-0005jD-00
2000-01-30 17:28:13 example.net [192.168.8.2]: Connection timed out
2000-01-30 17:28:13 harry@example.net: remote_smtp transport deferred:
  Connection timed out
```

Individual log files keep a copy of log entries for each message so you can easily inspect them. The same information could have been extracted from the main log file using the *exigrep* utility:

```
$ exigrep 12EwGE-0005jD-00 /var/log/exim/exim_mainlog
```

That would take longer, especially on a busy system where the log files can get quite big. The *exigrep* utility comes into its own when looking for information about more than one message. Its first argument is a regular expression, and it picks out all the log lines concerned with any messages that have at least one log line that matches the expression. Thus it can be used to pick out all messages for one specific address, or all those to or from a specific host.

You can keep a general watch on what a running Exim is doing by running *tail* on its main log file. Another way of doing this is to run the *eximon* utility that comes with Exim. This is an X11 application that puts up a scrolling display of the main log, and also shows a list of messages that are awaiting delivery, as well as some stripcharts about delivery activity.

Miscellaneous config Options

Here are a few of the more useful options you can set in the configuration file:

message_size_limit

Setting this option limits the size of message that Exim will accept.

return_size_limit

Setting this option limits the amount of an incoming message that Exim will return as part of a bounce message.

deliver_load_max

If the system load exceeds the value given for this option, all mail delivery is suspended, though messages are still accepted.

smtp_accept_max

This is the maximum number of simultaneous incoming SMTP calls Exim is prepared to accept.

log_level

This option controls the amount of material that is written to the log. There are also some options with names beginning with *log_* that control the logging of specific information.

Message Routing and Delivery

Exim splits up mail delivery into three different tasks: routing, directing, and transporting. There are a number of code modules of each type, and each is separately configurable. Usually a number of different routers, directors, and transports are set up in the configuration file.

Routers resolve remote addresses, determining which host the message should be sent to and which transport should be used. In Internet-connected hosts there is often just one router, which does the resolution by looking up the domain in the DNS. Alternatively, there may be one router that handles addresses destined for hosts on a local LAN, and a second to send any other addresses to a single *smart host*; for example, an ISP's mail server.

Local addresses are given to the directors, of which there are normally several, to handle aliasing and forwarding as well as identifying local mailboxes. Mailing lists can be handled by aliasing or forwarding directors. If an address gets aliased or forwarded, any generated addresses are handled independently by the routers or directors, as necessary. By far the most common case will be delivery to a mailbox, but messages may also be piped into a command or appended to a file other than the default mailbox.

A transport is responsible for implementing a method of delivery; for example, sending the message over an SMTP connection or adding it to a specific mailbox. Routers and directors select which transport to use for each recipient address. If a transport fails, Exim either generates a bounce message or defers the address for a later retry.

With Exim, you have a lot of freedom in configuring these tasks. For each of them, a number of drivers are available, from which you can choose those you need. You describe them to Exim in different sections of its configuration file. The transports are defined first, followed by the directors, and then the routers. There are no built-in defaults, though Exim is distributed with a default configuration file that covers simple cases. If you want to change Exim's routing policy or modify a transport, it is easiest to start from the default configuration and make changes rather than attempt to set up a complete configuration from scratch.

Routing Messages

When given an address to deliver, Exim first checks whether the domain is one that is handled on the local host by matching it against a list in the `local_domains` configuration variable. If this option is not set, the local host name is used as the only local domain. If the domain is local, the address is handed to the directors. Otherwise, it is handed to the routers to find out which host to forward a message to.*

Delivering Messages to Local Addresses

Most commonly, a local address is just a user's login name, in which case the message is delivered to the user's mailbox, */var/spool/mail/user-name*. Other cases include aliases, mailing list names, and mail forwarding by the user. In these cases, the local address expands to a new list of addresses, which may be either local or remote.

Apart from these "normal" addresses, Exim can handle other types of local message destinations, like filenames and pipe commands. When delivering to a file, Exim appends the message, creating the file if necessary. File and pipe destinations are not addresses in their own right, so you can't send mail to, say, */etc/passwd@vbrew.com* and expect to overwrite the password file; deliveries to a specific file are valid only if they come from forwarding or alias files. Note, however, that */etc/passwd@vbrew.com* is a syntactically valid email address, but if Exim received it, it would (typically) search for a user whose login name was */etc/passwd*, fail to find one, and bounce the message.

---

* This is a simplification. It is possible for directors to pass addresses to transports that deliver to remote hosts, and similarly, it is possible for routers to pass addresses to local transports that write the messsage to a file or a pipe. It is also possible for routers to pass addresses to the directors in some circumstances.

In an alias list or forwarding file, a *filename* is anything that begins with a slash (/) that does not parse as a fully qualified email address. For example, */tmp/junk* in a forwarding or alias file is interpreted as a file name, but */tmp/junk@vbrew.com* is an email address, though it is not likely to be a very useful one. However, valid addresses of this type are seen when sending mail through X.400 gateways, because X.400 addresses start with a slash.

Similarly, a *pipe command* may be any Unix command preceded by the pipe symbol (|), unless the string parses as a valid email address complete with domain. Unless you have changed the configuration, Exim does not use a shell to run the command; instead, it splits it up into a command name, arguments itself, and runs it directly. The message is fed to the command on its standard input.

For example, to gate a mailing list into a local newsgroup, you might use a shell script named *gateit,* and set up a local alias that delivers all messages from this mailing list to the script using `|gateit`. If the command line contains a comma, it and the preceding pipe symbol must be enclosed in double quotes.

Local users

A local address most commonly denotes a user's mailbox. This is normally located in */var/spool/mail* and has the name of the user, who also owns the file. If it does not exist, it is created by Exim.

In some configurations, the group is set to the user's group and the mode is 0600. In these cases, delivery processes are run as the user, and the user may delete the mailbox entirely. In other configurations, the mailbox's group is **mail**, and it has mode 660; delivery processes are run under a system uid and group **mail**, and users cannot delete their mailbox files, though they can empty them.

Note that although */var/spool/mail* is currently the standard place to put the mailbox files, some mail software may be compiled to use different paths, for example, */usr/spool/mail.* If delivery to users on your machine fails consistently, you should see if it helps to make this a symbolic link to */var/spool/mail.*

The addresses **MAILER-DAEMON** and **postmaster** should normally appear in your alias file, expanding into the email address of the system administrator. **MAILER-DAEMON** is used by Exim as the sender address in bounce messages. It is also recommended that **root** be set up as an alias for an administrator, especially when deliveries are being run under the permissions of the recipient users, in order to avoid running any delivery as **root**.

Forwarding

Users can redirect their mail to alternative addresses by creating a *.forward* file in their home directories. This contains a list of recipients separated by commas and/or newlines. All lines of the file are read and interpreted. Any type of address may be used. A practical example of a *.forward* file for vacations might be:

```
janet, "|vacation"
```

In other descriptions of *.forward* files, you might see the username at the start preceded by a backslash. This was necessary in some older MTAs to stop a search for a *forward* for the new name, which could lead to looping. The backslash is not necessary in Exim, which automatically avoids loops of this kind.* However, a backslash is permitted, and in fact it does make a difference in configurations where several domains are being handled at once. Without a backslash, an unqualified username is qualified with a default domain; with a backslash the incoming domain is preserved.

The first address in the forward file delivers the incoming message to **janet**'s mailbox, while the *vacation* command returns a short notification to the sender.†

In addition to supporting "traditional" forwarding files, Exim can be configured to allow more complex files called *filters*. Instead of being just a list of forwarding addresses, a filter file can contain tests on the contents of the incoming message so that, for example, messages could be forwarded only if the subject contained the message "urgent." The system administrator must decide whether to allow users this flexibility.

Alias Files

Exim is able to handle alias files compatible with Berkeley's *sendmail* alias files. Entries in the alias file can have the following form:

```
alias: recipients
```

`recipients` is a comma-separated list of addresses that will be substituted for the alias. The recipient list may be continued across newlines if the next line begins with whitespace.

A special feature allows Exim to handle mailing lists that are held separately from the alias file: if you specify `:include:`*filename* as a recipient, Exim reads the specified file and substitutes its contents as a list of recipients. An alternative to handling mailing lists is shown later in this chapter in "Mailing Lists."

The main aliases file is */etc/aliases*. If you make this file world-writable or group-writeable, Exim will refuse to use it and will defer local deliveries. You can control the test it applies to the file's permissions by setting *modemask* in the *system_aliases* director.

---

* A director is skipped if the address it is about to process is one that it has previously processed in the course of generating the present address.

† Please, if you choose to use a vacation program, make sure it will not reply to messages sent from mailing lists! It is very annoying to discover that someone has gone on vacation and find a vacation message for every message they've received. Mailing list administrators: this is a good example of why it is bad practice to force the `Reply-To:` field of mailing list messages to that of the list submission address.

This is a sample *aliases* file:

```
# vbrew.com /etc/aliases file
hostmaster: janet
postmaster: janet
usenet: phil
# The development mailing list.
development: joe, sue, mark, biff,
        /var/mail/log/development
owner-development: joe
# Announcements of general interest are mailed to all
# of the staff
announce: :include: /etc/Exim/staff,
        /var/mail/log/announce
owner-announce: root
# gate the ppp mailing list to a local newsgroup
ppp-list: "|/usr/local/bin/gateit local.lists.ppp"
```

When there are file names and pipe commands in an alias file, as here, Exim needs to be told which userid to run the deliveries under. The *user* option (and possibly *group*, too) must be set in Exim's configuration file, either on the director that is handling the aliases, or on the transports to which it directs these items.

If an error occurs while delivering to an address generated from the *aliases* file, Exim will send a bounce message to the sender of the message, as usual, but this might not be appropriate. The *errors_to* option can be used to specify that bounce messages are to be sent elsewhere; for example, to the postmaster.

Mailing Lists

Instead of the *aliases* file, mailing lists may also be managed by means a *forward-file* director. The lists are all kept in a single directory such as */etc/exim/lists/*, and a mailing list named `nag-bugs` is described by the file *lists/nag-bugs*. This should contain the members' addresses separated by commas or newlines. Lines beginning with a hash sign (#) are treated as comments. A simple director to use such data is as follows:

```
lists:
  driver = forwardfile
  file = /etc/exim/lists/${local_part}
  no_check_local_user
  errors_to = ${local_part}-request
```

When this director runs, the values of the *file* and *errors_to* options are *expanded*. Expansion causes certain portions of the strings beginning with dollar characters to be replaced every time the string is used. The simplest kind of expansion is the insertion of the value of one of Exim's variables, and this is what is happening here. The substring `${local_part}` substitutes the value of the `$local_part`, which is the local part of the address that is being processed.

For each mailing list, a user (or alias or mailing list) named `listname-request` should exist; any errors occurring when resolving an address or delivering to a list member are reported to this address.

Protecting Against Mail Spam

Mail spam, or unsolicited email advertising, is an annoying problem for many users. A project has been formed to address this problem called the Mail Abuse Protection System (MAPS), and a mechanism has been built that reduces the problem, called the Real Time Blackhole List (RBL). Information on how the MAPS RBL works can be obtained from its online documentation at *http://maps.vix.com/rbl/*. The idea is simple. Sites that are caught generating mail spam are added into the database and mail transfer agents like Exim are able to query the database to confirm that a source is not a spammer before accepting mail from it.

Since the advent of the RBL, several other similar lists have been created. One of the most useful is the Dial-Up List (DUL), which lists the IP addresses of dial-up hosts. These should normally send outgoing mail only to their ISP's mail servers. Many sites block mail from external dial-ups because when such a host avoids its own ISP's server, it is usually up to no good.

Exim provides support for the real-time and other blacklists. It is very easily configured. To enable it, add the following lines to your */etc/exim.conf* file:

```
# Vixie / MAPS RBL (http://maps.vix.com/rbl)
rbl_domains = rbl.maps.vix.com : dul.maps.vix.com
```

This example checks both the RBL and the DUL, rejecting any messages from hosts that are on either list. The *rbl_hosts* option allows you to specify groups of hosts to which RBL checking does (or does not) apply. The default setting is:

```
rbl_hosts = *
```

which means that all hosts are subject to RBL checking. If you wanted to override blacklisting and accept mail from a specific host without performing the RBL checking you could, for example, use:

```
rbl_hosts = ! nocheck.example.com : *
```

The exclamation mark before the first item in this list indicates a negated item: if the calling host is *nocheck.example.com,* it will match this item. But because of the negation, RBL checking is not performed. Any other host matches the second item in the list.

UUCP Setup

Exim does not have any specific code for transporting mail via UUCP, nor does it support UUCP bang path addresses. However, if domain addressing is being used, Exim can be interfaced to UUCP fairly simply. Here is a configuration fragment for sending certain domains to UUCP, taken from a real installation:

```
# Transport
uucp:
  driver = pipe
  user = nobody
  command = "/usr/local/bin/uux -r - \
    ${substr_-5:$host}!rmail ${local_part}"
  return_fail_output = true

# Router
uucphost:
  transport = uucp
  driver = domainlist
  route_file = /usr/exim/uucphosts
  search_type = lsearch
```

In a complete configuration file, the transport would be inserted among the other transports, and the router probably defined as the first router. The file */usr/exim/ uucphosts* contains entries like this:

```
darksite.example.com:          darksite.UUCP
```

which is interpreted to mean, "Send mail addressed to the domain **darksite.example.com** to the UUCP host **darksite**." This configuration could be set up more simply without the router adding the suffix .UUCP to **darksite** only to have the transport take it off again, but this way is useful because it makes clear the distinction between the domain name **darksite.example.com** and the UUCP host name **darksite**.

Whenever the router comes across a domain that is in the route file, it will send the address to the UUCP transport, which subsequently pipes it to the *uux* command (described in Chapter 16, *Managing Taylor UUCP*). If there is a problem, *uux* will generate some output and terminate with a non-zero error code. The setting of `return_fail_output` makes sure that the output is returned to the sender.

If incoming UUCP messages are grouped into files in batched SMTP format, they can be passed directly to Exim using a command like this:

```
exim -bS </var/uucp/incoming/001
```

However, there is one catch. When Exim receives a message locally, it insists that the sender is the logged-in user that calls it, but for a UUCP batch we want the senders to be taken from the incoming messages. Exim will do this if the process that calls it is running as a *trusted user*. If you arrange for incoming UUCP to be handled by a user called **uucp**, for example, you need to specify:

```
trusted_users = uucp
```

in the Exim configuration file to ensure that sender addresses are correctly handled.

## CHAPTER TWENTY

NETNEWS

Netnews, or Usenet news, remains one of the most important and highly valued services on computer networks today. Dismissed by some as a mire of unsolicited commercial email and pornography, Netnews still maintains several cases of the high-quality discussion groups that made it a critical resource in pre-web days. Even in these times of a billion web pages, Netnews is still a source for online help and community on many topics.

Usenet History

The idea of network news was born in 1979 when two graduate students, Tom Truscott and Jim Ellis, thought of using UUCP to connect machines for information exchange among Unix users. They set up a small network of three machines in North Carolina.

Initially, traffic was handled by a number of shell scripts (later rewritten in C), but they were never released to the public. They were quickly replaced by "A News," the first public release of news software.

A News was not designed to handle more than a few articles per group and day. When the volume continued to grow, it was rewritten by Mark Horton and Matt Glickman, who called it the "B" release (a.k.a. B News). The first public release of B News was version 2.1 in 1982. It was expanded continuously, with several new features added. Its current version is B News 2.11. It is slowly becoming obsolete; its last official maintainer switched to INN.

Geoff Collyer and Henry Spencer rewrote B News and released it in 1987; this is release "C," or C News. Since its release, there have been a number of patches to C News, the most prominent being the C News Performance Release. On sites that carry a large number of groups, the overhead involved in frequently invoking *relaynews*, which is responsible for dispatching incoming articles to other hosts, is significant. The Performance Release adds an option to *relaynews* that allows it to run in *daemon mode*, through which the program puts itself in the background. The Performance Release is the C News version currently included in most Linux releases. We describe C News in detail in Chapter 21, *C News*.

All news releases up to C were primarily targeted for UUCP networks, although they could be used in other environments, as well. Efficient news transfer over networks like TCP/IP or DECNet required a new scheme. So in 1986, the *Network News Transfer Protocol* (NNTP) was introduced. It is based on network connections and specifies a number of commands to interactively transfer and retrieve articles.

There are a number of NNTP-based applications available from the Net. One of them is the *nntpd* package by Brian Barber and Phil Lapsley, which you can use to provide newsreading service to a number of hosts inside a local network. *nntpd* was designed to complement news packages, such as B News or C News, to give them NNTP features. If you want to use NNTP with the C News server, you should read Chapter 22, *NNTP and the nntpd Daemon*, which explains how to configure the *nntpd* daemon and run it with C News.

An alternative package supporting NNTP is INN, or *Internet News*. It is not just a frontend, but a news system in its own right. It comprises a sophisticated news relay daemon that can maintain several concurrent NNTP links efficiently, and is therefore the news server of choice for many Internet sites. We discuss it in detail in Chapter 23, *Internet News*.

What Is Usenet, Anyway?

One of the most astounding facts about Usenet is that it isn't part of any organization, nor does it have any sort of centralized network management authority. In fact, it's part of Usenet lore that except for a technical description, you cannot define *what* it is; at the risk of sounding stupid, one might define Usenet as a collaboration of separate sites that exchange Usenet news. To be a Usenet site, all you have to do is find another Usenet site and strike an agreement with its owners and maintainers to exchange news with you. Providing another site with news is called *feeding* it, whence another common axiom of Usenet philosophy originates: "Get a feed, and you're on it."

The basic unit of Usenet news is the *article*. This is a message a user writes and "posts" to the net. In order to enable news systems to deal with it, it is prepended with administrative information, the so-called article header. It is very similar to the mail header format laid down in the Internet mail standard RFC-822, in that it consists of several lines of text, each beginning with a field name terminated by a colon, which is followed by the field's value.*

Articles are submitted to one or more *newsgroup*. One may consider a newsgroup a forum for articles relating to a common topic. All newsgroups are organized in a hierarchy, with each group's name indicating its place in the hierarchy. This often makes it easy to see what a group is all about. For example, anybody can see from the newsgroup name that *comp.os.linux.announce* is used for announcements concerning a computer operating system named Linux.

These articles are then exchanged between all Usenet sites that are willing to carry news from this group. When two sites agree to exchange news, they are free to exchange whatever newsgroups they like, and may even add their own local news hierarchies. For example, **groucho.edu** might have a news link to **barnyard.edu**, which is a major news feed, and several links to minor sites which it feeds news. Now Barnyard College might receive all Usenet groups, while GMU only wants to carry a few major hierarchies like *sci, comp,* or *rec.* Some of the downstream sites, say a UUCP site called **brewhq**, will want to carry even fewer groups, because they don't have the network or hardware resources. On the other hand, **brewhq** might want to receive newsgroups from the *fj* hierarchy, which GMU doesn't carry. It therefore maintains another link with **gargleblaster.com**, which carries all *fj* groups and feeds them to **brewhq**. The news flow is shown in Figure 20-1.

The labels on the arrows originating from **brewhq** may require some explanation, though. By default, it wants all locally generated news to be sent to **groucho.edu**. However, as **groucho.edu** does not carry the *fj* groups, there's no point in sending it any messages from those groups. Therefore, the feed from **brewhq** to GMU is labeled `all,!fj`, meaning that all groups except those below *fj* are sent to it.

How Does Usenet Handle News?

Today, Usenet has grown to enormous proportions. Sites that carry the whole of Netnews usually transfer something like a paltry 60 MB a day.‡ Of course, this requires much more than pushing files around. So let's take a look at the way most Unix systems handle Usenet news.

News begins when users create and post articles. Each user enters a message into a special application called a newsreader, which formats it appropriately for transmission to the local news server. In Unix environments the newsreader commonly uses the *inews* command to transmit articles to the newsserver using the TCP/IP protocol. But it's also possible to write the article directly into a file in a special

---

* The format of Usenet news messages is specified in RFC-1036, "Standard for interchange of USENET messages."

‡ Wait a minute: 60 Megs at 9,600 bps, that's 60 million multiplied by 1,024, that is... mutter, mutter... Hey! That's 34 hours!

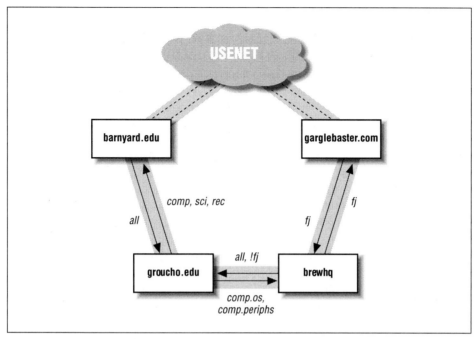

Figure 20-1. Usenet newsflow through Groucho Marx University

directory called the news spool. Once the posting is delivered to the local news server, it takes responsibility for delivering the article to other news users.

News is distributed through the net by various transports. The medium used to be UUCP, but today the main traffic is carried by Internet sites. The routing algorithm used is called *flooding.* Each site maintains a number of links (*news feeds*) to other sites. Any article generated or received by the local news system is forwarded to them, unless it has already been at that site, in which case it is discarded. A site may find out about all other sites the article has already traversed by looking at the `Path:` header field. This header contains a list of all systems through which the article has been forwarded in bang path notation.

To distinguish articles and recognize duplicates, Usenet articles have to carry a message ID (specified in the `Message-Id:` header field), which combines the posting site's name and a serial number into `<serial@site>`. For each article processed, the news system logs this ID into a *history* file, against which all newly arrived articles are checked.

The flow between any two sites may be limited by two criteria. For one, an article is assigned a distribution (in the `Distribution:` header field), which may be used to confine it to a certain group of sites. On the other hand, the newsgroups exchanged may be limited by both the sending and receiving systems. The set of newsgroups and distributions allowed to be transmitted to a site are usually kept in the *sys* file.

The sheer number of articles usually requires that improvements be made to the above scheme. On UUCP networks, systems collect articles over a period of time and combine them into a single file, which is compressed and sent to the remote site. This is called *batching*.

An alternative technique is the *ihave/sendme* protocol that prevents duplicate articles from being transferred, thus saving net bandwidth. Instead of putting all articles in batch files and sending them along, only the message IDs of articles are combined into a giant "ihave" message and sent to the remote site. The remote site reads this message, compares it to its history file, and returns the list of articles it wants in a "sendme" message. Only the requested articles are sent.

Of course, ihave/sendme makes sense only if it involves two big sites that receive news from several independent feeds each, and that poll each other often enough for an efficient flow of news.

Sites that are on the Internet generally rely on TCP/IP-based software that uses the Network News Transfer Protocol (NNTP). NNTP is described in RFC-977; it is responsible for the transfer of news between news servers and provides Usenet access to single users on remote hosts.

NNTP knows three different ways to transfer news. One is a real-time version of ihave/sendme, also referred to as *pushing* news. The second technique is called *pulling* news, in which the client requests a list of articles in a given newsgroup or hierarchy that have arrived at the server's site after a specified date, and chooses those it cannot find in its history file. The third technique is for interactive news-reading and allows you or your newsreader to retrieve articles from specified new-groups, as well as post articles with incomplete header information.

At each site, news is kept in a directory hierarchy below */var/spool/news*, each article in a separate file, and each newsgroup in a separate directory. The directory name is made up of the newsgroup name, with the components being the path components. Thus, *comp.os.linux.misc* articles are kept in */var/spool/news/comp/ os/linux/misc*. The articles in a newsgroup are assigned numbers in the order they arrive. This number serves as the file's name. The range of numbers of articles currently online is kept in a file called *active*, which at the same time serves as a list of newsgroups your site knows.

Since disk space is a finite resource, you have to start throwing away articles after some time.* This is called *expiring*. Usually, articles from certain groups and hierarchies are expired at a fixed number of days after they arrive. This may be overridden by the poster by specifying a date of expiration in the `Expires:` field of the article header.

You now have enough information to choose what to read next. UUCP users should read about C-News in Chapter 21. If you're using a TCP/IP network, read about NNTP in Chapter 22. If you need to transfer moderate amounts of news over TCP/IP, the server described in that chapter may be enough for you. To install a heavy-duty news server that can handle huge volumes of material, go on to read about InterNet News in Chapter 23.

---

* Some people claim that Usenet is a conspiracy by modem and hard disk vendors.

CHAPTER TWENTY-ONE

C NEWS

One of the most popular software packages for Netnews is C News. It was designed for sites that carry news over UUCP links. This chapter will discuss the central concepts of C News, basic installation, and maintenance tasks.

C News stores its configuration files in */etc/news*, and most of its binaries are kept below the */usr/lib/news/* directory. Articles are kept below */var/spool/news*. You should make sure that virtually all files in these directories are owned by user **news** or group **news**. Most problems arise from files being inaccessible to C News. Use *su* to become the user **news** before you touch anything in the directory. The only exception is the *setnewsids* command, which is used to set the real user ID of some news programs. It must be owned by **root** and have the setuid bit set.

In this chapter, we describe all C News configuration files in detail and show you what you have to do to keep your site running.

Delivering News

Articles can be fed to C News in several ways. When a local user posts an article, the newsreader usually hands it to the *inews* command, which completes the header information. News from remote sites, be it a single article or a whole batch, is given to the *rnews* command, which stores it in the */var/spool/news/in.coming* directory, from where it will be picked up at a later time by *newsrun*. With any of these two techniques, however, the article will eventually be handed to the *relaynews* command.

For each article, the *relaynews* command first checks if the article has already been seen at the local site by looking up the message ID in the *history* file. Duplicate articles are dropped. Then *relaynews* looks at the `Newsgroups:` header line to find out if the local site requests articles from any of these groups. If it does, and the newsgroup is listed in the *active* file, *relaynews* tries to store the article in the corresponding directory in the news spool area. If this directory does not exist, it is created. The article's message ID is then logged to the *history* file. Otherwise, *relaynews* drops the article.

Sometimes *relaynews* fails to store an incoming article because a group to which it has been posted is not listed in your *active* file. In this case, the article is moved to the *junk* group.* *relaynews* also checks for stale or misdated articles and reject them. Incoming batches that fail for any other reason are moved to */var/spool/news/in.coming/bad*, and an error message is logged.

After this, the article is relayed to all other sites that request news from these groups, using the transport specified for each particular site. To make sure an article isn't sent to a site that has already seen it, each destination site is checked against the article's `Path:` header field, which contains the list of sites the article has traversed so far, written in the UUCP-style bang-path source-routing style described in Chapter 17, *Electronic Mail*. If the destination site's name does not appear in this list, the article is sent to it.

C News is commonly used to relay news between UUCP sites, although it is also possible to use it in an NNTP environment. To deliver news to a remote UUCP site, either in single articles or whole batches, *uux* is used to execute the *rnews* command on the remote site and feed the article or batch to it on standard input. Refer to Chapter 16, *Managing Taylor UUCP*, for more information on UUCP.

Batching is the term used to describe sending large bundles of individual articles all in one transmission. When batching is enabled for a given site, C News does not send any incoming article immediately; instead, it appends its path name to a file, usually called *out.going/site/togo*. Periodically, a program is executed from a *crontab* entry by the *cron* program, which reads this file and bundles all of the listed articles into one or more file, optionally compressing them and sending them to *rnews* at the remote site.†

Figure 21-1 shows the news flow through *relaynews*. Articles may be relayed to the local site (denoted by `ME`), to a site named **ponderosa** via email, and a site named **moria**, for which batching is enabled.

---

* There may be a difference between the groups that exist at your site and those that your site is willing to receive. For example, the subscription list might specify *comp.all*, which should send all newsgroups below the *comp* hierarchy, but at your site you might not list several of the *comp* newsgroups in the *active* file. Articles posted to those groups will be moved to *junk*.

† Note that this should be the *crontab* of **news**; file permissions will not be mangled.

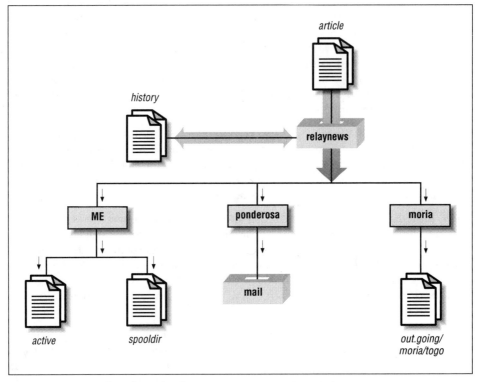

Figure 21-1. News flow through relaynews

Installation

C News should be available in a prepackaged format for any modern Linux distribution, so installation will be easy. If not, or if you want to install from the original source distribution, then of course you can.* No matter how you install it, you will need to edit the C News configuration files. Their formats are described in the following list:

sys The *sys* file controls which newsgroups your site receives and forwards. We discuss it in detail in the following section.

active
> Not usually edited by the administration; contains directions for handling articles in each newsgroup the site handles.

---

* You can obtain the C News source distribution from its home site at **ftp.cs.toronto.edu** */pub/c-news/c-news.tar.Z*

organization

This file should contain your organization's name, for example, "Virtual Brewery, Inc." On your home machine, enter "private site," or anything else you like. Most people will not consider your site properly configured if you haven't customized this file.

newsgroups

This file is a list of all newsgroups, with a one-line description of each one's purpose. These descriptions are frequently used by your newsreader when displaying the list of all groups to which you are subscribed.

mailname

Your site's mail name, e.g., **vbrew.com**.

whoami

Your site's name for news purposes. Quite often, the UUCP site name is used, e.g., **vbrew**.

explist

You should probably edit this file to reflect your preferred expiration times for special newsgroups. Disk space may play an important role in your choices.

To create an initial hierarchy of newsgroups, obtain *active* and *newsgroups* files from the site that feeds you. Install them in */etc/news*, making sure they are owned by **news** and have a mode of 644, using the *chmod* command. Remove all *to.** groups from the active file, and add *to.my-site*, *to.feed-site*, *junk*, and *control*. The *to.** groups are normally used for exchanging ihave/sendme messages, but you should list them regardless of whether you plan to use ihave/sendme or not. Next, replace all article numbers in the second and third field of *active* using the following commands:

```
# cp active active.old
# sed 's/ [0-9]* [0-9]* / 0000000000 00001 /' active.old > active
# rm active.old
```

The second command invokes the *sed* stream editor. This invocation replaces two strings of digits with a string of zeroes and the string 000001, respectively.

Finally, create the news spool directory and the subdirectories used for incoming and outgoing news:

```
# cd /var/spool
# mkdir news news/in.coming news/out.going news/out.master
# chown -R news.news news
# chmod -R 755 news
```

If you're using precompiled newsreaders sourced from a different distribution to the C News server you have running, you may find that some expect the news spool in */usr/spool/news* rather than */var/spool/news*. If your newsreader doesn't seem to find any articles, create a symbolic link from */usr/spool/news* to */var/spool/ news* like this:

```
# ln -sf /usr/spool/news /var/spool/news
```

Now you are ready to receive news. Note that you don't have to create the individual newsgroup spool directories. C News automatically creates spool directories for any newsgroup it receives an article for, if one doesn't already exist.

In particular, this happens to *all* groups to which an article has been cross-posted. So, after a while, you will find your news spool cluttered with directories for newsgroups you have never subscribed to, like *alt.lang.teco*. You may prevent this by either removing all unwanted groups from *active*, or by regularly running a shell script that removes all empty directories below */var/spool/news* (except *out.going* and *in.coming*, of course).

C News needs a user to send error messages and status reports to. By default, this is **usenet**. If you use the default, you have to set up an alias for it that forwards all of its mail to one or more responsible person. You may also override this behavior by setting the environment variable `NEWSMASTER` to the appropriate name. You have to do so in **news**'s *crontab* file, as well as every time you invoke an administrative tool manually, so installing an alias is probably easier. Mail aliases are described in Chapter 18, *Sendmail*, and Chapter 19, *Getting Exim Up and Running*.

While you're hacking */etc/passwd*, make sure that every user has her real name in the `pw_gecos` field of the password file (this is the fourth field). It is a question of Usenet netiquette that the sender's real name appears in the `From:` field of the article. Of course, you will want to do so anyway when you use mail.

The sys File

The *sys* file, located in */etc/news*, controls which hierarchies you receive and forward to other sites. Although there are maintenance tools named *addfeed* and *delfeed*, we think it's better to maintain this file by hand.

The *sys* file contains entries for each site to which you forward news, as well as a description of the groups you will accept. The first line is a `ME` entry that describes your system. It's a safe bet to use the following:

```
ME:all/all::
```

You also have to add a line for each site to which you feed news. Each line looks like this:

```
site[/exclusions]:grouplist[/distlist][:flags[:cmds]]
```

Entries may be continued across newlines using a backslash (\) at the end of the line to be continued. A hash sign (#) denotes a comment.

site

> This is the name of the site the entry applies to. One usually chooses the site's UUCP name for this. There has to be an entry for your site in the *sys* file too, or you will not receive any articles yourself.
>
> The special site name ME denotes your site. The ME entry defines all groups you are willing to store locally. Articles that aren't matched by the ME line will go to the *junk* group.
>
> C News rejects any articles that have already passed through this site to prevent loops. C News does this by ensuring that the local site name does not appear in the Path: of the article. Some sites may be known by a number of valid names. For example, some sites use their fully qualified domain name in this field, or an alias like `news.site.domain`. To ensure the loop prevention mechanism works, it is important to add all aliases to the exclusion list, separating them by commas.
>
> For the entry applying to site **moria**, for instance, the *site* field would contain `moria/moria.orcnet.org`. If **moria** were also by an alias of **news.orcnet.org**, then our *site* field would contain `moria/moria.orcnet.org,news.orcnet.org`.

grouplist

> This is a comma-separated subscription list of groups and hierarchies for this particular site. A hierarchy may be specified by giving the hierarchy's prefix (such as *comp.os* for all groups whose names start with this prefix), optionally followed by the keyword *all* (e.g., *comp.os.all*).
>
> You can exclude a hierarchy or group from forwarding by preceding it with an exclamation mark. If a newsgroup is checked against the list, the longest match applies. For example, if *grouplist* contains this list:
>
> `!comp,comp.os.linux,comp.folklore.computers`
>
> no groups from the *comp* hierarchy except *comp.folklore.computers* and all groups below *comp.os.linux* will be fed to that site.
>
> If the site requests to be forwarded all news you receive yourself, enter all as *grouplist*.

distlist

> This value is offset from the *grouplist* by a slash and contains a list of distributions to be forwarded. Again, you may exclude certain distributions by preceding them with an exclamation mark. All distributions are denoted by all. Omitting *distlist* implies a list of all.
>
> For example, you may use a distribution list of all, !local to prevent news meant only for local use from being sent to remote sites.
>
> There are usually at least two distributions: world, which is often the default distribution used when none is specified by the user, and local. There may

be other distributions that apply to a certain region, state, country, etc. Finally, there are two distributions used by C News only; these are `sendme` and `ihave`, and are used for the sendme/ihave protocol.

The use of distributions is a subject of debate. The distribution field in a news article can be created arbitrarily, but for a distribution to be effective, the news servers in the network must know it. Some misbehaving newsreaders create bogus distributions by simply assuming the top-level newsgroup hierarchy of the article destination is a reasonable distribution. For example, one might assume *comp* to be a reasonable distribution to use when posting to the *comp.os.linux.networking* newsgroup. Distributions that apply to regions are often questionable, too, because news may travel outside of your region when sent across the Internet.* Distributions applying to an organization, however, are very meaningful; e.g., to prevent confidential information from leaving the company network. This purpose, however, is generally served better by creating a separate newsgroup or hierarchy.

flags

This option describes certain parameters for the feed. It may be empty or a combination of the following:

F   This flag enables batching.

f   This is almost identical to the F flag, but allows C News to calculate the size of outgoing batches more precisely, and should probably be used in preference.

I   This flag makes C News produce an article list suitable for use by ihave/sendme. Additional modifications to the *sys* and the *batchparms* file are required to enable ihave/sendme.

n   This creates batch files for active NNTP transfer clients like *nntpxmit* (see Chapter 22, *NNTP and the nntpd Daemon*). The batch files contain the article's filename along with its message ID.

L   This tells C News to transmit only articles posted at your site. This flag may be followed by a decimal number *n*, which makes C News transfer articles posted only within *n* hops from your site. C News determines the number of hops from the `Path:` field.

u   This tells C News to batch only articles from unmoderated groups.

m   This tells C News to batch only articles from moderated groups.

You may use at most one of F, f, I, or n.

_____

* It is not uncommon for an article posted in say, Hamburg, to go to Frankfurt via **reston.ans.net** in the Netherlands, or even via some site in the U.S.

cmds

> This field contains a command that will be executed for each article, unless you enable batching. The article will be fed to the command on standard input. This should be used for very small feed only; otherwise, the load on both systems will be too high.
>
> The default command is:
>
> ```
> uux - -r -z remote-system!rnews
> ```
>
> This invokes *rnews* on the remote system, feeding it the article on standard input.
>
> The default search path for commands given in this field is */bin:/usr/bin:/usr/lib/news/batch*. The latter directory contains a number of shell scripts whose names start with *via*; they are briefly described later in this chapter.
>
> If batching is enabled using one of the F, f, I, or n flags, C News expects to find a filename in this field rather than a command. If the filename does not begin with a slash (/), it is assumed to be relative to */var/spool/news/out.going*. If the field is empty, it defaults to *remote-system/togo*. The file is expected to be in the same format as the *remote-system/togo* file and contain a list of articles to transmit.

When setting up C News, you will most probably have to write your own *sys* file. Here is a sample file for **vbrew.com**, from which you may copy what you need:

```
# We take whatever they give us.
ME:all/all::
# We send everything we receive to moria, except for local and
# brewery-related articles. We use batching.
moria/moria.orcnet.org:all,!to,to.moria/all,!local,!brewery:f:
# We mail comp.risks to jack@ponderosa.uucp
ponderosa:comp.risks/all::rmail jack@ponderosa.uucp
# swim gets a minor feed
swim/swim.twobirds.com:comp.os.linux,rec.humor.oracle/all,!local:f:
# Log mail map articles for later processing
usenet-maps:comp.mail.maps/all:F:/var/spool/uumaps/work/batch
```

The active File

The *active* file is located in */etc/*, and lists all groups known at your site and the articles currently online. You will rarely have to touch it, but we explain it nevertheless for sake of completion. Entries take the following form:

newsgroup high low perm

newsgroup is the group's name. *low* and *high* are the lowest and highest numbers of articles currently available. If none are available at the moment, *low* is equal to *high*+1.

At least that's what the *low* field is meant to do. However, for efficiency, C News doesn't update this field. This wouldn't be such a big loss if there weren't news-readers that depend on it. For instance, *trn* checks this field to see if it can purge any articles from its thread database. To update the *low* field, you therefore have to run the *updatemin* command regularly (or, in earlier versions of C News, the *upact* script).

`perm` is a parameter detailing the access users are granted to the group. It takes one of the following values:

y   Users are allowed to post to this group.

n   Users are not allowed to post to this group. However, the group may still be read.

x   This group has been disabled locally. This happens sometimes when news administrators (or their superiors) take offense at articles posted to certain groups.

   Articles received for this group are not stored locally, although they are forwarded to the sites that request them.

m   This denotes a moderated group. When a user tries to post to this group, an intelligent newsreader notifies her of this and send the article to the moderator instead. The moderator's address is taken from the *moderators* file in */var/lib/ news*.

`=real-group`
   This marks `newsgroup` as being a local alias for another group, namely `real-group`. All articles posted to `newsgroup` will be redirected to it.

In C News, you will generally not have to access this file directly. Groups can be added or deleted locally using *addgroup* and *delgroup* (see the section "Maintenance Tools and Tasks" later in this chapter). A `newgroup` control message adds a group for the whole of Usenet, while a `rmgroup` message deletes a group. *Never send such a message yourself!* For instructions on how to create a newsgroup, read the monthly postings in *news.announce.newusers*.

The *active.times* file is closely related to the *active* file. Whenever a group is created, C News logs a message to this file containing the name of the group created, the date of creation, whether it was done by a `newgroup` control message or locally, and who did it. This is convenient for newsreaders that may notify the user of any recently created groups. It is also used by the *NEWGROUPS* command of NNTP.

Article Batching

News batches follow a particular format that is the same for B News, C News, and INN. Each article is preceded by a line like this:

```
#! rnews count
```

`count` is the number of bytes in the article. When you use batch compression, the resulting file is compressed as a whole and preceded by another line, indicated by the message to be used for unpacking. The standard compression tool is *compress*, which is marked by:

```
#! cunbatch
```

Sometimes, when the news server sends batches via mail software that removes the eighth bit from all data, a compressed batch may be protected using what is called *c7-encoding*; these batches will be marked by *c7unbatch*.

When a batch is fed to *rnews* on the remote site, it checks for these markers and processes the batch appropriately. Some sites also use other compression tools, like *gzip*, and precede their gzipped files with the word *zunbatch* instead. C News does not recognize nonstandard headers like these; you have to modify the source to support them.

In C News, article batching is performed by */usr/lib/news/batch/sendbatches*, which takes a list of articles from the *site/togo* file and puts them into several newsbatches. It should be executed once per hour, or even more frequently, depending on the volume of traffic. Its operation is controlled by the *batchparms* file in */var/lib/news*. This file describes the maximum batch size allowed for each site, the batching and optional compression program to be used, and the transport for delivering it to the remote site. You may specify batching parameters on a per-site basis, as well as a set of default parameters for sites not explicitly mentioned.

When installing C News, you will most likely find a *batchparms* file in your distribution that contains a reasonable default entry, so there's a good chance that you won't have to touch the file. Just in case, we describe its format. Each line consists of six fields, separated by spaces or tabs:

```
site size max batcher muncher transport
```

`site`

    `site` is the name of the site to which the entry applies. The *togo* file for this site must reside in *out.going/togo* below the news spool. A site name of `/default/` denotes the default entry and is to match any site not directly specified with an entry unique to it.

`size`

    `size` is the maximum size of article batches created (before compression). For single articles larger than this, C News makes an exception and puts each in a single batch by itself.

max

> *max* is the maximum number of batches created and scheduled for transfer before batching stalls for this particular site. This is useful in case the remote site should be down for a long time, because it prevents C News from cluttering your UUCP spool directories with zillions of newsbatches.
>
> C News determines the number of queued batches using the *queuelen* script in */usr/lib/news/*. If you've installed C News in a prepackaged format, the script should not need any editing, but if you choose to use a different flavor of spool directories, for example, Taylor UUCP, you might have to write your own. If you don't care about the number of spool files (because you're the only person using your computer and you don't write articles by the megabyte), you may replace the script's contents by a simple *exit 0* statement.

batcher

> The *batcher* field contains the command used for producing a batch from the list of articles in the *togo* file. For regular feeds, this is usually *batcher*. For other purposes, alternative batchers may be provided. For instance, the ihave/sendme protocol requires the article list to be turned into *ihave* or *sendme* control messages, which are posted to the newsgroup *to.site*. This is performed by *batchih* and *batchsm*.

muncher

> The *muncher* field specifies the compression command. Usually, this is *comp-cun*, a script that produces a compressed batch.* Alternatively, suppose you create a muncher that uses *gzip*, say **gzipcun** (note that you have to write it yourself). You have to make sure that *uncompress* on the remote site is patched to recognize files compressed with *gzip*.
>
> If the remote site does not have an *uncompress* command, you may specify *nocomp*, which does not do any compression.

transport

> The last field, *transport*, describes the transport to be used. A number of standard commands for different transports are available; their names begin with *via*. *sendbatches* passes them the destination sitename on the command line. If the *batchparms* entry is not `/default/`, *sendbatches* derives the sitename from the *site* field by stripping it of anything after and including the first dot or slash. If the `batchparms` entry is `/default/`, the directory names in *out.going* are used.

---

* As shipped with C News, *compcun* uses *compress* with the 12-bit option, since this is the lowest common denominator for most sites. You may produce a copy of the script, say *compcun16*, for which you use 16-bit compression. The improvement is not too impressive, though.

To perform batching for a specific site, use the following command:

```
# su news -c "/usr/lib/news/batch/sendbatches site"
```

When invoked without arguments, *sendbatches* handles all batch queues. The interpretation of "all" depends on the presence of a default entry in *batchparms*. If one is found, all directories in */var/spool/news/out.going* are checked; otherwise, *sendbatches* cycles through all entries in *batchparms*, processing just the sites found there. Note that *sendbatches*, when scanning the *out.going* directory, takes only those directories that contain no dots or at signs (@) as sitenames.

There are two commands that use *uux* to execute *rnews* on the remote system: *viauux* and *viauuxz*. The latter sets the *−z* flag for *uux* to keep older versions from returning success messages for each article delivered. Another command, *viamail*, sends article batches to the user **rnews** on the remote system via mail. Of course, this requires that the remote system somehow feeds all mail for **rnews** to its local news system. For a complete list of these transports, refer to the *newsbatch* manual page.

All commands from the last three fields must be located in either *out.going/site* or */usr/lib/news/batch*. Most of them are scripts; you can easily tailor new tools for your personal needs. They are invoked through pipes. The list of articles is fed to the batcher on standard input, which produces the batch on standard output. This is piped into the muncher, and so on.

Here is a sample file:

```
# batchparms file for the brewery
# site         | size   |max    |batcher   |muncher    |transport
#--------------+--------+-------+----------+-----------+-----------
/default/       100000  22       batcher    compcun     viauux
swim            10000   10       batcher    nocomp      viauux
```

Expiring News

In B News, expiration needs to be performed by a program called *expire*, which took a list of newsgroups as arguments, along with a time specification after which articles had to be expired. To have different hierarchies expire at different times, you had to write a script that invoked *expire* for each of them separately. C News offers a more convenient solution. In a file called *explist*, you may specify newsgroups and expiration intervals. A command called *doexpire* is usually run once a day from *cron* and processes all groups according to this list.

Occasionally, you may want to retain articles from certain groups even after they have been expired; for example, you might want to keep programs posted to *comp.sources.unix*. This is called *archiving*. *explist* permits you to mark groups for archiving.

An entry in *explist* looks like this:

```
grouplist perm times archive
```

grouplist is a comma-separated list of newsgroups to which the entry applies. Hierarchies may be specified by giving the group name prefix, optionally appended with `all`. For example, for an entry applying to all groups below *comp.os*, enter either **comp.os** or **comp.os.all**.

When *expiring* news from a group, the name is checked against all entries in *explist* in the order given. The first matching entry applies. For example, to throw away the majority of *comp* after four days, except for *comp.os.linux.announce*, which you want to keep for a week, you simply have an entry for the latter, which specifies a seven-day expiration period, followed by an expiration period for *comp*, which specifies four days.

The `perm` field details if the entry applies to moderated, unmoderated, or any groups. It may take the values `m`, `u`, or `x`, which denote moderated, unmoderated, or any type.

The third field, `times`, usually contains only a single number. This is the number of days after which articles expire if they haven't been assigned an artificial expiration date in an `Expires:` field in the article header. Note that this is the number of days counting from its *arrival* at your site, not the date of posting.

The `times` field may, however, be more complex than that. It may be a combination of up to three numbers separated from one another by dashes. The first denotes the number of days that have to pass before the article is considered a candidate for expiration, even if the `Expires:` field would have it expire already. It is rarely useful to use a value other than zero. The second field is the previously mentioned default number of days after which it will be expired. The third is the number of days after which an article will be expired unconditionally, regardless of whether it has an `Expires:` field or not. If only the middle number is given, the other two take default values. These may be specified using the special entry `/bounds/`, which is described a little later.

The fourth field, `archive`, denotes whether the newsgroup is to be archived and where. If no archiving is intended, a dash should be used. Otherwise, you either use a full pathname (pointing to a directory) or an at sign (@). The at sign denotes the default archive directory, which must then be given to *doexpire* by using the −*a* flag on the command line. An archive directory should be owned by **news**. When *doexpire* archives an article from say, *comp.sources.unix*, it stores it in the directory *comp/sources/unix* below the archive directory, creating it if necessary. The archive directory itself, however, will not be created.

There are two special entries in your *explist* file that *doexpire* relies on. Instead of a list of newsgroups, they have the keywords `/bounds/` and `/expired/`. The `/bounds/` entry contains the default values for the three values of the `times` field described previously.

The /expired/ field determines how long C News will hold onto lines in the *history* file. C News will not remove a line from the history file once the corresponding article(s) have been expired, but will hold onto it in case a duplicate should arrive after this date. If you are fed by only one site, you can keep this value small. Otherwise, a couple of weeks is advisable on UUCP networks, depending on the delays you experience with articles from these sites.

Here is a sample *explist* file with rather tight expiry intervals:

```
# keep history lines for two weeks. No article gets more than three months
/expired/                         x       14      -
/bounds/                          x       0-1-90  -
# groups we want to keep longer than the rest
comp.os.linux.announce            m       10      -
comp.os.linux                     x       5       -
alt.folklore.computers            u       10      -
rec.humor.oracle                  m       10      -
soc.feminism                      m       10      -
# Archive *.sources groups
comp.sources,alt.sources          x       5       @
# defaults for tech groups
comp,sci                          x       7       -
# enough for a long weekend
misc,talk                         x       4       -
# throw away junk quickly
junk                              x       1       -
# control messages are of scant interest, too
control                           x       1       -
# catch-all entry for the rest of it
all                               x       2       -
```

Expiring presents several potential problems. One is that your newsreader might rely on the third field of the *active* file described earlier, which contains the number of the lowest article online. When expiring articles, C News does not update this field. If you need (or want) to have this field represent the real situation, you need to run a program called *updatemin* after each run of *doexpire*. (In older versions of C News, a script called *upact* did this.)

C News does not expire by scanning the newsgroup's directory, but simply checks the *history* file if the article is due for expiration.* If your history file somehow gets out of sync, articles may be around on your disk forever because C News has literally forgotten them.† You can repair this by using the *addmissing* script in */usr/lib/ news/maint*, which will add missing articles to the *history* file or *mkhistory*, which rebuilds the entire file from scratch. Don't forget to become user **news** before invoking it, or else you will wind up with a *history* file unreadable by C News.

---

* The article's date of arrival is kept in the middle field of the history line and given in seconds since January 1, 1970.

† I don't know *why* this happens, but it does from time to time.

Miscellaneous Files

There are a number of files that control the behavior of C News, but are not essential. All of them reside in */etc/news*. We describe them briefly here:

newsgroups

This is a companion file of *active* that contains a list of each newsgroup name along with a one-line description of its main topic. This file is automatically updated when C News receives a `checknews` control message.

localgroups

If you have a lot of local groups, you can keep C News from complaining about them each time you receive a `checkgroups` message by putting their names and descriptions in this file, just as they would appear in *newsgroups*.

mailpaths

This file contains the moderator's address for each moderated group. Each line contains the group name followed by the moderator's email address (offset by a tab).

Two special entries are provided as defaults: `backbone` and `internet`. Both provide, in bang-path notation, the path to the nearest backbone site and the site that understands RFC-822 style addresses (*user@host*). The default entries are:

```
internet            backbone
```

You do not have to change the `internet` entry if you have *exim* or *sendmail* installed; they understand RFC-822 addressing.

The `backbone` entry is used whenever a user posts to a moderated group whose moderator is not listed explicitly. If the newsgroup's name is *alt.sewer* and the `backbone` entry contains *path!%s*, C News will mail the article to *path!alt-sewer*, hoping that the backbone machine is able to forward the article. To find out which path to use, ask the news-admin at the site that feeds you. As a last resort, you can also use *uunet.uu.net!%s*.

distributions

This file is not really a C News file, but is used by some newsreaders and *nntpd*. It contains the list of distributions recognized by your site and a description of their (intended) effects. For example, Virtual Brewery has the following file:

```
world       everywhere in the world
local       Only local to this site
nl          Netherlands only
mugnet      MUGNET only
fr          France only
de          Germany only
brewery     Virtual Brewery only
```

log This file contains a log of all C News activities. It is culled regularly by running *newsdaily*; copies of the old log files are kept in *log.o*, *log.oo*, etc.

errlog

This is a log of all error messages created by C News. These messages do not include logs of articles junked due to being sent to an invalid wrong group or other user errors. This file is mailed to the newsmaster (**usenet** by default) automatically by *newsdaily* if it is not found empty.

errlog is cleared by *newsdaily*. *errlog.o* keeps old copies and companions.

batchlog

This file logs all runs of *sendbatches*. It is usually of scant interest. It is also attended by *newsdaily*.

watchtime

This is an empty file created each time *newswatch* runs.

Control Messages

The Usenet news protocol knows a special category of articles that evoke certain responses or actions by the news system. These are called *control* messages. They are recognized by the presence of a `Control:` field in the article header, which contains the name of the control operation to be performed. There are several types of them, all of which are handled by shell scripts located in */usr/lib/news/ctl*.

Most of these messages perform their action automatically at the time the article is processed by C News without notifying the newsmaster. By default, only `check-groups` messages will be handed to the newsmaster, but you may change this by editing the scripts.

The cancel Message

The most widely known message is `cancel`, with which a user can cancel an article sent earlier. This effectively removes the article from the spool directories, if it exists. The `cancel` message is forwarded to all sites that receive news from the groups affected, regardless of whether the article has been seen already. This takes into account the possibility that the original article has been delayed over the cancellation message. Some news systems allow users to cancel other people's messages; this is, of course, a definite no-no.

newgroup and rmgroup

Two messages dealing with creation or removal of newsgroups are the `newgroup` and `rmgroup` messages. Newsgroups below the "usual" hierarchies may be created only after a discussion and voting has been held among Usenet readers. The rules applying to the *alt* hierarchy allow for something close to anarchy. For more information, see the regular postings in *news.announce.newusers* and *news.announce.newgroups*. Never send a `newgroup` or `rmgroup` message yourself unless you definitely know that you are allowed to.

The checkgroups Message

`checkgroups` messages are sent by news administrators to make all sites within a network synchronize their *active* files with the realities of Usenet. For example, commercial Internet Service Providers might send out such a message to their customers' sites. Once a month, the "official" `checkgroups` message for the major hierarchies is posted to *comp.announce.newgroups* by its moderator. However, it is posted as an ordinary article, not as a control message. To perform the `checkgroups` operation, save this article to a file, say */tmp/check*, remove everything up to the beginning of the control message itself, and feed it to the `checkgroups` script using the following command:

```
# su news -c "/usr/lib/news/ctl/checkgroups" < /tmp/check
```

This will update your *newsgroups* file from the new list of groups, adding the groups listed in *localgroups*. The old *newsgroups* file will be moved to *newsgroups.bac*. Note that posting the message locally rarely works, because *inews*, the command that accepts and posts articles from users, refuses to accept that large an article.

If C News finds mismatches between the `checkgroups` list and the *active* file, it produces a list of commands that would bring your site up to date and mails it to the news administrator.

The output typically looks like this:

```
From news Sun Jan 30 16:18:11 1994
Date: Sun, 30 Jan 94 16:18 MET
From: news (News Subsystem)
To: usenet
Subject: Problems with your active file
The following newsgroups are not valid and should be removed.
        alt.ascii-art
        bionet.molbio.gene-org
        comp.windows.x.intrisics
        de.answers
You can do this by executing the commands:
        /usr/lib/news/maint/delgroup alt.ascii-art
        /usr/lib/news/maint/delgroup bionet.molbio.gene-org
        /usr/lib/news/maint/delgroup comp.windows.x.intrisics
        /usr/lib/news/maint/delgroup de.answers
The following newsgroups were missing.
        comp.binaries.cbm
        comp.databases.rdb
        comp.os.geos
        comp.os.qnx
```

```
comp.unix.user-friendly
misc.legal.moderated
news.newsites
soc.culture.scientists
talk.politics.crypto
talk.politics.tibet
```

When you receive a message like this from your news system, don't believe it automatically. Depending on who sent the **checkgroups** message, it may lack a few groups or even entire hierarchies; you should be careful about removing any groups. If you find groups are listed as missing that you want to carry at your site, you have to add them using the *addgroup* script. Save the list of missing groups to a file and feed it to the following little script:

```
#!/bin/sh
#
WHOIAM=`whoami`
if [ "$WHOIAM" != "news" ]
then
        echo "You must run $0 as user 'news'" >&2
        exit 1
fi
#
cd /usr/lib/news
while read group; do
    if grep -si "^$group[[:space:]].*moderated" newsgroup; then
        mod=m
    else
        mod=y
    fi
    /usr/lib/news/maint/addgroup $group $mod
done
```

sendsys, version, and senduuname

Finally, there are three messages that can be used to find out about the network's topology. These are **sendsys**, **version**, and **senduuname**. They cause C News to return the *sys* file to the sender, as well as a software version string and the output of *uuname*, respectively. C News is very laconic about **version** messages; it returns a simple, unadorned C.

Again, you should *never* issue such a message unless you have made sure that it cannot leave your (regional) network. Replies to **sendsys** messages can quickly bring down a UUCP network.*

---

* I wouldn't try this on the Internet, either.

C News in an NFS Environment

A simple way to distribute news within a local network is to keep all news on a central host and export the relevant directories via NFS so that newsreaders may scan the articles directly. The overhead involved in retrieving and threading articles is significantly lower than NNTP. NNTP, on the other hand, wins in a heterogeneous network where equipment varies widely among hosts, or where users don't have equivalent accounts on the server machine.

When you use NFS, articles posted on a local host have to be forwarded to the central machine because accessing adminstrative files might otherwise expose the system to race conditions that leave the files inconsistent. Also, you might want to protect your news spool area by exporting it read-only, which also requires forwarding to the central machine.

C News handles this central machine configuration transparently to the user. When you post an article, your newsreader usually invokes *inews* to inject the article into the news system. This command runs a number of checks on the article, completes the header, and checks the file *server* in */etc/news*. If this file exists and contains a hostname different from the local host's name, *inews* is invoked on that server host via *rsh*. Since the *inews* script uses a number of binary commands and support files from C News, you have to either have C News installed locally or mount the news software from the server.

For the *rsh* invocation to work properly, each user who posts news must have an equivalent account on the server system, i.e., one to which she can log in without being asked for a password.

Make sure that the hostname given in *server* literally matches the output of the *hostname* command on the server machine, or else C News will loop forever in an attempt to deliver the article. We discuss NFS is detail in Chapter 14, *The Network File System*.

Maintenance Tools and Tasks

Despite the complexity of C News, a news administrator's life can be fairly easy; C News provides you with a wide variety of maintenance tools. Some of these are intended to be run regularly from *cron*, like *newsdaily*. Using these scripts greatly reduces daily care and feeding requirements of your C News installation.

Unless stated otherwise, these commands are located in */usr/lib/news/maint*. (Note that you must become user **news** before invoking these commands. Running them as a superuser may render critical newsfiles inaccessible to C News.):

newsdaily
> The name already says it: run this once a day. It is an important script that helps you keep log files small, retaining copies of each from the last three

runs. It also tries to sense anomalies, like stale batches in the incoming and outgoing directories, postings to unknown or moderated newsgroups, etc. Resulting error messages are mailed to the newsmaster.

newswatch

This script should be run regularly to look for anomalies in the news system, once an hour or so. It is intended to detect problems that will have an immediate effect on the operability of your news system, in which case it mails a trouble report to the newsmaster. Things checked include stale lock files that don't get removed, unattended input batches, and disk space shortage.

addgroup

This script adds a group to your site locally. The proper invocation is:

```
addgroup groupname y|n|m|=realgroup
```

The second argument has the same meaning as the flag in the *active* file, meaning that anyone may post to the group (y), that no one may post (n), that it is moderated (m), or that it is an alias for another group (=`realgroup`). You might also want to use *addgroup* when the first articles in a newly created group arrive earlier than the `newgroup` control message that is intended to create it.

delgroup

This script allows you to delete a group locally. Invoke it as:

```
delgroup groupname
```

You still have to delete the articles that remain in the newsgroup's spool directory. Alternatively, you might leave it to the natural course of events (i.e., expiration) to make them go away.

addmissing

This script adds missing articles to the *history* file. Run it when there are articles that seem to hang around forever.

newsboot

This script should be run at system boot time. It removes any lock files left over when news processes were killed at shutdown, and closes and executes any batches left over from NNTP connections that were terminated when shutting down the system.

newsrunning

This script resides in */usr/lib/news/input* and may be used to disable unbatching of incoming news, for instance during work hours. You may turn off unbatching by invoking:

```
/usr/lib/news/input/newsrunning off
```

It is turned on by using on instead of off.

CHAPTER TWENTY-TWO

NNTP AND THE NNTPD DAEMON

Network News Transfer Protocol (NNTP) provides for a vastly different approach to news exchange from C News and other news servers without native NNTP support. Rather than rely on a batch technology like UUCP to transfer news articles between machines, it allows articles to be exchanged via an interactive network connection. NNTP is not a particular software package, but an Internet standard described in RFC-977. It is based on a stream-oriented connection, usually over TCP, between a client anywhere in the network and a server on a host that keeps Netnews on disk storage. The stream connection allows the client and server to interactively negotiate article transfer with nearly no turnaround delay, thus keeping the number of duplicate articles low. Together with the Internet's high-transfer rates, this adds up to a news transport that surpasses the original UUCP networks by far. While some years ago it was not uncommon for an article to take two weeks or more before it arrived in the last corner of Usenet; it is now often less than two days. On the Internet itself, it is even within the range of minutes.

Various commands allow clients to retrieve, send, and post articles. The difference between sending and posting is that the latter may involve articles with incomplete header information; it generally means that the user has just written the article.* Article retrieval may be used by news transfer clients as well as newsreaders. This makes NNTP an excellent tool for providing news access to many clients on a local network without going through the contortions that are necessary when using NFS.

NNTP also provides for an active and a passive way to transfer news, colloquially called "pushing" and "pulling." Pushing is basically the same as the ihave/sendme protocol used by C News (described in Chapter 21, *C News*). The client offers an article to the server through the *IHAVE msgid* command, and the server returns a response code that indicates whether it already has the article or if it wants it. If the server wants the article, the client sends the article, terminated by a single dot on a separate line.

---

* When posting an article over NNTP, the server always adds at least one header field, `NNTP-Posting-Host:`. The field contains the client's hostname.

Pushing news has the single disadvantage that it places a heavy load on the server system, since the system has to search its history database for every single article.

The opposite technique is pulling news, in which the client requests a list of all (available) articles from a group that have arrived after a specified date. This query is performed by the *NEWNEWS* command. From the returned list of message IDs, the client selects those articles it does not yet have, using the *ARTICLE* command for each of them in turn.

Pulling news needs tight control by the server over which groups and distributions it allows a client to request. For example, it has to make sure that no confidential material from newsgroups local to the site is sent to unauthorized clients.

There are also a number of convenience commands for newsreaders that permit them to retrieve the article header and body separately, or even single header lines from a range of articles. This lets you keep all news on a central host, with all users on the (presumably local) network using NNTP-based client programs for reading and posting. This is an alternative to exporting the news directories via NFS, as described in Chapter 21.

An overall problem of NNTP is that it allows a knowledgeable person to insert articles into the news stream with false sender specification. This is called *news faking* or *spoofing.** An extension to NNTP allows you to require user authentication for certain commands, providing some measure of protection against people abusing your news server in this way.

There are a number of NNTP packages. One of the more widely known is the NNTP daemon, also known as the *reference implementation.* Originally, it was written by Stan Barber and Phil Lapsley to illustrate the details of RFC-977. As with much of the good software available today, you may find it prepackaged for your Linux distribution, or you can obtain the source and compile it yourself. If you choose to compile it yourself, you will need to be quite familiar with your distribution to ensure you configure all of the file paths correctly.

The *nntpd* package has a server, two clients for pulling and pushing news, and an *inews* replacement. They live in a B News environment, but with a little tweaking, they will be happy with C News, too. However, if you plan to use NNTP for more than offering newsreaders access to your news server, the reference implementation is not really an option. We will therefore discuss only the NNTP daemon contained in the *nntpd* package and leave out the client programs.

If you wish to run a large news site, you should look at the *InterNet News* package, or INN, that was written by Rich Salz. It provides both NNTP and UUCP-based news transport. News transport is definitely better than *nntpd.* We discuss INN in detail in Chapter 23, *Internet News.*

---

* The same problem exists with the Simple Mail Transfer Protocol (SMTP), although most mail transport agents now provide mechanisms to prevent spoofing.

The NNTP Protocol

We've mentioned two NNTP commands that are key to how news articles are pushed or pulled between servers. Now we'll look at these in the context of an actual NNTP session to show you how simple the protocol is. For the purposes of our illustration, we'll use a simple *telnet* client to connect to an INN-based news server at the Virtual Brewery called **news.vbrew.com**. The server is running a minimal configuration to keep the examples short. We'll look at how to complete the configuration of this server in Chapter 23. In our testing we'll be very careful to generate articles in the *junk* newsgroup only, to avoid disturbing anyone else.

Connecting to the News Server

Connecting to the news server is a simple as opening a TCP connection to its NNTP port. When you are connected, you will be greeted with a welcome banner. One of the first commands you might try is `help`. The response you get generally depends upon whether the server believes you are a remote NNTP server or a newsreader, as there are different command sets required. You can change your operating mode using the *mode* command; we'll look at that in a moment:

```
$ telnet news.vbrew.com nntp
Trying 172.16.1.1...
Connected to localhost.
Escape character is '^]'.
200 news.vbrew.com InterNetNews server INN 1.7.2 08-Dec-1997 ready
help
100 Legal commands
        authinfo
                help
                ihave
                check
                takethis
                list
                mode
                xmode
                quit
                head
                stat
                xbatch
                xpath
                xreplic
For more information, contact "usenet" at this machine.
.
```

The responses to NNTP commands always end with a period (.) on a line by itself. The numbers you see in the output listing are *response codes* and are used by the server to indicate success or failure of a command. The response codes are described in RFC-977; we'll talk about the most important ones as we proceed.

Pushing a News Article onto a Server

We mentioned the *IHAVE* command when we talked about pushing news articles onto a news server. Let's now have a look at how the *IHAVE* command actually works:

```
ihave <123456@gw.vk2ktj.ampr.org>
335
From: terry@gw.vk2ktj.ampr.org
Subject: test message sent with ihave
Newsgroups: junk
Distribution: world
Path: gw.vk2ktj.ampr.org
Date: 26 April 1999
Message-ID: <123456@gw.vk2ktj.ampr.org>
Body:

This is a test message sent using the NNTP IHAVE command.

.
235
```

All NNTP commands are case insensitive, so you may enter them in either upper- or lowercase. The *IHAVE* command takes one mandatory argument, it being the Message ID of the article that is being pushed. Every news article is assigned a unique message ID when it is created. The *IHAVE* command provides a way of the NNTP server to say which articles it has when it wants to push articles to another server. The sending server will issue an *IHAVE* command for each article it wishes to push. If the command response code generated by the receiving NNTP server is in the "3xx" range, the sending NNTP server will transmit the complete article, including it's full header, terminating the article with a period on a line by itself. If the response code was in the "4xx" range, the receiving server has chosen not to accept this article, possibly because it already has it, or because of some problem, such as running out of disk space.

When the article has been transmitted, the receiving serve issues another response code indicating whether the article transmission was successful.

Changing to NNRP Reader Mode

Newsreaders use their own set of commands when talking to a news server. To activate these commands, the news server has to be operating in *reader* mode. Most news servers default to reader mode, unless the IP address of the connecting host is listed as a news-forwarding peer. In any case, NNTP provides a command to explicitly switch into reader mode:

```
mode reader
200 news.vbrew.com InterNetNews NNRP server INN 1.7.2 08-Dec-1997 ready/
    (posting ok).
```

```
help
100 Legal commands
  authinfo user Name|pass Password|generic <prog> <args>
  article [MessageID|Number]
  body [MessageID|Number]
  date
  group newsgroup
  head [MessageID|Number]
  help
  ihave
  last
  list [active|active.times|newsgroups|distributions|distrib.pats|/
      overview.fmt|subscriptions]
  listgroup newsgroup
  mode reader
  newgroups yymmdd hhmmss ["GMT"] [<distributions>]
  newnews newsgroups yymmddhhmmss ["GMT"] [<distributions>]
  next
  post
  slave
  stat [MessageID|Number]
  xgtitle [group_pattern]
  xhdr header [range|MessageID]
  xover [range]
  xpat header range|MessageID pat [morepat...]
  xpath MessageID
Report problems to <usenet@vlager.vbrew.com>
.
```

NNTP reader mode has a lot of commands. Many of these are designed to make the life of a newsreader easier. We mentioned earlier that there are commands that instruct the server to send the head and the body of articles separately. There are also commands that list the available groups and articles, and others that allow posting, an alternate means of sending news articles to the server.

Listing Available Groups

The *list* command lists a number of different types of information; notably the groups supported by the server:

```
list newsgroups
215 Descriptions in form "group description".
control               News server internal group
junk                  News server internal group
local.general         General local stuff
local.test            Local test group
.
```

Listing Active Groups

list active shows each supported group and provides information about them. The two numbers in each line of the output are the high-water mark and the low-water mark—that is, the highest numbered article and lowest numbered article in each group. The newsreader is able to form an idea of the number of articles in the group from these. We'll talk a little more about these numbers in a moment. The last field in the output displays flags that control whether posting is allowed to the group, whether the group is moderated, and whether articles posted are actually stored or just passed on. These flags are described in detail in Chapter 23. An example looks like this:

```
list active
215 Newsgroups in form "group high low flags".
control 0000000000 0000000001 y
junk 0000000003 0000000001 y
alt.test 0000000000 0000000001 y
.
```

Posting an Article

We mentioned there was a difference between pushing an article and posting an article. When you are pushing an article, there is an implicit assumption that the article already exists, that it has a message identifier that has been uniquely assigned to it by the server to which it was originally posted, and that it has a complete set of headers. When posting an article, you are creating the article for the first time and the only headers you supply are those that are meaningful to you, such as the Subject and the Newgroups to which you are posting the article. The news server you post the article on will add all the other headers for you and create a message ID that it will use when pushing the article onto other servers.

All of this means that posting an article is even easier than pushing one. An example posting looks like this:

```
post
340 Ok
From: terry@richard.geek.org.au
Subject: test message number 1
Newsgroups: junk
Body:

This is a test message, please feel free to ignore it.

.
240 Article posted
```

We've generated two more messages like this one to give our following examples some realism.

Listing New Articles

When a newsreader first connects to a new server and the user chooses a newsgroup to browse, the newsreader will want to retrieve a list of new articles, those posted or received since the last login by the user. The *newnews* command is used for this purpose. Three mandatory arguments must be supplied: the name of the group or groups to query, the start date, and the start time from which to list. The date and time are each specified as six-digit numbers, with the most significant information first; *yymmdd* and *hhmmss*, respectively:

```
newnews junk 990101 000000
230 New news follows
<7g2o5r$aa$6@news.vbrew.com>
<7g5bhm$8f$2@news.vbrew.com>
<7g5bk5$8f$3@news.vbrew.com>
.
```

Selecting a Group on Which to Operate

When the user selects a newsgroup to browse, the newsreader may tell the news server that the group was selected. This simplifies the interaction between newsreader and news server; it removes the need to constantly send the name of the newsgroup with each command. The *group* command simply takes the name of the selected group as an argument. Many following commands use the group selected as the default, unless another newsgroup is specified explicitly:

```
group junk
211 3 1 3 junk
```

The *group* command returns a message indicating the number of active messages, the low-water mark, the high-water mark, and the name of the group, respectively. Note that while the number of active messages and the high-water mark are the same in our example, this is not often the case; in an active news server, some articles may have expired or been deleted, lowering the number of active messages but leaving the high-water mark untouched.

Listing Articles in a Group

To address newsgroup articles, the newsreader must know which article numbers represent active articles. The *listgroup* command offers a list of the active article numbers in the current group, or an explicit group if the group name is supplied:

```
listgroup junk
211 Article list follows
1
2
3
.
```

Retrieving an Article Header Only

The user must have some information about an article before she can know whether she wishes to read it. We mentioned earlier that some commands allow the article header and body to be transferred separately. The *head* command is used to request that the server transmit just the header of the specified article to the newsreader. If the user doesn't want to read this article, we haven't wasted time and network bandwidth transferring a potentially large article body unnecessarily.

Articles may be referenced using either their number (from the *listgroup* command) or their message identifier:

```
head 2
221 2 <7g5bhm$8f$2@news.vbrew.com> head
Path: news.vbrew.com!not-for-mail
From: terry@richard.geek.org.au
Newsgroups: junk
Subject: test message number 2
Date: 27 Apr 1999 21:51:50 GMT
Organization: The Virtual brewery
Lines: 2
Message-ID: <7g5bhm$8f$2@news.vbrew.com>
NNTP-Posting-Host: localhost
X-Server-Date: 27 Apr 1999 21:51:50 GMT
Body:
Xref: news.vbrew.com junk:2
.
```

Retrieving an Article Body Only

If, on the other hand, the user decides she does want to read the article, her newsreader needs a way of requesting that the message body be transmitted. The *body* command is used for this purpose. It operates in much the same way as the *head* command, except that only the message body is returned:

```
body 2
222 2 <7g5bhm$8f$2@news.vbrew.com> body
This is another test message, please feel free to ignore it too.
.
```

Reading an Article from a Group

While it is normally most efficient to separately transfer the headers and bodies of selected articles, there are occasions when we are better off transferring the complete article. A good example of this is in applications through which we want to transfer all of the artices in a group without any sort of preselection, such as when we are using an NNTP cache program like *leafnode.*[*]

Naturally, NNTP provides a means of doing this, and not surprisingly, it operates almost identically to the *head* command as well. The *article* command also accepts an article number or message ID as an argument, but returns the whole article including its header:

```
article 1
220 1 <7g2o5r$aa$6@news.vbrew.com> article
Path: news.vbrew.com!not-for-mail
From: terry@richard.geek.org.au
Newsgroups: junk
Subject: test message number 1
Date: 26 Apr 1999 22:08:59 GMT
Organization: The Virtual brewery
Lines: 2
Message-ID: <7g2o5r$aa$6@news.vbrew.com>
NNTP-Posting-Host: localhost
X-Server-Date: 26 Apr 1999 22:08:59 GMT
Body:
Xref: news.vbrew.com junk:1

This is a test message, please feel free to ignore it.

.
```

If you attempt to retrieve an unknown article, the server will return a message with an appropriately coded response code and perhaps a readable text message:

```
article 4
423 Bad article number
```

We've described how the most important NNTP commands are used in this section. If you're interested in developing software that implements the NNTP protocol, you should refer to the relevant RFC documents; they provide a great deal of detail that we couldn't include here.

Let's now look at NNTP in action through the **nntpd** server.

Installing the NNTP Server

The NNTP server (**nntpd**) may be compiled in two ways, depending on the expected load on the news system. There are no compiled versions available, because of some site-specific defaults that are hardcoded into the executable. All configuration is done through macros defined in *common/conf.h*.

---

[*] *leafnode* is available by anonymous FTP from **wpxx02.toxi.uni-wuerzburg.de** in the */pub/* directory.

nntpd may be configured as either a standalone server that is started at system boot time from an *rc* file, or a daemon managed by *inetd*. In the latter case, you have to have the following entry in */etc/inetd.conf*:

```
nntp    stream tcp nowait    news    /usr/etc/in.nntpd    nntpd
```

The *inetd.conf* syntax is described in detail in Chapter 12, *Important Network Features*. If you configure *nntpd* as standalone, make sure that any such line in *inetd.conf* is commented out. In either case, you have to make sure the following line appears in */etc/services*:

```
nntp    119/tcp    readnews untp    # Network News Transfer Protocol
```

To temporarily store any incoming articles, *nntpd* also needs a *.tmp* directory in your news spool. You should create it using the following commands:

```
# mkdir /var/spool/news/.tmp
# chown news.news /var/spool/news/.tmp
```

Restricting NNTP Access

Access to NNTP resources is governed by the file *nntp_access* in */etc/news*. Lines in this file describe the access rights granted to foreign hosts. Each line has the following format:

```
site    read|xfer|both|no    post|no    [!exceptgroups]
```

If a client connects to the NNTP port, **nntpd** attempts to obtain the host's fully qualified domain name from its IP address using reverse lookup. The client's hostname and IP address are checked against the `site` field of each entry in the order in which they appear in the file. Matches may be either partial or exact. If an entry matches exactly, it applies; if the match is partial, it applies only if there is no other match following it that is at least as good. `site` may be specified in one of the following ways:

Hostname
> This is a fully qualified domain name of a host. If this matches the client's canonical hostname literally, the entry applies, and all following entries are ignored.

IP address
> This is an IP address in dotted quad notation. If the client's IP address matches this, the entry applies, and all following entries are ignored.

Domain name
> This is a domain name, specified as **.domain*. If the client's hostname matches the domain name, the entry matches.

Network name
> This is the name of a network as specified in */etc/networks*. If the network number of the client's IP address matches the network number associated with the network name, the entry matches.

Default
> The string `default` matches any client.

Entries with a more general site specification should be specified earlier, because any matches will be overridden by later, more exact matches.

The second and third fields describe the access rights granted to the client. The second field details the permissions to retrieve news by pulling (`read`), and transmit news by pushing (`xfer`). A value of `both` enables both; `no` denies access altogether. The third field grants the client the right to post articles, i.e., deliver articles with incomplete header information, which is completed by the news software. If the second field contains `no`, the third field is ignored.

The fourth field is optional and contains a comma-separated list of groups to which the client is denied access.

This is a sample *nntp_access* file:

```
#
# by default, anyone may transfer news, but not read or post
default                 xfer            no
#
# public.vbrew.com offers public access via modem. We allow
# them to read and post to any but the local.* groups
public.vbrew.com        read            post    !local
#
# all other hosts at the brewery may read and post
*.vbrew.com             read            post
```

NNTP Authorization

The *nntpd* daemon provides a simple authorization scheme. If you capitalize any of the access tokens in the *nntp_access* file, *nntpd* requires authorization from the client for the respective operation. For instance, when specifying a permission of `Xfer` or `XFER`, (as opposed to `xfer`), *nntpd* will not let the client transfer articles to your site unless it passes authorization.

The authorization procedure is implemented by means of a new NNTP command named *AUTHINFO*. Using this command, the client transmits a username and a password to the NNTP server. *nntpd* validates them by checking them against the */etc/passwd* database and verifies that the user belongs to the **nntp** group.

The current implementation of NNTP authorization is only experimental and has therefore not been implemented very portably. The result of this is that it works only with plain-style password databases; shadow passwords are not recognized. If you are compiling from source and have the PAM package installed, the password check is fairly simple to change.

nntpd Interaction with C News

When *nntpd* receives an article, it has to deliver it to the news subsystem. Depending on whether it was received as a result of an *IHAVE* or *POST* command, the article is handed to *rnews* or *inews*, respectively. Instead of invoking *rnews*, you may also configure it (at compile time), to batch the incoming articles and move the resulting batches to */var/spool/news/in.coming*, where they are left for *relaynews* to pick them up at the next queue run.

nntpd has to have access to the *history* file to be able to properly perform the ihave/sendme protocol. At compile time, you have to make sure the path to that file is set correctly. If you use C News, make sure that C News and *nntpd* agree on the format of your history file. C News uses *dbm* hashing functions to access it; however, there are quite a number of different and slightly incompatible implementations of the *dbm* library. If C News has been linked with a different *dbm* library than you have in your standard *libc*, you have to link *nntpd* with this library, too.

nntpd and C news disagreement sometimes produces error messages in the system log that *nntpd* can not open it properly, or you might see duplicate articles being received via NNTP. A good test of a malfunctioning news transfer is to pick an article from your spool area, telnet to the **nntp** port, and offer it to *nntpd* as shown in the next example. Of course, you have to replace `msg@id` with the message ID of the article you want to feed to *nntpd*:

```
$ telnet localhost nntp
Trying 127.0.0.1...
Connected to localhost
Escape characters is '^ ]'.
201 vstout NNTP[auth] server version 1.5.11t (16 November 1991) ready at
Sun Feb 6 16:02:32 1194 (no posting)
IHAVE msg@id
435 Got it.
QUIT
```

This conversation shows *nntpd's* proper reaction; the message `Got it` tells you that it already has this article. If you get a message of *335 Ok* instead, the lookup in the history file failed for some reason. Terminate the conversation by typing Ctrl-D. You can check what has gone wrong by checking the system log; *nntpd* logs all kinds of messages to the `daemon` facility of *syslog*. An incompatible *dbm* library usually manifests itself in a message complaining that *dbminit* failed.

INTERNET NEWS

The Internet News daemon (INN) is arguably the most popular Netnews server in use today. INN is extremely flexible and is suitable for all but the smallest news sites.* INN scales well and is suited to large news server configurations.

The INN server comprises a number of components, each with their own configuration files that we will discuss in turn. Configuration of INN can be a little involved, but we'll describe each of the stages in this chapter and arm you with enough information to make sense of the INN manual pages and documentation and build configurations for just about any application.

Some INN Internals

INN's core program is the *innd* daemon. *innd*'s task is to handle all incoming articles, storing them locally, and to pass them on to any outgoing newsfeeds if required. It is started at boot time and runs continually as a background process. Running as a daemon improves performance because it has to read its status files only once when starting. Depending on the volume of your news feed, certain files such as *history* (which contain a list of all recently processed articles) may range from a few megabytes to tens of megabytes.

Another important feature of INN is that there is always only one instance of *innd* running at any time. This is also very beneficial to performance, because the daemon can process all articles without having to worry about synchronizing its

---

* Very small news sites should consider a caching NNTP server program like *leafnode*, which is available at *http://wpxx02.toxi.uni-wuerzburg.de/~krasel/leafnode.html*.

internal states with other copies of *innd* rummaging around the news spool at the same time. However, this choice affects the overall design of the news system. Because it is so important that incoming news is processed as quickly as possible, it is unacceptable that the server be tied up with such mundane tasks as serving newsreaders accessing the news spool via NNTP, or decompressing newsbatches arriving via UUCP. Therefore, these tasks have been broken out of the main server and implemented in separate support programs. Figure 23-1 attempts to illustrate the relationships between *innd*, the other local tasks, and remote news servers and newsreaders.

Today, NNTP is the most common means of transporting news articles around, and *innd* doesn't directly support anything else. This means that *innd* listens on a TCP socket (port 119) for connections and accepts news articles using the "ihave" protocol.

Articles arriving by transports other than NNTP are supported indirectly by having another process accept the articles and forward them to *innd* via NNTP. News-batches coming in over a UUCP link, for instance, are traditionally handled by the *rnews* program. INN's *rnews* decompresses the batch if necessary, and breaks it up into individual articles; it then offers them to *innd* one by one.

Newsreaders can deliver news when a user posts an article. Since the handling of newsreaders deserves special attention, we will come back to this a little later.

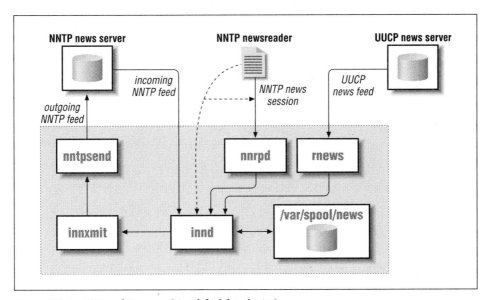

Figure 23-1. INN architecture (simplified for clarity)

When receiving an article, *innd* first looks up its message ID in the *history* file. Duplicate articles are dropped and the occurrences are optionally logged. The same goes for articles that are too old or lack some required header field, such as `Subject:`.* If *innd* finds that the article is acceptable, it looks at the `News-groups:` header line to find out what groups it has been posted to. If one or more of these groups are found in the *active* file, the article is filed to disk. Otherwise, it is filed to the special group *junk*.

Individual articles are kept below */var/spool/news*, also called the *news spool*. Each newsgroup has a separate directory, in which each article is stored in a separate file. The file names are consecutive numbers, so that an article in *comp.risks* may be filed as *comp/risks/217*, for instance. When *innd* finds that the directory it wants to store the article in does not exist, it creates it automatically.

Apart from storing articles locally, you may also want to pass them on to outgoing feeds. This is governed by the *newsfeeds* file that lists all downstream sites along with the newsgroups that should be fed to them.

Just like *innd*'s receiving end, the processing of outgoing news is handled by a single interface, too. Instead of doing all the transport-specific handling itself, *innd* relies on various backends to manage the transmission of articles to other news servers. Outgoing facilities are collectively dubbed *channels*. Depending on its purpose, a channel can have different attributes that determine exactly what information *innd* passes on to it.

For an outgoing NNTP feed, for instance, *innd* might fork the *innxmit* program at startup, and, for each article that should be sent across that feed, pass its message ID, size, and filename to *innxmit*'s standard input. For an outgoing UUCP feed, on the other hand, it might write the article's size and file name to a special logfile, which is head by a different process at regular intervals in order to create batches and queue them to the UUCP subsystem.

Besides these two examples, there are other types of channels that are not strictly outgoing feeds. These are used, for instance, when archiving certain newsgroups, or when generating overview information. Overview information is intended to help newsreaders thread articles more efficiently. Old-style newsreaders had to scan all articles separately in order to obtain the header information required for threading. This would put an immense strain on the server machine, especially when using NNTP; furthermore, it was very slow.† The overview mechanism alleviates this problem by prerecording all relevant headers in a separate file (called *.overview*) for each newsgroup. This information can then be picked up by newsreaders either by reading it directly from the spool directory, or by using the *XOVER* command when connected via NNTP. INN has the *innd* daemon feed all articles to the *overchan* command, which is attached to the daemon through a channel. We'll see how this is done when we discuss configuring news feeds later.

---

* This is indicated by the *Date:* header field; the limit is usually two weeks.

† Threading 1,000 articles when talking to a loaded server could easily take around five minutes, which only the most dedicated Usenet addict would find acceptable.

Newsreaders and INN

Newsreaders running on the same machine as the server (or having mounted the server's news spool via NFS) can read articles from the spool directly. To post an article composed by the user, they invoke the *inews* program, which adds any header fields that are missing and forwards them to the daemon via NNTP.

Alternatively, newsreaders can access the server remotely via NNTP. This type of connection is handled differently from NNTP-based news feeds, to avoid tying up the daemon. Whenever a newsreader connects to the NNTP server, *innd* forks a separate program called *nnrpd*, which handles the session while *innd* returns to the more important things (receiving incoming news, for example).* You may be wondering how the *innd* process can distinguish between an incoming news feed and a connecting newsreader. The answer is quite simple: the NNTP protocol requires that an NNTP-based newsreader issue a *mode reader* command after connecting to the server; when this command is received, the server starts the *nnrpd* process, hands the connection to it, and returns to listening for connections from another news server. There used to be at least one DOS-based newsreader which was not configured to do this, and hence failed miserably when talking to INN, because *innd* itself does not recognize any of the commands used to read news if it doesn't know the connection is from a news reader.

We'll talk a little more about newsreader access to INN under "Controlling Newsreader Access," later in the chapter.

Installing INN

Before diving into INN's configuration, let's talk about its installation. Read this section, even if you've installed INN from one of the various Linux distributions; it contains some hints about security and compatibility.

Linux distributions included Verson INN-1.4sec for quite some time. Unfortunately, this version had two subtle security problems. Modern versions don't have these problems and most distributions include a precompiled Linux binary of INN Version 2 or later.

If you choose, you can build INN yourself. You can obtain the source from **ftp.isc.org** in the */isc/inn/* directory. Building INN requires that you edit a configuration file that tells INN some detail about your operating system, and some features may require minor modifications to the source itself.

Compiling the package itself is pretty simple; there's a script called *BUILD* that will guide you through the process. The source also contains extensive documentation on how to install and configure INN.

---

* The name apparently stands for NetNews Read & Post Daemon.

After installing all binaries, some manual fixups may be required to reconcile INN with any other applications that may want to access its *rnews* or *inews* programs. UUCP, for instance, expects to find the *rnews* program in */usr/bin* or */bin*, while INN installs it in */usr/lib/bin* by default. Make sure */usr/lib/bin/* is in the default search path, or that there are symbolic links pointing to the actual location of the *rnews* and *inews* commands.

Configuring INN: the Basic Setup

One of the greatest obstacles beginners may face is that INN requires a working network setup to function properly, even when running on a standalone host. Therefore, it is essential that your kernel supports TCP/IP networking when running INN, and that you have set up the loopback interface as explained in Chapter 5, *Configuring TCP/IP Networking*.

Next, you have to make sure that *innd* is started at boot time. The default INN installation provides a script file called *boot* in the */etc/news/* directory. If your distribution uses the SystemV-style *init* package, all you have to do is create a symbolic link from your */etc/init.d/inn* file pointing to */etc/news/boot*. For other flavors of *init*, you have to make sure */etc/news/boot* is executed from one of your *rc* scripts. Since INN requires networking support, the startup script should be run *after* the network interfaces are configured.

INN Configuration Files

Having completed these general tasks, you can now turn to the really interesting part of INN: its configuration files. All these files reside in */etc/news*. Some changes to configurations files were introduced in Version 2, and it is Version 2 that we describe here. If you're running an older version, you should find this chapter useful to guide you in upgrading your configuration. During the next few sections, we will discuss them one by one, building the Virtual Brewery's configuration as an example.

If you want to find out more about the features of individual configuration files, you can also consult the manual pages; the INN distribution contains individual manual pages for each of them.

Global Parameters

There are a number of INN parameters that are global in nature; they are relevant to all newsgroups carried.

The inn.conf file

INN's main configuration file is *inn.conf*. Among other things, it determines the name by which your machine is known on Usenet. Version 2 of INN allows a baffling number of parameters to be configured in this file. Fortunately, most parameters have default values that are reasonable for most sites. The *inn.conf(5)* file details all of the parameters, and you should read it carefully if you experience any problems.

A simple example *inn.conf* might look like:

```
# Sample inn.conf for the Virtual Brewery
server:         vlager.vbrew.com
domain:         vbrew.com
fromhost:       vbrew.com
pathhost:       news.vbrew.com
organization:   The Virtual Brewery
mta:            /usr/sbin/sendmail -oi %s
moderatormailer: %s@uunet.uu.net
#
# Paths to INN components and files.
#
pathnews:               /usr/lib/news
pathbin:                /usr/lib/news/bin
pathfilter:             /usr/lib/news/bin/filter
pathcontrol:            /usr/lib/news/bin/control
pathdb:                 /var/lib/news
pathetc:                /etc/news
pathrun:                /var/run/news
pathlog:                /var/log/news
pathhttp:               /var/log/news
pathtmp:                /var/tmp
pathspool:              /var/spool/news
patharticles:           /var/spool/news/articles
pathoverview:           /var/spool/news/overview
pathoutgoing:           /var/spool/news/outgoing
pathincoming:           /var/spool/news/incoming
patharchive:            /var/spool/news/archive
pathuniover:            /var/spool/news/uniover
overviewname:           .overview
```

The first line tells the programs *rnews* and *inews* which host to contact when delivering articles. This entry is absolutely crucial; to pass articles to *innd*, they have to establish an NNTP connection with the server.

The `domain` keyword should specify the domain portion of the host's fully qualified domain name. A couple of programs must look up your host's fully qualified domain name; if your resolver library returns the unqualified hostname only, the name given in the `domain` attribute is tacked onto it. It's not a problem to configure it either way, so it's best to define `domain`.

The next line defines what hostname *inews* is going to use when adding a `From:` line to articles posted by local users. Most newsreaders use the `From:` field when composing a reply mail message to the author of an article. If you omit this field, it will default to your news host's fully qualifed domain name. This is ot always the best choice. You might, for example, have news and mail handled by two different hosts. In this case, you would supply the fully qualified domain name of your mail host after the `fromhost` statement.

The `pathhost` line defines the hostname INN is to add to the `Path:` header field whenever it receives an article. In most cases, you will want to use the fully quali-fied domain name of your news server; you can then omit this field since that is the default. Occasionally you may want to use a generic name, such as **news.vbrew.com**, when serving a large domain. Doing this allows you to move the news system easily to a different host, should you choose to at some time.

The next line contains the `organization` keyword. This statement allows you to configure what text *inews* will put into the `Organization:` line of articles posted by your local users. Formally, you would place a description of your orga-nization or your organization's name in full here. Should you not wish to be so formal, it is fashionable for organizations with a sense of humor to exhibit it here.

The `organization` keyword is mandatory and specifies the pathname of the mail transport agent that will be used for posting moderator messages. `%s` is replaced by the moderator email address.

The `moderatormailer` entry defines a default address used when a user tries to post to a moderated newsgroup. The list of moderator addresses for each news-group is usually kept in a separate file, but you will have a hard time keeping track of all of them. The `moderatormailer` entry is therefore consulted as a last resort; if it is defined, *inews* will replace the `%s` string with the (slightly trans-formed) newsgroup name and send the entire article to this address. For instance, when posting to *soc.feminism*, the article is mailed to *soc-feminism@uunet.uu.net*, given the above configuration. At UUNET, there should be a mail alias installed for each of these submissions addresses that automatically forwards all messages to the appropriate moderator.

Finally, each of the remaining entries specifies the location of some component file or executable belonging to INN. If you've installed INN from a package, these paths should have been configured for you. If you're installing from source, you'll need to ensure that they reflect where you've installed INN.

Configuring Newsgroups

The news administrator on a system is able to control which newsgroups users have access to. INN provides two configuration files that allow the administrator to decide which newsgroups to support and provide descriptions for them.

The active and newsgroups files

The *active* and *newsgroups* files are used to store and describe the newsgroups hosted by this news server. They list which newsgroups we are interested in receiving and serving articles for, and administrative information about them. These files are found in the */var/lib/news/* directory.

The *active* file determines which newsgroups this server supports. Its syntax is straightforward. Each line in the *active* file has four fields delimited by whitespace:

```
name himark lomark flags
```

The *name* field is the name of the newsgroup. The *himark* field is the highest number that has been used for an article in that newsgroup. The *lomark* field is the lowest active number in use in the newsgroup. To illustrate how this works, consider the follow scenario. Imagine that we have a newly created newsgroup: *himark* and *lowmark* are both 0 because there are no articles. If we post 5 articles, they will be numbered 1 through 5. *himark* will now equal 5, the highest numbered article, and *lowmark* will equal 1, the lowest active article. If article 5 is cancelled there will be no change; *himark* will remain at 5 to ensure that that article number is not reallocated and *lowmark* will remain at 1, the lowest active article. If we now cancel article 1, *himark* will remain unchanged, but *lowmark* will now equal 2, because 1 is no longer active. If we now post a new article, it will be assigned article number 6, so *himark* will now equal 6. Article 5 has been in use, so we won't reassign it. *lowmark* remains at 2. This mechanism allows us to easily allocate unique article numbers for new articles and to calculate approximately how many active articles there are in the group: *himark–lowmark*.

The field may contain one of the following:

y Posting directly to this news server is allowed.

n Posting directly to this news server is not allowed. This prevents newsreaders from posting directly to this news server. New articles may only be received from other news servers.

m The group is moderated. Any articles posted to this newsgroup are forwarded to the newsgroup moderator for approval before they enter the newsgroup. Most newsgroups are unmoderated.

j Articles in this group are not kept, but only passed on. This causes the news server to accept the article, but all it will do with it is pass it to the "up-stream" news servers. It will not make the articles available to newsreaders reading from this server.

x   Articles cannot be posted to this newsgroup. The only way that news articles are delivered to this server is by feeding them from another news server. Newsreaders may not directly write articles to this server.

=foo.bar
    Articles are locally filed into the "foo.bar" group.

In our simple server configuration we'll carry a small number of newsgroups, so our */var/lib/news/active* file will look like:

```
control 0000000000 0000000001 y
junk 0000000000 0000000001 y
rec.crafts.brewing 0000000000 0000000001 y
rec.crafts.brewing.ales 0000000000 0000000001 y
rec.crafts.brewing.badtaste 0000000000 0000000001 y
rec.crafts.brewing.brandy 0000000000 0000000001 y
rec.crafts.brewing.champagne 0000000000 0000000001 y
rec.crafts.brewing.private 0000000000 0000000001 y
```

The *himark* and *lomark* numbers in this example are those you would use when creating new newsgroups. The *himark* and *lomark* numbers will look quite different for a newsgroup that has been active for some time.

The *newsgroups* file is even simpler. It provides one-line descriptions of newsgroups. Some newsreaders are able to read and present this information to a user to help them decide whether they want to subscribe.

The format of the *newsgroups* file is simply:

```
name description
```

The *name* field is the name of a newsgroup, and the *<description* is a single line description of that newsgroup.

We want to describe the newsgroups that our server supports, so we'll build our *newsgroups* file as follows:

```
rec.crafts.brewing.ales        Home brewing Ales and Lagers
rec.crafts.brewing.badtaste    Home brewing foul tasting brews
rec.crafts.brewing.brandy      Home brewing your own Brandy
rec.crafts.brewing.champagne   Home brew your own Champagne
rec.crafts.brewing.private     The Virtual Brewery home brewers group
```

Configuring Newsfeeds

INN provides the news administrator the ability to control which newsgroups are forwarded on to other news servers and how they will be forwarded. The most common method uses the NNTP protocol described earlier, but INN also allows newsfeeds via other protocols, such as UUCP.

The newsfeeds file

The *newsfeeds* file determines where news articles will be sent. It normally resides in the */etc/news/* directory.

The format of the *newsfeeds* is a little complicated at first. We'll describe the general layout here, and the *newsfeeds(5)* manual page describes what we leave out. The format is as follows:

```
# newsfeeds file format
site:pattern:flags:param
site2:pattern2\
      :flags2:param2
```

Each news feed to a site is described by a single line, or may be spread across multiple lines using the \ continuation character. The : characters delimit the fields in each line. The # character at the start of a line marks that line as a comment.

The `site` field names the site to which this feed description relates. The sitename can be coded any way you like and doesn't have to be the domain name of the site. The site name will be used later and will refer to an entry in a table that supplies the hostname to the *innxmit* program that transmits the news articles by NNTP to the remote server. You may have multiple entries for each site; each entry will be treated individually.

The `pattern` field specifies which news groups are to be sent to this site. The default is to send all groups, so if that is what you want, just make this field empty. This field is usually a comma-delimited list of pattern-matching expressions. The * character matches zero or more of any character, the . character has no special significance, the ! character (if used at the start of an expression) performs a logical NOT, and the @ character at the start of a newsgroup name means "Do not forward any articles that are posted or crossposted to this group." The list is read and parsed from left to right, so you should ensure that you place the more specific rules first. The pattern:

```
rec.crafts.brewing*,!rec.crafts.brewing.poison,@rec.crafts.brewing.private
```

would send all of the *rec.crafts.brewing* news heirarchy *except* the *rec.crafts.brewing.poison*. It would not feed any articles that were either posted or crossposted to the *rec.crafts.brewing.private* newsgroup; these articles will be trapped and available only to those people who use this server. If you reversed the first two patterns, the first pattern would be overridden by the second and you would end up feeding articles for the *rec.crafts.brewing.poison* newsgroup. The same is true of the first and last patterns; you must always place the more specific patterns before any less specific patterns for them to take effect.

`flags` controls and places constraints on the feed of news articles to this site. The `flags` field is a comma delimited list can contain any of the items from the following list, delimited by commands:

`<size`
> Article must be less then size bytes.

`Aitems`
> Article checks. *items* can be one or more of d (must have Distribution header) or p (don't check for site in Path header).

`Bhigh/low`
> Internal buffer size before writing to output.

`H[count]`
> Article must have less then *count* hops; the default is 1.

`Isize`
> Internal buffer size (for a file feed).

`Mpattern`
> Only moderated groups that match the pattern.

`Npattern`
> Only unmoderated groups that match the pattern.

`Ssize`
> Start spooling if more than size bytes get queued.

`Ttype`
> Feed types: f (file), m (funnel; the `param` field names the entry that articles will be funneled to), p (pipe to program), c (send to stdin channel of the `param` field's subprocess), and x (like c, but handles commands on stdin).

`Witems`
> What to write: b (article bytesize), f (full path), g (first newsgroup), m (Message ID), n (relative path), s (site that fed article), t (time received), * (names of funnel feed-ins or all sites that get the article), N (newsgroups header), D (distribution header), H (all headers), O (overview data), and R (replication data).

The `param` field has special coding that is dependent on the type of feed. In the most common configuration it is where you specify the name of the output file to which you will write the outgoing feed. In other configurations you can leave it out. In yet other configurations it takes on different meanings. If you want to do something unusual, the *newsfeeds(5)* manual page will explain the use of the `param` field in some detail.

There is a special site name that should be coded as ME and should be the first entry in the file. This entry is used to control the default settings for your news feeds. If the ME entry has a distribution list associated with it, this list will be prepended to each of the other site entries before they are sent. This allows you to, for example, declare some newsgroups to be automatically fed, or automatically blocked from feeding, without having to repeat the pattern in each site entry.

We mentioned earlier that it was possible to use some special feeds to generate thread data that makes the newsreader's job easier. We'll do this by exploiting the *overchan* command that is part of the INN distribution. To do this, we've created a special local feed called `overview` that will pass the news articles to the *overchan* command for processing into overview data.

Our news server will provide only one external news feed, which goes to the Groucho Marx University, and they receive articles for all newsgroups except the *control* and *junk* newsgroups, the *rec.crafts.brewing.private* newsgroup, which will be kept locally, and the *rec.crafts.brewing.poison* newsgroup, which we don't want people from our brewery seen posting to.

We'll use the *nntpsend* command to transport the news via NNTP to the **news.groucho.edu** server. *nntpsend* requires us to use the "file" delivery method and to write the article's pathname and article ID. Note that we've set the **param** field to the name of the output file. We'll talk a little more about the *nntpsend* command in a moment. Our resulting newsfeed's configuration is:

```
# /etc/news/newsfeeds file for the Virtual Brewery
#
# Send all newsgroups except the control and junk ones by default
ME:!control,!junk::
#
# Generate overview data for any newsreaders to use.
overview::Tc,WO:/usr/lib/news/bin/overchan
#
# Feed the Groucho Marx University everything except our private newsgroup
# and any articles posted to the rec.crafts.brewing.poison newsgroup.
gmarxu:!rec.crafts.brewing.poison,@rec.crafts.brewing.private:\
        Tf,Wnm:news.groucho.edu
#
```

The nntpsend.ctl file

The *nntpsend* program manages the transmission of news articles using the NNTP protocol by calling the *innxmit* command. We saw a simple use of the *nntpsend* command earlier, but it too has a configuration file that provides us with some flexibility in how we configure our news feeds.

The *nntpsend* command expects to find batch files for the sites it will feed. It expects those batch files to be named */var/spool/news/out.going/sitename*. *innd* creates these batch files when acting on an entry in the *newsfeeds*, which we saw in the previous sections. We specified the sitename as the filename in the **param** field, and that satisfies the *nntpsend* command's input requirements.

The *nntpsend* command has a configuration file called *nntpsend.ctl* that is usually stored in the */etc/news/* directory.

The *nntpsend.ctl* file allows us to associate a fully qualified domain name, some news feed size constraints, and a number of transmission parameters with a news feed site name. The sitename is a means of uniquely identifying a logical feed of articles. The general format of the file is:

```
sitename:fqdn:max_size:[args]
```

The following list describes the elements of this format:

sitename
> The sitename as supplied in the *newsfeeds* file

fqdn
> The fully qualified domain name of the news server to which we will be feeding the news articles

max_size
> The maximum volume of news to feed in any single transfer

args
> Additional arguments to pass to the *innxmit* command

Our sample configuration requires a very simple *nntpsend.ctl* file. We have only one news feed. We'll restrict the feed to a maximum of 2 MB of traffic and we'll pass an argument to the *innxmit* that sets a 3-minute (180 second) timeout. If we were a larger site and had many news feeds, we'd simply create new entries for each new feed site that looked much the same as this one:

```
# /etc/news/nntpsend.ctl
#
gmarxu:news.groucho.edu:2m:-t 180
#
```

Controlling Newsreader Access

Not so many years ago, it was common for organizations to provide public access to their news servers. Today it is difficult to locate public news servers; most organizations carefully control who has access to their servers, typically restricting access to users supported on their network. INN provides configuration files to control this access.

The incoming.conf file

We mentioned in our introduction to INN that it achieves some of its efficiency and size by separating the news feed mechanism from the newsreading mechanism. The */etc/news/incoming.conf* file is where you specify which hosts will be feeding you news using the NNTP protocol, as well as where you define some parameters that control the way articles are fed to you from these hosts. Any host not listed in this file that connects to the news socket will not be handled by the *innd* daemon; instead, it will be handled by the *nnrpd* daemon.

The */etc/news/incoming.conf* file syntax is very simple, but it takes a moment to come to terms with. Three types of valid entries are allowed: key/value pairs, which are how you specify attributes and their values; peers, which is how you specify the name of a host allowed to send articles to us using NNTP; and groups, a means of applying key/value pairs to groups of peers. Key/value pairs can have three different types of scope. Global pairs apply to every peer defined in the file. Group pairs apply to all peers defined within that group. Peer pairs apply only to that one peer. Specific definitions override less specific ones: therefore, peer definitions override group definitions, which in turn override global pairs.

Curly brace characters ({}) are used to delimit the start and end of the `group` and `peer` specifications. The # character marks the rest of the line it appears on as a comment. Key/value pairs are separated by the colon character and appear one to a line.

A number of different keys may be specified. The more common and useful are:

hostname
> This key specifies a comma-separated list of fully qualifed names or IP addresses of the peers that we'll allow to send us articles. If this key is not supplied, the hostname defaults to the label of the peer.

streaming
> This key determines whether streaming commands are allowed from this host. It is a Boolean value that defaults to `true`.

max-connections
> This key specifies the maximum number of connections allowed from this group or peer. A value of zero means unlimited (which can also be specified using `none`).

password
> This key allows you to specify the password that must be used by a peer if it is to be allowed to transfer news. The default is to not require a password.

patterns
> This key specifies the newsgroups that we accept from the associated peer. This field is coded according to precisely the same rules as we used in our *newsfeeds* file.

In our example we have only one host that we are expecting to feed us news: our upstream news provider at Groucho Marx University. We'll have no password, but we will ensure that we don't accept any articles for our private newsgroup from outside. Our *hosts.nntp* looks like:

```
# Virtual Brewery incoming.conf file.

# Global settings
streaming:      true
max-connections: 5
```

```
# Allow NNTP posting from our local host.
peer ME {
    hostname: "localhost, 127.0.0.1"
}

# Allow groucho to send us all newsgroup except our local ones.
peer groucho {
    hostname: news.groucho.edu
    patterns: !rec.crafts.brewing.private
}
```

The nnrp.access file

We mentioned earlier that newsreaders, and in fact any host not listed in the *hosts.nntp*, that connect to the INN news server are handled by the *nnrpd* program. *nnrpd* uses the */etc/news/nnrp.access* file to determine who is allowed to make use of the news server, and what permissions they should have.

The *nnrp.access* file has a similar structure to the other configuration files we've looked at. It comprises a set of patterns used to match against the connecting host's domain name or IP address, and fields that determine what access and permission it should be given. Each entry should appear on a line by itself, and fields are separated by colons. The last entry in this file that matches the connecting host will be the one used, so again, you should put general patterns first and follow them with more specific ones later in the file. The five fields of each entry in the order they should appear are:

Hostname or IP address
> This field conforms to *wildmat(3)* pattern-matching rules. It is a pattern that describes the connecting host's name or IP address.

Permissions
> This field determines what permissions the matching host should be granted. There are two permissons you may configure: R gives read permissions, and P gives posting permissions.

Username
> This field is optional and allows you to specify a username that an NNTP client must log into the server before being allowed to post news articles. This field may be left blank. No user authentication is required to read articles.

Password
> This field is optional and is the password accompanying the **username** field. Leaving this field blank means that no password is required to post articles.

Newsgroups

> This field is a pattern specifying which newsgroups the client is allowed to access. The pattern follows the same rules as those used in the *newsfeeds* file. The default for this field is no newsgroups, so you would normally have a pattern configured here.

In the virtual brewery example, we will allow any NNTP client in the Virtual Brewery domain to both read and post to all newsgroups. We will allow any NNTP client read-only access to all newsgroups except our private internal newsgroup. Our *nnrp.access* file will look like this:

```
# Virtual Brewery - nnrp.access
# We will allow public reading of all newsgroups except our private one.
*:R:::*,!rec.crafts.brewing.private

# Any host with the Virtual Brewery domain may Read and Post to all
# newsgroups
*.vbrew.com:RP::*
```

Expiring News Articles

When news articles are received by a news server, they are stored to disk. News articles need to be available to users for some period of time to be useful, so a large operating news server can consume lots of disk space. To ensure that the disk space is used effectively, you can opt to delete news articles automatically after a period of time. This is called *article expiration*. Naturally, INN provides a means of automatically expiring news articles.

The expire.ctl file

The INN server uses a program called *expire* to delete expired news articles. The *expire* program in turn uses a file called */etc/news/expire.ctl* to configure the rules that govern article expiration.

The syntax of */etc/news/expire.ctl* is fairly simple. As with most configuration files, empty lines or lines beginning with the # character are ignored. The general idea is that you specify one rule per line. Each rule defines how article expiration will be performed on newsgroups matching a supplied pattern. The rule syntax looks like this:

pattern:modflag:keep:default:purge

The following list describes the fields:

pattern

> This field is a comma-delimited list of patterns matching names of newsgroups. The *wildmat*(3) routine is used to match these patterns. The last rule matching a newsgroup name is the one that is applied, so if you want to specify wildcard (*) rules, they should be listed first in this file.

modflag

> This flag describes how this rule applies to moderated newsgroups. It can be coded with an M to mean that this rule applies only to moderated newsgroups, a U to mean that this rule applies only to unmoderated newsgroups, or an A to mean that this rule ignores the moderated status and applies to all groups.

keep

> This field allows you to specify the minimum time an article with an "Expires" header will be kept before it is expired. The units are days, and are a floating point, so you may specify values like 7.5 for seven-and-a-half days. You may also specify never if you wish articles to stay in a newsgroup forever.

default

> This field is the most important. This field allows you to specify the time an article without an Expires header will be kept. Most articles won't have an Expires header. This field is coded in the same way as the *keep* field, with never meaning that articles without Expires headers will never be expired.

purge

> This field allows you to specify the maximum time an article with an Expires header will be kept before it is expired. The coding of this field is the same as for the keep field.

Our requirements are simple. We will keep all articles in all newsgroups for 14 days by default, and between 7 and 21 days for articles that have an Expires header. The *rec.crafts.brewing.private* newsgroup is our internal newsgroup, so we'll make sure we don't expire any articles from it:

```
# expire.ctl file for the Virtual Brewery

# Expire all articles in 14 days by default, 7-21 days for those with
# Expires: headers
*:A:7:14:21

# This is a special internal newsgroup, which we will never expire.
rec.crafts.brewing.private:A:never:never:never
```

We will mention one special type of entry you may have in your */etc/news/ expires.ctl* file. You may have exactly one line that looks like this:

```
/remember/:days
```

This entry allows you to specify the minimum number of days that an article will be remembered in the history file, irrespective of whether the article itself has been expired or not. This might be useful if one of the sites that is feeding you articles is infrequent and has a habit of sending you old articles every now and again. Setting the */remember/* field helps to prevent the upstream server from sending you the article again, even if it has already been expired from your server.

If your server remembers it has already received the article, it will reject attempts to resend it. It is important to remember that this setting has no effect at all on article expiration; it affects only the time that details of an article are kept in the history database.

Handling Control Messages

Just as with C News, INN can automatically process control messages. INN provides a powerful configuration mechanism to control what action will occur for each of a variety of control messages, and an access control mechanism to control who can initiate actions against which newsgroups.

The control.ctl file

The *control.ctl* file is fairly simple in structure. The syntax rules for this file are much the same as for the other INN configuration files. Lines beginning with # are ignored, lines may be continued using /, and fields are delimited by :.

When a control message is received, it is tested against each rule in turn. The last rule in the file that matches the message is the rule that will be used, so you should put any generic rules at the start of the file and more specific rules at the end of the file. The general syntax of the file is:

```
message:from:newsgroups:action
```

The meanings of each of the fields are:

message
> This is the name of the control message. Typical control messages are described later.

from
> This is a shell-style pattern matching the email address of the person sending the message. The email address is converted to lowercase before comparison.

newsgroups
> If the control message is `newgroup` or `rmgroup`, this field is a shell-style pattern matching the newsgroup created or removed.

action
> This field specifies what action to take for any message matching the rule. There are quite a number of actions we can take; they are described in the next list.

The *message* field of each line can have one of the following values:

checkgroups
> This message requests that news administrators resynchonrize their active newsgroups database against the list of newsgroups supplied in the control message.

newgroup
> This message requests the creation of a new newsgroup. The body of the control message should contain a short description of the purpose of the newsgroup to be created.

rmgroup
> requests that a newsgroup be removed.

sendsys
> This message requests that the *sys* file of this news server be transmitted by mail to the originator of the control message. RFC-1036 states that it is a requirement of Usenet membership that this information be publicly available because it is used to keep the map of Usenet up to date.

version
> This message requests that the hostname and version of news server software be returned to the originator of the control message.

all This is a special coding that will match any control message.

The `message` field may include the following actions:

doit
> The requested command is performed. In many cases, a mail message will be sent to the administrator to advise them that the action has taken place.

doit=file
> This is the same as the `doit` action except that a log message will be written to the *file* log file. If the specified file is *mail*, the log entry is sent by email. If the specified file is the null string, the log message is written to */dev/null* and is equivalent to using the unqualified `doit` action. If the *file* name begins with a / character, the name is taken to be an absolute filename for the logfile; otherwise, the specified name is translated to */var/log/news/file.log*.

doifarg
> The requested command is performed if the command has an argument. If the command has no argument, the control message is ignored.

drop
> The requested command is ignored.

log A log message is sent to the `stderr` output of the *innd* process. This is normally directed out to the */var/log/news/errlog* file.

log=file
> This is the same as a `log` action, except the logfile is specified as per the rules given for the `doit=file` action.

mail

> An email message is sent to the news administrator containing the requested command details. No other action takes place.

verify-*

> If an action begins with the string "`verify-`", then the control message is authenticated using PGP (or GPG).*

So that you can see what a *control.ctl* file would look like in practice, here is a very short illustrative sample:

```
##  Sample /etc/news/control.ctl
##
## Warning: You should not use this file, it is illustrative only.

##      Control Message Handling
all:*:*:mail
checkgroups:*:*:mail
ihave:*:*:drop
sendme:*:*:drop
sendsys:*:*:log=sendsys
senduuname:*:*:log=senduuname
version:*:*:log=version
newgroup:*:*:mail
rmgroup:*:*:mail


##  Handle control messages for the eight most important news heirarchies
##  COMP, HUMANITIES, MISC, NEWS, REC, SCI, SOC, TALK
checkgroups:*:comp.*|humanities.*|misc.*|news.*|rec.*|sci.*|soc.*|talk.*:drop
newgroup:*:comp.*|humanities.*|misc.*|news.*|rec.*|sci.*|soc.*|talk.*:drop
rmgroup:*:comp.*|humanities.*|misc.*|news.*|rec.*|sci.*|soc.*|talk.*:drop
checkgroups:group-admin@isc.org:*:verify-news.announce.newgroups
newgroup:group-admin@isc.org:comp.*|misc.*|news.*:verify-news.announce.newgroups
newgroup:group-admin@isc.org:rec.*|sci.*|soc.*:verify-news.announce.newgroups
newgroup:group-admin@isc.org:talk.*|humanities.*:verify-news.announce.newgroups
rmgroup:group-admin@isc.org:comp.*|misc.*|news.*:verify-news.announce.newgroups
rmgroup:group-admin@isc.org:rec.*|sci.*|soc.*:verify-news.announce.newgroups
rmgroup:group-admin@isc.org:talk.*|humanities.*:verify-news.announce.newgroups


## GNU ( Free Software Foundation )
newgroup:gnu@prep.ai.mit.edu:gnu.*:doit
newgroup:news@*ai.mit.edu:gnu.*:doit
rmgroup:gnu@prep.ai.mit.edu:gnu.*:doit
rmgroup:news@*ai.mit.edu:gnu.*:doit


## LINUX (Newsfeed from news.lameter.com)
checkgroups:christoph@lameter.com:linux.*:doit
```

---

* PGP and GPG are tools designed to authenticate or encrypt messages using public key techniques. GPG is the GNU free version of PGP. GPG may be found at *http://www.gnupg.org/*, and PGP may be found at *http://www.pgp.com/*.

```
newgroup:christoph@lameter.com:linux.*:doit
rmgroup:christoph@lameter.com:linux.*:doit
```

Running INN

The *inn* source package provides a script suitable for starting *inn* at boot time. The script is usually called */usr/lib/news/bin/rc.news*. The script reads arguments from another script, usually called */usr/lib/news/innshellvars*, which contains definitions of the filenames and filepaths that *inn* will use to locate components it needs. It is generally considered a good idea to execute *inn* with the permissions of a non-root user, such as **news**.

To ensure that *inn* is started at boot time, you should check that */usr/lib/news/ innshellvars* is configured correctly and then call the */usr/lib/news/bin/rc.news* script from a script executed at boot time.

Additionally, there are administrative tasks that must be performed periodically. These tasks are usually configured to be executed by the *cron* command. The best way to do this is to add the appropriate commands to your */etc/crontab* file, or even better, create a file suitable for the */etc/cron.d* directory, if your distribution provides one. An example of such a file might look like:

```
# Example /etc/cron.d/inn file, as used in the Debian distribution.
#
SHELL=/bin/sh
PATH=/usr/lib/news/bin:/sbin:/bin:/usr/sbin:/usr/bin

# Expire old news and overview entries nightly, generate reports.

15 0 * * *      news    news.daily expireover lowmark delayrm

# Every hour, run an rnews -U. This is not only for UUCP sites, but
# also to process queued up articles put there by in.nnrpd in case
# innd wasn't accepting any articles.

10 * * * *      news    rnews -U
```

These commands will ensure that old news is automatically expired each day, and that any queued articles are processed each hour. Note also that they are executed with the permissions of the **news** user.

Managing INN: The ctlinnd Command

The INN news server comes with a command to manage its day-to-day operation. The *ctlinnd* command can be used to manipulate newsgroups and newsgroup feeds, to obtain the status, of the server, and to reload, stop, and start the server.

You'd normally get a summary of the *ctlinnd* command syntax using:

```
# ctlinnd -h
```

We'll cover some of the more important uses of *ctlinnd* here; please consult the *ctlinnd* manual page for more detail.

Add a New Group

Use the following syntax to add a new group:

```
ctlinnd newgroup group rest creator
```

The arguments are defined as follows:

group
> The name of the group to create.

rest
> This argument should be coded in the same way as the *flags* field of the *active* file. It defaults to y if not supplied.

creator
> The name of the person creating the group. Enclose it in quotes if there are any spaces in the name.

Change a Group

Use the following syntax to change a group:

```
ctlinnd changegroup group rest
```

The arguments are defined as follows:

group
> The name of the group to change.

rest
> This argument should be coded in the same way as the *flags* field of the *active* file.

This command is useful to change the moderation status of a group.

Remove a Group

Use the following syntax to remove a group:

```
ctlinnd rmgroup group
```

The argument is defined as follows:

group
> The name of the group to remove.

This command removes the specified newsgroup from the *active* file. It has no effect on the news spool. All articles in the spool for the specified group will be expired in the usual fashion, but no new articles will be accepted.

Renumber a Group

Use the following syntax to renumber a group:

```
ctlinnd renumber group
```

The argument is defined as follows:

group
> The name of the group to renumber. If a *group* is an empty string, all groups are renumbered.

This command updates the low-water mark for the specified group.

Allow/Disallow Newsreaders

Use the following syntax to allow or disallow newsreaders:

```
ctlinnd readers flag text
```

The arguments are defined as follows:

flag
> Specifying n causes all newsreader connections to be disallowed. Specifying y allows newsreader connections.

text
> The text supplied will be given to newsreaders who attempt to connect, and usually describes the reason for disabling newsreader access. When reenabling newsreader access, this field must be either an empty string or a copy of the text supplied when the newsreader was disabled.
>
> This command does not affect incoming newsfeeds. It only controls connections from newsreaders.

Reject Newsfeed Connections

Use the following syntax to reject newsfeed connections:

```
ctlinnd reject reason
```

The argument is defined as follows:

reason
> The text supplied should explain why incoming connections to *innd* are rejected.

This command does not affect connections that are handed off to *nnrpd* (i.e., newsreaders); it only affects connections that would be handled by *innd* directly, such as remote newsfeeds.

Allow Newsfeed Connections

Use the following syntax to allow newsfeed connections:

```
ctlinnd allow reason
```

The argument is defined as follows:

reason
> The supplied text must be the same as that supplied to the preceding *reject* command or an empty string.

This command reverses the effect of a *reject* command.

Disable News Server

Use the following syntax to disable the news server:

```
ctlinnd throttle reason
```

The argument is defined as follows:

reason
> The reason for throttling the server.

This command is simultaneously equivalent to a `newsreaders no` and a `reject`, and is useful when emergency work is performed on the news database. It ensures that nothing attempts to update it while you are working on it.

Restart News Server

Use the following syntax to restart the news server:

```
ctlinnd go reason
```

The argument is defined as follows:

reason
> The reason given when stopping the server. If this field is an empty string, the server will be reenabled unconditionally. If a reason is given, only those functions disabled with a reason matching the supplied text will be restarted.

This command is used to restart a server function after a *throttle, pause,* or *reject* command.

Display Status of a Newsfeed

Use the following syntax to display the status of a newsfeed:

```
ctlinnd feedinfo site
```

The argument is defined as follows:

site
> The site name (taken from the *newsfeeds* file) for which you wish to display the newsfeed's status.

Drop a Newsfeed

Use the following syntax to drop a newsfeed:

```
ctlinnd drop site
```

The argument is defined as follows:

site
> The name of the site (taken from the *newsfeeds* file) to which feeds are dropped. If this field is an empty string, all active feeds will be dropped.

Dropping a newsfeed to a site halts any active feeds to the site. It is not a permanent change. This command would be useful if you've modified the feed details for a site and a feed to that site is active.

Begin a Newsfeed

Use the following syntax to begin a newsfeed:

```
ctlinnd begin site
```

The argument is defined as follows:

site
> The name of the site from the *newsfeeds* file to which feeds are started. If a feed to the site is already active, a *drop* command is done first automatically.

This command causes the server to reread the *newsfeeds* file, locate the matching entry, and commence a newsfeed to the named site using the details found. You can use this command to test a new news feed to a site after you've added or modified its entry in the *newsfeeds* file.

Cancel an Article

Use the following syntax to cancel an article:

```
ctlinnd cancel Message-Id
```

The argument is defined as follows:

Message-ID
   The ID of the article to be cancelled.

This command causes the specified article to be deleted from the server. It does not generate a cancel message.

CHAPTER TWENTY-FOUR

NEWSREADER CONFIGURATION

A *newsreader* is a program that users invoke to view, store, and create news articles. Several newsreaders have been ported to Linux. We will describe the basic setup for the three most popular newsreaders: *tin*, *trn*, and *nn*.

One of the most effective newsreaders is:

```
$ find /var/spool/news -name '[0-9]*' -exec cat {} \; | more
```

This is the way Unix die-hards read their news.

Most newsreaders, however, are much more sophisticated. They usually offer a full-screen interface with separate levels for displaying all groups the user has subscribed to, an overview of all articles in each group, and individual articles. Many web browsers double as newsreaders, but if you want to use a standalone newsreader, this chapter explains how to configure two classic ones: *trn* and *nn*.

At the newsgroup level, most newsreaders display a list of articles, showing their subject lines and authors. In big groups, it is difficult for the user to keep track of articles relating to each other, although it is possible to identify responses to earlier articles.

A response usually repeats the original article's subject, prepending it with `Re:`. Additionally, the `References:` header line should include the message ID of the article on which the response is directly following up. Sorting articles by these two criteria generates small clusters (in fact, trees) of articles, which are called *threads*. One of the tasks of writing a newsreader is devising an efficient scheme of threading, because the time required for this is proportional to the square of the number of articles.

We will not go into how the user interfaces are built here. All newsreaders currently available for Linux have a good help function; please refer to it for more details.

In the following sections, we will deal only with administrative tasks. Most of these relate to the creation of threads databases and accounting.

tin Configuration

The most versatile newsreader with respect to threading is *tin*. It was written by Iain Lea and is loosely modeled on an older newsreader named *tass* (written by Rich Skrenta). It does its threading when the user enters the newsgroup, and it is pretty fast unless you're getting posts via NNTP.

On a 486DX50, it takes roughly 30 seconds to thread 1,000 articles when reading directly from disk. It would take more than 5 minutes over NNTP to reach a loaded news server.* You may improve this time by regularly updating your index file by invoking *tin* with the *−u* option, so that when you next start *tin* to read news the threads already exist. Alternatively, you can invoke *tin* with the *−U* option to read news. When invoked this way, *tin* forks a background process to build the index files while you are reading news.

Usually, *tin* dumps its threading databases in the user's home directory below *.tin/ index*. This may be costly in terms of resources, however, so you should keep a single copy of them in a central location. This may be achieved by making *tin* setuid to **news**, for example. *tin* will then keep all thread databases below */var/ spool/news/.index*. For any file access or shell escape, it will reset its effective uid to the real uid of the user who invoked it.†

The version of *tin* included in some Linux distributions is compiled without NNTP support, but most do have it now. When invoked as *rtin* or with the *−r* option, *tin* tries to connect to the NNTP server specified in the file */etc/nntpserver* or in the **NNTPSERVER** environment variable. The *nntpserver* file simply contains the server's name on a single line.

trn Configuration

trn is also the successor to an older newsreader, namely *rn* (which means *read news*). The "t" in its name stands for "threaded." It was written by Wayne Davidson.

Unlike *tin*, *trn* has no provision for generating its threading database at runtime. Instead, it uses those prepared by a program called *mthreads* that has to be invoked regularly from *cron* to update the index files.

---

* Things improve drastically if the NNTP server does the threading itself and lets the client retrieve the threads databases; INN does this, for instance.

† This is the reason why you will get ugly error messages when invoking *tin* as superuser. But you shouldn't do routine work as **root**, anyway.

You can still access new articles if you're not running *mthreads*, but you will have all those "A GENUINE INVESTMENT OPPORTUNITY" articles scattered across your article selection menu, instead of a single thread you may easily skip.

To turn on threading for particular newsgroups, invoke *mthreads* with the list of newsgroups on the command line. The format of the list is the same as the one in the C News *sys* file:

```
$ mthreads 'comp,rec,!rec.games.go'
```

This command enables threading for all of *comp* and *rec*, except for *rec.games.go* (people who play Go don't need fancy threads). After that, you simply invoke *mthreads* with no options at all to make it thread any newly arrived articles. Threading of all groups found in your *active* file can be turned on by invoking *mthreads* with a group list of *all*.

If you're receiving news during the night, you will customarily run *mthreads* once in the morning, but you can also to do so more frequently if necessary. Sites that have very heavy traffic may want to run *mthreads* in daemon mode. When it is started at boot time using the *–d* option, it puts itself in the background, wakes up every ten minutes to check if there are any newly arrived articles, and threads them. To run *mthreads* in daemon mode, put the following line in your *rc.news* script:

```
/usr/local/bin/rn/mthreads -deav
```

The *–a* option makes *mthreads* automatically turn on threading for new groups as they are created; *–v* enables verbose log messages to the *mthreads* log file *mt.log* in the directory where you have *trn* installed.

Old articles that are no longer available must be removed from the index files regularly. By default, only articles with a number below the low-water mark will be removed.* Articles above this number that have been expired (because the oldest article has been assigned a long expiration date by an `Expires:` header field) may nevertheless be removed by giving *mthreads* the *–e* option to force an "enhanced" expiry run. When *mthreads* is running in daemon mode, the *–e* option makes *mthreads* put in such an enhanced expiry run once a day, shortly after midnight.

nn Configuration

nn, written by Kim F. Storm, claims to be a newsreader whose ultimate goal is not to read news. Its name stands for "No News," and its motto is "No news is good news. *nn* is better."

---

* Note that C News (described in Chapter 21, *C News*) doesn't update this low-water mark automatically; you have to run *updatemin* to do so.

To achieve this ambitious goal, *nn* comes with a large assortment of maintenance tools that not only allow thread generation, but also extensive database consistency checks, accounting, gathering of usage statistics, and access restrictions. There is also an administration program called *nnadmin*, which allows you to perform these tasks interactively. It is very intuitive, so we will not dwell on these aspects, but deal only with the generation of the index files.

The *nn* threads database manager is called *nnmaster*. It is usually run as a daemon, started from an *rc* file at boot time. It is invoked as:

```
/usr/local/lib/nn/nnmaster -l -r -C
```

This enables threading for all newsgroups present in your *active* file.

Equivalently, you may invoke *nnmaster* periodically from *cron*, giving it a list of groups to act upon. This list is very similar to the subscription list in the *sys* file, except that it uses blanks instead of commas. Instead of the fake group name **all**, an empty argument of `" "` should be used to denote all groups. A sample invocation looks like this:

```
# /usr/local/lib/nn/nnmaster !rec.games.go rec comp
```

Note that the order is significant. The leftmost group specification that matches always wins. Thus, if we had put `!rec.games.go` after `rec`, all articles from this group would have been threaded nevertheless.

nn offers several methods to remove expired articles from its databases. The first is to update the database by scanning the newsgroup directories and discarding the entries whose corresponding article has exceeded its expiration date. This is the default operation obtained by invoking *nnmaster* with the *−E* option. It is reasonably quick, unless you're doing this via NNTP.

The second method behaves exactly like a default expiration run of *mthreads*; it removes only those entries that refer to articles with numbers below the low-water mark in the *active* file. It may be enabled using the *−e* option.

Finally, the third strategy discards the entire database and recollects all articles. It may be enabled using the *−E3* option.

The list of groups to be expired is given by the *−F* option in the same fashion as above. However, if you have *nnmaster* running as daemon, you must kill it (using *−k*) before expiration can take place, and restart it with the original options afterward. Thus the proper command to run expiration on all groups using the first method is:

```
# nnmaster -kF ""
# nnmaster -lrC
```

There are many more flags that fine-tune the *nn*'s behavior. If you are concerned about removing bad articles or assembling article digests, read the *nnmaster* manual page.

nnmaster relies on a file named *GROUPS*, which is located in */var/lib/nn*. If it does not exist when *nnmaster* is first run, it is created. For each newsgroup, it contains a line that begins with the group's name, optionally followed by a time stamp and flags. You may edit these flags to enable certain behavior for the group in question, but you may not change the order in which the groups appear.* The flags allowed and their effects are detailed in the *nnmaster* manual page, too.

---

* Their order has to agree with that of the entries in the (binary) *MASTER* file.

EXAMPLE NETWORK: THE VIRTUAL BREWERY

Throughout this book we've used the following example that is a little less complex than Groucho Marx University and may be closer to the tasks you will actually encounter.

The Virtual Brewery is a small company that brews, as the name suggests, virtual beer. To manage their business more efficiently, the virtual brewers want to network their computers, which all happen to be PCs running the brightest and shiniest production Linux kernel. Figure A-1 shows the network configuration.

On the same floor, just across the hall, there's the Virtual Winery, which works closely with the brewery. The vintners run an Ethernet of their own. Quite naturally, the two companies want to link their networks once they are operational. As a first step, they want to set up a gateway host that forwards datagrams between the two subnets. Later, they also want to have a UUCP link to the outside world, through which they exchange mail and news. In the long run, they also want to set up PPP connections to connect to offsite locations and to the Internet.

The Virtual Brewery and the Virtual Winery each have a class C subnet of the Brewery's class B network, and gateway to each other via the host **vlager**, which also supports the UUCP connection. Figure A-2 shows the configuration.

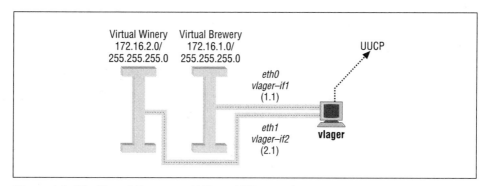

Figure A-1. The Virtual Brewery and Virtual Winery subnets

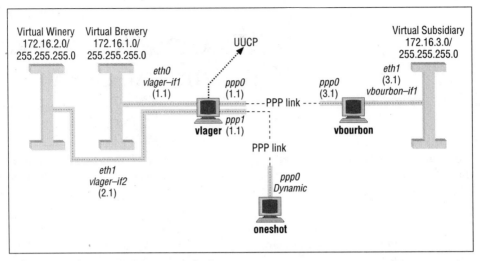

Figure A-2. The Virtual Brewery Network

Connecting the Virtual Subsidiary Network

The Virtual Brewery grows and opens a branch in another city. The subsidiary runs an Ethernet of its own using the IP network number **172.16.3.0**, which is subnet 3 of the Brewery's class B network. The host **vlager** acts as the gateway for the Brewery network and will support the PPP link; its peer at the new branch is called **vbourbon** and has an IP address of **172.16.3.1**. This network is illustrated in Figure A-2.

USEFUL CABLE CONFIGURATIONS

If you wish to connect two computers together and you don't have an Ethernet network, you will need either a serial null modem cable, or a PLIP parallel cable.

These cables can be bought off the shelf, but are much cheaper and fairly simple to make yourself.

A PLIP Parallel Cable

To make a parallel cable to use for PLIP, you will need two 25-pin connectors (called DB-25) and a cable with at least eleven conductors. The cable must not be any longer than 15 meters (50 feet). The cable may or may not have a shield, but if you are building a long cable, it is probably a good idea to have one.

If you look at the connector, you should be able to read tiny numbers at the base of each pin—from 1 for the pin at the top left (if you hold the broader side up) to 25 for the pin at the bottom right. For the null printer cable, you have to connect the following pins of both connectors with each other, as shown in Figure B-1.

All remaining pins remain unconnected. If the cable is shielded, the shield should be connected to the DB-25's metallic shell on just *one* end.

A Serial NULL Modem Cable

A serial null modem cable will work for both SLIP and PPP. Again, you will need two DB-25 connectors. This time your cable requires only eight conductors.

You may have seen other NULL modem cable designs, but this one allows you to use hardware flow control—which is far superior to XON/XOFF flow control—or none at all. The conductor configuration is shown in Figure B-2:

Again, if you have a shield, you should connect it to the first pin at one end only.

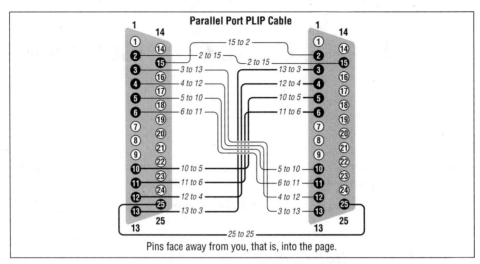

Figure B-1. Parallel PLIP cable

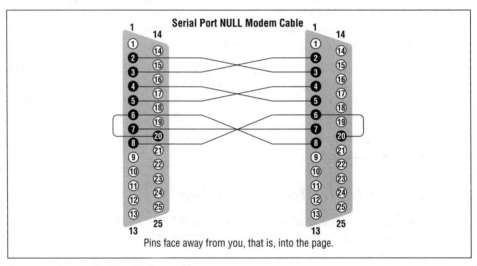

Figure B-2. Serial NULL-Modem cable

LINUX NETWORK ADMINISTRATOR'S GUIDE, SECOND EDITION COPYRIGHT INFORMATION

0. Preamble

The purpose of this License is to make a manual, textbook, or other written document "free" in the sense of freedom: to assure everyone the effective freedom to copy and redistribute it, with or without modifying it, either commercially or noncommercially. Secondarily, this License preserves for the author and publisher a way to get credit for their work, while not being considered responsible for modifications made by others.

This License is a kind of "copyleft," which means that derivative works of the document must themselves be free in the same sense. It complements the GNU General Public License, which is a copyleft license designed for free software.

We have designed this License in order to use it for manuals for free software, because free software needs free documentation: a free program should come with manuals providing the same freedoms that the software does. But this License is not limited to software manuals; it can be used for any textual work, regardless of subject matter or whether it is published as a printed book. We recommend this License principally for works whose purpose is instruction or reference.

1. Applicability and Definitions

This License applies to any manual or other work that contains a notice placed by the copyright holder saying it can be distributed under the terms of this License. The "Document," below, refers to any such manual or work. Any member of the public is a licensee, and is addressed as "you."

A "Modified Version" of the Document means any work containing the Document or a portion of it, either copied verbatim, or with modifications and/or translated into another language.

A "Secondary Section" is a named appendix or a front-matter section of the Document that deals exclusively with the relationship of the publishers or authors of the Document to the Document's overall subject (or to related matters) and contains nothing that could fall directly within that overall subject. (For example, if the Document is in part a textbook of mathematics, a Secondary Section may not explain any mathematics.) The relationship could be a matter of historical connection with the subject or with related matters, or of legal, commercial, philosophical, ethical or political position regarding them.

The "Invariant Sections" are certain Secondary Sections whose titles are designated, as being those of Invariant Sections, in the notice that says that the Document is released under this License.

The "Cover Texts" are certain short passages of text that are listed, as Front-Cover Texts or Back-Cover Texts, in the notice that says that the Document is released under this License.

A "Transparent" copy of the Document means a machine-readable copy, represented in a format whose specification is available to the general public, whose contents can be viewed and edited directly and straightforwardly with generic text editors or (for images composed of pixels) generic paint programs or (for drawings) some widely available drawing editor, and that is suitable for input to text formatters or for automatic translation to a variety of formats suitable for input to text formatters. A copy made in an otherwise Transparent file format whose markup has been designed to thwart or discourage subsequent modification by readers is not Transparent. A copy that is not "Transparent" is called "Opaque."

Examples of suitable formats for Transparent copies include plain ASCII without markup, Texinfo input format, LaTeX input format, SGML or XML using a publicly available DTD, and standard-conforming simple HTML designed for human modification. Opaque formats include PostScript, PDF, proprietary formats that can be read and edited only by proprietary word processors, SGML or XML for which the DTD and/or processing tools are not generally available, and the machine-generated HTML produced by some word processors for output purposes only.

The "Title Page" means, for a printed book, the title page itself, plus such following pages as are needed to hold, legibly, the material this License requires to appear in the title page. For works in formats that do not have any title page as such, "Title Page" means the text near the most prominent appearance of the work's title, preceding the beginning of the body of the text.

2. Verbatim Copying

You may copy and distribute the Document in any medium, either commercially or noncommercially, provided that this License, the copyright notices, and the license notice saying this License applies to the Document are reproduced in all copies, and that you add no other conditions whatsoever to those of this License. You may not use technical measures to obstruct or control the reading or further copying of the copies you make or distribute. However, you may accept compensation in exchange for copies. If you distribute a large enough number of copies you must also follow the conditions in section 3.

You may also lend copies, under the same conditions stated above, and you may publicly display copies.

3. Copying in Quantity

If you publish printed copies of the Document numbering more than 100, and the Document's license notice requires Cover Texts, you must enclose the copies in covers that carry, clearly and legibly, all these Cover Texts: Front-Cover Texts on the front cover, and Back-Cover Texts on the back cover. Both covers must also clearly and legibly identify you as the publisher of these copies. The front cover must present the full title with all words of the title equally prominent and visible. You may add other material on the covers in addition. Copying with changes limited to the covers, as long as they preserve the title of the Document and satisfy these conditions, can be treated as verbatim copying in other respects.

If the required texts for either cover are too voluminous to fit legibly, you should put the first ones listed (as many as fit reasonably) on the actual cover, and continue the rest onto adjacent pages.

If you publish or distribute Opaque copies of the Document numbering more than 100, you must either include a machine-readable Transparent copy along with each Opaque copy, or state in or with each Opaque copy a publicly-accessible computer-network location containing a complete Transparent copy of the Document, free of added material, which the general network-using public has access to download anonymously at no charge using public-standard network protocols. If you use the latter option, you must take reasonably prudent steps, when you begin distribution of Opaque copies in quantity, to ensure that this Transparent copy will remain thus accessible at the stated location until at least one year after the last time you distribute an Opaque copy (directly or through your agents or retailers) of that edition to the public.

It is requested, but not required, that you contact the authors of the Document well before redistributing any large number of copies, to give them a chance to provide you with an updated version of the Document.

4. Modifications

You may copy and distribute a Modified Version of the Document under the conditions of sections 2 and 3 above, provided that you release the Modified Version under precisely this License, with the Modified Version filling the role of the Document, thus licensing distribution and modification of the Modified Version to whoever possesses a copy of it. In addition, you must do these things in the Modified Version:

A. Use in the Title Page (and on the covers, if any) a title distinct from that of the Document, and from those of previous versions (which should, if there were any, be listed in the History section of the Document). You may use the same title as a previous version if the original publisher of that version gives permission.

B. List on the Title Page, as authors, one or more persons or entities responsible for authorship of the modifications in the Modified Version, together with at least five of the principal authors of the Document (all of its principal authors, if it has less than five).

C. State on the Title page the name of the publisher of the Modified Version, as the publisher.

D. Preserve all the copyright notices of the Document.

E. Add an appropriate copyright notice for your modifications adjacent to the other copyright notices.

F. Include, immediately after the copyright notices, a license notice giving the public permission to use the Modified Version under the terms of this License, in the form shown in the Addendum below.

G. Preserve in that license notice the full lists of Invariant Sections and required Cover Texts given in the Document's license notice.

H. Include an unaltered copy of this License.

I. Preserve the section entitled "History," and its title, and add to it an item stating at least the title, year, new authors, and publisher of the Modified Version as given on the Title Page. If there is no section entitled "History" in the Document, create one stating the title, year, authors, and publisher of the Document as given on its Title Page, then add an item describing the Modified Version as stated in the previous sentence.

J. Preserve the network location, if any, given in the Document for public access to a Transparent copy of the Document, and likewise the network locations given in the Document for previous versions it was based on. These may be placed in the "History" section. You may omit a network location for a work that was published at least four years before the Document itself, or if the original publisher of the version it refers to gives permission.

K. In any section entitled "Acknowledgements" or "Dedications," preserve the section's title, and preserve in the section all the substance and tone of each of the contributor acknowledgements and/or dedications given therein.

L. Preserve all the Invariant Sections of the Document, unaltered in their text and in their titles. Section numbers or the equivalent are not considered part of the section titles.

M. Delete any section entitled "Endorsements." Such a section may not be included in the Modified Version.

N.   Do not retitle any existing section as "Endorsements" or to conflict in title with any Invariant Section.

If the Modified Version includes new front-matter sections or appendices that qualify as Secondary Sections and contain no material copied from the Document, you may at your option designate some or all of these sections as invariant. To do this, add their titles to the list of Invariant Sections in the Modified Version's license notice. These titles must be distinct from any other section titles.

You may add a section entitled "Endorsements," provided it contains nothing but endorsements of your Modified Version by various parties—for example, statements of peer review or that the text has been approved by an organization as the authoritative definition of a standard.

You may add a passage of up to five words as a Front-Cover Text, and a passage of up to 25 words as a Back-Cover Text, to the end of the list of Cover Texts in the Modified Version. Only one passage of Front-Cover Text and one of Back-Cover Text may be added by (or through arrangements made by) any one entity. If the Document already includes a cover text for the same cover, previously added by you or by arrangement made by the same entity you are acting on behalf of, you may not add another; but you may replace the old one, on explicit permission from the previous publisher that added the old one.

The author(s) and publisher(s) of the Document do not by this License give permission to use their names for publicity for or to assert or imply endorsement of any Modified Version.

5. Combining Documents

You may combine the Document with other documents released under this License, under the terms defined in section 4 above for modified versions, provided that you include in the combination all of the Invariant Sections of all of the original documents, unmodified, and list them all as Invariant Sections of your combined work in its license notice.

The combined work need only contain one copy of this License, and multiple identical Invariant Sections may be replaced with a single copy. If there are multiple Invariant Sections with the same name but different contents, make the title of each such section unique by adding at the end of it, in parentheses, the name of the original author or publisher of that section if known, or else a unique number. Make the same adjustment to the section titles in the list of Invariant Sections in the license notice of the combined work.

In the combination, you must combine any sections entitled "History" in the various original documents, forming one section entitled "History"; likewise combine any sections entitled "Acknowledgements," and any sections entitled "Dedications." You must delete all sections entitled "Endorsements."

6. Collections of Documents

You may make a collection consisting of the Document and other documents released under this License, and replace the individual copies of this License in the various documents with a single copy that is included in the collection, provided that you follow the rules of this License for verbatim copying of each of the documents in all other respects.

You may extract a single document from such a collection, and distribute it individually under this License, provided you insert a copy of this License into the extracted document, and follow this License in all other respects regarding verbatim copying of that document.

7. Aggregation with Independent Works

A compilation of the Document or its derivatives with other separate and independent documents or works, in or on a volume of a storage or distribution medium, does not as a whole count as a Modified Version of the Document, provided no compilation copyright is claimed for the compilation. Such a compilation is called an "aggregate," and this License does not apply to the other self-contained works thus compiled with the Document, on account of their being thus compiled, if they are not themselves derivative works of the Document.

If the Cover Text requirement of section 3 is applicable to these copies of the Document, then if the Document is less than one quarter of the entire aggregate, the Document's Cover Texts may be placed on covers that surround only the Document within the aggregate. Otherwise they must appear on covers around the whole aggregate.

8. Translation

Translation is considered a kind of modification, so you may distribute translations of the Document under the terms of section 4. Replacing Invariant Sections with translations requires special permission from their copyright holders, but you may include translations of some or all Invariant Sections in addition to the original versions of these Invariant Sections. You may include a translation of this License provided that you also include the original English version of this License. In case of a disagreement between the translation and the original English version of this License, the original English version will prevail.

9. Termination

You may not copy, modify, sublicense, or distribute the Document except as expressly provided for under this License. Any other attempt to copy, modify, sublicense or distribute the Document is void, and will automatically terminate your rights under this License. However, parties who have received copies, or rights, from you under this License will not have their licenses terminated so long as such parties remain in full compliance.

10. Future Revisions of this License

The Free Software Foundation may publish new, revised versions of the GNU Free Documentation License from time to time. Such new versions will be similar in spirit to the present version, but may differ in detail to address new problems or concerns. See *http://www.gnu.org/copyleft/*.

Each version of the License is given a distinguishing version number. If the Document specifies that a particular numbered version of this License "or any later version" applies to it, you have the option of following the terms and conditions either of that specified version or of any later version that has been published (not as a draft) by the Free Software Foundation. If the Document does not specify a version number of this License, you may choose any version ever published (not as a draft) by the Free Software Foundation.

SAGE: THE SYSTEM ADMINISTRATORS GUILD

If you are not getting everything you need from posting to *comp.os.linux.** groups and reading documentation, maybe it's time to consider joining SAGE, the System Administrators Guild, sponsored by USENIX. The main goal of SAGE is to advance system administration as a profession. SAGE brings together system and network administrators to foster professional and technical development, share problems and solutions, and communicate with users, management, and vendors on system administration topics.

Current SAGE initiatives include:

- Co-sponsoring the highly successful annual System Administration Conferences (LISA) with USENIX.

- Publishing *Job Descriptions for System Administrators*, edited by Tina Darmohray, the first in a series of very practical booklets and resource guides covering system administration issues and techniques.

- Creating an archive site, **ftp.sage.usenix.org**, for papers from the System Administration Conferences and sysadmin-related documentation.

- Establishing working groups in areas important to system administrators, such as jobs, publications, policies, electronic information distribution, education, vendors, and standards.

To learn more about the USENIX Association and its Special Technical Group, SAGE, contact the USENIX Association office at (510) 528-8649 in the U.S., or by email to *office@usenix.org*. To receive information electronically, contact *info@usenix.org*. Annual SAGE membership is $25 (you must also be a member of USENIX). Members enjoy free subscriptions to *login:* and *Computing Systems*, a quarterly refereed technical journal; discounts on conference and symposia registration; and savings on SAGE publication purchases and other services.

INDEX

About the Authors

Olaf Kirch has a degree in Mathematics but turned his back on category theory and compact continuous lattices after booting his first Linux kernel some time in '92. He vividly recalls the joy of learning Unix by reading Linux kernel code.

Since that time, he has participated in various Linux projects, including writing large parts of its NFS implementation, and running the first Linux security mailing list with Jeff Uphoff in '95.

He currently works for Caldera Systems, where he is responsible for much of the network-related stuff as well as security issues, and sometimes finds himself wondering whether he's dreaming or if all this is real.

In his spare time, he enjoys being with Maren and their daughter Jule. And in case you actually read the bio in the first edition of the Network Administrator's Guide—Olaf does have a driving license now.

Terry Dawson is an amateur radio operator and longtime Linux enthusiast. He is the author of a number of network-related HOWTO documents for the Linux Documentation Project, and is an active participant in a number of other Linux projects.

Terry has 15 years of professional experience in telecommunications and is currently engaged in network management research in the Telstra Research Laboratories. Terry lives in Sydney with his wife Maggie, and son Jack.

Colophon

Our look is the result of reader comments, our own experimentation, and feedback from distribution channels. Distinctive covers complement our distinctive approach to technical topics, breathing personality and life into potentially dry subjects.

The cover image of a cowboy is adapted from a 19th-century engraving from *Marvels of the New West: A Vivid Portrayal of the Stupendous Marvels in the Vast Wonderland West of the Missouri River*, by William Thayer (The Henry Bill Publishing Co., Norwich, CT, 1888). Lar Kaufman suggested the western theme for O'Reilly's Linux series.

Maureen Dempsey copyedited *Linux Network Administrator's Guide, Second Edition*; Ann Schirmer proofread the text. Claire Cloutier, Catherine Morris, and Mary Sheehan provided quality control. Robert Romano and Rhon Porter created the illustrations using Adobe Photoshop 5 and Macromedia FreeHand 8. Judy Hoer wrote the index. Compositors include Ann Schirmer, Mary Sheehan, Gabe Weiss, and Sarah Jane Shangraw.

Hanna Dyer designed the cover layout based on a series design by Edie Freedman. Emma Colby produced the cover with QuarkXPress 3.32 and Adobe Photoshop 5.5 software, using the ITC Garamond Condensed font. Alicia Cech and David Futato designed the interior layouts, based on a series design created by Edie Freedman and Jennifer Niederst and modified by Nancy Priest. Chapter opening graphics are from the Dover Pictorial Archive and *Marvels of the New West*.

Whenever possible, our books use RepKover™, a durable and flexible lay-flat binding. If the page count exceeds RepKover's limit, perfect binding is used.

Interior fonts are Adobe ITC Garamond and ConstantWillison. Text was prepared in SGML using the DocBook 2.1 DTD. The print version of this book was created by translating the SGML source into a set of *gtroff* macros using a filter developed at O'Reilly by Norman Walsh. Steve Talbott designed and wrote the underlying macro set on the basis of the GNU *gtroff –gs* macros; Lenny Muellner adapted the macros to SGML and implemented the book design. The GNU *groff* text formatter version 1.09 was used to generate PostScript output; this output was distilled to PDF for use at press.

 # More Titles from O'Reilly

Linux

Linux in a Nutshell, 2nd Edition

By Ellen Siever &
the Staff of O'Reilly & Associates
2nd Edition February 1999
628 pages, ISBN 1-56592-585-8

This complete reference covers the core
commands available on common Linux
distributions. It contains all user, programming,
administration, and networking commands with
options, and also documents a wide range of
GNU tools. New material in the second edition includes popular LILO
and Loadlin programs used for dual-booting, a Perl quick-reference,
and RCS/CVS source control commands.

Linux Multimedia Guide

By Jeff Tranter
1st Edition September 1996
386 pages, ISBN 1-56592-219-0

Linux is increasingly popular among
computer enthusiasts of all types, and one
of the applications where it is flourishing
is multimedia. This book tells you how to
program such popular devices as sound cards,
CD-ROMs, and joysticks. It also describes the best free software
packages that support manipulation of graphics, audio, and video
and offers guidance on fitting the pieces together.

The Cathedral & the Bazaar

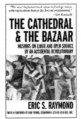

By Eric S. Raymond
1st Edition October 1999
288 pages, ISBN 1-56592-724-9

After Red Hat's stunning IPO, even people
outside the computer industry have now
heard of Linux and open-source software.
This book contains the essays, originally
published online, that led to Netscape's
decision to release their browser as open
source, put Linus Torvalds on the cover of Forbes Magazine and
Microsoft on the defensive, and helped Linux to rock the world
of commercial software. These essays have been expanded and
revised for this edition, and are in print for the first time.

Running Linux, 3rd Edition

By Matt Welsh, Matthias Kalle Dalheimer &
Lar Kaufman
3rd Edition August 1999
752 pages, ISBN 1-56592-469-X

This book explains everything you need to
understand, install, and start using the Linux
operating system. It includes an installation
tutorial, system maintenance tips, document
development and programming tools, and guidelines for network,
file, printer, and Web site administration. New topics in the third
edition include KDE, Samba, PPP, and revised instructions for
installation and configuration (especially for the Red Hat, SuSE
and Debian distributions).

Linux Device Drivers

By Alessandro Rubini
1st Edition February 1998
442 pages, ISBN 1-56592-292-1

This practical guide is for anyone who
wants to support computer peripherals
under the Linux operating system or who
wants to develop new hardware and run it
under Linux. It shows step-by-step how to
write a driver for character devices, block devices, and network
interfaces, illustrated with examples you can compile and run.
Focuses on portability.

Learning the bash Shell, 2nd Edition

By Cameron Newham & Bill Rosenblatt
2nd Edition January 1998
336 pages, ISBN 1-56592-347-2

This second edition covers all of the features
of bash Version 2.0, while still applying to
bash Version 1.x. It includes one-dimensional
arrays, parameter expansion, more pattern-
matching operations, new commands, security
improvements, additions to ReadLine, improved configuration and
installation, and an additional programming aid, the bash shell
debugger.

O'REILLY®

TO ORDER: **800-998-9938** • *order@oreilly.com* • *http://www.oreilly.com/*
OUR PRODUCTS ARE AVAILABLE AT A BOOKSTORE OR SOFTWARE STORE NEAR YOU.
FOR INFORMATION: **800-998-9938** • **707-829-0515** • *info@oreilly.com*

Linux

Using Samba

By Peter Kelly, Perry Donham &
David Collier-Brown
1st Edition November 1999
416 pages, Includes CD-ROM
ISBN 1-56592-449-5

Samba turns a UNIX or Linux system into a
file and print server for Microsoft Windows
network clients. This complete guide to
Samba administration covers basic 2.0 configuration, security,
logging, and troubleshooting. Whether you're playing on one note
or a full three-octave range, this book will help you maintain an
efficient and secure server. Includes a CD-ROM of sources and
ready-to-install binaries.

Learning Red Hat Linux

By Bill McCarty
1st Edition September 1999
394 pages, Includes CD-ROM
ISBN 1-56592-627-7

Learning Red Hat Linux will guide any new
Linux user through the installation and use
of the free operating system that is shaking
up the world of commercial software. It
demystifies Linux in terms familiar to Windows users and gives
readers only what they need to start being successful users of
this operating system.

MySQL & mSQL

By Randy Jay Yarger, George Reese & Tim King
1st Edition July 1999
506 pages, ISBN 1-56592-434-7

This book teaches you how to use MySQL
and mSQL, two popular and robust database
products that support key subsets of SQL on
both Linux and UNIX systems. Anyone who
knows basic C, Java, Perl, or Python can
write a program to interact with a database, either as a standalone application or through a Web page. This book takes you
through the whole process, from installation and configuration to
programming interfaces and basic administration. Includes ample
tutorial material.

Programming with Qt

By Matthias Kalle Dalheimer
1st Edition April 1999
384 pages, ISBN 1-56592-588-2

This indispensable guide teaches you how
to take full advantage of Qt, a powerful,
easy-to-use, cross-platform GUI toolkit, and
guides you through the steps of writing your
first Qt application. It describes all of the
GUI elements in Qt, along with advice about when and how to
use them. It also contains material on advanced topics like 2D
transformations, drag-and-drop, and custom image file filters.

Open Sources:
Voices from the Open Source Revolution

Edited by Chris DiBona,
Sam Ockman & Mark Stone
1st Edition January 1999
280 pages, ISBN 1-56592-582-3

In *Open Sources*, leaders of Open Source
come together in print for the first time
to discuss the new vision of the software
industry they have created, through essays
that explain how the movement works, why it succeeds, and
where it is going. A powerful vision from the movement's spiritual
leaders, this book reveals the mysteries of how open development
builds better software and how businesses can leverage freely
available software for a competitive business advantage.

Programming with GNU Software

By Mike Loukides & Andy Oram
1st Edition December 1996
260 pages, Includes CD-ROM
ISBN 1-56592-112-7

This book and CD combination is a complete
package for programmers who are new to
UNIX or who would like to make better use
of the system. The tools come from Cygnus
Support, Inc., and Cyclic Software, companies that provide support
for free software. Contents include GNU Emacs, gcc, C and C++
libraries, gdb, RCS, and make. The book provides an introduction
to all these tools for a C programmer.

UNIX Basics

Learning the UNIX Operating System, 4th Edition

By Jerry Peek, Grace Todino & John Strang
4th Edition December 1997
106 pages, ISBN 1-56592-390-1

If you are new to UNIX, this concise introduction will tell you just what you need to get started and no more. The new fourth edition covers the Linux operating system and is an ideal primer for someone just starting with UNIX or Linux, as well as for Mac and PC users who encounter a UNIX system on the Internet. This classic book, still the most effective introduction to UNIX in print, now includes a quick-reference card.

Learning the vi Editor, 6th Edition

By Linda Lamb & Arnold Robbins
6th Edition October 1998
348 pages, ISBN 1-56592-426-6

This completely updated guide to editing with vi, the editor available on nearly every UNIX system, now covers four popular vi clones and includes command summaries for easy reference. It starts with the basics, followed by more advanced editing tools, such as ex commands, global search and replacement, and a new feature, multi-screen editing.

Learning the Korn Shell

By Bill Rosenblatt
1st Edition June 1993
360 pages, ISBN 1-56592-054-6

A thorough introduction to the Korn shell, both as a user interface and as a programming language. This book provides a clear explanation of the Korn shell's features, including ksh string operations, co-processes, signals and signal handling, and command-line interpretation. *Learning the Korn Shell* also includes real-life programming examples and a Korn shell debugger (kshdb).

Learning GNU Emacs, 2nd Edition

By Debra Cameron, Bill Rosenblatt &
Eric Raymond
2nd Edition September 1996
560 pages, ISBN 1-56592-152-6

Learning GNU Emacs is an introduction to Version 19.30 of the GNU Emacs editor, one of the most widely used and powerful editors available under UNIX. It provides a solid introduction to basic editing, a look at several important "editing modes" (special Emacs features for editing specific types of documents, including email, Usenet News, and the World Wide Web), and a brief introduction to customization and Emacs LISP programming. The book is aimed at new Emacs users, whether or not they are programmers. Includes quick-reference card.

Using csh and tcsh

By Paul DuBois
1st Edition August 1995
242 pages, ISBN 1-56592-132-1

Using csh and tcsh describes from the beginning how to use these shells interactively to get your work done faster with less typing. You'll learn how to make your prompt tell you where you are (no more pwd); use what you've typed before (history); type long command lines with few keystrokes (command and filename completion); remind yourself of filenames when in the middle of typing a command; and edit a botched command without retyping it.

Volume 3M: X Window System User's Guide, Motif Edition, 2nd Edition

By Valerie Quercia & Tim O'Reilly
2nd Edition January 1993
956 pages, ISBN 1-56592-015-5

The X Window System User's Guide, Motif Edition orients the new user to window system concepts and provides detailed tutorials for many client programs, including the xtermterminal emulator and the twm, uwm, and mwmwindow managers. Later chapters explain how to customize the X environment. Revised for Motif 1.2 and X11 Release 5.

How to stay in touch with O'Reilly

1. Visit Our Award-Winning Web Site

http://www.oreilly.com/

★ "Top 100 Sites on the Web" —*PC Magazine*
★ "Top 5% Web sites" —*Point Communications*
★ "3-Star site" —*The McKinley Group*

Our web site contains a library of comprehensive product information (including book excerpts and tables of contents), downloadable software, background articles, interviews with technology leaders, links to relevant sites, book cover art, and more. File us in your Bookmarks or Hotlist!

2. Join Our Email Mailing Lists

New Product Releases

To receive automatic email with brief descriptions of all new O'Reilly products as they are released, send email to:
listproc@online.oreilly.com
Put the following information in the first line of your message (*not* in the Subject field):
subscribe oreilly-news

O'Reilly Events

If you'd also like us to send information about trade show events, special promotions, and other O'Reilly events, send email to:
listproc@online.oreilly.com
Put the following information in the first line of your message (*not* in the Subject field):
subscribe oreilly-events

3. Get Examples from Our Books via FTP

There are two ways to access an archive of example files from our books:

Regular FTP

- ftp to:
  ftp.oreilly.com
  (login: anonymous
  password: your email address)
- Point your web browser to:
  ftp://ftp.oreilly.com/

FTPMAIL

- Send an email message to:
  ftpmail@online.oreilly.com
  (Write "help" in the message body)

4. Contact Us via Email

order@oreilly.com
To place a book or software order online. Good for North American and international customers.

subscriptions@oreilly.com
To place an order for any of our newsletters or periodicals.

books@oreilly.com
General questions about any of our books.

software@oreilly.com
For general questions and product information about our software. Check out O'Reilly Software Online at **http://software.oreilly.com/** for software and technical support information. Registered O'Reilly software users send your questions to: **website-support@oreilly.com**

cs@oreilly.com
For answers to problems regarding your order or our products.

booktech@oreilly.com
For book content technical questions or corrections.

proposals@oreilly.com
To submit new book or software proposals to our editors and product managers.

international@oreilly.com
For information about our international distributors or translation queries. For a list of our distributors outside of North America check out:
http://www.oreilly.com/www/order/country.html

5. Work with Us

Check out our website for current employment opportunites:
www.jobs@oreilly.com
Click on "Work with Us"

O'Reilly & Associates, Inc.
101 Morris Street, Sebastopol, CA 95472 USA
TEL   707-829-0515 or 800-998-9938
         (6am to 5pm PST)
FAX   707-829-0104

Titles from O'Reilly

WEB

Advanced Perl Programming
Apache: The Definitive Guide,
  2nd Edition
ASP in a Nutshell
Building Your Own Web Conferences
Building Your Own Website™
CGI Programming with Perl
Designing with JavaScript
Dynamic HTML:
  The Definitive Reference
Frontier: The Definitive Guide
HTML: The Definitive Guide,
  3rd Edition
Information Architecture
  for the World Wide Web
JavaScript Pocket Reference
JavaScript: The Definitive Guide,
  3rd Edition
Learning VB Script
Photoshop for the Web
WebMaster in a Nutshell
WebMaster in a Nutshell,
  Deluxe Edition
Web Design in a Nutshell
Web Navigation:
  Designing the User Experience
Web Performance Tuning
Web Security & Commerce
Writing Apache Modules

PERL

Learning Perl, 2nd Edition
Learning Perl for Win32 Systems
Learning Perl/TK
Mastering Algorithms with Perl
Mastering Regular Expressions
Perl5 Pocket Reference, 2nd Edition
Perl Cookbook
Perl in a Nutshell
Perl Resource Kit—UNIX Edition
Perl Resource Kit—Win32 Edition
Perl/TK Pocket Reference
Programming Perl, 2nd Edition
Web Client Programming with Perl

GRAPHICS & MULTIMEDIA

Director in a Nutshell
Encyclopedia of Graphics
  File Formats, 2nd Edition
Lingo in a Nutshell
Photoshop in a Nutshell
QuarkXPress in a Nutshell

USING THE INTERNET

AOL in a Nutshell
Internet in a Nutshell
Smileys
The Whole Internet for Windows95
The Whole Internet:
  The Next Generation
The Whole Internet
  User's Guide & Catalog

JAVA SERIES

Database Programming with
  JDBC and Java
Developing Java Beans
Exploring Java, 2nd Edition
Java AWT Reference
Java Cryptography
Java Distributed Computing
Java Examples in a Nutshell
Java Foundation Classes in a Nutshell
Java Fundamental Classes Reference
Java in a Nutshell, 2nd Edition
Java in a Nutshell, Deluxe Edition
Java I/O
Java Language Reference, 2nd Edition
Java Media Players
Java Native Methods
Java Network Programming
Java Security
Java Servlet Programming
Java Swing
Java Threads
Java Virtual Machine

UNIX

Exploring Expect
GNU Emacs Pocket Reference
Learning GNU Emacs, 2nd Edition
Learning the bash Shell, 2nd Edition
Learning the Korn Shell
Learning the UNIX Operating System,
  4th Edition
Learning the vi Editor, 6th Edition
Linux in a Nutshell
Linux Multimedia Guide
Running Linux, 2nd Edition
SCO UNIX in a Nutshell
sed & awk, 2nd Edition
Tcl/Tk in a Nutshell
Tcl/Tk Pocket Reference
Tcl/Tk Tools
The UNIX CD Bookshelf
UNIX in a Nutshell, System V Edition
UNIX Power Tools, 2nd Edition
Using csh & tsch
Using Samba
vi Editor Pocket Reference
What You Need To Know:
  When You Can't Find Your
  UNIX System Administrator
Writing GNU Emacs Extensions

SONGLINE GUIDES

NetLaw	NetResearch
NetLearning	NetSuccess
NetLessons	NetTravel

SOFTWARE

Building Your Own WebSite™
Building Your Own Web Conference
WebBoard™ 3.0
WebSite Professional™ 2.0
PolyForm™

SYSTEM ADMINISTRATION

Building Internet Firewalls
Computer Security Basics
Cracking DES
DNS and BIND, 3rd Edition
DNS on WindowsNT
Essential System Administration
Essential WindowsNT
  System Administration
Getting Connected:
  The Internet at 56K and Up
Linux Network Administrator's Guide
Managing IP Networks with
  Cisco Routers
Managing Mailing Lists
Managing NFS and NIS
Managing the WindowsNT Registry
Managing Usenet
MCSE: The Core Exams in a Nutshell
MCSE: The Electives in a Nutshell
Networking Personal Computers
  with TCP/IP
Oracle Performance Tuning,
  2nd Edition
Practical UNIX & Internet Security,
  2nd Edition
PGP: Pretty Good Privacy
Protecting Networks with SATAN
sendmail, 2nd Edition
sendmail Desktop Reference
System Performance Tuning
TCP/IP Network Administration,
  2nd Edition
termcap & terminfo
The Networking CD Bookshelf
Using & Managing PPP
Virtual Private Networks
WindowsNT Backup & Restore
WindowsNT Desktop Reference
WindowsNT Event Logging
WindowsNT in a Nutshell
WindowsNT Server 4.0 for
  Netware Administrators
WindowsNT SNMP
WindowsNT TCP/IP Administration
WindowsNT User Administration
Zero Administration for Windows

X WINDOW

Vol. 1: Xlib Programming Manual
Vol. 2: Xlib Reference Manual
Vol. 3M: X Window System
  User's Guide, Motif Edition
Vol. 4M: X Toolkit Intrinsics
  Programming Manual,
  Motif Edition
Vol. 5: X Toolkit Intrinsics
  Reference Manual
Vol. 6A: Motif Programming Manual
Vol. 6B: Motif Reference Manual
Vol. 8 : X Window System
  Administrator's Guide

PROGRAMMING

Access Database Design and
  Programming
Advanced Oracle PL/SQL
  Programming with Packages
Applying RCS and SCCS
BE Developer's Guide
BE Advanced Topics
C++: The Core Language
Checking C Programs with lint
Developing Windows Error Messages
Developing Visual Basic Add-ins
Guide to Writing DCE Applications
High Performance Computing,
  2nd Edition
Inside the Windows 95 File System
Inside the Windows 95 Registry
lex & yacc, 2nd Edition
Linux Device Drivers
Managing Projects with make
Oracle8 Design Tips
Oracle Built-in Packages
Oracle Design
Oracle PL/SQL Programming,
  2nd Edition
Oracle Scripts
Oracle Security
Palm Programming:
  The Developer's Guide
Porting UNIX Software
POSIX Programmer's Guide
POSIX.4: Programming
  for the Real World
Power Programming with RPC
Practical C Programming, 3rd Edition
Practical C++ Programming
Programming Python
Programming with curses
Programming with GNU Software
Pthreads Programming
Python Pocket Reference
Software Portability with imake,
  2nd Edition
UML in a Nutshell
Understanding DCE
UNIX Systems Programming for SVR4
VB/VBA in a Nutshell: The Languages
Win32 Multithreaded Programming
Windows NT File System Internals
Year 2000 in a Nutshell

USING WINDOWS

Excel97 Annoyances
Office97 Annoyances
Outlook Annoyances
Windows Annoyances
Windows98 Annoyances
Windows95 in a Nutshell
Windows98 in a Nutshell
Word97 Annoyances

OTHER TITLES

PalmPilot: The Ultimate Guide
Palm Programming:
  The Developer's Guide

International Distributors

UK, EUROPE, MIDDLE EAST AND AFRICA (EXCEPT FRANCE, GERMANY, AUSTRIA, SWITZERLAND, LUXEMBOURG, LIECHTENSTEIN, AND EASTERN EUROPE)

INQUIRIES
O'Reilly UK Limited
4 Castle Street
Farnham
Surrey, GU9 7HS
United Kingdom
Telephone: 44-1252-711776
Fax: 44-1252-734211
Email: information@oreilly.co.uk

ORDERS
Wiley Distribution Services Ltd.
1 Oldlands Way
Bognor Regis
West Sussex PO22 9SA
United Kingdom
Telephone: 44-1243-779777
Fax: 44-1243-820250
Email: cs-books@wiley.co.uk

FRANCE

INQUIRIES
Éditions O'Reilly
18 rue Séguier
75006 Paris, France
Tel: 33-1-40-51-52-30
Fax: 33-1-40-51-52-31
Email: france@editions-oreilly.fr

ORDERS
GEODIF
61, Bd Saint-Germain
75240 Paris Cedex 05, France
Tel: 33-1-44-41-46-16 (French books)
Tel: 33-1-44-41-11-87 (English books)
Fax: 33-1-44-41-11-44
Email: distribution@eyrolles.com

GERMANY, SWITZERLAND, AUSTRIA, EASTERN EUROPE, LUXEMBOURG, AND LIECHTENSTEIN

INQUIRIES & ORDERS
O'Reilly Verlag
Balthasarstr. 81
D-50670 Köln
Germany
Telephone: 49-221-973160-91
Fax: 49-221-973160-8
Email: anfragen@oreilly.de (inquiries)
Email: order@oreilly.de (orders)

CANADA (FRENCH LANGUAGE BOOKS)

Les Éditions Flammarion ltée
375, Avenue Laurier Ouest
Montréal (Québec) H2V 2K3
Tel: 00-1-514-277-8807
Fax: 00-1-514-278-2085
Email: info@flammarion.qc.ca

HONG KONG

City Discount Subscription Service, Ltd.
Unit D, 3rd Floor, Yan's Tower
27 Wong Chuk Hang Road
Aberdeen, Hong Kong
Tel: 852-2580-3539
Fax: 852-2580-6463
Email: citydis@ppn.com.hk

KOREA

Hanbit Media, Inc.
Chungmu Bldg. 201
Yonnam-dong 568-33
Mapo-gu
Seoul, Korea
Tel: 822-325-0397
Fax: 822-325-9697
Email: hant93@chollian.dacom.co.kr

PHILIPPINES

Global Publishing
G/F Benavides Garden
1186 Benavides Street
Manila, Philippines
Tel: 632-254-8949/637-252-2582
Fax: 632-734-5060/632-252-2733
Email: globalp@pacific.net.ph

TAIWAN

O'Reilly Taiwan
No. 3, Lane 131
Hang-Chow South Road
Section 1, Taipei, Taiwan
Tel: 886-2-23968990
Fax: 886-2-23968916
Email: taiwan@oreilly.com

CHINA

O'Reilly Beijing
Room 2410
160, FuXingMenNeiDaJie
XiCheng District
Beijing, China PR 100031
Tel: 86-10-66412305
Fax: 86-10-86631007
Email: beijing@oreilly.com

INDIA

Computer Bookshop (India) Pvt. Ltd.
190 Dr. D.N. Road, Fort
Bombay 400 001 India
Tel: 91-22-207-0989
Fax: 91-22-262-3551
Email: cbsbom@giasbm01.vsnl.net.in

JAPAN

O'Reilly Japan, Inc.
Yotsuya Y's Building
7 Banch 6, Honshio-cho
Shinjuku-ku
Tokyo 160-0003 Japan
Tel: 81-3-3356-5227
Fax: 81-3-3356-5261
Email: japan@oreilly.com

ALL OTHER ASIAN COUNTRIES

O'Reilly & Associates, Inc.
101 Morris Street
Sebastopol, CA 95472 USA
Tel: 707-829-0515
Fax: 707-829-0104
Email: order@oreilly.com

AUSTRALIA

Woodslane Pty., Ltd.
7/5 Vuko Place
Warriewood NSW 2102
Australia
Tel: 61-2-9970-5111
Fax: 61-2-9970-5002
Email: info@woodslane.com.au

NEW ZEALAND

Woodslane New Zealand, Ltd.
21 Cooks Street (P.O. Box 575)
Waganui, New Zealand
Tel: 64-6-347-6543
Fax: 64-6-345-4840
Email: info@woodslane.com.au

LATIN AMERICA

McGraw-Hill Interamericana
Editores, S.A. de C.V.
Cedro No. 512
Col. Atlampa
06450, Mexico, D.F.
Tel: 52-5-547-6777
Fax: 52-5-547-3336
Email: mcgraw-hill@infosel.net.mx

O'REILLY®

TO ORDER: **800-998-9938** • **order@oreilly.com** • **http://www.oreilly.com/**

OUR PRODUCTS ARE AVAILABLE AT A BOOKSTORE OR SOFTWARE STORE NEAR YOU.

FOR INFORMATION: **800-998-9938** • **707-829-0515** • **info@oreilly.com**